Doing Business After Brexit: A Practical Guide to the Legal Changes

Efallai nad yw'r wybodaeth
sydd yn y rhifyn hwn yn
adlewyrchu
DEDDFWRIAETH
BRESENNOL

Information contained within
this edition may not be
CURRENT LAW

Doing Business After Brexit: A Practical Guide to the Legal Changes

Helen Tse BA (Hons) Cantab, MA (Hons) Cantab, DPhil, MBE
Partner, Corporate, Clarke Willmott LLP, Manchester

Bloomsbury Professional

Bloomsbury Professional
An imprint of Bloomsbury Publishing Plc

Bloomsbury Professional Ltd	Bloomsbury Publishing Plc
41–43 Boltro Road	50 Bedford Square
Haywards Heath	London
RH16 1BJ	WC1B 3DP
UK	UK

www.bloomsbury.com

BLOOMSBURY and the Diana logo are trademarks of

Bloomsbury Publishing Plc

© Bloomsbury Professional Ltd 2017

While every care has been taken to ensure the accuracy of this work, no responsibility for loss or damage occasioned to any person acting or refraining from action as a result of any statement in it can be accepted by the authors, editors or publishers.

British Library Cataloguing-in-Publication Data

A catalogue record for this book is available from the British Library.

ISBN:	PB:	978 1 78451 936 0
	Epdf:	978 1 78451 938 4
	Epub:	978 1 78451 937 7

Typeset by Phoenix Photosetting, Chatham, Kent
Printed and bound by CPI Group (UK) Ltd, Croydon, CRO 4YY

To find out more about our authors and books visit www.bloomsburyprofessional.com. Here you will find extracts, author information, details of forthcoming events and the option to sign up for our newsletters

Dedication

I dedicate this book to God and my dearest family including my husband Colin Wong, Mabel Tse, Eric Tse, Lisa Tse, Janet Tse, Jimmy Tse, Peter, Kitty Kat and Sam.

Acknowledgements

Thank you to my colleagues at Clarke Willmott for supporting me, in particular Ed Foulkes, Stephen Rosser, Margaret Mann, Simon Thomas, Siobhan Birket, John Irving, Perry Swanson, Ian Nash, Emma Collins, Emma Hamnett, Susan Hall, Andrew Stone, John Flint, Roy Crozier, Lindsay Felstead, Emma Ramsden, Harley-Jayne Marshall and my secretary Janet Norman. I also dedicate this book to every professional involved in or advising on Brexit related matters – we're all in it for the long haul so let's share best practice for the sake of our clients.

Last but not at all least, I thank all the contributors to this book for their expertise and insight – their dedication and knowledge is unparalleled.

Preface

A number of my clients called me in a panic the day after the Brexit Referendum results were announced and asked nervously what were the effects of Brexit on their business deals, employees, supply agreements and contracts and financing – the questions went on and on. That same day Lloyds Bank stopped processing all the mortgages they were funding. A number of acquisitions stopped dead in their tracks. Uncertainty is bad for business and Brexit brought a huge amount of uncertainty to the business arena, causing the value of the pound sterling to drop significantly overnight. My clients had valid questions and I too wanted answers. When I started to research their questions no one had actually written in detail about this – probably because no one really could believe Brexit would occur – which prompted me to take up the mantle. I decided to invite leading lawyers in their specialist fields to contribute to this book and examine the legal issues arising from Brexit. I also believed it was important to interview thought leaders from various sectors – retail, manufacturing, pensions, finance, science and academia – to get a finger on the pulse of the UK nation. I was also very grateful to Prime Minister Theresa May, David Davies MP, Secretary of State for Exiting the European Union and the Foreign Secretary, Boris Johnson MP, all of whom have contributed to this book by way of their speeches.

Doing Business After Brexit aims to be a guidance book, a mind map and a prompt, providing you with an insight as to what I anticipate may be the legal changes in the event of a hard Brexit. This book is not prescriptive and nor should it be relied upon as legal advice. However, it should give you some pointers as to what to look out for and ask your legal advisers to review. It is always good business practice to regularly review your business. Cars go for an annual MOT. By comparison, how often do you conduct a business MOT? Your business is far more valuable than your car and it should be good practice to regularly check your legal documents regarding commercial ventures to ensure the contracts are still profitable and worthwhile, and if they are not, how can they be terminated? How about your employees – do they still have the right to work in the UK? With the pound sterling depreciating, how has that affected your finances, stock prices and ultimate sale prices? Do you have an EU Trademark? If so, if in the event of a Brexit where the UK will no longer be covered under the EU Trademark, this intellectual property will need to be registered under the UK Intellectual Property Office regime to protect your priority in the UK. How about property, finance, insurance, tax, data requirements? Will these need to be revised or monitored in the event of Brexit? Whilst these questions are raised in the context of Brexit, I would stress that these questions are not just Brexit related – they are commercially and legally important issues to think about to ensure your business is in the best possible long-term health and maintains stability in the uncertainty of the business world – whether it concerns Brexit, Trump coming into power in the USA or other political changes in the world.

This book will be a living, breathing publication which will need revision in the future. The range of expertise on which it is based is considerable, involving practitioners from commercial law, intellectual property, media, employment law, tax, employment and insolvency. The contributors to this book have given freely of their time to serve the public interest by helping to manage the impact of Brexit on business and by promoting legal education about Brexit and its consequences.

This book will not take a position on leaving or remaining in the EU but when interviewing CEOs and business leaders they are free to give their views if they so choose and their thoughts are in the Thought Leadership section. It's a fascinating take on these business leaders' thoughts on Brexit and their views on how one should adapt to the changing political and economic landscape. We can learn much from how these business leaders do business and it is extremely valuable to have their input into this book.

As a representative for my fellow lawyers, I wrote this book to identify the key legal issues which my colleagues and I believe need to be addressed by businesses in order to facilitate a transition that minimises the risk of legal uncertainty, the loss of rights, and possible adverse consequences to the national economy, and capitalises on the opportunities for post-Brexit global Britain.

It is clear that there is a great deal of work to be done. This book gives an insight into the scale of the task that lies ahead and pleads for businesses to be vigilant rather than just burying their heads in the sand and thinking Brexit will bypass them. Brexit will affect everyone and every business.

My interest is in helping businesses ensure that they are ready for the world post-Brexit and not to be caught out. I sincerely hope that when I review my client's business, I can deliver the best deal possible for them. Given the ever changing scene, to provide you with the most up to date news on Brexit, may I refer you to our dedicated website www.brexitbrexitbrexit.com.

Finally, the content of this book is intended to provide a general guide to the subject matter. Specialist legal advice should be sought about your specific circumstances.

This book is up to date to 30 April 2017 but later developments have been incorporated where possible.

Helen Tse

5 April 2017

Contents

Contents

Contents

Contributors

Helen Tse, Clarke Willmott

Helen Tse, lawyer, is the first port of call for SME companies, high net worth individuals and entrepreneurs regarding corporate and commercial law matters. Helen herself is an entrepreneur, a published author and the recipient of the coveted MBE from Her Majesty the Queen in 2014.

A graduate in Law from Cambridge University with a professional career spanning Clifford Chance, London & Hong Kong, PricewaterhouseCoopers and Walkers in the Cayman Islands, Helen Tse is an authority in the world of law and business. Helen is a corporate partner with Clarke Willmott, a multi-disciplinary national law firm with 700 lawyers across seven offices. Her practice includes mergers and acquisitions, private equity and China investments. For more information contact: helen.tse@clarkewillmott.com or helenthelawyer@gmail.com.

Philip Brooks, ORC International

Philip Brooks is Financial Services Research Director at ORC International (www.orcinternational.com). Phil's experience spans the sector, working with clients from general and life insurers, retail and investment banks, through to building societies, online aggregators and regulators.

Phil helps his clients to innovate and explore new market opportunities by providing both primary and secondary research on market sizing, NPD and customer needs, alongside helping clients to understand and enhance their customer experience through customer journey mapping, monitoring and relationship assessment.

With close to 20 years of experience, Phil was previously Head of Financial Services Research at Harris Interactive and has written for a number of sector publications, spoken at industry conferences alongside the City UK.

Both MHP Communications and ORC International are both part of the Engine Group www.enginegroup.com

John Denis-Smith, 39 Essex Chambers

John Denis-Smith is a London- based construction law specialist barrister, practising out of 39 Essex Chambers for the past 11 years. He previously worked as a solicitor with construction and infrastructure international firms Herbert Smith and Fenwick Elliott. He is a Fellow of the Chartered Institute of Arbitrators.

Andy Fleming, MHP Communications

Andy Fleming is a Director on the asset management and pensions teams at MHP Communications (http://www.mhpc.com). He has worked with a number of major UK pension funds and advisors, as well as investment management specialists.

Previously he was Head of Communications at the National Association of Pension Funds (now PLSA), helping to build the organisation's media profile in the key areas of pensions reform and corporate governance.

Andy has over 20 years of experience in financial PR, and was formerly a press spokesman for the ONS, the DWP and the FCA.

Steve Kuncewicz, Slater and Gordon

Steve is a principal lawyer in the business advisory team at Slater and Gordon Lawyers in Manchester.

He specialises in intellectual property, media and social media law with a particular emphasis on the creative, digital and technology sector. Steve is listed as a recommended lawyer' in tier 2 of the *Legal 500 2014, 2015,* and *2016,* North West Technology, Media & Telecoms section.

He is a regular spokesperson, and has given interviews to the local and national press through BBC Breakfast, Sky News, ITV, BBC Radio 2, BBC Radio 4, BBC Radio 5 Live and LBC London.

Steve's first book, *Legal Issues of Web 2.0 and Social Media*, was published in June 2011 and his second book *Legal Issues of Corporate Communication in the Online World* was published in June 2012.

Jane Lambert, 4–5 Gray's Inn Square

Jane Lambert was born in Manchester and educated at St Paul's School, the University of St Andrews and the University of California, Los Angeles. Before coming to the Bar she worked first for the Economist Intelligence Unit as a research consultant and editor of one of its specialist publications and later as an investment analyst for stockbrokers Vivian Gray. She was called to the Bar by Lincoln's Inn and underwent pupillage with Roger Cox (later HH Judge Cox) in the chambers of Roy Beldam QC (later Lord Justice Beldam) and Robert Reid (later HH Judge Reid QC) in the chambers of Paul Baker QC (later HH Judge Baker QC). She acquired her expertise in intellectual property and technology law as legal advisor to VISA International for Europe, the Middle East and Africa. Returning to Manchester she practised in the chambers of Peter Watkins building up a practice in IP and related areas of law. In 1997 she set up NIPC as the first and so far only patent chambers outside London. She has been counsel in several important cases and has authored or contributed to several specialist publications. In 2013 she joined 4–5 Gray's Inn Square together with the majority of her members. She is ranked in *Chambers* Guide to the Bar as a Tier 1 practitioner for IP in the regions,

Gary McIndoe, Latitude Law

Gary qualified as a solicitor in 2000 after training with David Gray and Company in Newcastle-upon-Tyne. He returned to his home city of Manchester where he joined specialist immigration practice Thornhill Ince. He was appointed Director of the Greater Manchester Immigration Aid Unit, a not-for-profit legal advice agency, in 2002.

Gary founded Latitude Law in December 2007. He is a Trustee for RAPAR and is currently Chair of the Electronic Immigration Network, a charity providing online information in the field of immigration and asylum.

Maura McIntosh, Herbert Smith Freehills LLP

Maura is a professional support consultant in the general commercial litigation team at Herbert Smith Freehills. In that role she provides technical advice on issues of both substantive law and court procedure.

Maura is an editor of the firm's 'Litigation notes' blog and also edits the firm's online privilege and jurisdiction materials and its contract disputes practical guides series. She is also Deputy Chair of the Civil Justice Council's Civil Litigation Review working group. Her particular areas of interest include privilege, costs and funding issues, contract law and conflict of laws.

Howard Morris, Morrison & Foerster

Howard Morris is head of the London arm of the Business Restructuring & Insolvency Group at Morrison & Foerster. Howard has more than 20 years' experience in UK and international restructuring and insolvency work. He has acted for banks and other secured and unsecured creditors, committees of bondholders, trade creditors, debtors and acquirers of business and assets from insolvent companies. He has experience in international asset tracing and recovery, as well as a strong background in banking and finance.

Howard's experience extends to matters involving the UK, the United States, where he lived for some years, and a number of other jurisdictions, including continental Europe, central Asia, Russia, Africa, the Middle East and offshore financial centres. He is a member of the International Insolvency Institute, the Association of Business Recovery Professionals (R3), and serves on the Brexit working groups of the Law Society of England Wales and R3 as well as its General Technical Committee.

Howard had a long career with Dentons where he served two terms as Chief Executive and was most recently their Global Integration Partner. Howard is an accredited CEDR mediator, particularly interested in mediating disputes arising out of restructurings and insolvency proceedings.

Anna Pertoldi, Herbert Smith Freehills LLP

Anna is a partner in the dispute resolution team at Herbert Smith Freehills. She is a general commercial litigator by background and is the partner responsible for litigation know-how in London.

Anna lectures and writes regularly on litigation topics, in particular on privilege and jurisdiction law and developments, and is an editor of the firm's 'Litigation notes' blog (http://hsfnotes.com/litigation/). She has written extensively on Brexit-related issues and also contributes to *Blackstone's Civil Practice.*

Shara Pledger, Latitude Law

Shara is a solicitor, accredited by the Law Society as a level 2 senior caseworker. She joined Latitude Law from Eversheds in 2010. Shara has gained considerable expertise handling sponsor licensing applications for employers and specialises in complex PBS applications and issues.

Kevin Poulter, Child & Child

Kevin Poulter is a partner and head of the employment team at Child & Child. He advises commercial and not for profit organisations, senior employees and directors on the full range of employment issues. Kevin is respected for providing clear, practical, commercial advice to clients and has a special interest in discrimination and workplace issues involving social media.

Kevin is a popular and engaging speaker and is frequently called upon to provide insight and opinion on legal, digital and diversity issues for broadcast news and current affairs shows. Kevin has written for numerous print and online publications and was the first Editor at Large of the Solicitors Journal.

Kevin is a 'Business Expert' for SAGE and maintains a blog on social media and the law at www.kevinpoulter.com.

Kevin is a member of the Employment Lawyers Association.

Dimitrios Syrrakos, Manchester Metropolitan University

Dimitrios Syrrakos joined the Department of Accounting Finance and Economics at Manchester Metropolitan University in 2001. Since then, he has delivered numerous units such as Macroeconomics, Economics of European Monetary Union and Advanced Economic Theory. He completed his PhD on European monetary integration in 2008. The thesis focused on the varying extents to which countries were prepared to join the Euro and the prospects of the Eurozone. Since then he has researched and published on the Eurozone debt crisis in Inter-economics, Comparative Economic Studies and International Journal of Green Economics. He has been repeatedly invited onto media as a featured Eurozone commentator (including BBC World News, BBC Radio 5 Live and BBC Radio Manchester) and to international conferences in the UK, France and Poland to present his work. Other research interests include fiscal policy in Eurozone countries, exchange rate economics and international monetary relations.

Etienne Wong, Old Square Tax Chambers

Etienne Wong qualified as a solicitor in 1990, and was a partner and head of the international VAT unit at Clifford Chance LLP from 1999 to 2014. He was called to the Bar in 2014. He has been advising on all aspects of VAT since 1989 (particularly in relation to financing transactions, real estate transactions, funds, private equity transactions, outsourcing transactions, e-commerce, new media and transactions in the power and energy sectors).

Alex Wright, Latitude Law

Alex joined Latitude Law in July 2011 having completed his LPC at the College of Law and his LLB at the University of Birmingham. In 2012 he completed his Masters in Law at Manchester Metropolitan University, and was awarded a distinction for his dissertation on rights of free movement for same-sex couples within the EU. He qualified as a solicitor with the firm in January 2016.

Table of UK Legislation

STATUTES

STATUTORY INSTRUMENTS

Table of Cases

Part I
Potential Impact of Brexit

INTRODUCTION

BREXIT SPEECH: THERESA MAY, PRIME MINISTER OF GREAT BRITAIN, LANCASTER HOUSE, 17 JANUARY 2017

'A little over six months ago, the British people voted for change. They voted to shape a brighter future for our country. They voted to leave the European Union and embrace the world.

And they did so with their eyes open: accepting that the road ahead will be uncertain at times, but believing that it leads towards a brighter future for their children – and their grandchildren too.

And it is the job of this Government to deliver it. That means more than negotiating our new relationship with the EU. It means taking the opportunity of this great moment of national change to step back and ask ourselves what kind of country we want to be.

My answer is clear. I want this United Kingdom to emerge from this period of change stronger, fairer, more united and more outward-looking than ever before. I want us to be a secure, prosperous, tolerant country – a magnet for international talent and a home to the pioneers and innovators who will shape the world ahead. I want us to be a truly Global Britain – the best friend and neighbour to our European partners, but a country that reaches beyond the borders of Europe too. A country that goes out into the world to build relationships with old friends and new allies alike.

I want Britain to be what we have the potential, talent and ambition to be. A great, global trading nation that is respected around the world and strong, confident and united at home.

A PLAN FOR BRITAIN

That is why this Government has a Plan for Britain. One that gets us the right deal abroad but also ensures we get a better deal for ordinary working people at home. It's why that plan sets out how we will use this moment of change to build a stronger economy and a fairer society by embracing genuine economic and social reform.

Why our new Modern Industrial Strategy is being developed, to ensure every nation and area of the United Kingdom can make the most of the opportunities ahead. Why we will go further to reform our schools to ensure every child has the knowledge and the skills they need to thrive in post-Brexit Britain. Why as we continue to bring the deficit down, we will take a balanced approach by investing in our economic infrastructure – because it can transform the growth potential of our economy, and improve the quality of people's lives across the whole country.

It's why we will put the preservation of our precious Union at the heart of everything we do. Because it is only by coming together as one great union of nations and people that we can make the most of the opportunities ahead. The result of the referendum was not a decision to turn inward and retreat from the world. Because Britain's history and culture is profoundly internationalist.

We are a European country – and proud of our shared European heritage – but we are also a country that has always looked beyond Europe to the wider world. That is why we are one of the most racially diverse countries in Europe, one of the most multicultural members of the European Union, and why – whether we are talking about India, Pakistan, Bangladesh, America, Australia, Canada, New Zealand, countries in Africa or those that are closer to home in Europe – so many of us have close friends and relatives from across the world.

Instinctively, we want to travel to, study in, trade with countries not just in Europe but beyond the borders of our continent. Even now as we prepare to leave the EU, we are planning for the next biennial Commonwealth Heads of Government meeting in 2018 – a reminder of our unique and proud global relationships.

A MESSAGE FROM BRITAIN TO THE REST OF EUROPE

And it is important to recognise this fact. June the 23rd was not the moment Britain chose to step back from the world. It was the moment we chose to build a truly Global Britain. I know that this – and the other reasons Britain took such a decision – is not always well understood among our friends and allies in Europe. And I know many fear that this might herald the beginning of a greater unravelling of the EU.

But let me be clear: I do not want that to happen. It would not be in the best interests of Britain. It remains overwhelmingly and compellingly in Britain's national interest that the EU should succeed. And that is why I hope in the months and years ahead we will all reflect on the lessons of Britain's decision to leave.

So let me take this opportunity to set out the reasons for our decision and to address the people of Europe directly. It's not simply because our history and culture is profoundly internationalist, important though that is. Many in Britain have always felt that the United Kingdom's place in the European Union came at the expense of our global ties, and of a bolder embrace of free trade with the wider world.

There are other important reasons too.

Our political traditions are different. Unlike other European countries, we have no written constitution, but the principle of Parliamentary Sovereignty is the basis of our unwritten constitutional settlement. We have only a recent history of devolved governance – though it has rapidly embedded itself – and we have little history of coalition government. The public expect to be able to hold their governments to account very directly, and as a result supranational institutions as strong as those created by the European Union sit very uneasily in relation to our political history and way of life.

And, while I know Britain might at times have been seen as an awkward member state, the European Union has struggled to deal with the diversity of its member countries and their interests. It bends towards uniformity, not flexibility. David Cameron's negotiation was a valiant final attempt to make it work for Britain – and I want to thank all those elsewhere in Europe who helped him reach an agreement – but the blunt truth, as we know, is that there was not enough flexibility on many important matters for a majority of British voters.

Now I do not believe that these things apply uniquely to Britain. Britain is not the only member state where there is a strong attachment to accountable and democratic government, such a strong internationalist mindset, or a belief that diversity within Europe should be celebrated. And so I believe there is a lesson in Brexit not just for Britain but, if it wants to succeed, for the EU itself.

Because our continent's great strength has always been its diversity. And there are two ways of dealing with different interests. You can respond by trying to hold things together by force, tightening a vice-like grip that ends up crushing into tiny pieces the very things you want to protect. Or you can respect difference, cherish it even, and reform the EU so that it deals better with the wonderful diversity of its member states.

So to our friends across Europe, let me say this.

Our vote to leave the European Union was no rejection of the values we share. The decision to leave the EU represents no desire to become more distant to you, our friends and neighbours. It was no attempt to do harm to the EU itself or to any of its remaining member states. We do not want to turn the clock back to the days when Europe was less peaceful, less secure and less able to trade freely. It was a vote to restore, as we see it, our parliamentary democracy, national self-determination, and to become even more global and internationalist in action and in spirit.

We will continue to be reliable partners, willing allies and close friends. We want to buy your goods and services, sell you ours, trade with you as freely as possible, and work with one another to make sure we are all safer, more secure and more prosperous through continued friendship.

You will still be welcome in this country as we hope our citizens will be welcome in yours. At a time when together we face a serious threat from our enemies, Britain's unique intelligence capabilities will continue to help to keep people in Europe safe from terrorism. And at a time when there is growing concern about European security, Britain's servicemen and women, based in European countries including Estonia, Poland and Romania, will continue to do their duty.

We are leaving the European Union, but we are not leaving Europe.

And that is why we seek a new and equal partnership – between an independent, self-governing, Global Britain and our friends and allies in the EU.

Not partial membership of the European Union, associate membership of the European Union, or anything that leaves us half-in, half-out. We do not seek to adopt a model already enjoyed by other countries. We do not seek to hold on to bits of membership as we leave.

No, the United Kingdom is leaving the European Union. And my job is to get the right deal for Britain as we do.

OBJECTIVES AND AMBITIONS

So today I want to outline our objectives for the negotiation ahead. 12 objectives that amount to one big goal: a new, positive and constructive partnership between Britain and the European Union.

And as we negotiate that partnership, we will be driven by some simple principles: we will provide as much certainty and clarity as we can at every stage. And we will take this opportunity to make Britain stronger, to make Britain fairer, and to build a more Global Britain too.

CERTAINTY AND CLARITY

1. Certainty

The first objective is crucial. We will provide certainty wherever we can.

We are about to enter a negotiation. That means there will be give and take. There will have to be compromises. It will require imagination on both sides. And not everybody will be able to know everything at every stage. But I recognise how important it is to provide business, the public sector, and everybody with as much certainty as possible as we move through the process.

So where we can offer that certainty, we will do so. That is why last year we acted quickly to give clarity about farm payments and university funding. And it is why, as we repeal the European Communities Act, we will convert the 'acquis' – the body of existing EU law – into British law.

This will give the country maximum certainty as we leave the EU. The same rules and laws will apply on the day after Brexit as they did before. And it will be for the British Parliament to decide on any changes to that law after full scrutiny and proper Parliamentary debate.

And when it comes to Parliament, there is one other way in which I would like to provide certainty. I can confirm today that the Government will put the final deal that is agreed between the UK and the EU to a vote in both Houses of Parliament, before it comes into force.

A STRONGER BRITAIN

Our second guiding principle is to build a stronger Britain.

2. Control of our own laws

That means taking control of our own affairs, as those who voted in their millions to leave the European Union demanded we must. So we will take back control of our laws and bring an end to the jurisdiction of the European Court of Justice in Britain. Leaving the European Union will mean that our laws will be made in Westminster, Edinburgh, Cardiff and Belfast. And those laws will be interpreted by judges not in Luxembourg but in courts across this country. Because we will not have truly left the European Union if we are not in control of our own laws.

3. Strengthen the Union

A stronger Britain demands that we do something else – strengthen the precious union between the four nations of the United Kingdom. At this momentous time, it is more important than ever that we face the future together, united by what makes us strong: the bonds that unite us as a people, and our shared interest in the UK being an open, successful trading nation in the future. And I hope that same spirit of unity will apply in Northern Ireland in particular over the coming months in the Assembly elections, and the main parties there will work together to re-establish a partnership government as soon as possible.

Foreign affairs are of course the responsibility of the UK Government, and in dealing with them we act in the interests of all parts of the United Kingdom. As Prime Minister, I take that responsibility seriously. I have also been determined from the start that the devolved administrations should be fully engaged in this process.

That is why the Government has set up a Joint Ministerial Committee on EU Negotiations, so ministers from each of the UK's devolved administrations can contribute to the process of planning for our departure from the European Union. We have already received a paper from the Scottish Government, and look forward to receiving a paper from the Welsh Government shortly. Both papers will be considered as part of this important process. We won't agree on everything, but I look forward to working with the administrations in Scotland, Wales and Northern Ireland to deliver a Brexit that works for the whole of the United Kingdom.

Part of that will mean working very carefully to ensure that – as powers are repatriated from Brussels back to Britain – the right powers are returned to Westminster, and the right powers are passed to the devolved administrations of Scotland, Wales and Northern Ireland.

As we do so, our guiding principle must be to ensure that – as we leave the European Union – no new barriers to living and doing business within our own Union are created, that means maintaining the necessary common standards and frameworks for our own domestic market, empowering the UK as an open, trading nation to strike the best trade deals around the world, and protecting the common resources of our islands. And as we do this, I should equally be clear that no decisions currently taken by the devolved administrations will be removed from them.

4. Maintain the Common Travel Area with Ireland

We cannot forget that, as we leave, the United Kingdom will share a land border with the EU, and maintaining that Common Travel Area with the Republic of Ireland will be an important priority for the UK in the talks ahead. There has been a Common Travel Area between the UK and the Republic of Ireland for many years. Indeed, it was formed before either of our two countries were members of the European Union. And the family ties and bonds of affection that unite our two countries mean that there will always be a special relationship between us.

So we will work to deliver a practical solution that allows the maintenance of the Common Travel Area with the Republic, while protecting the integrity of the United Kingdom's immigration system. Nobody wants to return to the borders of the past, so we will make it a priority to deliver a practical solution as soon as we can.

A FAIRER BRITAIN

The third principle is to build a fairer Britain. That means ensuring it is fair to everyone who lives and works in this country.

5. Control of immigration

And that is why we will ensure we can control immigration to Britain from Europe. We will continue to attract the brightest and the best to work or study in Britain – indeed openness to international talent must remain one of this country's most distinctive assets – but that process must be managed properly so that our immigration system serves the national interest. So we will get control of the number of people coming to Britain from the EU. Because while controlled immigration can bring great benefits – filling skills shortages, delivering public services, making British businesses the world-beaters they often are – when the numbers get too high, public support for the system falters.

In the last decade or so, we have seen record levels of net migration in Britain, and that sheer volume has put pressure on public services, like schools, stretched our infrastructure, especially housing, and put a downward pressure on wages for working class people. As Home Secretary for six years, I know that you cannot control immigration overall when there is free movement to Britain from Europe.

Britain is an open and tolerant country. We will always want immigration, especially high-skilled immigration, we will always want immigration from Europe, and we will always welcome individual migrants as friends. But the message from the public before and during the referendum campaign was clear: Brexit must mean control of the number of people who come to Britain from Europe. And that is what we will deliver.

6. Rights for EU nationals in Britain, and British nationals in the EU

Fairness demands that we deal with another issue as soon as possible too. We want to guarantee the rights of EU citizens who are already living in Britain, and the rights of British nationals in other member states, as early as we can. I have told other EU leaders that we could give people the certainty they want straight away, and reach such a deal now. Many of them favour such an agreement – one or two others do not – but I want everyone to know that it remains an important priority for Britain – and for many other member states – to resolve this challenge as soon as possible. Because it is the right and fair thing to do.

7. Protect workers' rights

And a fairer Britain is a country that protects and enhances the rights people have at work. That is why, as we translate the body of European law into our domestic regulations, we will ensure that workers rights are fully protected and maintained.

Indeed, under my leadership, not only will the Government protect the rights of workers' set out in European legislation, we will build on them. Because under this Conservative Government, we will make sure legal protection for workers keeps pace with the changing labour market – and that the voices of workers are heard by the boards of publicly-listed companies for the first time.

A TRULY GLOBAL BRITAIN

But the great prize for this country – the opportunity ahead – is to use this moment to build a truly Global Britain. A country that reaches out to old friends and new allies alike. A great, global, trading nation. And one of the firmest advocates for free trade anywhere in the world.

8. Free trade with European markets

That starts with our close friends and neighbours in Europe. So as a priority, we will pursue a bold and ambitious Free Trade Agreement with the European Union. This agreement should allow for the freest possible trade in goods and services between Britain and the EU's member states. It should give British companies the maximum freedom to trade with and operate within European markets – and let European businesses do the same in Britain. But I want to be clear. What I am proposing cannot mean membership of the Single Market.

European leaders have said many times that membership means accepting the 'four freedoms' of goods, capital, services and people. And being out of the EU but a member of the Single Market would mean complying with the EU's rules and regulations that implement those freedoms, without having a vote on what those rules and regulations are. It would mean accepting a role for the European Court of Justice that would see it still having direct legal authority in our country.

It would to all intents and purposes mean not leaving the EU at all. And that is why both sides in the referendum campaign made it clear that a vote to leave the EU would be a vote to leave the Single Market. So we do not seek membership of the Single Market. Instead we seek the greatest possible access to it through a new, comprehensive, bold and ambitious Free Trade Agreement.

That Agreement may take in elements of current Single Market arrangements in certain areas – on the export of cars and lorries for example, or the freedom to provide financial services across national borders – as it makes no sense to start again from scratch when Britain and the remaining Member States have adhered to the same rules for so many years.

But I respect the position taken by European leaders who have been clear about their position, just as I am clear about mine. So an important part of the new strategic partnership we seek with the EU will be the pursuit of the greatest possible access to the Single Market, on a fully reciprocal basis, through a comprehensive Free Trade Agreement.

And because we will no longer be members of the Single Market, we will not be required to contribute huge sums to the EU budget. There may be some specific European programmes in which we might want to participate. If so, and this will be for us to decide, it is reasonable that we should make an appropriate contribution. But the principle is clear: the days of Britain making vast contributions to the European Union every year will end.

9. New trade agreements with other countries

But it is not just trade with the EU we should be interested in. A Global Britain must be free to strike trade agreements with countries from outside the European Union too. Because important though our trade with the EU is and will remain, it is clear that the UK needs to increase significantly its trade with the fastest growing export markets in the world.

Since joining the EU, trade as a percentage of GDP has broadly stagnated in the UK. That is why it is time for Britain to get out into the world and rediscover its role as a great, global, trading nation. This is such a priority for me that when I became Prime Minister I established, for the first time, a Department for International Trade, led by Liam Fox.

We want to get out into the wider world, to trade and do business all around the globe. Countries including China, Brazil, and the Gulf States have already expressed their interest in striking trade deals with us. We have started discussions on future trade ties with countries like Australia, New Zealand and India. And President Elect Trump has said Britain is not 'at the back of the queue' for a trade deal with the United States, the world's biggest economy, but front of the line.

I know my emphasis on striking trade agreements with countries outside Europe has led to questions about whether Britain seeks to remain a member of the EU's Customs Union. And it is true that full Customs Union membership prevents us from negotiating our own comprehensive trade deals. Now, I want Britain to be able to negotiate its own trade agreements. But I also want tariff-free trade with Europe and cross-border trade there to be as frictionless as possible.

That means I do not want Britain to be part of the Common Commercial Policy and I do not want us to be bound by the Common External Tariff. These are the elements of the Customs Union that prevent us from striking our own comprehensive trade agreements with other countries. But I do want us to have a customs agreement with the EU.

Whether that means we must reach a completely new customs agreement, become an associate member of the Customs Union in some way, or remain a signatory to some elements of it, I hold no preconceived position. I have an open mind on how we do it. It is not the means that matter, but the ends.

And those ends are clear: I want to remove as many barriers to trade as possible. And I want Britain to be free to establish our own tariff schedules at the World Trade Organisation, meaning we can reach new trade agreements not just with the European Union but with old friends and new allies from outside Europe too.

10. The best place for science and innovation

A Global Britain must also be a country that looks to the future. That means being one of the best places in the world for science and innovation. One of our great strengths as a nation is the breadth and depth of our academic and scientific communities, backed up by some of the world's best universities. And we have a proud history of leading and supporting cutting-edge research and innovation.

So we will also welcome agreement to continue to collaborate with our European partners on major science, research, and technology initiatives. From space exploration to clean energy to medical technologies, Britain will remain at the forefront of collective endeavours to better understand, and make better, the world in which we live.

11. Cooperation in the fight against crime and terrorism

And a Global Britain will continue to cooperate with its European partners in important areas such as crime, terrorism and foreign affairs. All of us in Europe face the challenge of cross-border crime, a deadly terrorist threat, and the dangers presented by hostile states. All of us share interests and values in common, values we want to see projected around the world.

With the threats to our common security becoming more serious, our response cannot be to cooperate with one another less, but to work together more. I therefore want our future relationship with the European Union to include practical arrangements on matters of law enforcement and the sharing of intelligence material with our EU allies. I am proud of the role Britain has played and will continue to play in promoting Europe's security. Britain has led Europe on the measures needed to keep our continent secure – whether it is implementing sanctions against Russia following its action in Crimea, working for peace and stability in the Balkans, or securing Europe's external border. We will continue to work closely with our European allies in foreign and defence policy even as we leave the EU itself.

A PHASED APPROACH
12. A smooth, orderly Brexit

These are our objectives for the negotiation ahead – objectives that will help to realise our ambition of shaping that stronger, fairer, Global Britain that we want to see. They are the basis for a new, strong, constructive partnership with the European Union – a partnership of friends and allies, of interests and values. A partnership for a strong EU and a strong UK.

But there is one further objective we are setting. For as I have said before – it is in no one's interests for there to be a cliff-edge for business or a threat to stability, as we change from our existing relationship to a new partnership with the EU. By this, I do not mean that we will seek some form of unlimited transitional status, in which we find ourselves stuck forever in some kind of permanent political purgatory. That would not be good for Britain, but nor do I believe it would be good for the EU.

Instead, I want us to have reached an agreement about our future partnership by the time the two-year Article Fifty process has concluded. From that point onwards, we believe a phased process of implementation, in which both Britain and the EU institutions and member states prepare for the new arrangements that will exist between us will be in our mutual self-interest. This will give businesses enough time to plan and prepare for those new arrangements.

This might be about our immigration controls, customs systems or the way in which we cooperate on criminal justice matters. Or it might be about the future legal and regulatory framework for financial services. For each issue, the time we need to phase-in the new arrangements may differ. Some might be introduced very quickly, some might take longer. And the interim arrangements we rely upon are likely to be a matter of negotiation.

But the purpose is clear: we will seek to avoid a disruptive cliff-edge, and we will do everything we can to phase in the new arrangements we require as Britain and the EU move towards our new partnership.

THE RIGHT DEAL FOR BRITAIN

So, these are the objectives we have set. Certainty wherever possible. Control of our own laws. Strengthening the United Kingdom. Maintaining the Common Travel Area with Ireland. Control of immigration. Rights for EU nationals in Britain, and British nationals in the EU. Enhancing rights for workers. Free trade with European markets. New trade agreements with other countries. A leading role in science and innovation. Cooperation on crime, terrorism and foreign affairs. And a phased approach, delivering a smooth and orderly Brexit.

This is the framework of a deal that will herald a new partnership between the UK and the EU. It is a comprehensive and carefully considered plan that focuses on the ends, not just the means – with its eyes fixed firmly on the future, and on the kind of country we will be once we leave. It reflects the hard work of many in this room today who have worked tirelessly to bring it together and to prepare this country for the negotiation ahead.

And it will, I know, be debated and discussed at length. That is only right. But those who urge us to reveal more – such as the blow-by-blow details of our negotiating strategy, the areas in which we might compromise, the places where we think there are potential trade-offs – will not be acting in the national interest.

Because this is not a game or a time for opposition for opposition's sake. It is a crucial and sensitive negotiation that will define the interests and the success of our country for many years to come. And it is vital that we maintain our discipline.

That is why I have said before – and will continue to say – that every stray word and every hyped up media report is going to make it harder for us to get the right deal for Britain. Our opposite numbers in the European Commission know it, which is why they are keeping their discipline. And the ministers in this Government know it too, which is why we will also maintain ours.

So however frustrating some people find it, the Government will not be pressured into saying more than I believe it is in our national interest to say. Because it is not my job to fill column inches with daily updates, but to get the right deal for Britain. And that is what I intend to do.

A NEW PARTNERSHIP BETWEEN BRITAIN AND EUROPE

I am confident that a deal – and a new strategic partnership between the UK and the EU – can be achieved.

This is firstly because, having held conversations with almost every leader from every single EU member state; having spent time talking to the senior figures from the European institutions, including President Tusk, President Juncker, and President Schulz; and after my Cabinet colleagues David Davis, Philip Hammond and Boris Johnson have done the same with their interlocutors, I am confident that the vast majority want a positive relationship between the UK and the EU after Brexit. And I am confident that the objectives I am setting out today are consistent with the needs of the EU and its Member States.

That is why our objectives include a proposed Free Trade Agreement between Britain and the European Union, and explicitly rule out membership of the EU's Single Market. Because when the EU's leaders say they believe the four freedoms of the Single Market are indivisible, we respect that position. When the 27 Member States say they want to continue their journey inside the European Union, we not only respect that fact but support it. Because we do not want to undermine the Single Market, and we do not want to undermine the European Union. We want the EU to be a success and we want its remaining member states to prosper. And of course we want the same for Britain.

And the second reason I believe it is possible to reach a good deal is that the kind of agreement I have described today is the economically rational thing that both Britain and the EU should aim for. Because trade is not a zero sum game: more of it makes us all more prosperous. Free trade between Britain and the European Union means more trade, and more trade means more jobs and more wealth creation. The erection of new barriers to trade, meanwhile, means the reverse: less trade, fewer jobs, lower growth.

The third and final reason I believe we can come to the right agreement is that cooperation between Britain and the EU is needed not just when it comes to trade but when it comes to our security too. Britain and France are Europe's only two nuclear powers. We are the only two European countries with permanent seats on the United Nations Security Council. Britain's armed forces are a crucial part of Europe's collective defence.

And our intelligence capabilities – unique in Europe – have already saved countless lives in very many terrorist plots that have been thwarted in countries across our continent. After Brexit, Britain wants to be a good friend and neighbour in every way, and that includes defending the safety and security of all of our citizens.

So I believe the framework I have outlined today is in Britain's interests. It is in Europe's interests. And it is in the interests of the wider world. But I must be clear. Britain wants to remain a good friend and neighbour to Europe. Yet I know there are some voices calling for a punitive deal that punishes Britain and discourages other countries from taking the same path. That would be an act of calamitous self-harm for the countries of Europe. And it would not be the act of a friend. Britain would not – indeed we could not – accept such an approach. And while I am confident that this scenario need never arise – while I am sure a positive agreement can be reached – I am equally clear that no deal for Britain is better than a bad deal for Britain.

Because we would still be able to trade with Europe. We would be free to strike trade deals across the world. And we would have the freedom to set the competitive tax rates and embrace the policies that would attract the world's best companies and biggest investors to Britain. And – if we were excluded from accessing the Single Market – we would be free to change the basis of Britain's economic model.

But for the EU, it would mean new barriers to trade with one of the biggest economies in the world. It would jeopardise investments in Britain by EU companies worth more than half a trillion pounds. It would mean a loss of access for European firms to the financial services of the City of London. It would risk exports from the EU to Britain worth around £290 billion every year. And it would disrupt the sophisticated and integrated supply chains upon which many EU companies rely.

Important sectors of the EU economy would also suffer. We are a crucial – profitable – export market for Europe's automotive industry, as well as sectors including energy, food and drink, chemicals, pharmaceuticals, and agriculture. These sectors employ millions of people around Europe. And I do not believe that the EU's leaders will seriously tell German exporters, French farmers, Spanish fishermen, the young unemployed of the Eurozone, and millions of others, that they want to make them poorer, just to punish Britain and make a political point.

For all these reasons – and because of our shared values and the spirit of goodwill that exists on both sides – I am confident that we will follow a better path. I am confident that a positive agreement can be reached. It is right that the Government should prepare for every eventuality – but to do so in the knowledge that a constructive and optimistic approach to the negotiations to come is in the best interests of Europe and the best interests of Britain.

CONCLUSION

We do not approach these negotiations expecting failure, but anticipating success. Because we are a great, global nation with so much to offer Europe and so much to offer the world. One of the world's largest and strongest economies. With the finest intelligence services, the bravest armed forces, the most effective hard and soft power, and friendships, partnerships and alliances in every continent.

And another thing that's important. The essential ingredient of our success. The strength and support of 65 million people willing us to make it happen. Because after all the division and discord, the country is coming together.

The referendum was divisive at times. And those divisions have taken time to heal. But one of the reasons that Britain's democracy has been such a success for so many years is that the strength of our identity as one nation, the respect we show to one another as fellow citizens, and the importance we attach to our institutions means that when a vote has been held we all respect the result. The victors have the responsibility to act magnanimously. The losers have the responsibility to respect the legitimacy of the outcome. And the country comes together.

And that is what we are seeing today. Business isn't calling to reverse the result, but planning to make a success of it. The House of Commons has voted overwhelmingly for us to get on with it. And the overwhelming majority of people – however they voted – want us to get on with it too.

So that is what we will do. Not merely forming a new partnership with Europe, but building a stronger, fairer, more Global Britain too. And let that be the legacy of our time. The prize towards which we work. The destination at which we arrive once the negotiation is done.

And let us do it not for ourselves, but for those who follow. For the country's children and grandchildren too. So that when future generations look back at this time, they will judge us not only by the decision that we made, but by what we made of that decision.

They will see that we shaped them a brighter future. They will know that we built them a better Britain.'

CHAPTER 1

WHAT IS BREXIT?

Helen Tse, Clarke Willmott LLP

INTRODUCTION

Brexit is a mixture of the words 'Britain' and 'exit' to describe Britain leaving Europe. The word itself appears to have first been identified in 2012, coined by EURACTIV in a blog post by Peter Wilding.[1] There has been much talk of whether the UK will implement a 'Hard Brexit' or a 'Soft Brexit' – describing the level of withdrawal Britain will make from Europe. It was very shortly after Parliament voted overwhelmingly to give the Prime Minister the power to trigger Article 50 and start the process of the UK formally leaving the EU that the government presented its formal policy paper detailing how it is proposed that the UK will make its Brexit.

The Prime Minister's hard-line proposals were set out in the Lancaster House speech in January 2017 and White Paper of February 2017 entitled 'The United Kingdom's exit from and new partnership with the European Union' which amount to a list of key objectives of effecting a successful Brexit, some of which may not be easy to achieve in practice. The White Paper pulls together a firm 12-point plan outlining the main aims of achieving a successful Brexit as follows:

1   to provide certainty and clarity;
2   to take control of our own laws;
3   to strengthen the union;
4   to protect our strong historic ties with Ireland and maintain the common travel area;
5   to control immigration;
6   to secure rights for EU nationals in the UK, and UK nationals in the EU;
7   to protect workers' rights;
8   to ensure free trade with European markets;
9   to secure new trade agreements with other countries;
10   to ensure the UK remains the best place for science and innovation;
11   to cooperate in the fight against crime and terrorism; and
12   to deliver a smooth, orderly exit from the EU.

It remains to be seen whether the hard-line proposals as set out in the Prime Minister's White Paper will result in a 'Hard Brexit' or a 'Soft Brexit'. 'Hard Brexit' could mean the UK ending its trading agreement with the 27 EU countries and the free movement of people ending. 'Soft Brexit' might include the UK being part of an EU single market for goods and services but with limitations on immigration and the free movement of people. As at the time of writing, the

---

1   P Wilding in BlogActiv.eu (Blog) 15 May (OED Archive) *Stumbling towards the Brexit: Britain, a referendum and an ever-closer reckoning.*

political stage is wrought with uncertainty and so it remains unclear as to which is to be the preferred method as to the UK formally leaving the EU. This position will hopefully become clearer in the coming weeks and months to ensure the country is able to meet its plan for Brexit as set out in the Prime Minister's White Paper.

1.1   A BRIEF HISTORY OF THE UK'S RELATIONSHIP WITH THE EU

1957 – The Treaty of Rome created the European Economic Community (EEC) – the UK was not party to it.

1963 and 1967 – The UK tried to join the EEC but this was denied by the French President Charles de Gaulle stating the UK's agricultural practices were not compatible with Europe.

1969 – President Charles de Gaulle resigned and the UK's third attempt to join the EEC was successful.

1972 – January 1972, the UK Prime Minister, Edward Heath (Conservative) signed the Treaty of Accession.

1973 – 1 January – the UK joined the EEC

1975 – The UK held a referendum on whether the UK should remain in the EEC. On 5 June 1975, the electorate were asked to vote yes or no on the question: 'Do you think the UK should stay in the European Community (Common Market)?' Approximately 64% of the UK population voted and of that, 67.2% voted to stay in the EEC.[1] The data shows that support for the UK to leave the EU in 1975 appears unrelated to the support for Leave in the 2016 referendum.[2]

1979 – The UK opted out of the newly formed European Exchange Rate Mechanism (ERM) which was the precursor to the creation of the euro.

1985 – The UK ratified the Single European Act, the first major revision to the Treaty of Rome without a referendum with the full support HM Government of Margaret Thatcher.

1990 – In October, the UK joined the ERM with the pound sterling pegged to the deutschmark. In November 1990 Prime Minister Margaret Thatcher resigned amid internal divisions within the Conservative Party arising partly from her increasingly Eurosceptic views.

1992 – Black Wednesday happened and the UK was forced to withdraw from the ERM after the pound sterling came under pressure from currency speculators costing the UK taxpayers over £3 billion.

---

1   *'Research Briefings – The 1974–75 UK Renegotiation of EEC Membership and Referendum'.* Parliament of the United Kingdom.

2   'Who Voted for Brexit? A comprehensive district level analysis'. Becker, Fetzer, Novy, University of Warwick. Retrieved 22 Nov 2016.

1993 – Under the Maastricht Treaty, the EEC became the European Union on 1 November 1993, reflecting the economic and political union.

2009 – On 1 December, the Lisbon Treaty came into force. The Maastricht Treaty is now known, in updated form as, the Treaty on European Union (2007) or TEU, and the Treaty of Rome is now known, in updated form, as the Treaty on the Functioning of the European Union (2007) or TFEU.

The NatCen Social Research and its British Social Attitudes (BSA) survey offered various choices to the respondents for the Britain's relationship with the European Union:

1   to withdraw from the EU;
2   to remain within the EU and attempt to diminish its power;
3   to leave things as they are;
4   to stay within the EU and try to broaden its power; or
5   to work for the formation of a single European government

22% of the respondents agreed with option 1 and 43% with option 2. 65% either desire to break ties or decrease the EU's legislative influence and only 38% supported both option 1 and 2. Euroscepticism has been increasing since 1993.

1.2   2016 REFERENDUM

1.2.1   Negotiations for EU reform

In 2012, there were calls for a referendum on the UK's EU membership which was rejected by the then Prime Minister David Cameron. However, he pacified critics with the possibility of a future referendum on the point. According to the BBC, 'The prime minister acknowledged the need to ensure the UK's position within the European Union had "the full-hearted support of the British people" but they needed to show "tactical and strategic patience".'

One of David Cameron's promises was a referendum on Europe if he were elected in 2015. As a consequence, the referendum pursuant to the European Union Referendum Act 2015 was held in 2016 which led to Brexit.

David Cameron tried to reform the obligations of the UK in remaining as an EU member by focusing on four key points: protection of the single market for non-Eurozone countries, reduction of 'red tape', exempting Britain from 'ever-closer union', and restricting EU immigration.

In February 2016, the negotiations of David Cameron were limited; in-work benefits for new EU immigrants were agreed, but before they could be applied, a country such as the UK would have to get permission from the European Commission and then from the European Council.

On that basis David Cameron announced a referendum date of 23 June 2016 to address a renegotiation of the UK's EU membership. David Cameron said that if a leave vote won, he would trigger Article 50 immediately giving the UK a 'two-year time period to negotiate the arrangements for exit.'

1.2.2 Referendum result

On 24 June 2016, the referendum result was 51.9% in favour of leaving the EU and 48.1% in favour of remaining a member of the European Union. There was shock regarding the result especially amongst the business world and four million people signed a petition requesting a second referendum. This was rejected by the government on 9 July 2016.

United Kingdom European Union membership referendum, 2016		
Choice	Votes	%
Leave the EU	17,410,742	51.89
Remain a member of the EU	16,141,241	48.11
Valid votes	33,551,983	99.92
Invalid or blank votes	25,359	0.08
Total votes	33,577,342	100.00
Registered voters and turnout	46,500,001	72.21
Voting age population and turnout	51,356,768	65.38
Source: Electoral Commission[55]; UNDESA (UK VAP); US Census Bureau (Gibraltar VAP)		

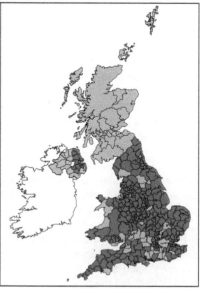

Results by region (left) and by local council district (right)

■ Leave ■ Remain

1.3 REVIEW OF THE LAW AND POTENTIAL IMPACTS OF BREXIT

1.3.1 Political effects

Brexit was the beginning of much political upheaval. David Cameron, the UK Prime Minister resigned on 13 July 2016 and was replaced by Theresa May. The Chancellor George Osborne was replaced by Philip Hammond. David Davis was appointed as the Secretary of State for Exiting the European Union (the Brexit Minister) and Boris Johnson, formerly the Mayor of London became the Secretary of State for Foreign and Commonwealth Affairs. In the Labour party, their leader Jeremy Corbyn lost a vote of confidence among his parliamentary party but has subsequently remained as leader. On 4 July 2016 the head of UKIP, Nigel Farage, resigned.

1.3.2 The procedure to leave the EU: 'Article 50'

The 2016 referendum (just like the 1975 referendum) does not trigger Article 50 nor does it force the Government to act in a prescribed manner. However, before the 2016 referendum, the UK Government sent out a flyer stating 'This is your decision. The Government will implement what you decide.'[1] During the 2016 Referendum campaign David Cameron said he would invoke Article 50 if the leave vote won,[2] but surprisingly the Civil Service did not make any contingency plans for a favourable outcome for the leave vote. The Foreign Affairs Select Committee described this omission as 'an act of gross negligence.'[3] David Cameron resigned and said that it would be for the incoming Prime Minister to invoke Article 50 and start the formal and legal process of the UK leaving the EU.[4]

In *Miller and Santos v Secretary of State* [2016] EWHC 2768 (Admin), paras 105–106 it was asked who has the power to give a notification under Article 50. The Secretary of State didn't argue that the Referendum Act 2015 gave a statutory power to the Crown to give notice under Article 50. The court stated:

'... a referendum on any topic can only be advisory for the lawmakers in Parliament unless very clear language to the contrary is in the referendum legislation in question. No such language is used in the 2015 Referendum Act. Further, the 2015 Referendum Act was passed against a background including a clear briefing paper to parliamentarians explaining that the referendum would have advisory effect only.'

---

1   HM Government. 'Why the Government believes that voting to remain in the European Union is the best decision for the UK. The EU referendum, Thursday, 23 June 2016.
2   Staunton, Denis (23 February 2016). 'David Cameron: no second referendum if UK votes for Brexit'. The Irish Times.
3   Patrick Wintour (20 July 2016). 'Cameron accused of 'gross negligence' over Brexit contingency plans'. The Guardian.
4   Brexit: David Cameron to quit after UK votes to leave EU'. BBC. Retrieved 24 June 2016.

1.3.3 Article 50

No member state has ever invoked Article 50 of the Treaty on European Union and wanted to leave.[1] Article 50 of the Treaty on European Union is the mechanism for a member state to leave the EU by giving notice to the European Council. It was triggered on 29 March 2017 and the UK has two years to negotiate with the 27 EU member states regarding treaties. Otherwise, such treaties will no longer apply. The leaving agreement may be agreed by qualified majority voting.[2] The Council of the European Union has not unanimously agreed to an extension, so the UK will have two years from when the country gives official notice to the EU to leave the EU. During the two years, it would be useful for the new treaties to be agreed but that might not happen practically given it takes time to negotiate treaties. The most recent treaty with Canada has taken ten years for the UK to agree and finalise. Some aspects, such as new trade agreements, may be difficult to negotiate until after the UK has formally left the EU. Under Article 50, the withdrawal must be in accordance with the member state's constitution, and uncertainty exists as to the constitutional requirements in the UK.

On 28 June 2016, an EU Parliament motion called for the UK to trigger Article 50 as soon as possible to exit the EU. However, the prerogative to trigger Article 50 remains with the UK and not the EU. Whilst the UK Government does not trigger Article 50, the UK remains in the EU and must abide by EU treaties. If the UK were to significantly breach EU law, there are legal provisions under the Lisbon Treaty to allow the EU to cancel membership but this test has a high threshold and unlikely for the UK.[3] Breaches of EU law wouldn't result in the UK being rejected from the EU, rather, certain rights would be restricted, eg free trade, free movement and voting rights.

The Article 50 debate has been wrought with arguments from the business world, academics and politicians. Alan Renwick of the Constitution Unit of University College London stated that Article 50 negotiations could not be used to renegotiate the conditions of future membership and Article 50 did not provide the legal basis of withdrawing a decision to leave.

On the other hand, Udo Di Fabio, a retired German Supreme Court judge on constitutional law has argued[4] that:

> 'The Lisbon Treaty does not forbid an exiting country to withdraw its application for leaving, because the Vienna Convention on the Law of Treaties prescribes an initial notification procedure, a kind of period of notice. Before a contract under international law such as the Lisbon Treaty, which had been agreed without specifying details of giving notice, can be effectively cancelled, it is required that the intention to do so is expressed 12 months

---

1   Greenland left the EU in 1985, prior to the introduction of Article 50, and as an autonomous country within the Danish Realm, not as a sovereign member state.
2   Article 50(3) of the Treaty on European Union.
3   Rankin, Jennifer (25 June 2016). 'What is Article 50 and why is it so central to the Brexit debate?'. The Guardian.
4   FAZ Artikel: Zukunft-der-europaeischen-union Kopf-hoch.

in advance: in this matter there exists the principle of preserving existing agreements and international organisations. In this light, the declaration of the intention to leave would itself be, under EU law, not a notice of cancellation.

Separate negotiations of the EU institutions with pro-EU regions London, Scotland or Northern Ireland would constitute a violation of the Lisbon Treaty, according to which the integrity of a member country is explicitly put under protection.'

The European Parliament set out their thoughts in a note dated February 2016. If the UK left the EU, from that date, the application of the EU Treaties would also end. The UK at that stage would have to adopt any EU Law to transition such laws in the UK. This is an extensive and on-going task and there are currently teams looking at how to transition the laws to ensure a smooth Brexit.[1] The EU has exclusive laws regarding the Common Fisheries Policy, customs union, competition rules, monetary policy and concluding international agreements which will need to be considered before Article 50 is invoked.[2]

1.3.4 Invoking Article 50

10 DOWNING STREET
LONDON SW1A 2AA

THE PRIME MINISTER   29 March 2017

Dear President Tusk

On 23 June last year, the people of the United Kingdom voted to leave the European Union. As I have said before, that decision was no rejection of the values we share as fellow Europeans. Nor was it an attempt to do harm to the European Union or any of the remaining member states. On the contrary, the United Kingdom wants the European Union to succeed and prosper. Instead, the referendum was a vote to restore, as we see it, our national self-determination. We are leaving the European Union, but we are not leaving Europe – and we want to remain committed partners and allies to our friends across the continent.

---

1   Eva-Maria Poptcheva, Article 50 TEU: Withdrawal of a Member State from the EU, Briefing
     Note for European Parliament.(Note: 'The content of this document is the sole responsibility
     of the author and any opinions expressed therein do not necessarily represent the official
     position of the European Parliament.)'
2   http://ec.europa.eu/citizens-initiative/public/competences/faq#q1.

Earlier this month, the United Kingdom Parliament confirmed the result of the referendum by voting with clear and convincing majorities in both of its Houses for the European Union (Notification of Withdrawal) Bill. The Bill was passed by Parliament on 13 March and it received Royal Assent from Her Majesty The Queen and became an Act of Parliament on 16 March.

Today, therefore, I am writing to give effect to the democratic decision of the people of the United Kingdom. I hereby notify the European Council in accordance with Article 50(2) of the Treaty on European Union of the United Kingdom's intention to withdraw from the European Union. In addition, in accordance with the same Article 50(2) as applied by Article 106a of the Treaty Establishing the European Atomic Energy Community, I hereby notify the European Council of the United Kingdom's intention to withdraw from the European Atomic Energy Community. References in this letter to the European Union should therefore be taken to include a reference to the European Atomic Energy Community.

The UK Prime Minister Theresa May invoked Article 50 on 29 March 2017 (for the Prime Minister's Commons statement on triggering Article 50, see Appendix 1 at p 367).

1.3.5 'Great Repeal Bill'

Theresa May promised a 'Great Repeal Bill', described as an essential step in the process of the UK leaving the EU, which would repeal the European Communities Act 1972 and restate all enactments of UK law previously in force. This essentially means that EU law would no longer apply in the UK.

The government's White Paper was published on 30 March 2017 and sets out the government's proposals for ensuring a functioning statute book once we have left the EU. The government in the UK is keen to ensure a black hole in our statute book is avoided given the implications and disruption that this could have on UK businesses and individual citizens as the Brexit process takes place. However, the process of putting the Great Repeal Bill in place is likely to be one of the largest legislative projects undertaken in UK history and so it is not to be thought of lightly.

A controversial feature of the Great Repeal Bill is that the government proposes to create powers to correct the statute book where it is considered necessary to do so without full parliamentary scrutiny. There has been opposition to this sweeping power to make ill thought-out legislation and understandably so.

A further issue is borne out of timing – the government's negotiations to effect Brexit will be taking place simultaneously with the Great Repeal Bill's passage through parliament. Those negotiations could inevitably shape what our country's legal landscape looks like post-Brexit although the Great Repeal Bill will need to have been fully dealt with by the day that the UK leaves the EU.

The Great Repeal Bill will need to work its way through both Houses of Parliament but to become law only at the point of the UK's departure from the EU, which under the current timetable is due for March 2019 unless otherwise extended.

The government has estimated that between 800 and 1,000 statutory instruments will be needed to be implemented to ensure the success and proper functioning of the Great Repeal Bill and I would envisage that until the clauses of the Act have been fully considered, all laws will remain in force until specifically repealed.[1] This book will look at the hypothetical situations if certain laws were abolished and the effects which may be had on your business.

1.3.6   Negotiating positions

Various leaders from EU countries had decided to refrain from any negotiations with the UK. until the UK invoked Article 50. Jean-Claude Juncker was particularly stern and ordered all members of the EU Commission (EC) not to negotiate with UK parties regarding Brexit.[2] In October 2016, he said he was annoyed that the UK, despite being in the EU for 40 years, was not closer to Europe. Mr Juncker was bullish about Brexit and rejected it being the beginning of the demise of the EU. Rather he said he would develop an EU defence policy without the British after Brexit, and rejected a suggestion that the EC should negotiate in such a way that Britain would be able to hold a second referendum. On 5 November 2016, a number of European businesses wanted to make agreements with the British government to protect their commercial trading arrangements and Juncker warned: 'I am telling them [companies] that they should not interfere in the debate, as they will find that I will block their path.'[3]

On 29 June 2016, the European Council president Donald Tusk told the UK that the UK would not be allowed access to the European Single Market unless they accepted its four freedoms of movement for goods, capital, services, and people.[4]

On 4 November 2016, Boris Johnson, the British Foreign Secretary, met his counterpart, the German Minister for Foreign Affairs, Frank-Walter Steinmeier and tried to emphasise the importance of British-German relationships, but Steinmeier bluntly responded that the German view was that the UK should have voted to stay in the EU and that the German priority now was to preserve the remaining union of 27 members. There could be no negotiations before the UK formally gives notice. A long delay before beginning negotiations would be detrimental. Great Britain could not keep the advantages of the common market but at the same time cancel the 'less pleasant rules'.

1   Mason, Rowena (3 October 2016). 'UK and Scotland on course for great 'constitutional bust-up''. BBC.
2   https://www.rt.com/uk/348683-article-50-eu-brexit/.
3   http://derstandard.at/2000047020439/Juncker-warnt-Firmen-vor-eigenen-Brexit-Deals   (In German).
4   http://www.express.co.uk/news/politics/684528/Brexit-Donald-Tusk-Britain-free-movement-access-EU-single-market-David-Cameron.

The First Minister of Scotland, Nicola Sturgeon, stated that Scotland might refuse consent for legislation required to leave the EU, though some lawyers argue that Scotland cannot block Brexit.

Newly appointed PM Theresa May made it clear that negotiations with the EU required a 'UK-wide approach'. On 15 July 2016, she said: 'I have already said that I won't be triggering Article 50 until I think that we have a UK approach and objectives for negotiations – I think it is important that we establish that before we trigger Article 50.'

Nick Clegg MP said the figures showed the Civil Service was unprepared for the very complex negotiations ahead.[1] This uncertainty will undoubtedly impact business negatively and I hope that in reviewing your business based on the proposed hypothetical situations raised in this book, it will strengthen and prepare your business for the worst case scenario.

1.4   CONSEQUENCES OF WITHDRAWAL FOR THE UNITED KINGDOM

1.4.1   Relationship with remaining EU members

Political system of the European Union

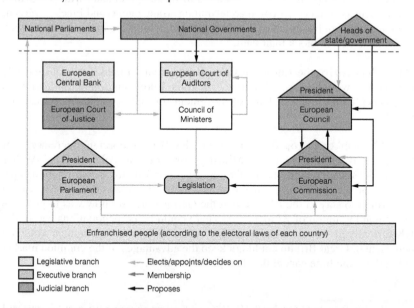

The UK leaving the EU could take various forms. For businesses, the key is can the UK stay or have access to the EU internal market?

---

1   Laura Hughes (9 September 2016). 'Brexit department spends more than £250,000 on legal advice in just two months'. Daily Telegraph.

1.4.2   Alternative Brexit models

	EU membership	Norway	Switzerland	Canada	Turkey	WTO
Single market member?	Full	Full	Partial	No	No	No
Tariffs?	None	None	None	Reduced tariffs through free trade deal	None on industrial goods	Yes
Accept free movement?	Yes	Yes	Yes	No	No	No
In the customs union	Yes	No	No	No	Yes	No
Makes EU budget contributions	Yes	Yes	Yes (but smaller than Norway)	No	No	No

In the event the UK leaves the EU, would that result in an automatic withdrawal from the EEA or does it need notice under Article 127 of the EEA Agreement – and, if the courts so decide, would such notice given by the UK require an Act of Parliament?

'Access to' and 'membership of' the single market are sometimes used interchangeably but they mean very different things.

The single market currently has 28 full members and full membership provides four freedoms: free movement of goods, services, capital, and people in the EU.

The European Economic Area (EEA) on the other hand is a limited model – granting an internal market between the EU and Norway, Iceland, and Liechtenstein and is governed by the EEA Agreement. The limited members have to abide by EU law in certain areas but they have to allow free movement of people.

Chancellor Philip Hammond has said if the UK is 'closed off' in trade terms by the rest of the EU, it could be forced into adopting a 'new economic model', comments interpreted as suggesting cuts to corporation tax to allow the UK to entice business from elsewhere in Europe.

Various models have been considered and discussed to ascertain whether the UK could stay in the EEA as a European Free Trade Association (EFTA) member (alongside Iceland, Liechtenstein and Norway), or seek to negotiate bilateral terms more along the Swiss model with a series of interdependent sectoral agreements. Since 1973, the UK has not negotiated a trade agreement in its own right so is being assisted by myself and the private sector advisers.

As an EFTA member the UK would be bound by EU law in relation to the internal market but would not be allowed to vote on such law – only provide development suggestions as the EU is required to conduct extensive consultations with non-EU members before issuing EU law.

The EEA Agreement (EU and EFTA members except Switzerland) does not include Common Agriculture and Fisheries Policies, Customs Union, Common Trade Policy, Common Foreign and Security Policy, direct and indirect taxation, and Police and Judicial Co-operation in Criminal Matters. Therefore if the UK were an EFTA members it would be allowed to legislate its own laws in these areas. However, as a EFTA country the UK as consideration to access the internal market, it would be required to contribute to the EU Budget.[1]

In addition, as an EATA member, the UK would not be subject to European Court of Justice rulings. The EFTA Court has their own jurisdiction to resolve disputes between the EU, EU Member states, and the EFTA Member States.[2]

Liechtenstein model

Perhaps the Liechtenstein model may be a solution as it has restricted the free movement of people using Article 114 of the EEA Agreement.

Switzerland model

Switzerland's agreement covers free movement of goods, and free movement of people. Brexit came about because many UK voters wanted to restrict the freedom of movement of people. Therefore, the EEA Agreement as it stands which allows the free movement for EU and EEA citizens in return for allowing EFTA members to access the internal market wouldn't work for the UK. Switzerland has agreed provisions to allow for the free movement for EU citizens. The Swiss immigration referendum in February 2014 voted narrowly in favour of an end to the 'free movement' agreement, by February 2017. However, the bilateral treaties between Switzerland and the European Union are all co-dependent: if one is terminated then all are terminated. Therefore, if Switzerland chose unilaterally to cancel the 'free movement' agreement then all its agreements with the EU would lapse unless a compromise was found.

A UK new model: Prime Minister's letter to Donald Tusk triggering Article 50

On 29 March 2017, the UK Prime Minister Theresa May wrote to European Council President Donald Tusk to notify him of the UK's intention to leave the EU (for the full text of the Prime Minister's letter, see Appendix 2 at p 371).

---

1   Glencross, Andrew (March 2015). 'Why a British referendum on EU membership will not solve the Europe question'. International Affairs. 91 (2): 303–17.
2   http://www.allenovery.com/Brexit-Law/Documents/Macro/EU/AO_BrexitLaw_-_EEA_Membership_Jul_2016.PDF.

1.4.3   British citizens living and working in the EU

Several thousand British citizens resident in other EU countries have, after the referendum, applied for citizenship where they live, since they fear losing the right to work there.

1.5   CONSEQUENCES OF WITHDRAWAL FOR THE EU

Brexit has caused concern amongst the EU nations. The German Parliament published a paper looking at the economic and political impact of Brexit on the EU. The paper said The UK is the third largest export market of German goods of approximately 120 billion euros annually, which is about 8% of German exports, with Germany achieving a trade surplus with Britain worth €36.3 billion (2014). A 'hard Brexit' would mean German exports would be subject to World Trade Organization (WTO) customs and tariffs, affecting German car exports, where duties of about 10% would have to be paid to Britain. In Germany, 750,000 jobs depend upon export to Britain, while on the British side about 3 million jobs depend on export to the EU. The paper concluded the consequences of withdrawal from the EU by the UK would be negative and create much uncertainty.

Pursuant to the Lisbon Treaty 2009, EU Council decisions can only be blocked by four or more members. The thinking of this was to prevent the three most populous members (Germany, France and Britain) from dominating the EU Council. Brexit will result in Germany and like-minded northern European countries (the Dutch, Scandinavians and Baltic states) losing an ally and therefore also their blocking minority. Without this blocking minority, other EU states could potentially be more powerful as they could overrule Germany and its allies in questions of EU budget discipline or the recruitment of German banks to guarantee deposits in troubled southern European banks.

The UK leaving the EU is a massive blow to the EU as the UK has the third-largest population, the second largest net contributor to the EU budget (of €11.5 billion) and the financial centre of the world. The EU would have to find a way to plug the deficit. Brexit also is a disadvantage for the UK who would no longer be a shareholder (currently holding 16%) in the European Investment Bank, in which only EU members can participate. Furthermore, Britain is one of only two members (the other being France) that possess nuclear weapons and have a veto in the Security Council of the United Nations.

A report by Tim Oliver of the German Institute for International and Security Affairs expanded analysis of what a British withdrawal could mean for the EU: the report argues that a UK withdrawal 'has the potential to fundamentally change the EU and European integration. On the one hand, a withdrawal could tip the EU towards protectionism, exacerbate existing divisions, or unleash centrifugal forces leading to the EU's unravelling. Alternatively, the EU could free itself of its most awkward member, making the EU easier to lead and more effective.'

Brexit sent shockwaves through the EU with concerns that other members would want to leave the EU. However it has been argued that most member states have a greater dependence on the EU than Britain, and that the economies of many of the smaller countries would struggle greatly to survive outside of the EU.

1.6 SUMMARY: KEY STATISTICS

1.6.1 Social

Population, 2016	million	% of EU total	Unemployment rate (%), Q1 2016	%	Rank (1=highest)
EU incl. UK	510.1	100%	EU incl. UK	8.8	..
Germany	82.2	16%	UK	5.0	25
UK	65.3	13%	Greece	24.3	1
France*	63.7	12%	Spain	20.4	2
Italy	60.7	12%	Germany	4.3	27
Spain	46.4	9%	Czech Rep.	4.2	28

* Figure from 2013, excluding overseas territories

1.6.2 Economy

Gross Domestic Product, 2015	£ billion	% of EU total	GDP growth (annual average, 2010–2015)	%
EU incl. UK	10,625	100%	EU incl. UK	1.2
UK	1,870	18%	UK	2.0
Germany	2,197	21%	Germany	2.0
France	1,583	15%	France	1.1
Italy	1,188	11%	Italy	-0.3
US	12,208	..	US	2.0

1.6.3 Trade

UK's largest export markets, 2014	£ billion	% of total	UK's largest import markets, 2014	£ billion	% of total
Total EU	228.9	44.4%	Total EU	290.6	52.9%
USA	88.0	17.1%	Germany	70.6	12.8%
Germany	43.3	8.4%	USA	51.6	9.4%

Netherlands	34.1	6.6%	China	38.3	7.0%
France	30.6	5.9%	France	37.0	6.7%
Ireland	27.9	5.4%	Netherlands	36.1	6.6%

1.6.4   EU budget contributions

Highest net contributions, 2014		Highest net contributions per head, 2014		
£ billion			£	
Germany	14.2	Netherlands	305	
France	6.0	Sweden	218	
UK	5.7	Germany	177	
Netherlands	5.1	Denmark	143	
Italy	4.2	UK	89	(8th highest)

Note: EU budget contributions include EU receipts to the private sector. This is the main reason why the UK's net contribution is lower than the £9.8 billion reported by HM Treasury.

Sources: Eurostat (social and economy); ONS, *Pink Book 2015* (trade); Commons Library briefing, *EU budget and the UK's contribution*; HMRC for exchange rates

CHAPTER 2

ECONOMIC IMPACT AND MANUFACTURING

Dimitrios Syrrakos, Manchester Metropolitan University[1]

INTRODUCTION

The Chapter consists of four parts. The first evaluates the implications of the PM's Speech on 17 January and the EU responses it prompted. The second assesses the current UK-EU macroeconomic framework and changes to it brought about by the Referendum and the impeding Brexit negotiations. The third part draws on Brexit's impact on SMEs from changes in the trade relations between the UK and the other 27 EU member states. Finally, the fourth section focuses on the UK manufacturing sector and the strategies that could be adopted to mitigate the impact of Brexit, while seeking to take advantage of new opportunities.

2.1 PM's SPEECH – IMPLICATIONS AND EU RESPONSES

The Maastricht Treaty of 1992 identified the conditions that EU countries should observe once they have joined the EU's Single Market. These conditions are based on the principles of free movement of capital, goods, services and labour. By the second half of the 1990s, free movement of labour had come to imply free movement of people.

Trade relations between the UK and the rest of the EU, while the former remains an EU member, represent the optimal trade relations the UK can secure with other countries, in this case other EU members. The PM's speech on 17 January at Lancaster House, by ruling out continuation of single market membership, implied that the outcome of the negotiations the UK government is about to embark upon with the rest of the EU cannot resemble the current trade relations. As a result, only a second or third best is attainable. In the words of Conservative MP and Chair of the Commons Education Committee, Neil Carmichael:

'The Prime Minister's commitment to trading as freely as possible with the EU is welcome, but the best possible trading arrangement with the EU is full participation in the single market. No other arrangement is comparable, and so if the Government abandons membership of the single market, they will start the negotiations opting for second best.' (The Independent)

The UK's macroeconomic arrangements and trade relations with other EU countries are depicted in Table 1 below. Exchange rate arrangements are presented horizontally at the top and trade relations are depicted vertically on the left. Brexit,

---

1   The author would like to express his thanks to Prof Chris Pyke for help with data and referencing.

with curbing immigration implications, as reinforced by the PM Speech will inevitably place the UK under different (less advanced) trade arrangements with *all* of the 27 remaining EU countries. This second best scenario, a variation of 'hard-Brexit', will see the UK's trade relations with the rest of the EU downgraded to retaining access to (a much needed) customs union.

Table 1

EU Trade Relations and Exchange Rate Arrangements

European Union macroeconomic framework			
	Currency - exchange rate relations		
Trade relations	**Flexible**	**Fixed**	**Common**
	Exchange rates	**Exchange rates**	**Currency - euro**
World Trade Organisation			
	Cliff-edge		
Free trade area	↑		
Common internal	**Very-hard**		
tariffs and quotas	**Brexit**		
	↑		
Customs Union			
Common internal	**Turkey?**		
and external	**Hard Brexit**		
tariffs and quotas	↑		
Single market	↑ **Soft Brexit -**	Poland	France, Germany
Common internal	accessing single	Denmark	Italy, Spain, Lux.
and external tariffs	market	Sweden	Austria, Ireland
and quotas		Bulgaria	Belgium, Portugal
Plus	**UK**	Romania	Finland, Cyprus
Coordination of		Hungary	Holland, Greece
macroeconomic policies			Slovakia, Slovenia
and/or reduction of			Lithuania, Latvia
exchange rate volatility			Estonia, Malta

The PM's speech, despite demarcating the UK's negotiating framework, based on the 12 objectives provided, did not explicitly clarify the type of trade relations the UK seeks to establish with the EU in the post-Brexit environment. For example, objectives 8 and 9 are inherently inconsistent. Objective 8, called for the UK to seek a 'Comprehensive Free Trade Agreement with the European Union'. At the same time though, the PM said:

'But I want to be clear. What I am proposing cannot mean membership of the Single Market'.

The UK government's stance causes confusion and often dismay to EU officials. If an EU country acknowledges that curbing immigration implies no single market membership, then that country cannot have access to the specific single market's elements in certain areas of interest. Preferential access (access *a la carte*) cannot be granted. This is the case, not because the EU wants to punish the UK, but because it would undermine that functioning of the single market itself. If the UK is able to export cars to EU's single market (eg to France and Germany), without paying its contributions to EU, why should not other EU countries have the same deal, while losing market share to the UK automobile industry? As a consequence, there cannot be the greatest possible access, (or any access) to the Single Market. Effectively this means that the nature of Brexit is going to be hard.

However, regardless of the clarity provided concerning the UK's negotiating stance, in terms of not seeking continuation of single market membership, further confusion was caused in relation to customs union membership.

As full membership of a customs union precludes establishing free trade areas independently with third parties, it can only be concluded that the UK is contemplating leaving the EU's customs union. To understand why this is the case consider the following scenario, which is highly likely to emerge if objectives 8 and 9 as set out by the PM were implemented. Assume the UK, following Brexit, is granted full access to the EU's customs union, and at the same time exceptionally permitted to join trade agreements with other countries. Soon after, the UK and the USA could create their own customs union. This implies that the UK would be party to two separate customs unions, and as a result, imported products from the USA could flood the EU customs union via the UK.

This would clearly undermine the functioning of the EU's customs union and would not be viable. Eventually, the UK would either be requested to apply the EU's external tariff and non-tariff trade barriers to USA goods and services (effectively dissolving its customs union with the USA), or leave the EU's customs union. This example, illustrates why not a single country is party to two customs unions. Going back to the example, the only way for this to be the case, is for all other EU countries to accept the terms and conditions of a USA and UK customs union. This would then imply that the two customs unions have merged to one customs union including the EU, the UK and the USA.

This rules out the PM's proposal for a new customs agreement, as any agreement would have to be inferior to the EU's customs union. However, it does not rule out, limited or preferential access. Assuming good will from the part of the EU, limited access to the EU's customs union could form the basis for an agreement. And this is exactly what the PM offered and clarified in her speech. The crucial issue therefore, that the negotiations would focus on is what markets such an agreement would include. Ultimately, compromises would have to be made by the UK's negotiating team, in particular concerning financial services. To conclude, the PM's speech provided clarity by recognising that soft Brexit is no longer an option (ruling out the small arrow on the left hand side in Table 1, and moving to somewhere between the two middle arrows). This would point to

35

an agreement that falls short of full access to EU's customs union but is much superior to a free trade area. This is relatively encouraging as it conveys the message to the EU that the UK is ready to negotiate on the grounds of an inferior variant of the EU's customs union agreement. By doing so, the PM's Speech shifted the debate away from 'soft vs hard' Brexit, to one over 'hard vs very hard' Brexit, while pointing its preference for a consensus closer to the former.

Notwithstanding the difficulties in making a prediction for the final agreement the framework set by the PM indicates that it could resemble in some ways the EU-Turkey customs union subject to differences in the sectors it would include.

It needs to be noted though, that the Common Market guidelines regulate only around 40% of the EU member countries' economic activity with areas such as financial services and insurance largely not included. Hence, the UK government's proposals for, in effect a 'sector-by-sector' access to the single market. Such an approach would make sense, provided the European Commission (EC) allows individual EU countries to negotiate bilateral trade agreements with the UK on specific sectors, such as insurance. However, given that the EC's objective is to enlarge the single market competency areas and to include as many industries as possible, this is highly unlikely.[1] As Chancellor Merkel pointed out in response to the PM's Speech: 'The main thing is that Europe does not let itself be divided and we will make sure of that via very intensive dialogue'. A consensus similar to the trade agreement between Switzerland and the EU should not be ruled out, ensuring access to specific single market areas. This of course would involve a compromise from the UK government as it would limit its ability to reduce immigration from the EU and it would also have to continue making contributions to the EU.

Failure to secure access to the single market and the customs union will lead the UK's trade relations with the rest of the EU to a free trade area, or a 'very hard' Brexit. Failure to agree even on a free trade area between the UK and the EU's free trade area, will relegate the UK's trade relations to World Trade Organisation (WTO) regulations that broadly allow free trade but subject to countries' unilateral tariffs and quotas.

Much desired flexibility from the rest of the EU countries and the European Commission could facilitate an agreement, based on a version of the EU's customs union, permitting some curbing of immigration. However, as a customs union implies the adoption of common external tariffs and quotas it would be impossible to forge trade relations with other parts of the world, such as the USA, China, India and Australia.

Early signs from EU officials are not encouraging. Guy Verhofstadt, the EU Parliament's representative in the negotiations (and former Belgian PM), summed up the PM's 12 objectives the day after the PM delivered her speech, as:

---

1   Morales, A. (2017) 'Merkel Seen Putting EU Values Ahead of Car Lobby in Brexit Talks': https://www.bloomberg.com/politics/articles/2017-01-18/merkel-seen-putting-eu-values-ahead-of-car-lobby-in-brexit-talks downloaded 18/01/2017

'creating an illusion that you can go out of the single market and the customs union and you can cherry pick and still have a number of advantages […]. He went on to add 'I think this will not happen. We shall never accept a situation in which it is better to be outside the single market than be a member of the European Union'.[1]

While visiting Washington, on 26 of January, Mr Verhofstadt also stated that:

'The UK PM announced a very radical Brexit because she knows that the EU will never accept a situation in which the status of a country outside the union is more favourable than to be a member of the European Union'.[2]

On the prospects of a new trade deal between the UK and the EU-27 to be delivered by 2019, pledged by the PM, Mr Verhofstadt called it 'impossible'.

Sir Andrew Cahn, former single market advisor to the UK government and one of the architects of the EU's single market foresees a 'bitter' divorce. He also points out that:

The EU side, after all, in a way, have already won the first round of this negotiation because they have forced the UK to say 'no, we won't be in the single market'.[3]

The volumes of trade involved are vital. The UK exported to the EU approximately £230 billion in 2015, which is equal to 47% of the £490 billion of total UK exports.[4] The rest of the EU exported £290 billion to the UK (thus leaving a UK deficit to the rest of the EU of £60 billion).

Let us assume that Brexit negotiations and a final 'hard Brexit' agreement lead to a 20% reduction in the intra EU-UK volumes of trade. A 20% reduction in the UK exports to EU, will lead to a decrease by £46 billion from £230 billion to £184 billion. However, more importantly it would also reduce total UK exports from £490 bn to (490 − 46) = £ 444 bn, or **9.4%** of total UK exports. On the other hand, a 20% reduction in the EU exports to the UK will see them reduced by £58 billion to from £290 billion to £232 billion. This would also reduce total EU exports from £1.812 trillion to £1.754 trillion, or **3.2%** of total EU exports.

1   Khan, S. (2017) 'EU Brexit negotiator Guy Verhofstadt says Theresa May can't 'cherry pick benefits of the European Union': http://www.independent.co.uk/news/world/europe/chief-eu-brexit-negotiator-guy-verhofstadt-theresa-may-cherry-pick-illusionspeech-benefits-european-a7531971.html downloaded 18/01/2017

2   Wishart, I. (2017) 'Seven Brexit Strategies Theresa May Could Use to Erode EU Unity': https://www.bloomberg.com/news/articles/2017-01-12/seven-brexit-strategies-theresa-may-could-use-to-erode-eu-unity downloaded 12/01/2017.

3   Merrick, R. (2017) 'EU wins first round of Brexit battle by 'forcing UK out of single market', former adviser warns Theresa May': http://www.independent.co.uk/news/uk/politics/brexit-battle-eu-theresa-may-single-market-free-trade-deal-negotiations-sir-andrew-cahn-uk-economy-a7532791.html downloaded 18/01/2017.

4   Confederation of British Industry (2016) 'Making Success of Brexit: A whole-Economy view of the UK-EU negotiations' December, 2016, CBI-Duncanprint.

As a result, while a hard Brexit will prove detrimental for both the UK and the EU, it would approximately be three time costlier for the UK in terms of net exports. The same result is arrived at when comparing the intra EU-UK volumes of exports relative to their respective GDP. UK exports to EU equal 12% of the UK's GDP, whereas EU exports to the UK equals 3.5% of the EU's GDP (excluding the UK). Reflecting on the same issue, Ulrich Hoppe, the head of the German-British Chamber of Industry and Commerce, claimed that:

> 'Germany's trade surplus with the U.K. amounts to about *1 percent* of the gross domestic product of Europe's biggest economy, and if 1 percent of German GDP grows slightly less or slightly more, it doesn't really matter to the German economy. So the idea that Germany from a business point of view will be very flexible towards the U.K. in the Brexit negotiations is a dream.' (Italics provided).

The other side of this argument of course, is that the loss in net exports to the EU, will be more than compensated by the devaluation of the pound, which will boost the value of export orders and thus the quantity of exports. Thus, while profit margins may be reduced per unit of exports due to potential tariffs, increased sales could generate more profits on aggregate. This may be the case for as long as the UK remains in the single market. Post-Brexit it would depend on the nature of the tariffs and the extent of the pound's depreciation, the combined impact of which is almost impossible to predict. The exchange rate dimension to the argument is addressed in the following section.

2.2 THE UK–EU MACROECONOMIC FRAMEWORK

2.2.1 Exchange rate arrangements

The European Commission (EC) perceives exchange rate volatility as a barrier to trade. Its elimination is therefore conducive to the completion of the single market. Countries in the Eurozone (EZ) for example have chosen the most advanced type of fixed exchange rate regime – that of a currency union – and have thus contributed to this aim. The UK on the other hand, while accepting the need for exchange rate stability, in this case in the pound-to-euro exchange rate, has maintained its monetary independence. This means that the Bank of England (BE) has retained the right to set the 'base rate' and target the Money Supply (MS) in line with the needs of the UK economy. This right was exercised soon after the recession of 2008 hit the UK economy. From spring 2009 – when the BE was convinced of the severity of the recession – to autumn 2012, the BE pursued unconventional monetary policies involving lowering the rate of interest to unprecedented levels, and adopting a Quantitative Easing (QE) programme that led to the injection of an additional £375 billion into UK financial institutions in four rounds.

This helped UK financial institutions to increase their capital and reserve requirements. However, it did not lead to increases in lending in the short run. As confidence to the UK was shattered, following the deficit's increase to 10.5% in 2009/10, the new coalition government adopted a fiscal consolidation programme to accompany BE's expansionary monetary policy. The initial objective was deficit elimination by 2015, when the next general election was due to take place. The policy framework of contractionary fiscal and expansionary monetary policy was considered the most appropriate by the UK coalition government.

However, the private sector's response to expansionary monetary policy was not the one anticipated. Banks and private sector companies hoarded money, instead of investing, given the prospects of another recession in 2012. Eventually, as the deficit was gradually reduced, albeit not to the extent initially projected, confidence was gradually restored leading the UK economy becoming the fastest growing among the G7 during 2014/15. External developments, such as the Eurozone's debt crisis peak in 2011/12, saw the UK's safe haven status been restored. However, it has to be noted that positive developments in the UK economy were taking place against a background of unconventional monetary policy and productivity not recovering its 2008 rates. As in the long run it is productivity rates that determine whether countries become wealthier or poorer, a lot more work was/is required to take place in terms of infrastructure investment, education, R&D etc.[1] Overall though, the QE programme's effectiveness and the pound's depreciation in 2008 reaching 30% against the US dollar and the Euro, are considered to have had a relatively positive effect on the UK economy at a time of considerable hardship. Gradually, after seven long years, towards the end of 2014 and 2015 the focus shifted away from unconventional policies, to forming expectations of when the BE will start raising the base rate towards more 'normal' rates. Overall, according to BE's estimations the QE programme, added 1 percent growth annually between 2010 and 2015.

However, the BEs QE programme, while helpful to the UK economy, had wider implications in the EU context. It placed the UK in a unique position. In order to understand why this is the case, we need to resort to exchange rate definitions.

At a basic level the exchange rate is the rate at which a currency, eg the domestic currency (£)-converts to another currency (eg £1 = €1.15). This is the bilateral exchange rate, ie the units of another currency that £1 can buy. Another definition is based on the real effective exchange rate. This is based on a weighted average of the exchange rates of the most important trading partners of the country under perspective. As a result, the real effective exchange rate provides an objective way of judging the relative strength of the domestic currency against a basket of other currencies. For example, by focusing only on a particular bilateral exchange rate, eg the pound to South African rand, it is very difficult to assess the overall impact of the Brexit vote on the pound's performance. This is particularly the case, when contrasting trends are observed in bilateral exchange rates. For example, the value of the pound has declined significantly in relation to the euro since June but has remained relative stable in relation to the Russian ruble. Thus, it becomes very difficult to pass judgement on the overall performance of a currency by drawing on specific bilateral exchange rates. The real effective

---

1   Cadman, E (2016) 'Carney issues stark warning with package to ease Brexit downturn' FT: http://www.ft.com/cms/s/0/0d729692-5a1a-11e6-9f7badea1b336d4.html#axzz4GQotgOYv downloaded 05/08/2016.

exchange rate resolves this problem, but focusing on the trends of the bilateral rates of the currencies of the 24 (or 26) most important trading partners. In this way, the effects of an 'outlier' bilateral exchange rate trend are minimised.

The real effective exchange rate raises the question over the definition of the real exchange rate. The Real Exchange Rate (RER) equals the bilateral-(nominal) exchange rate multiplied by the ratio of the price of exports over the price of imports.

$$\text{Real ER} = \text{Nominal ER} \times \frac{P_{Exports}}{P_{Imports}} \quad (1)$$

In a fixed exchange rate regime, the bilateral-nominal exchange rate is irrevocably fixed and any adjustment to economic shocks has to come by the price ratio of exports over imports.

Fixed Exchange Rates

$$\text{Real ER} = \text{Nominal ER} \times \frac{P_{Exports}}{P_{Imports}}$$

This reflects the need for the domestic economy to become competitive in the short term by reducing the cost of production in the productive sectors of the economy, such as export industries. This reduces export prices, and as such, the export-to-import price ratio will decline, causing an overall reduction in the RER. This mechanism provides the main theoretical rationale in favour of fiscal cuts in Southern Eurozone. Overall, the nominal exchange rate (which is fixed and cannot be adjusted) will be multiplied by a lower export-to -import price ratio and it will lead to a depreciation in the RER, stimulating further the volume of exports.

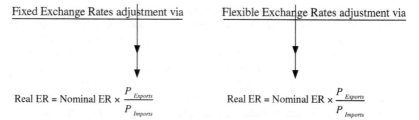

Fixed Exchange Rates adjustment via

$$\text{Real ER} = \text{Nominal ER} \times \frac{P_{Exports}}{P_{Imports}}$$

Flexible Exchange Rates adjustment via

$$\text{Real ER} = \text{Nominal ER} \times \frac{P_{Exports}}{P_{Imports}}$$

On the other hand, under flexible exchange rates, the adjustment to economic shocks *in the short term*, is delivered from the depreciation in the nominal exchange rate, without requiring an immediate adjustment to the exports-to-imports price ratio. The depreciation (or devaluation) reduces the nominal exchange rate thus causing a decline to nominal ER × export-to-import prices. Overall, the RER declines, facilitating the restoration in competitiveness caused by the shock. As a result, the adjustment of the UK economy to the Brexit outcome of the EU Referendum in June was facilitated by the significant depreciation in the nominal exchange rate of the pound. This has already boosted orders for domestically-produced goods and services from the rest of the EU and the US in particular. This is particularly the case for the UK manufacturing sector.

The above analysis does not imply that the exports-to-imports price ratio would not adjust in the medium-to-long term even under flexible exchange rates. The crucial issue is that this adjustment does not need to take place immediately, so that flexible exchange rates provide more time for the domestic economy to adjust to the newly emerged environment. This provides one of the main advantages of flexible exchange rates.

The above discussion on the adjustment mechanisms under fixed and flexible exchange rates respectively, leads to the question of what drives the (nominal) price of a currency to decline. In order to account for this, the determinants of the exchange rate need to be presented. The main determinants of the value of the domestic currency include:

(i) the volumes and composition of trade (Balance of Payments);
(ii) the rate of interest in relation to the rates of interest in other major economies;
(iii) the domestic price level;
(iv) growth performance; and
(v) economic fundamentals.

Increased volumes and favourable terms of trade — ie exports exceeding imports – would lead to surpluses in the UK's balance of payments, putting upward pressure on the value of the pound. On the other hand, persistent decreases in the volume of exports accompanied by increases in imports, would lead to deficits in the UK's balance of payments, putting downward pressure on the value of the pound. The rate of interest is the main short-term determinant of the value of the domestic currency. An increase in the BE's interest rate (base discount rate) would lead to an increase in the value of the pound, in the absence of interest rate changes abroad. Likewise, a decrease in the base rate, would lead to a depreciation. Higher inflation in the UK than abroad leads to a depreciation in the value of the pound in the long term. In the short-run, however, it can prompt an appreciation if it leads domestic residents to expect an increase in the base rate, to counter inflationary pressures.

Lastly, a deterioration in the domestic economy's fundamentals would lead to a depreciation. Economic fundamentals include industrial production, cost of production per unit of output, technological innovation and adaptation to production, among others.

The determinants of the exchange rate should not be viewed in isolation. Assume for example, that there is persistently higher inflation in the UK than in France. This implies that, year-on-year, producing the same product in the UK would gradually become more expensive than producing it in France. As a result, sales of the product made in France would increase in international markets, at the expense of the sales of the UK product. This would have a negative impact on the volume of UK exports, and therefore on the terms of trade, in particular the current account of the balance of payments. It would also have a negative impact on the UK growth potential. This would cause the value of the pound to depreciate.

Likewise, when the Bank of England supplied more pounds to the economy, the pound's value would decrease, causing a reduction in the cost of production in the UK in international terms, in the short term. In the medium to long term, import push inflation will pass through the production process and the UK's competitive advantages emanating from the devaluation would be reduced if not eliminated.[1] These are the kind of inflationary pressures the UK economy is currently experiencing.[2]

To summarise, the supply of money therefore presumes a free-floating exchange rate and independent monetary authorities. Countries that chose to join a fixed exchange rate regime and replaced their currencies with a common currency (eg France, Germany, Italy etc), surrendered monetary independence in the sense that they cannot increase the money supply for domestic policy objectives. Reducing exchange rate volatility, which can be facilitated by joining a fixed exchange rate regime with another country's currency, would be conducive to enhancing the volumes of trade between the two countries in the regime (eg France and Germany).

The only EU country that has retained full monetary independence is the UK. The UK economy as a result functions within a macroeconomic framework featuring free movements of capital, labour movements, free trade (including free movements of goods and services) and flexible exchange rates. The Eurozone member countries' economies on the other hand, are in an environment of irrevocably fixed exchange rates (EZ), free capital and labour movements and free trade. These arrangements place the BE in a unique position within the EU framework. It has the right to engage in expansionary monetary policy without the consent of the other EU countries to mitigate the negative impact of recessions, like the recession of 2008/09 and the surprise Brexit referendum result in 2016. The schematics of the UK's positioning in the EU context is presented below. As it can be observed the UK's current arrangements in the EU lead to Pound-to-Euro exchange rate volatility.

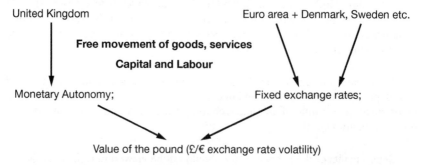

United Kingdom   Euro area + Denmark, Sweden etc.

Free movement of goods, services

Capital and Labour

Monetary Autonomy;   Fixed exchange rates;

Value of the pound (£/€ exchange rate volatility)

1   Meakin, L. (2017) 'Carney Sees Brexit Consumer Slowdown Ahead After Strength' : https://www.bloomberg.com/news/articles/2017-01-16/carney-sees-brexit-consumer-slowdown-coming-after-strong-2016 downloaded 17/01/2017.

2   Office for National Statistics, (2017a) 'UK consumer price inflation: Dec 2016': https://www.ons.gov.uk/economy/inflationandpriceindices/bulletins/consumerpriceinflation/latest

Such volatility has been observed since 2008. During 2014/15 the pound appreciated considerably, leading to a pound-to-euro exchange rate of 1.42 and to a pound-to-dollar exchange rate of 1.45 in December 2015. The significant appreciation in the value of the pound during this period, reflected the gradual restoration of confidence in the UK economy, prompted partly by the halving of the 2010 deficit, and partly due to the growth performance of the UK economy which, as mentioned above, registered the highest growth of the G7 countries. On the other hand, this favourable macroeconomic environment took place against a background of low productivity and unbalanced growth, both in terms of its drivers and regional performance.[1] Growth was driven primarily by services and less so by construction and exports and was heavily focused on the south, with many regions around the country not recovering their 2008 output loses.

This trend has persisted well into 2016. The latest preliminary growth figures for Q4 2016, while confirming the UK's strong growth momentum (0.6% in Qs 2,3 and 4 and 2% for 2016) also reflect its unbalanced nature, as its major driver was services.[2] Other major international organisations have also confirmed this trend and their short-term forecasts point to a slowdown in growth while Brexit negotiations are under way. The International Monetary Fund projects a growth of 1.1% for 2017, a rate echoed by the World Bank that expects growth of 1.2% for the current year, and 1.3% in 2018. The Bank of England, slightly more optimistic, anticipates growth to slow to 1.4% in 2017 and 1.5% in 2018. The Office for Budget Responsibility forecasted a growth rate of 1.4% for 2017 and 1.7% for 2018.There is consensus for the reasons for the slowdown in growth including Brexit negotiations, and its unbalanced nature.[3]

2.2.2   BE's 2% inflation target – the pound

The Bank of England adhere to the principle of flexible inflation targeting. While inflation in the UK has been maintained below the 2% inflation target since 2013, the pound's drop in value since July 2016 has caused import prices to increase in £ terms. As import-push inflation passes through into the UK production process, via, eg higher food prices, eventually this will lead/has led to higher inflation in the UK. The BE in its **August 2016** Inflation Report, produced a forecast for a rate of inflation of 2.7% in 2017. BE Governor Mark Carney and the Monetary Policy Committee have already communicated that they will not increase the base rate in the case of a one-off violation of the 2% inflation target provided it is maintained at reasonable levels. However, the forecast assumed no further depreciation in the value of the pound. Major financial institutions such

---

1   Smith, W. A. (2017) Theresa May needs to focus on changing the attitudes of British businesses as much as she does on Brexit: http://www.independent.co.uk/voices/brexit-theresa-may-speech-philip-hammond-productivity-andy-haldane-a7529721.html downloaded 17/01/2017.

2   Office for National Statistics, (2017b) 'Gross domestic product, preliminary estimate: Oct to Dec 2016': https://www.ons.gov.uk/economy/grossdomesticproductgdp/bulletins/grossdomesticproductpreliminaryestimate/octtodec2016 downloaded 29/01/2017.

3   Cox, J. (2017b) 'World Bank cuts UK growth forecast in first review since Brexit vote' : http://www.independent.co.uk/news/business/news/world-bank-cuts-uk-growth-forecast-brexit-first-review-economy-prediction-a7521146.html.

as HSBC and Deutsche Bank, Germany's Central Bank, expect the pound to further, depreciate another 5 and 10% respectively, reaching a low of $1.10. This was attributed first to political uncertainty and second to the UK's wide external imbalances that persists, at least so far, despite the devaluation that took place in the aftermath of the referendum.[1]

Overall, in the medium to long term the pound's depreciation will lead to a re-allocation of resources from small and medium-sized enterprises (SMEs) (and sectors of the economy) that are exposed to the increase in import-push inflation to SMEs (and sectors of the economy) that are not. Assume an SME firm, SME-A, is less exposed to import-push inflation and not dependent on the influx of less skilled labour from EU countries. It would, eventually, be in a competitive advantage in relation to another SME, SME-B that is exposed to import-push inflation and is dependent on less skilled labour from eastern EU countries. If SME-A's main export market is the USA, whereas SME-B's main export market is France or Germany the competitive advantage would widen even further. It could also be the case that SME-A is not an export-orientated company but entirely dependent on developments in the UK economy (eg a construction firm). The extent of the resource re-allocation away from SME-B to SME-A would be dependent on the final Brexit agreement.

Following the Brexit outcome delivered in the referendum the pound dropped significantly in particular in relation to the US dollar and the euro. The decline has been more significant against the dollar to levels not seen since the mid-1980s. In relation to the euro, the pound has dropped back to its 2011 level. To date the depreciation has reached 20% against the dollar and 13% against the euro, against its January 2016 value.

2.2.3 Pound-to-dollar

One of the interesting features of the exchange rate volatility in the value of the pound, post-referendum has been its dramatic decline in relation to the USA dollar. What has prompted this decline? There are three main reasons.

First, it is the outcome of the referendum, which caused, and continues to cause, uncertainty in foreign exchange markets leading to a decline in most of the pound's bilateral exchange rates, and as a result, a decline in the pound's Real Exchange Rate. However, this reason alone cannot account for the magnitude of decline in relation to the US dollar. A second reason relates to the UK's record current account deficit in in 2015 that reached an overall 5.2%.[2] From a purely economic perspective, this reflects that the appreciation of the pound during 2014 and 2015 was not sustainable. Even this, though does not suffice to

---

1   Spezzati, S. (2017) 'Pound Rescued by May Faces Choppy Waters as Political Risks Loom': https://www.bloomberg.com/news/articles/2017-01-18/pound-rescued-by-may-faces-choppy-waters-as-political-risks-loom downloaded 18/01/2017.

2   Albanese, C., Krajewski, A. and Karamanis, V. (2017) 'What Charts Say About the Pound's Brexit Test': https://www.bloomberg.com/news/articles/2017-01-17/pound-s-brexit-driven-acid-test-intensifies-what-charts-show downloaded 17/01/2017.

fully explain the pound's depreciation against the dollar, in excess of its decline against other currencies.

Why, for example, has the pound only receded to its 2011/12 value against the euro, whereas it has dropped to levels not seen since the 1980s against the dollar? At this point, emphasis needs to be placed on events in the USA. The growth potential in the US economy has gathered enough pace to prompt the Federal Reserve to increase rates for the first time in 2016. While there are still underlying problems in the USA economy, (eg labour market participation rate in the USA is 63–64% against the UK's rate of 74.5%), developments point to monetary policy divergence between the USA and the UK. The August decision by the BE to reduce the base rate to 0.25% conveyed a signal to markets that the adjustment of the UK economy to the Brexit environment would take priority for the BE over short term considerations of the rate of inflation. The Governor of the BE has also acknowledged that a one-off inflation overshooting above the 2% target will be tolerated by the Bank in the short to the medium run, in particular as Brexit negotiations are taking place.

Assuming therefore that BE's inflation forecast for a 2.7% inflation in 2017 proves correct this will strengthen the market's perception of a monetary policy divergence between the UK and the USA in the short to the medium term. This prognosis is of course in line with the Chancellor's extension of the deficit elimination period, which has been pushed beyond 2020, as emphasis is placed on the adjustment of the economy to the Brexit challenges.

Lastly, as 'Trumpenomics' raises the prospect for an even stronger USA growth performance, this reinforces market's expectations pointing to further interest rate hikes in the USA during 2017 and 2018. Thus, divergence in USA and UK monetary policy, could lead to higher interest rate differential between the two countries, could precipitate capital inflows to the USA. This, combined with the above two reasons explains the sharp depreciation of the pound in relation to the US dollar.

As mentioned above, the forecast for 2.7% inflation in the UK is based on the assumption that the value of the pound will be maintained at its current levels. Given the markets' focus on the politics of Brexit, a further depreciation in the value of the pound cannot be ruled out.[1] The pound-to-dollar exchange rate will be crucial to companies exporting to the USA, as it would, and indeed has, boosted orders for UK goods and services. Given that the UK is about to embark on a process that will see it departing from the EU, relations in broad terms, but also trade relations in particular with the USA, will be vital. This is the case as the USA will provide an obvious candidate country with which the UK should seek to enhance its trade ties. A prospect which already seems to be

---

1   Albanese, (2017) 'Pimco Bets Pound Plunge Is Far From Over as Brexit Clouds Gather': https://www.bloomberg.com/news/articles/2017-01-12/pimco-bets-pound-plunge-is-far-from-over-as-brexit-clouds-gather downloaded 14/01/2017.

reciprocal from the new USA administration.[1] There are obvious obstacles that could hinder this process, such as the inevitable delays in reaching a new trade agreement. However, given the political willingness in the USA, increases in the UK–USA volumes of trade should be targeted.[2]

2.3 SMALL AND MEDIUM-SIZED ENTERPRISES (SMEs)

In terms of timely and adequate preparations for a smooth adjustment to a Brexit environment, SMEs must assess, if they have not done so already, their exposure to Brexit negotiations. SMEs focusing primarily on domestic markets, such as construction companies, are by definition not dependent on sales to EU markets and are thus very well placed to adjust to the Brexit environment. The long-run threat to SMEs in this category relates to the deterioration on the purchasing power of UK households and increases in the price of oil. The higher the inflationary overshooting from the BE's 2% inflation target and the longer its duration beyond 2017, the more the purchasing power is going to be reduced.[3] In this case, in the long term SMEs in this category will suffer from the decline in households' real wages, which will sooner or later translate to less spending. In the short-to-medium term, spending may be sustained as households are prepared to take on more credit, or withdraw from savings to maintain their current standards of living. However, as credit accelerates, credit constraints will manifest themselves, leading to less spending. Given the discussion above concerning the depreciation in the pound, SMEs in this category, should also develop contingency plans for rates of inflation reaching or exceeding the 5% threshold. Indeed, the substantial drop in retail sales in December 2016, the biggest since 2012, enhances the legitimacy of the argument.[4]

SMEs that are not dependent on exporting to EU could still experience difficulties emanating from labour shortages, in particular shortages of less skilled labour. This, apart from driving higher labour costs, as firms would compete for labour from a relatively fixed labour market could also hurt overall production. In this case, access to the EU labour market could be rendered possible, depending on the final Brexit agreement, and assuming that the brunt of the cost of a job permits scheme, would be met by the UK government. This is an area that would

---

1   Editorial The Independent (2017) 'Let's not be naïve – Trump has the upper hand over Theresa May in trade negotiations The first is that America will put America first. The harsh message from the President does at least have the virtue of clarity' 22/01/2017: http://www.independent.co.uk/voices/editorials/trump-has-the-upper-hand-over-theresa-may-in-trade-negotiations-a7540306.html downloaded 22/01/2017.

2   Ross-Thomas, E. (2017) 'Trump Offers Britain Quick Trade Accord as He Shuns Europe' : https://www.bloomberg.com/news/articles/2017-01-15/trump-offers-u-k-quick-trade-deal-as-may-plans-visit-times downloaded 16/01/2017.

3   Ward, J. (2017a) 'UK Retail-Sales Slump Hints at Cracks in Brexit Boom' Bloomberg, 20/01/2017: Ward, J. (2017b) 'U.K. Economy's Brexit Success Still Leaves Companies Fretting': https://www.bloomberg.com/news/articles/2017-01-25/u-k-economy-s-brexit-success-still-leaves-companies-fretting downloaded 25/01/2017.

4   Goodman, D. (2017) 'Pound Slides as UK Retail Sales Drop Most Since 2012': https://www.bloomberg.com/news/articles/2017-01-20/pound-slides-as-u-k-retail-sales-drop-most-since-2012-chart downloaded 22/01/2017.

require lobbying from SMEs. In the long term, due to the potentially higher costs of accessing funds and financial services SMEs need to put aside funds to support these services once Brexit materialises. This is particularly the case, if there is no interim agreement in place following the two years' negotiation period, as stipulated by Article-50.

SMEs that have trade links with the USA should seek the UK government's assistance in terms of further enhancing them. For their part, such SMEs should seize this unique opportunity and start to plan immediately, detailing steps that would facilitate such an enhancement. SMEs with limited access to USA markets, or that do not have ties with the USA, should identify whether these are possible to establish. In this case, they should prepare draft feasibility strategies on whether trade ties with the USA can be developed. In case these strategies have the potential to be fruitful, they should seek grants (research grants, transport costs coverage, etc) from the UK (and perhaps the USA) government as they seek USA markets. This can be the case in particular for SMEs that have strong existing ties with EU countries and, as a result of Brexit, aim to diversify their markets. Minimising losses in the single market, subject to Brexit negotiations, and maximising sales to the USA is the obvious long-term objective.

SMEs that depend on the single market will be affected more severely. In the short term though (2017–19), they should take advantage of the pound's drop in value and maximise sales (and profits) before import push inflation erodes their price advantage against other competitors located in other EU countries, and in particular in the Eurozone, and before the current trade arrangements cease to exist. From this perspective it is in the interest of these SMEs, if some access to the customs union is maintained. As following the PM's Speech full access to the single market is highly improbable, access to EU's customs union could provide a viable way forward for a large number of SMEs that would face obstacles while trying to reach EU markets, but could mitigate these by the competitive advantage provided by the pound's drop. As a result, joining the existing EU's Customs union arrangements after 2019, in the absence of a Brexit agreement *is vital*. A (hard) Brexit agreement could provide access to UK goods and services in the EU customs union. However, contingency plans for a very hard Brexit should be in place, by the end of 2019 at the latest. These, should include plans for mitigating accelerating inflation to levels of 4.5–5.5%.

Finally, in this context, it becomes vital for all SMEs to avoid a 'cliff-edge', where following an unsuccessful two-year period of negotiations access to Single market is lost, and there are no trade agreements with other countries (USA, India and EU). It is of paramount importance therefore all SMEs lobby the UK government and its negotiating team in particular for such a catastrophic scenario to be prevented. Contingency plans for a 'cliff-edge' should be prepared as early as possible, but they should not be viewed as the central scenario, for the present. They would amount to WTO rules and regulations for the UK exports for the EU markets and non-EU markets.

Table 2: Summary of SMEs' Response

	Small and Medium Enterprises
Not exposed to EU markets	Short term: Identify the impact of declines in the purchasing power of UK households, following inflationary pressures
	Medium term: Identify shortages in less skilled labour.
	Long term: Contingency plans for higher cost of financial services and inflation ranging from 4.5%–5.5% – Lobby to avoid 'cliff-edge'
Exporting to EU	Short term: Maximise benefits from the pound's decline – Minimising cost from import-push inflation/oil dependency
	Medium term: Identify problems-break down in supply lines
	Long term: Contingency plans for higher cost of financial services and Outcome depending on final Brexit agreement:
	1. Soft Brexit: Access to customs union maintained – modest EU market losses that could be mitigated by the Pound's decline.
	2. Hard Brexit: A free trade area with EU is put in place. Considerably losses in EU markets – further declines in the Pound likely Contingency plans for inflation ranging 4.5–5.5%
	3. Very Hard Brexit: WTO rules are put in place with EU. Considerable losses in EU markets from tariffs and non-tariff trade barriers – further declines in the Pound most likely – SMEs to hedge against foreign exchange exposure – Possible ties with the USA need to be identified
	Contingency plans for inflation ranging 4.5–5.5%/Balance of Payments crisis Lobby to avoid 'cliff-edge'

2.3.1   UK debt – SMEs

The UK has been borrowing money at historically low interest rates since 2011. This could change quite considerably post Brexit and in particular in the foreign holders of UK debt view the pound's decline as permanent in nature, as a consequence of Brexit. As approximately 27% of the UK's £1.6 trillion debt (approximately 84% of the UK's GDP) is owed by non-UK residents (approximately £430 billion), a similar ratio by the BE and the rest by UK residents or UK-based firms, pensions funds etc, the effects of non-UK residents selling UK debt could be significant. Indeed, the increase in inflation has already caused a decline in bond prices and increased the yield of UK debt.[1] At modest rates of inflation, this should not be a problem.

---

1   Burton, S. and Mogi, C. (2016) 'A Weaker Currency Is No Longer Economic Elixir It Once Was': http://www.bloomberg.com/news/articles/2016-09-25/a-weaker-currency-is-no-longer-the-economic-elixir-it-once-was downloaded 26/09/2016.

Uncertainty over Brexit negotiations could prompt a continuation of this trend, so that the yield could increase further from the current 1.35%. While this is not likely – in particular if non-UK resident holders of UK debt view the pound's drop as temporary – it should be born in mind by SMEs. Given the complexities in the Brexit process, and unless markets expect an upward trend in the value of the pound in the next three to five years, an event which is highly unlikely, a declining ratio of foreign to domestic holders could cause an increase in the cost of borrowing and reduced access to funds. In addition, in this case the cost of borrowing could increase substantially, with an adverse impact on economic growth. This is not a likely scenario, but one that SMEs need to be aware of. Therefore, SMEs need to identify whether a (permanent) depreciation in the value of the pound to current (or even lower levels in the short to medium term) and the potential increase in the cost of borrowing could be mitigated by the increase in the orders and the volumes of exports that accompany such a depreciation.[1]

Whether the pound's depreciation would cause a deterioration in its reserve currency status – something that could lead to an even higher cost of borrowing – remains to be seen.[2] With the US dollar (63%) and the euro (20%) accounting for 83% of reserve currency use, the pound (4.5%), and the Japanese yen (4.5%) as minor reserve currencies count for another 9%. The remaining 8% is accounted by the Canadian and Australian dollars, the Swiss franc and other currencies. The 4.5% allocation to the pound corresponds to approximately £280 billion of reserves held in pounds sterling.[3]

2.4 THE CASE FOR UK MANUFACTURING – A POSITIVE BREXIT IMPACT?

Manufacturing in the UK has long been in decline, both in absolute and relative terms. A variety of factors including de-industrialisation in the 1960s, 1970s and 1980s, international pricing competition from South Asia and East Europe since the early 1990s, automation processes, IT innovations and their application in the production process, globalisation and a truly international supply chain are among the most important. Membership of the EU since 1973, has also contributed by preventing the adoption of a 'national' industrial policy that could have favoured UK manufacturing. Competing in pricing was thus very

---

1   Syed, S. (2017) Brexit could cut wages by 30% over next two decades, says private equity boss Guy Hands: http://www.independent.co.uk/news/business/news/brexit-guy-hands-says-cut-wages-30-percent-twenty-years-private-equity-a7540986.html downloaded 23/01/2017.

2   Chu, B. (2017) Is the pound in danger of losing its reserve currency status because of Brexit? What does this mean? Why would it matter? And is it even true?
    http://www.independent.co.uk/news/business/news/is-the-pound-in-danger-of-losing-its-reserve-currency-status-a7549886.html downloaded 27/01/2017.

3   International Monetary Fund, (2017) 'IMF Data Access to Macroeconomic and Financial Data. Currency Composition of Official Foreign Exchange Reserves (COFER)'. : http://data.imf.org/?sk=E6A5F467-C14B-4AA8-9F6D-5A09EC4E62A4 downloaded 28/01/2017

difficult even in the 1970s. This acted against UK manufacturing due to the high cost of production, in relation to France and Germany. Later on in the 1980s, the UK government placed more emphasis on financial services, as they were viewed more promising in the long run.

This led to a declining role for the manufacturing sector, which also suited the political objectives of the Thatcher conservative governments, aiming to reduce trades unions' powers. Manufacturing featured the strongest trades union activity. Many firms that survived the 1970s and 1980s, found it extremely hard to do so in the 1990s due to the downturn in 1991/92 and new extreme pricing pressures from international competitors in Eastern Europe and South East Asia. Support from the Major and Blair governments could have not been enough. Even if New Labour wanted to provide further assistance from 1997–2010 this would have violated the EU's single market regulations. UK manufacturing firms that survived focused more on quality rather than pricing.

However, a combination of the 2008 recession, that hit harder in the UK than in the USA, France and Germany due to the reliance of the UK economy on financial services, and the EU referendum outcome will provide barriers to the UK's financial sector growth. These barriers will emerge due to the emergence of new macroeconomic conditions. The BE in its August inflation report, while forecasting the impact of the referendum on the UK economy and acknowledging the difficulties with forecasting in such a fluid environment, took for granted that Brexit will lead to *lower* capital mobility.[1] At present, EU governments are not allowed to apply capital restrictions, as this will distort efficiency in European capital markets, most of which are located in London.[2]

This does not mean that Brexit will render the UK a closed economy, but it does mean some distortion in European financial markets, with its nature and magnitude almost impossible to anticipate, as it would depend on the market's reaction to the negotiation process and the final Brexit agreement. The PM's Lancaster House speech also pointed to a hard Brexit. The impact of the new conditions (hard Brexit plus lower degree of capital mobility between the UK and the remaining 27 EU member states) implies that capital efficiency would become very difficult to improve, and profits from the financial sector could suffer as a result. In addition, the potential loss of passporting rights which are likely to be downgraded to 'equivalence' for the UK banks and financial institutions with the EU single market will render the provision of financial services to the rest of the EU more costly once Brexit has materialised, with detrimental effects on

---

1   Bank of England (2016) 'Inflation Report': http://www.bankofengland.co.uk/publications/
     Documents/inflationreport/2016/aug.pdf.
2   Greece is the only exception to this rule due to ongoing mitigating circumstances. Brexit will
     inevitably lead to minor capital restrictions between the UK-EU27 capital transactions.

the UK financial services.[1] A decline in the financial sector's contribution to the UK's GDP is likely. This presents manufacturing as an obvious candidate based on which the UK economy could/needs to be restructured.

2.4.1 Why is manufacturing important in post-Brexit Britain?

The contribution of manufacturing to the UK economic performance is vital, as it accounts for almost 10% of the country's GDP. Further, and most important in the context of the UK–EU negotiations, it is the leading sector of the economy in terms of exports, accounting for 40–45% of all UK exports, 58% of which are sold to EU markets. Manufacturing also generates the majority (almost 70%) of the UK's research and development. Further, of all sectors of the UK economy it is the most highly integrated with the rest of EU, in particular in supply chain production.[2] It is therefore the sector that would be influenced the most by Brexit and the final Brexit agreement.

Overall, six sectors (construction, education, hospitality, housing and real estate, manufacturing, professional and business services and retail) generate almost 75%of UK employment. However, a (hard) Brexit will have a different impact on each sector. For example, the obvious winner from the referendum's Brexit outcome and the pound's depreciation is hospitality, leisure and tourism. The sector has already benefited from the pound's depreciation and will most likely continue to do so by potential further depreciations once Brexit negotiations commence.[3] The sector will only need a fast visa Process to become available to all tourists from the remaining 27 EU member states post Brexit. Other sectors, such as education and construction will be influenced negatively in the period leading to Brexit, but their non-tradeable nature implies they do not contribute to the volumes of trade.

As it can be observed in Table 3, *Construction* for example will be influenced by increases in the cost of labour, as it could suffer from shortages of less skilled labour. However, the sector accounts for exports and imports worth only £1.6 billion and £1.2 billion respectively. Education and real estate, while they generate five million jobs, are non-tradable. Financial services is the sector with the highest surpluses, generating £54.9 billion. The loss of financial institutions' passporting rights, could cause a significant reduction in these surpluses.

---

1   Cox, J. (2017a) 'Optimism in financial services sector hits crisis era-low as Brexit concerns top worry list for banks Ninety per cent of banks questioned said that preparing for the impact of Brexit was their top challenge': http://www.independent.co.uk/news/business/news/optimism-financial-services-sector-banks-crisis-era-low-brexit-concerns-top-worry-list-for-banks-a7540936.html downloaded 23/01/2017: Finch, G. and Glover, J. (2017) 'Goodbye Passport, Hello Equivalence? Brexit Banks Lower Sights': https://www.bloomberg.com/politics/articles/2017-01-13/goodbye-passport-hello-equivalence-brexit-banks-lower-sights.

2   Confederation of British Industry (2016) 'Making Success of Brexit: A whole-Economy view of the UK-EU negotiations' December, 2016, CBI-Duncanprint.

3   BBC (2017) 'UK economy grows by 0.6% in fourth quarter': http://www.bbc.co.uk/news/business-38755242 downloaded 27/01/2017.

Table 3: The UK economy and different sectors' contribution

UK Economy Sector	Employees mn	GVA bn and %	Exports bn	Imports bn	Exports – Imports
Agriculture	0.476	8.5	18	38.5	-20.5
Aviation	0.961	52/3.4	26		26
Chemicals and Plastics	0.277	17.5/1.1	26.9	27.8	-0.9
Construction	**2.2**	102.3/6.2	**1.6**	**1.2**	0.4
Creative Industries	1.9	87.4/5.3	19.8	8.7	11.1
Education	**2.9**	98.1/5.9	–	–	–
Energy	0.14	36.2/2.2	76.7 tn	154.8 tn	–
Financial Services	1.1	119.2/7.2	63.7	8.8	**54.9**
Food & Drink	0.444	26/1.7	18.2	38.5	-20.3
Hospitality, Leisure and Tourism	**3.1**	121.1/7.1	22	42.4	-20.4
Housing and Real Estate	**2.1**	101.6/6.1	–	–	–
Life Sciences	0.053	6.4/0.4	20.7	19.6	1.1
Manufacturing	**2.7**	162.4/9.8	**228.9**	**313.3**	**-84.4**
Professional and Business Services	**5.8**	204.4/12.3	**70.5**	**40.4**	**30.1**
Retail	**5**	182/10.9	11.4	**6.1**	5.3
Technology	1.2	95.5/5.7	20.8	29	-8.2
Transport, Distribution. and Logistics	1.5	76.8/4.6	24.1	21.7	2.4
Utilities & Environmental Services	0.414	46.9/2.8	6.4	4.7	1.7
TOTAL	**32.265**		**579**	**600.7**	

Table and calculations – author's own work, data from CBI. Sectors generating more than 2 million jobs in bold.

As it can be also observed, Manufacturing accounts for 2.7 million employees, (8.3% of total UK employment). Despite therefore of its deficit of £84.4 billion, manufacturing remains by far the most important exporting sector of the UK economy with exports worth £228.9 billion. To make the point clear, the second most export-orientated sector, that of professional and business ervices, generates £70.5 billion. And while professional and business services together with Retail generate almost 11 million jobs, they generate exports worth only £81.9 billion, exceeding slightly a third of manufacturing.

As 40–45% of all UK exports are manufactured goods and services, and 58% of them are sold to EU markets, the sector exports to the EU from £134.3 billion to 151.1 billion. As a result, approximately *a* quarter of all UK exports are manufactured goods and services sold to EU markets. Therefore, after Brexit, and in particular in the case of a 'hard' Brexit, that the PM alluded to in her Lancaster House speech, the UK stands to lose a big proportion of that quarter of its exports on a permanent basis. The actual percentage is impossible to estimate, as it would depend on the final Brexit agreement. The point to be made, however, is that put simply, the UK government cannot 'ignore' manufacturing performance.

As a result, whether the adjustment of the UK's economy to the new economic environment prompted by the EU referendum outcome and the impending lengthy Brexit negotiations is smooth or not depends largely on the adjustment of the UK's manufacturing sector to the post-Brexit environment and its responsiveness to the pound's depreciation in the interim period. Further, as already mentioned, the extension of the period that would lead to a balanced budget beyond 2020/21, confirmed by the Chancellor of the Exchequer in the pre-Budget report 'creates' a new macro-economic framework that places more emphasis on the adjustment of the economy rather than on fiscal consolidation, while acknowledging fiscal constraints'. Or rather, renders fiscal consolidation contingent to a smooth post-Brexit adjustment. Crucial to this is the adjustment of the manufacturing sector to the Brexit conditions, given that almost half of the UK's exports are sold to EU markets.

As such, it is the author's view that, out of all sectors in the UK economy bar hospitality, leisure and tourism, manufacturing stands out as a *potential* Brexit winner, subject to appropriate policies been designed in the short-run and implemented in post-Brexit Britain. Certainly, the sector should receive most attention from all UK institutions.

Manufacturing *could* emerge as a Brexit winner, as EU membership forbids the adoption of a national industrial policy, viewed as favouritism towards domestic firms and overall distorting competition within the EU context. This became a highly contentious issue when the UK authorities tried to rescue Tata Steel's operations in the UK during 2014/16, but EU regulations provided an obstacle in doing so. Offering state support, for example for a domestic firm, not only puts pressure on fiscal policy and public finances by committing taxpayers' money, but it also discriminates against other firms in the EU, and overall reduces European consumers' surplus. The same rationale applies to EU regulations not permitting the Italian government to provide a rescue fund for Alitalia etc.

Brexit is also likely to reinforce the trend away from sources of direct taxation. Given that in the EU context, striking the correct balance between direct and indirect taxation is constrained by economic policies pursued by other EU governments, Brexit will 'free' the hands of UK governments to 'pursue' a competitive tax policy.[1] Hence, the Chancellor's comments for potentially

---

1   Wishart, I. (2017) 'Seven Brexit Strategies Theresa May Could Use to Erode EU Unity': https://www.bloomberg.com/news/articles/2017-01-12/seven-brexit-strategies-theresa-may-could-use-to-erode-eu-unity downloaded 12/01/2017.

lowering corporation tax in the case of an unfavourable trade agreement with the remaining 27 member states. Accompanying a lower corporation tax with lower business rates and tax incentives for the manufacturing sector will provide a complete set of tax policies to accommodate Britain's post Brexit economy.

Further, the manufacturing sector's contribution to the narrowing of the UK's current account deficit would be vital. Given the unprecedented current account deficit exceeded 5% of GDP in 2015 and 2016, revenue sources and the fiscal policy mix would also have to be adjusted, albeit ensuring a delayed return to a balanced budget.[1] The Bank of England has estimated that the current account deficit will be halved from 5.2% to around 2.5-2.6% by 2019, as a result of the pound's depreciation.[2] The estimate was based on a 9% depreciation in the value of the pound. This optimistic forecast is based on the nature of the UK's current account deficit, which while unprecedented is not alarming. This nature points more to a decline in earnings on dividends and interest on foreign assets by UK residents during 2011–2015, in relation to payments to foreigners for their UK holdings over the same period.[3] As companies that raise their profits abroad, in particular in US dollars or euros, are placed in a very strong position when they translate these in pounds (eg FTSE 100) the current account deficits are bound to be significantly reduced as early as 2017.

Further, the impact of the depreciation will imply that domestic demand and exports will be even more important for future growth, as people in the UK will increase (proportionally) their purchase of domestically produced goods and services in relation to imported goods and services. As almost half exports are manufactured goods and services manufacturing will have to draw the UK government's attention. In addition, tax revenue sources and the contribution from direct and indirect taxation needs to reflect the new reality. Revenue sources have to be adjusted in the light of the return to a national industrial policy and significant volatility of the sterling/euro and sterling/dollar exchange rates.

As these policies were impossible to pursue in the EU context, but are an essential policy instrument of any post Brexit government, regardless of political background, new 'national' sources of finance *have* to become available. This requires a reshaping of the UK's macroeconomic policy based on government intervention, not previously permitted in the EU context. This new type of interventionist policy at a national level (whatever its political nature), would need to be financed, by direct and indirect taxation. Above all, it would/should aim at reducing the productivity gap between the UK and other advanced

---

1   King, S. (2016) 'The UK's balance of payments conundrum': http://blogs.ft.com/the-exchange/2016/07/20/the-uks-balance-of-payments-conundrum/?siteedition=intl#rec ommended-h-504491470546859260: Albanese, C., Krajewski, A. and Karamanis, V. (2017) 'What Charts Say About the Pound's Brexit Test': https://www.bloomberg.com/ news/articles/2017-01-17/pound-s-brexit-driven-acid-test-intensifies-what-charts-show downloaded 17/01/201

2   Bank of England (2016) 'Inflation Report': http://www.bankofengland.co.uk/publications/ Documents/inflationreport/2016/aug.pdf

3   Giles, C. and Fray, K. (2016) 'Eight charts showing state of UK economy before Bank of England rate decision', FT. http://www.ft.com/cms/s/0/fd522642-5596-11e6-9664e0bdc13c3bef.html#axzz4GQotgOYv downloaded on 07/11/16

economies including France and Germany. The productivity gap is reflected by the fact that the UK recovered its 2008 productivity rates per worker only in the second half of 2015/early 2016.[1] UK productivity also lags in relation to France and Germany by 20% and 30% respectively, as noted in the Chancellor's pre-Budget Report.[2]

As a result, UK manufacturing firms should develop a preliminary assessment of the impact of:

- Potential break down in supply chains with production processes located in-part in other EU countries, from double-tariffs and quotas;
- Links between supply chains in manufacturing and financial services located to EU-27. This is essential as it could potentially have a detrimental impact on raising funds for the manufacturing sector and infrastructure investment. Such links need to be reviewed alongside the increased cost of servicing national debt and the volatile exchange rate against the euro. The former would lead to higher cost of borrowing money for private sector firms, the latter would render contracts with European partners based on forward exchange rates difficult to agree. As result, convincing European partners to renew contracts, or commit to new ones would become a much more difficult process than it was in the past.
- Their responsiveness and impact from the pound's depreciation and higher inflation.
- Adapt and incorporate digital technology in the production process – seek government subsidies to build digital capacity and enhance digital training skills.

A UK national manufacturing policy could/should involve a two-tier system of regional and national financial assistance to firms and companies with a strong (or potentially strong) exporting capacity. The UK manufacturing firms in collaboration with the UK authorities should:

1. Identify regional or national best practice;[3]
2. Identify best practices from such best practice and try to extrapolate to other cases;
3. Improve productivity in the production process by business investment programmes, adaptations and staff re-training (to be subsidised by the government);

1   Giles, C. and Fray, K. (2016) 'Eight charts showing state of UK economy before Bank of England rate decision', FT: http://www.ft.com/cms/s/0/fd522642-5596-11e6-9664e0bdc13c3bef.html#axzz4GQotgOYv downloaded on 07/11/16
2   Smith, W. A. (2017) Theresa May needs to focus on changing the attitudes of British businesses as much as she does on Brexit: http://www.independent.co.uk/voices/brexit-theresa-may-speech-philip-hammond-productivity-andy-haldane-a7529721.html downloaded 17/01/2017
3   Hutton, R and Morales, Al. (2017) 'May Industrial Strategy Seeks to Pick Winning Areas for U.K.': http://www.independent.co.uk/news/business/news/brexit-latest-news-uk-three-years-slow-growth-rising-unemployment-reduced-incomes-ernst-young-ey-a7541016.html downloaded 23/01/2017

4. Adopt the best-possible tax incentives (business rates, corporation tax, re-investment tax breaks etc);
5. Seek regional subsidies where possible, with an inclusive approach to Wales, Scotland and Northern Ireland;
6. Prepare a country case study, drawing on the existing arrangements with countries that could resemble the UK's status in relation to the EU, such as Norway, Switzerland, Turkey etc, and a detailed evaluation of their industrial policies. Emphasis would be placed on the rules, regulations and policies that can be adopted in the context of the UK economy.
7. Identify new markets for UK manufacturers, such as the USA-NAFTA, and seek to reduce barriers to trade with these as much as possible.
8. Manufacturing can be used as a tool by the UK government-authorities to reduce regional disparities and economic inequalities and performance across the UK.
9. Review education programmes in the light of the Brexit reality, eg adapt higher education programmes and unit syllabuses and enhance skills training in colleges and technical education;
10. Where possible, identify Brexit losers and ways that government policy could partly compensate them. For example, the UK automobile industry and its adjustment to a 'hard' Brexit.

Events so far, and a series of impeding elections in EU countries in 2017, including France, the Netherlands, Germany and possibly Italy, point to a delayed hard-Brexit, most likely to occur at 2020, at the earliest. Therefore, the adjustment of the manufacturing sector in two periods, from 2017-Brexit, and then to the post-Brexit period is vital. Existing data on the volumes of trade between the UK and the EU should inform policies pre-Brexit that is within the existing EU framework subjected to high Pound-to-Euro exchange rate volatility. As such, the adjustment of the UK' manufacturing sector during 2017-Brexit will be dependent on: the pound's depreciation, the extent to which the depreciation would improve the UK's balance of payments deficit and the impact of the pound's depreciation on the rates of inflation.

Given that each 1% depreciation in the value of the pound, leads to an increase in exports by 0.2%–0.3%, it is expected that the depreciation in the value of the pound by 16%–18%, will cause an increase in exports by 3.2%–5.4%. This increase in exports would alleviate the current account deficit but it would suffice to eliminate it. As a result, the manufacturing sector should prepare for a negotiating period featuring high uncertainty and a further depreciation in the value of the pound. Coupled with appropriate post-Brexit policies, the manufacturing sector could play a key role in reshaping the UK's national accounts.

Ultimately, post-Brexit, the adjustment of the manufacturing sector would depend on whether the UK retains access to specific areas of the EU's customs union and industrial policies pursued by the UK authorities. These policies should *not* be subject to political developments in the UK. Therefore, the UK government could consider the establishment of an across party 'Institute of national-industrial policy' alongside existing government departments to facilitate the above aims.

As such, the main policy recommendation for the UK authorities is to focus on attaining the best possible trade agreement with the remaining 27 member states, and not viewing free trade areas with other countries/regions around the world, as a substitute for UK-EU trade relations. While agreeing on the general principles of such trade relations should be very welcome, the UK cannot legally bind itself to these, up until it has officially exited EU. This includes the UK-EU new trade deal. As such, new trade agreements should be secondary to the new UK-EU trade relations. Joining for example, the North American Free Trade Agreement (FAFTA), a free trade area that includes Mexico, Canada and the USA (Raphael, 2017) will be conducive to boosting UK exports to these three countries, but it cannot compensate for trade losses from a 'bad' trade agreement with the EU that would involve WTO tariffs and quotas. Given that, as mentioned above, a quarter of all UK exports are sold to EU markets, the geographical barrier between the UK and the three NAFTA members, is going to increase transport costs for UK exports. As the overwhelming majority of UK-manufactured products are goods (eg cars), shipping these to the USA, Canada and Mexico is going to increase transport costs quite considerably in relation to shipping these to the Netherlands or Germany.

The UK could also seek to boost financial services exports to the USA, as in this market geographical distance no longer presents the barrier it used to. However, this would be subject to fierce competition from USA firms in the same sector. Further, bilateral agreements establishing free trade areas, are bound to encounter the exchange rate volatility between the pound and the currencies under perspective, whereas trade with EU essentially involves only the pound-to-euro exchange rate, as the rest of the EU currencies are in a fixed exchange rate regime with the Euro (eg Swedish and Danish krone, Polish zloty, Bulgarian lev etc).

To conclude, while the UK negotiates its departure from the EU, it should develop an industrial strategy based on four main pillars:

i.   Develop a national industrial policy to be implemented immediately after leaving the EU (if possible the day after!);
ii. Compensate for the loss of trade with the remaining 27 EU member states which the new trade agreement will bring about by ensuring trade volumes with them do not decline considerably;
iii. In order to facilitate (ii), this would imply a considerable depreciation in the value of the pound, considerably lower than the current pound-to-euro rates and policies as described above;
iv. Develop and join free trade areas/associations with other countries/ regions, as a means of achieving (ii).

CHAPTER 3

A LEGAL CONTINGENCY PLAN FOR BREXIT

Helen Tse, Clarke Willmott LLP

INTRODUCTION

However we voted, we all have to accept the outcome of Brexit. All businesses should assess what impact Brexit will have on their contracts, operations, people and future. The Brexit Referendum result has in the short term already created uncertainty and impacted the value of the pound sterling. As the UK plans to exit the EU, you should do a Brexit MOT and I have set out a checklist for you to think about. Businesses that don't manage the risks or seize the opportunities will face strategic challenges as Brexit unfolds. Ultimately, many of the questions that Brexit throws up should be considered when doing an annual review on the strategy of your business. It's not just reaping the rewards in the good times. It's planning for the future, preparing for the potential difficulties and making your business as robust as possible to withstand whatever is thrown at it.

3.1 BREXIT MOT

My Brexit MOT has three simple premises:

Understand the proposed changes: The Brexit process will be continuously changing and as of the date of writing, the detail of Brexit has not yet been fully revealed. The best way to keep abreast of the proposed changes is to keep referring back to www.brexitbrexitbrexit.com which will provide the most up to date changes.

Review how those changes may affect you: I have prepared a comprehensive checklist for you to work through to see how proposed changes may affect you.

Prepare to adapt, change and be flexible: This book is a mindmap for you to take action. Do contact your professional advisers and make plans. Just like every person should have a will, or a power of attorney, so should every business have a Brexit MOT plan.

Mike Cherry, national chairman at the Federation of Small Businesses (FSB) said:

> 'Nearly a quarter of FSB members export, with the majority exporting to the single market. Access to the single market means access to 500 million potential consumers, more than 26m businesses and is worth €11tn.'

If you export to the EU and are suddenly adversely impacted by tariffs, do you have a back-up plan? Just like you would prepare in the event that you might lose a big customer, so too should you have a back-up plan in the event Brexit causes financial hardship to your business.

For those in IT, such businesses hoped the EU would create a single digital market which they could benefit from. Brexit now puts a potential brake on such developments. Will Brexit put a question mark on the UK overall and deter business with UK businesses? How about lending? Will the pound sterling continue to be adversely affected? Is the drop in the valuation of the pound sterling just a short-term problem as the 'real' UK economy is essentially strong?

Suzi Woolfson of business advisory and accountancy firm PwC, says that small businesses will lead the recovery.

> 'We should expect a bumpier economic climate in the short term, but as Mark Carney has commented, we have a resilient UK financial system and the 'real economy' will adjust. Private businesses and SMEs are at the heart of the real economy and they are nothing if not resilient, flexible and adaptable. I am confident that they are well equipped to weather the changes.'

I want businesses to continue robustly and believe it is business as usual, but with a back up plan. Businesses and entrepreneurs in the UK grasp opportunities even in the midst of uncertainty and threats – as echoed by the CEOs who have contributed to the Thought Leadership section of this book. A legal contingency plan isn't an option, it is a must. This checklist aims to set out the what ifs?, how abouts? and whens? and suggests steps in outline which are fleshed out in more detail in the following chapters. All businesses need to identify the risks and opportunities of Brexit.

3.2 CHECKLIST

	Yes/No
Data protection	
Is your personal data, customer data, payroll data or HR data transferred between the UK and other EU member states?	
For data held in the EU, is it protected by data protection law?	
If you are holding data in the cloud, ask the cloud provider do they hold your data in an EU member state?	
Regarding your payroll, if you outsource that to a payroll service provider do they hold your payroll data in an EU member state?	
Where are the key decisions regarding data made in the UK or in an EU Member State or elsewhere?	
Have you checked regarding your data's security and protection?	

	Yes/No
External marketing	
If your business is listed, do you need to make disclosures re Brexit to the public?	
For annual or interim reports do you need to make a statement on how Brexit may affect your business?	
Have you communicated or investigated whether your clients and contacts are affected by Brexit?	
Have you spoken to your staff especially those who are from the EU about the business's strategy post Brexit?	
Environmental law	
Do you claim for emissions allowances under the EU Emission Trading System?	
EU grants and funding	
Do you receive EU funding or grants?	
Do you borrow or receive a guarantee from the European Investment Bank, the European Investment Fund or any other EU institution?	
Where EU funding and grants end, have you got alternative funders ready to step in?	
Contracts	
Have you reviewed existing contracts, future contracts and standard forms and considered all the issues that might arise due to Brexit? Do such contracts need to be amended?	
Where do the risks lie in the contracts and is the risk allocated fairly?	
Are there any references to the EU or EU laws?	
Are any of the contracts with EU public authorities or utilities?	
Is there exclusivity granted or received regarding an EU member state?	
Look at the force majeure, material adverse change or change in law provisions. Has the contract been frustrated?	
Is the contract still financially beneficial or is it loss making due to tariffs and rising costs? Can you terminate the contract?	
Are you buying or selling a business (shares or assets) – do any of the conditions or termination rights apply so a party could refuse to complete on the deal?	
Can you enforce the contract against assets located in an EU Member State?	

	Yes/No
Financing	
Have you had your financing documents reviewed? In particular look at whether any termination rights or conditions apply. Do your creditors have any Brexit flex rights?	
Has your business been adversely affected by the exchange rate or interest rate movements?	
Have you reduced your exposure to exchange rate fluctuations?	
Have any financial covenants been breached (eg if your business has been adversely affected)? If so, have your material adverse effect clauses been triggered? How can you make good the situation?	
Have you valued your assets? Has there been a fall in the value of your assets? If so will your loan to value ratios need to be recalculated?	
Have you checked your financial ratios with your accountant?	
Do you need to refinance?	
If the EU loan and debt capital markets are not providing the best rates, do you have alternative providers?	
If a target business suddenly is a more attractive price because eg the drop in valuation of the pound sterling, do you have sufficient finance to acquire this M&A opportunity?	
If the UK's credit rating changes, would this affect your business or finance?	
Employees	
Are any of your non-EU employees on the Tier 2 Work Permit Scheme?	
Do you know the requirements for a Tier 2 Work Permit Sponsorship and Work Permit?	
Do you hire EU nationals?	
Will your EU nationals need visas and will they meet the visa requirements of say a Tier 2 Work Permit? If not, do you have sufficient employees to cover the work?	
Do you need to recruit staff or back-up staff?	
Do you need to revise your recruitment plans?	
Do you have procedures to ensure 'no discrimination' rules when hiring?	
Have you considered the costs and on-going operations and how to reduce any risks?	

	Yes/No
Insurance	
Have you checked with your insurance company or your insurance broker about your insurance policy?	
Are there any references to the EU or EU laws?	
Have you met all warranties and conditions precedent?	
Do you need a higher level of insurance (eg if sterling devalued and you suffered a loss)?	
Do your policies cover the risk of a deal collapsing, assets being devalued, an insolvency?	
Do your policies cover claims for other aspects eg professional indemnity?	
Do your policies cover the scenario where there maybe changes in corporate governance, regulation and employment law?	
If your asset values changed or there are changes in business premises or staff, do the insurers need to be notified?	
Intellectual property	
Do you own, use or have applied for EU trademarks? After Brexit to protect your IP in the UK, ensure you register the IP with the UK IPO office.	
Do you licence other people's IP rights that are granted from EU Member States?	
Do you have a website with .eu?	
Have you had any IP protected by the EU courts?	
Are you currently seeking or planning to seek an injunction only from a UK court in order to protect your IP rights in other EU Member States?	
Do you need to review and amend your licences or IP documents regarding their geographical scope and the IP rights covered?	
Do your internal controls and compliance policies need to be reviewed and amended if there is a change in IP law between EU and the UK?	
Premises	
Can you negotiate a reduction in rent or the same rent if there is less demand for leases?	
Do you need premises in the EU to do business in the EU?	
Public procurement	
Do you undertake public procurement tenders in EU member states relating to industries where non-EU parties may be excluded from the process?	

	Yes/No
Public procurement – *contd*	
What percentage of your business relies on public procurement in the EU?	
If those opportunities end, do you have other pipeline work to replace the public procurement work?	
Supply of goods	
Do you supply goods between the UK and EU member states?	
If you need to adhere to CE marks for the goods to meet health and safety requirements check the standards and see if there are new requirements.	
If tariffs are imposed will your trade deals still be commercially viable? If not, have you got alternative customers and clients?	
Do you supply goods which need to adhere to EU regulations? If the standards change for UK and EU, will you have costed the change in standards required to meet either or both?	
Do you want to continue to sell to the EU and at what cost?	
Supply of services	
Do you depend on passporting to supply your services from the UK to EU Member States and vice versa?	
Can you supply your services to other non-EU countries?	
Do you need to relocate to an EU member state to continue to supply your services?	
If you do need to relocate, what are the legal consequences in doing so – staffing, clients, tax, regulations, timescales?	
Tax	
Is your tax rate improved by EU law and, if so, if these benefits are stopped do you need to review your tax structure regarding capital and profit repatriation?	
If the Capital Duties Directive is no longer applicable, will this affect your ability to raise capital using clearance services or depositary receipt systems?	
Other parties	
Will the parties with whom you work or sell to be affected by Brexit?	
If so, can you continue in business as profitably?	

CHAPTER 4

TAX (INCLUDING VAT)

Etienne Wong, 15 Old Square Chambers

Shortly after this chapter was completed, the Government published the European Union (Withdrawal) Bill (formerly known as the 'Great Repeal Bill') (on 13 July 2017).

4.1 BREXIT – THE TAX IMPLICATIONS

I cannot recall the last time I heard the government mention tax when discussing Brexit – it is not high on their agenda. Indeed, many are surprised to learn UK tax, and how it operates, would even be affected by Brexit.

In this Chapter, we look first at how EU law has interacted with UK tax to date, and then we explore how the position may change as and when the UK actually leaves the EU. We will focus on 'direct taxes' (such as income tax and corporation tax) and VAT. Although we will not be looking at any other taxes (or tax areas), that is not to say they will not be affected by Brexit. To provide an overview of how they may be impacted, we include an extract from Paper 18 (titled 'UK Tax') part of the Brexit Papers from the Bar Council Brexit Working Group (written 'to help the government evaluate a range of pressing public interest concerns arising from the UK's decision to withdraw from the EU ').[1] This is set out as Appendix 3, at p 377.

4.2 EU LAW AND 'DIRECT TAXATION'

The EU is a legal arrangement under which member states transfer their powers in certain areas to EU institutions and, in doing so, agree to limit their sovereign rights in those areas.[2] EU laws become an integral part of the legal systems of the member states, which their courts are obliged to apply, binding both their nationals and themselves.[3] In the UK, this was achieved via the European Communities Act 1972, which:

> 'creates a hierarchy of law within the United Kingdom's legal system, by making European Union law part of and supreme over United Kingdom law'.[4]

---

1   See   http://www.barcouncil.org.uk/media-centre/publications/2017/2017/june/the-brexit-papers-third-edition.
2   See *Van Gend en Loos*, Case C-26/62.
3   See *Costa v ENEL*, Case C-6/64.
4   See House of Commons Library Briefing Paper number 7793, dated 23 February 2017 and titled 'Legislating for Brexit: the Great Repeal Bill' (or the Great Repeal Bill Briefing Paper), at page 12.

'Direct taxation' (the fiscal species that encompasses income tax, capital gains tax and corporation tax) is an area in which member states have retained their sovereign rights. Nevertheless, they do not have absolute discretion in the exercise of such rights. This is because they are still bound by the Treaties that form the constitutional basis of the EU – the Treaty on European Union (or TEU), for example, and the Treaty on the Functioning of the European Union (or TFEU) – and these Treaties set out certain principles (such as the principle of non-discrimination on grounds of nationality[1]) and provide for a number of fundamental freedoms. Each member state, as a signatory to these Treaties, is bound by these principles and freedoms, and thus obliged to exercise even its (retained) sovereign rights in compliance with them (and EU law generally).[2]

Where it is considered by one of its nationals that it has not done so – eg where it has introduced a tax measure that is considered to be incompatible with EU law – it may be challenged before one of its own courts, and the court must then either interpret the measure in such a way as to avoid inconsistency with EU law[3] or, if that is not possible, set the measure aside.[4] In doing so, the court may (and, in certain circumstances, must) refer questions on the interpretation of EU law to the European Court of Justice (CJEU).[5]

Where a measure is set aside, the member state has then to decide whether to abandon the measure altogether or revise its terms so as to bring it in line with EU law.

The European Commission can also challenge member states by bringing infringement proceedings itself where it considers they have introduced measures that are inconsistent with EU law.[6]

4.3   THE FUNDAMENTAL FREEDOMS

The fundamental freedoms are:

- the freedom of establishment;[7]
- the free movement of capital;[8]
- the free movement of goods;[9]
- the freedom to provide services;[10] and
- the free movement of persons.[11]

---

1   See TFEU, Article 18.
2   See *Manninen*, Case C-319/02.
3   See *Marleasing*, Case C-106/89.
4   See *Simmenthal*, Case C-106/77.
5   See TFEU, Article 267.
6   See TFEU, Article 258.
7   See TFEU, Articles 49 to 55.
8   See TFEU, Articles 63 to 66.
9   See TFEU, Articles 28 to 37.
10   See TFEU, Articles 56 to 62.
11   See TFEU, Articles 20 and 21, and 45 to 48.

Member states are generally prohibited from restricting fundamental freedoms.[1] This is to ensure that a member state does not discriminate against nationals of any other member state, or hinder the exercise by any of its own nationals of any right or freedom available under EU law in any other member state.

The freedom of establishment, for example, confers a right on any national of any member state to set up and manage businesses in any other member state.[2] A company incorporated under the laws of member state Q, therefore, has the right to set up business in any other member state, including the right to transfer its business from member state Q to any other member state. If member state Q introduces a measure that subjects a company incorporated under its laws, on any transfer of its place of management, to immediate taxation on any unrealised capital gains on the assets being transferred – but only where the transfer is to another country – companies incorporated under the laws of member state Q may be deterred from transferring their businesses to another member state. They may be deterred from exercising their freedom of establishment. Notwithstanding, therefore, that it is within the retained sovereign rights of member state Q to introduce the measure, because it makes the exercise of a fundamental freedom less attractive, the measure would be treated as a restriction[3] in breach of member state Q's obligations under the Treaties.[4]

'Direct tax' measures in the UK that have been treated as restrictions include the group relief provisions (under which claims may be made to set the losses of one company against the profits of another member of the same corporate group for corporation tax purposes).

Example: Marks & Spencer had been incurring losses in its EU subsidiaries, and sought to set the losses of its subsidiaries established in Belgium, France and Germany against the profits of their parent company (established in the UK). Its claims were rejected by HMRC on the basis that the UK's group relief provisions (at the time) only permitted the use of losses of companies that were established in the UK. In response, Marks & Spencer claimed that such group relief provisions were a restriction on its freedom of establishment, and thus contrary to EU law. In 2005, the CJEU ruled[5] that the provisions were indeed such a restriction, but also that they were justified, although they went beyond what was appropriate and necessary in certain respects.[6] Perhaps not surprisingly, that was not the end of the story. Disputes continued between Marks & Spencer and HMRC.[7] To complicate matters even further, the European Commission

---

1　Although there are circumstances when restrictions pursue a legitimate objective compatible with EU law and are justified – eg where there is an overriding reason in the public interest. Such restrictions are permitted to stand (to the extent they do not go beyond what is appropriate and necessary to achieve the objective pursued). Discussion of these scenarios is, however, beyond the scope of this Chapter.
2　See TFEU, Article 49.
3　See *Caixa-Bank France*, Case C-442/02.
4　Although, as mentioned in footnote 2 (p 64), the restriction may be justified.
5　In *Marks & Spencer*, Case C-446/03.
6　See footnote 1.
7　See *Marks & Spencer* [2013] UKSC 30 and [2014] UKSC 11, for example.

challenged the legislation the UK introduced[1] in response to the 2005 ruling from the CJEU, on the ground that even that was in contravention of the freedom of establishment. This culminated in a second CJEU ruling (in favour of the UK, rejecting the Commission's arguments) – more than nine years after the first.[2]

Another 'direct tax' measure that has been treated as a restriction on a fundamental freedom is the UK's provisions on 'controlled foreign companies', which are provisions designed (broadly) to address the diversion of profits from the UK to lower tax jurisdictions. In 2006, the CJEU ruled[3] that the provisions at the time were a restriction on the freedom of establishment but also that they could be justified, but only if they were properly framed (which they were not at the time). In response, the UK introduced changes via FA 2007. The European Commission considered the changes to be inadequate. This led to further changes, and eventually, the introduction of a new, and extremely complex, 'controlled foreign companies' regime in FA 2012.

4.4 BREXIT AND 'DIRECT TAXATION'

On 2 October 2016, the Secretary of State for Exiting the European Union released a statement saying that the 'Great Repeal Bill' (the central plank in the Government's legislative package to implement Brexit):

> 'will convert existing [EU] law into domestic [UK] law, while allowing Parliament to amend, repeal, or improve any law after appropriate scrutiny and debate.'

EU law comprises its Treaties, laws in the form of Regulations and Directives, and CJEU rulings. Treaties and Regulations are directly applicable (and do not need to be implemented via any UK legislation to have effect in the UK), whereas Directives are not (and have to be implemented into UK law via primary or secondary legislation). Some EU laws are already in Acts of Parliament (or secondary legislation), while others are not, and these latter laws will cease to have effect in the UK on Brexit unless incorporated into UK law via UK legislation. This is what the Great Repeal Bill (eventually the Great Repeal Act) will do. The Great Repeal: White Paper[4] was published on 30 March 2017.

It explains[5] how the Great Repeal Bill will ensure that, wherever possible, the same rules and laws apply on the day after the UK leaves the EU as before by:

- converting directly-applicable EU law (such as Regulations) into UK law;
- preserving all the laws the UK has made to implement its EU obligations;

---

1   Via FA 2006.
2   See *Commission v UK*, Case C-172/13.
3   See *Cadbury Schweppe*, Case C-196/04.
4   Legislating for the United Kingdom's withdrawal from the European Union, Cm 9446.
5   In the box headed 'What does the Great Repeal Bill convert into UK Law?' on page 14.

- providing for the continued availability of Treaty rights that can be relied on directly in court by individuals (by incorporating these into UK law); and
- giving the same binding, or precedent, status in UK courts to historic CJEU case law as accorded to decisions of the Supreme Court.

The White Paper clarifies[1] that Regulations will not be 'copied out into UK law Regulation by Regulation. Instead, the Great Repeal Bill will convert Regulations as they apply in the UK the moment before it leaves the EU into domestic law, so they continue to apply until legislators in the UK decide otherwise.

Despite what is stated in the White Paper, it is not generally expected that the Great Repeal Bill will transpose all EU laws to UK law. In her Lancaster House speech, 'Plan for Britain'[2] the Prime Minster said what she was proposing in terms of post-Brexit Britain 'cannot mean membership of the single market' because being:

> 'a member of the single market would mean complying with the EU's rules and regulations that implement [the fundamental] freedoms, without having a vote on what those rules and regulations are', [and it would mean] 'accepting a role for the European Court of Justice that would see it still having direct legal authority in [the UK]. It would to all intents and purposes mean not leaving the EU at all.'

It follows from this that free movement of persons will not survive Brexit (especially given the political imperative of controlling immigration from the EU to the UK). As for free movement of goods (and the prohibition on customs duties on imports and exports within the EU), it is as yet unclear whether the UK will remain a member of the EU customs union, although the Prime Minister has said[3] she wanted some form of customs agreement with the EU:

> '[w]hether that means [the UK] must reach a completely new customs agreement, become an associate member of the Customs Union in some way, or remain a signatory to some elements of it'.[4]

The Prime Minister's speech highlights the key problem with Brexit. Ultimately, it is not a question of what the UK wants; it is a question of what it can agree. There is no immediately obvious economic or fiscal reason, for example, why it would want to discriminate against non-UK nationals carrying on business in the UK, or discourage UK nationals from setting up business in the EU. There is no reason, therefore, why the freedom of establishment should not be transposed to UK law. The concern is that for their part, the EU may feel less constrained discriminating against the UK and UK nationals. The Prime Minister even acknowledged in her 'Plan for Britain' speech[5] that 'there are

---

1   At para **2.8**.
2   On 17 January 2017.
3   In her 'Plan for Britain' speech on 17 January 2017.
4   The White Paper mentions (at paragraph 1.22) that the Government will introduce a customs bill to establish a framework to implement a UK customs regime.
5   On 17 January 2017.

some voices calling for a punitive deal that punishes Britain and discourages other countries from taking the same path [ie leaving the EU]'. She made clear that 'no deal for Britain is better than a bad deal for Britain', and that 'if [the UK] were excluded from accessing the single market – [it] would be free to change the basis of Britain's economic model'. Implicit in this is a veiled reference to (potentially aggressive) tax competition, in which case the focus would no longer be on how much EU law would be retained, abandoned or changed on or after Brexit, but how much the UK tax system as a whole could be and should be changed on a fundamental level. Even in that scenario, however, it is not easy to see how inherently protectionist measures such as restrictions on the freedom of establishment would help to 'attract the world's best companies and biggest investors'[1], as the Prime Minister wants, or be consistent with her stated vision of a 'profoundly internationalist' Britain.[2]

The White Paper acknowledges that EU law is not construed in the same way as English law. At paragraph 2.10, it states:

'For example, in interpreting an EU measure it may be relevant to look at its aim and content, as revealed by its legal basis as found in the treaties ... Once we have left the EU, our courts will continue to be able to look to the treaty provisions in interpreting EU laws that are preserved.'

And although the Great Repeal Bill will not provide any role for the CJEU, even in relation to the interpretation of EU-derived law, and UK courts will no longer be required to consider the CJEU's jurisprudence, the White Paper accepts[3] that:

'... for as long as EU-derived law remains on the UK statute book, it is essential that there is a common understanding of what that law means. The Government believes that this is best achieved by providing for continuity in how that law is interpreted before and after exit day. To maximise certainty, therefore, the [Great Repeal] Bill will provide that any question as to the meaning of EU-derived law will be determined in the UK courts by reference to the CJEU's case law as it exists on the day [the UK] leave[s] the EU. Everyone will have been operating on the basis that the law means what the CJEU has already determined it does, and any other starting point would be to change the law. Insofar as case law concerns an aspect of EU law that is not being converted into UK law, that element of the case law will not need to be applied by the UK courts.

For example ... CJEU case law has over the past four decades clarified what is and is not subject to VAT, and failing to follow that case law in [the UK's] own legal system would create new uncertainties about the application of VAT.

This approach maximises legal certainty at the point of departure, but the intention is not to fossilise the past decisions of the CJEU forever. As such, [the Government] propose[s] that the [Great Repeal] Bill will provide that

---

1   See the Prime Minister's 'Plan for Britain' speech on 17 January 2017.
2   See her 'Plan for Britain' speech on 17 January 2017.
3   At paragraphs 2.14 to 2.17.

historic CJEU case law be given the same binding, or precedent, status in our courts as decisions of [the UK's] own Supreme Court. It is very rare for the Supreme Court to depart from one of its own decisions or that of its predecessor, the House of Lords. The circumstances in which it will, exceptionally, do so, derive from a Practice Statement made by the House of Lords in 1966, and adopted by the Supreme Court in 2010. That Statement set out, among other things, that while treating its former decisions as normally binding, it will depart from its previous decisions "when it appears right to do so".

... the Supreme Court [is expected] to take a similar, sparing approach to departing from CJEU case law. [The Government is] also examining whether it might be desirable for any additional steps to be taken to give further clarity about the circumstances in which such a departure might occur. Parliament will be free to change the law, and therefore overturn case law, where it decides it is right to do so.'

Irrespective of how much EU law is preserved by the Great Repeal Bill, it is inevitable that the relevant (EU-derived) provisions will, over time, become more UK and less EU. Long-running sagas such as what happened in *Marks & Spencer*[1] (with the group relief provisions) and *Cadbury Schweppes*[2] (with the 'foreign controlled companies' provisions) should be things of the past. The taxpayer will no longer be able to avail of the CJEU. Even if the freedom of establishment, for example, were transposed 'as is' to UK law on Brexit, Parliament would be 'free – subject to international agreements and treaties with other countries and the EU on matters such as trade – to amend, repeal and improve any law it chooses'.[3] The government would, therefore, have the power to qualify or override the freedom, or make exceptions to it for any new tax measures that may be considered a restriction.

And the European Commission will no longer have any standing to object.

4.5 DIRECTIVES

Directives that impact on 'direct taxation' include:

- the Parent-Subsidiary Directive;[4]
- the Interest and Royalty Directive;[5]
- the Merger Directive;[6] and
- the Anti-Tax Avoidance Directive.[7]

---

1   See Case C-446/03, [2013] UKSC 30 and [2014] UKSC 11 and *Commission v UK*, Case C-172/13.
2   See Case C-196/04.
3   See the Prime Minister's speech announcing the Great Repeal Bill on 2 October 2016.
4   Directive 2011/96/EU.
5   Directive 2003/49/EC.
6   Directive 2009/133/EU.
7   Directive (EU) 2016/1164.

The purpose and effect of these Directives are to harmonise (to an extent) the 'direct tax' rules in member states in the areas specified. For example, the Parent-Subsidiary Directive provides for a subsidiary in one member state to pay dividends and other profit distributions to its parent in another member state without having to withhold any amount from such dividends or distributions by way of tax. It also prevents such income from being taxed twice at the level of the parent (ie once in the member state of payment, and again in the member state of receipt).

There is little economic or fiscal reason to change the status quo, but Brexit is first and foremost a political initiative, and the extent to which the effect of the Directives would be preserved (both on Brexit, and in the medium term thereafter) will depend on how negotiations between the UK and the EU proceed.

Of particular interest is the Anti-Tax Avoidance Directive (or the ATAD). This was only adopted by the European Council on 12 July 2016. As a Directive, it is not directly applicable and needs, therefore, to be implemented into law by each member state. The deadline for implementation of the majority of the measures provided for in the ATAD is 1 January 2019.[1] This means that, in the normal course of events,[2] the UK would still be part of the EU by the time the deadline arrives.

The ATAD contains five measures to address what are regarded as 'common forms of aggressive tax planning' so as to ensure 'a fairer and more stable environment for businesses'.[3] The five measures relate to

- 'interest limitation' (ie restricting deductions of net borrowing costs by reference to EBITDA);[4]
- exit taxes (that bite on the transfer of businesses and assets cross-border);[5]
- a GAAR (ie a general anti-avoidance rule to address non-genuine arrangements);[6]
- 'controlled foreign companies';[7] and
- 'hybrid mismatches' (ie arrangements that result in an item being deducted twice for tax purposes (eg in two member states) or 'deduction without inclusion' (eg an item being deducted in the member state in which it is paid without also being taken into account for tax purposes in the member state in which it is received)).[8]

The extent to which implementation of the ATAD would impact on the existing tax system of a member state would depend on whether that member state already

---

1   See ATAD, Article 11.
2   As the Government notified the European Council (under TEU, Article 50) of its intention to withdraw on 29 March 2017, actual exit should occur two years later, on 29 March 2019.
3   See https://ec.europa.eu/taxation_customs/business/company-tax/anti-tax-avoidance-package/anti-tax-avoidance-directive_en.
4   See ATAD, Article 4.
5   See ATAD, Article 5.
6   See ATAD, Article 6.
7   See ATAD, Articles 7 and 8.
8   See ATAD, Article 9.

has provisions on the five areas to which the measures in the ATAD relate, and how aligned or divergent such provisions are with such measures. In the UK, its own GAAR,[1] for example, may be regarded as being already compliant with the GAAR measure in the ATAD, although its 'controlled foreign companies' provisions[2] may be regarded as being in need of amendment if they are to be in line with the corresponding measure in the ATAD.

While it is difficult to see the UK, which has been on its own campaign against aggressive tax planning, adopting a position after Brexit that is materially different from that provided for in the ATAD (at least in purpose and effect, if not in detail), it is also impossible to ignore the inherent competitiveness in having more taxpayer-friendly rules than the whole of the EU. Ultimately, it is a question of politics, and how negotiations between the UK and the other member states proceed.

4.6 VAT

In *Royal and Sun Alliance* [2003] UKHL 29, Lord Walker of Gestingthorpe said:

'Value added tax ('VAT') is essentially an EU tax ...'

This is because it derives from a Directive (now, the Principal VAT Directive (or the PVD)[3]), implemented in the UK via (what is now) the Value Added Tax Act 1994 (or the VATA). Unlike 'direct tax', which only really intersects with EU law where a fundamental freedom is engaged or a Directive applies, almost every aspect of VAT is suffused with EU law.

The more fervent Brexiteer might have hoped that when the UK left the EU, it would also leave this EU tax behind. This will not happen, if only because VAT brings in so much for the Exchequer.[4]

Much of the VAT law applicable in the UK is already in the VATA and related secondary legislation; the rest will be transposed to UK law via the Great Repeal Bill. The expectation is that, in the main, the UK VAT system will continue to operate as if it were still part of the common EU VAT system, at least in the short to medium term following Brexit. Preserving the rules of the common EU VAT system, however, would itself result in changes in how certain VAT rules apply in the UK. This is because VAT law draws a line between the EU and the rest of the world, and on Brexit, the UK will find itself on the other side of the fence.

---

1   See FA 2013, Part 5.
2   See the Taxation (International and Other Provisions) Act 2010, Part 9A.
3   Directive 2006/112/EC.
4   According to the HMRC document dated 21 February 2017 and titled 'HMRC Tax & NIC Receipts: Monthly and annual historical record', '[o]ver the last decade IT, CGT & NICs (Income tax, Capital Gains Tax and National Insurance Contributions) combined made up on average 56 per cent of total receipts. Value Added Tax (VAT) and Corporation Tax, Bank Levy and Petroleum Revenue Tax (CT, BL and PRT) are the next biggest, contributing an average 20 per cent and 10 per cent of total receipts respectively' – see https://www.gov.uk/government/uploads/system/uploads/attachment_data/file/592842/Jan17_Receipts_NS_Bulletin_Final.pdf.

For example, where goods are removed from one country to another, a layman may describe the transaction as an export/importation, but for VAT purposes, it would only be an export/importation where one country is in the EU and the other is outside the EU; where both are in the EU, the transaction would be a dispatch/acquisition (and not an export/importation).[1] On Brexit, transactions between the UK and the EU would no longer be dispatches / acquisitions – they would all be exports/importations – and the rules that apply will be different.[2]

Another example is where 'digital services' (such as the sale of music, films, games, magazines or books via download) are supplied to 'consumers' (ie non-business customers) in the EU. A business, whether it is established in or outside the EU, that provides such services is required to register for, and pay, VAT in each EU country in which it has 'consumers'; alternatively, it could opt to take advantage of the Mini One Stop Shop (or MOSS).[3] A business established in the US that is registered under the UK MOSS scheme, for example, would submit only one return (the MOSS return), as opposed to one return in every relevant EU country, and make only one VAT payment to (in this example) HMRC, with HMRC then forwarding the relevant parts of the return and the relevant portions of the payment to the tax authorities in the relevant EU countries.[4] The MOSS scheme, therefore, saves the US business the administrative burden of having to register, and account, for VAT in what could be a large number of countries. On Brexit, the UK itself will be outside the EU, and it will no longer be able to offer MOSS. The US business in the above example will have to re-register under the MOSS scheme of another – ie an EU – country. Businesses established in the UK that provide 'digital services' would be in the same position, and will have to decide whether to register, and account, for VAT in each EU country in which it has 'consumers' or opt for the MOSS scheme of a particular EU country.

Another area where UK VAT laws will need to be modified on Brexit is where certain types of services (such as most financial or insurance services) are provided to a client in another country. Under the common EU VAT system, how that transaction is treated for VAT purposes depends on whether the client is established in a EU country or outside the EU. Pre-Brexit, a bank established in the UK making a loan to a borrower established in France, for example, would be making an exempt supply of services for VAT purposes,[5] and it would not be able to recover any of the VAT it incurs for the purposes of making that loan.[6] A bank established in France making a loan to a borrower established in the UK would be in the same position. Post-Brexit, the bank established in France would be treated as making a supply of services that falls outside the scope of VAT[7] and it would be entitled to recover the VAT it incurs for the purposes of

---

1   See https://www.gov.uk/guidance/vat-exports-dispatches-and-supplying-goods-abroad, for example.
2   See https://www.gov.uk/guidance/vat-exports-dispatches-and-supplying-goods-abroad, for example.
3   See https://www.gov.uk/guidance/register-and-use-the-vat-mini-one-stop-shop, for example.
4   See https://www.gov.uk/guidance/register-and-use-the-vat-mini-one-stop-shop, for example.
5   See PVD, Articles 44 & 135 and VATA, section 7A & Schedule 9, Group 5.
6   See PVD, Article 168 and VATA, section 26.
7   See PVD, Articles 44 and VATA, section 7A.

making the loan.[1] It is expected that UK VAT law will be modified so that the bank established in the UK would be in the same position.

4.7 WHAT WAS OLD IS ... NEW AGAIN?

The above is a (non-exhaustive) list of changes that will need to be made to UK VAT laws in order for the UK VAT system to continue functioning in parallel to the common EU VAT system (which is considered preferable – ensuring consistency so as to promote certainty and avoid double or no taxation, at least for the short or medium term). The more intriguing question, of course, is whether, in the long term – ie once Brexit has settled – UK VAT law will change more significantly in a deliberate move away from the common EU VAT system.

There have been a number of cases where the UK wanted to frame its VAT laws in a particular way but was prevented from doing so because the measures in question were in breach of EU VAT laws. The provision of construction services, for example, is standard rated. There are exceptions – for example, where they are provided in the course of constructing a building that is intended solely for use by a charity for a 'non-business' purpose, in which case their supply is zero-rated – ie charged to VAT at 0% – and not standard rated.[2] However, once upon a time, construction services provided in the course of constructing any new building were zero-rated, even a building intended for wholly commercial or industrial use. The relevant provisions were changed after the CJEU ruled they were in breach of EU VAT law.[3] After Brexit, it would be possible for the UK to reinstate the original provisions. Charities that currently have to pay VAT on construction services – for example, where they are not using the building for a purpose that is considered 'non-business' for VAT purposes – would no doubt welcome such a change-back (because in most cases, they are not able to recover VAT, and so would prefer not to pay any). The issue, of course, is that if the UK made too many generous change-backs in favour of the tax bearer, the very reason for retaining the tax in the first place would be undermined.[4]

Change-backs do not, however, have to favour the tax bearer. The UK used to exempt management services supplied to open-ended investment companies, but not management services supplied to investment trust companies (or ITCs). This was ruled by the CJEU to be incompatible with EU VAT law,[5] and the UK had to extend the exemption to management services supplied to ITCs. If, after Brexit, the UK were to change the relevant provisions back to what they were before the CJEU ruling, that would be one instance where the change-back would be unlikely to reduce the tax-take.

---

1   See PVD, Article 169 and VATA, section 26.
2   See VATA, Schedule 8, Group 5.
3   See *Commission v United Kingdom*, Case C-416/85.
4   As noted in House of Commons Library Briefing Paper number CBP7630, dated 6 February 2017 and titled 'Tax after the EU referendum', 'the relative importance of VAT to the Exchequer ... suggests that future governments would be unlikely to substantially increase ... reliefs or abolish the tax, even while exit from the EU would give them this power'.
5   See *Claverhouse*, Case C-363/05.

The provisions discussed above are UK provisions that were challenged, either by the European Commission or UK nationals, and which had to be changed because, as drafted at the time, they were incompatible with EU VAT law. There are also cases where the provisions under challenge were not UK provisions, but provisions under the VAT laws of another EU country. Where the provisions under challenge are not UK provisions, when they are ruled by the CJEU to be incompatible with EU VAT law, there is less need for a direct and immediate response from the UK. However, the UK must still take account of the ruling, because it may mean that the corresponding UK provisions, too, are incompatible with EU VAT law and have to be changed.

Arthur Andersen,[1] for example, was a Dutch referral, on which the CJEU ruled as far back as 2005. HMRC has long acknowledged that the ruling meant the exemptions provided under UK VAT law for certain insurance transactions[2] were wider than the PVD allowed. No changes have, however, been made. Brexit could mean that no such changes would ever be made, should the UK so choose.

Similarly, following the more recent CJEU ruling on a Swedish referral,[3] questions have arisen as to whether the UK rules on VAT grouping are impacted and need to be changed.[4] HMRC already takes the view that the ruling does not require any changes to the UK rules.[5] The European Commission or the CJEU may, however, disagree. This, of course, would fall away as a viable concern on Brexit.

4.8 EUROPEAN PRINCIPLES

The common EU VAT system is built on a bed of EU legal principles. Some of these are set out expressly in Treaties, while others are unwritten (or, at least, not written in any statute book). They include:

- the principle of fiscal neutrality;[6]
- the principles of legal certainty and the protection of legitimate expectations;[7]
- the principle of subsidiarity and proportionality;[8]
- the principle of equivalence;[9]
- the principle of effectiveness;[10] and
- the principle of VAT and abuse of rights.[11]

---

1   See Case C-472/03.
2   See VATA, Schedule 9, Group 2.
3   See *Skandia America Corp*, Case C-7/13.
4   See   https://www.gov.uk/government/publications/revenue-and-customs-brief-2-2015-vat-grouping-rules-and-the-skandia-judgment/revenue-and-customs-brief-2-2015-vat-grouping-rules-and-the-skandia-judgment, for example.
5   See   https://www.gov.uk/government/publications/revenue-and-customs-brief-18-2015-vat-grouping-rules-and-the-skandia-judgement/revenue-and-customs-brief-18-2015-vat-grouping-rules-and-the-skandia-judgement.
6   See PVD, Recital 7, and *Commission v France*, Case C-481/98, for example.
7   See *Ampafrance*, Case C-177/99, for example.
8   See TEU, Article 5 and *Ampafrance*, Case C-177/99, for example.
9   See *Fantask*, Case C-188/95, for example.
10 See *Aprile*, Case C-228/96, for example.
11 See *Halifax*, Case C-255/02.

The Great Repeal Bill is expected to transpose most of these principles to UK law. Some, like the principle of equivalence (which requires member states to ensure that the remedies and procedural rules in relation to claims based on EU law are at least equivalent to (ie no less favourable than) those in relation to claims based on national law) and the principle of effectiveness (which prohibits member states from making it practically impossible (or excessively difficult) for their nationals to exercise EU rights), would probably not be transposed, because, after Brexit, UK nationals are expected no longer to be able to invoke EU laws or rights.[1]

Other principles, such as the principle of fiscal neutrality, are central to the common EU VAT system, and is expected to be transposed in whole to ensure the proper functioning of the UK VAT system. The question is how this will be achieved.

The principle of fiscal neutrality encapsulates:[2]

- the principle of VAT uniformity; and
- the principle of elimination of distortion in competition.[3]

It prohibits treating 'similar' items (whether they are goods or services), which are in competition with each other, differently for VAT purposes.[4] It applies, for example, where the supply of item A is subject to VAT at the standard rate, whereas the supply of item B, being a 'similar' item, is treated as exempt from VAT or subject to VAT at only the zero rate (or the reduced rate) – the overall effect being that the supply of item B is favoured over the supply of item A. To determine whether any two items are 'similar' for these purposes, one takes the point of view of a typical consumer, the question being whether the items have similar characteristics (ie whether their use is comparable) and whether they meet the same needs from the consumer's point of view (ie whether the differences between them have a significant influence on the consumer's decision to use one or the other).[5] It is not necessary, however, to show the two items are actually in competition, or that the difference in VAT treatment has actually resulted in distortion of competition.[6]

The above is only a high-level description of the principle. A single clause in the Great Repeal Bill saying simply that the EU principle of fiscal neutrality as it exists on Brexit Day is transposed to UK law in its entirety would clearly be unsatisfactory – it would beg too many questions – but it would appear from the White Paper that that is precisely what is intended.

---

1   Subject to any transitional provisions the UK and the EU may agree as part of any withdrawal agreement.
2   See *Ampafrance*, Case C-177/99, for example.
3   See PVD, Recital 7 and *Commission v France*, Case C-481/98, for example.
4   See *Commission v France*, Case C-481/98.
5   See *The Rank Group*, Case C-259/10.
6   See *The Rank Group*, Case C-259/10.

4.9 EUROPEAN COURT OF JUSTICE

The PVD has been enacted into UK law via the VATA. There is, therefore, no need for it to be transposed again (by the Great Repeal Bill) on Brexit. One question that arises is what should happen if it only transpires after Brexit that a provision in the VATA has not correctly implemented the corresponding provision in the PVD.

Pre-Brexit, a taxpayer may seek to rely on the provision in the PVD directly, and not the provision in the VATA, and they would be entitled to do so provided the provision in the PVD is unconditional and sufficiently precise.[1] In theory, the taxpayer would continue to be able to do so, by relying on the (expected) effect of the Great Repeal Bill, and the fact that, at the time the provision in the VATA was enacted, the UK was still part of the EU (and subject to EU VAT law). The White Paper states[2] that:

'If, after exit, a conflict arises between two pre-exit laws, one of which is an EU-derived law and the other not, then the EU-derived law will continue to take precedence over the other pre-exit law ...'

However, the taxpayer will no longer be able to avail of the CJEU. Nor will the UK courts be bound to follow any rulings handed down by the CJEU after Brexit (even though they may, and are in the short to medium term likely to, find them of persuasive value).

The common EU VAT system will continue to evolve, as would the UK VAT system. The question is whether the two will develop in tandem.

For example, a concept used in EU law where the relevant provision does not refer expressly to the law of the member states for its meaning and scope would normally be given an independent and uniform interpretation throughout the EU, so as to ensure uniform application of EU law across all the member states.[3] The exemptions provided for under EU VAT law[4] are examples of such a concept.[5] It is almost certain that, immediately after Brexit, the UK will continue to take account of the 'independent and uniform interpretation' that applies across the EU; the question is how long it will continue to do so.

4.10 OPPORTUNITIES

Because, pre-Brexit, UK VAT law has to cleave to EU VAT law, there has until now been little point in lobbying the Government for fundamental changes to the UK VAT system – it just cannot happen without also making the same fundamental changes to the common EU VAT system. This all changes, of course, on Brexit.

---

1   See *Becker*, Case C-8/81, for example.
2   At paragraph 2.20.
3   See *EKRO*, Case C-327/82, for example.
4   See PVD, Articles 135 and VATA, Schedule 9.
5   See *CPP*, Case C-349/96, for example.

For example, in *Longridge on the Thames,*[1] the Court of Appeal noted:

> 'There is no special rule for a charity. A charity does not enjoy blanket relief from VAT for its activities. Its liability to VAT will depend on whether its activities are economic activities. It may not be able to claim relief simply because it is carrying out a charitable activity ...'

With Brexit now visible on the horizon, there is no reason why the charities sector should not consider lobbying the government now for special rules to be introduced in two years' time to confer charities-specific reliefs (for example).

The opportunity for change is not, of course, restricted to the charities sector – it is open to any taxpayer or any tax bearer in any sector, and even HMRC itself.

In this connection, the White Paper states[2] that:

> 'The Great Repeal Bill will not aim to make major changes to policy or establish new legal frameworks in the UK beyond those which are necessary to ensure the law continues to function properly from day one ...'

The future is almost here, and if the referendum has shown us anything, there will be surprises.

---

1   [2016] EWCA Civ 930.
2   At paragraph 1.21.

CHAPTER 5

FINANCIAL SERVICES

Philip Brooks, ORC International and Andy Fleming, MHP Communications

(Also read the thought leadership piece by Paul Grainger CEO of Comply Port Limited.)

INTRODUCTION

Is Brexit good or bad for those working with financial services providers?

Confidence, of course, plays a significant role when making investment decisions and according to the OECD Business Confidence Index (BCI), confidence in the UK was flat immediately after the vote (from June 2016 to September 2016), but steadily rose from September 2016 to January 2017.[1]

More importantly, the performance of the UK economy since the vote has also been robust. The year finished strongly, solid levels of growth were reported as we ended 2016, and the UK Government's monthly borrowing hit its lowest level in 17 years due to higher than expected tax receipts.[2] With all these metrics combined, it would be fair to say the doomsday scenario of a Leave vote did not happen – or at least, hasn't happened yet.

However, that does not mean that we are better off than we would have been had Remain won. We are still a long way from leaving the EU. Those whose businesses are based on exports to the EU still face an uncertain future until trade deals are struck. The depreciation of the pound, although potentially boosting exports, is being felt by consumers as prices begin to rise without wage growth managing to keep up. In addition to rising inflation, we see higher interest rates and lower consumer spending.

The fact is, never has a quote by Donald Rumsfeld, which at the time was somewhat mocked, been so apt.

'There are known knowns; there are things we know we know.

'We also know there are known unknowns; that is to say we know there are some things we do not know.

---

1   OECD: Business confidence index (BCI)
     https://data.oecd.org/leadind/business-confidence-index-bci.htm?context=iLibrary
2   UK government surplus gives Philip Hammond pre-budget boost
     https://www.theguardian.com/business/2017/feb/21/bumper-tax-receipts-swell-public-finances-in-january

'But there are also unknown unknowns – the ones we don't know we don't know.

'And if one looks throughout the history of our country and other free countries, it is the latter category that tend to be the difficult ones.'

We know that the UK is going to leave the EU. We don't know what sort of agreement, if any, will be reached. Especially in relation to financial services. One thing is for certain – there will be wider, far reaching implications for business and trade that simply no one will have had the foresight to consider.

5.1   IMAGINE THE UK WITHOUT THE FINANCIAL SERVICES SECTOR

The importance of the financial services sector to the UK economy is significant, contributing around 7% towards UK GDP and directly employing 1.1 million people.[1]

Many may assume, incorrectly as it happens, that the majority of those employed within financial services are based in London. But the benefits of the financial services sector can be felt far wider, with two thirds of those employed actually being based outside of London.

The sector generates 12% of PAYE income tax and national insurance contributions alongside 15% of onshore corporation tax. If we add on related professional services (ie management consultants, legal services, accounting services etc) the total employment figure increases to 2.2 million.[2]

Its importance to the UK economy was described quite succinctly by Anthony Brown, CEO of the British Bankers Association whilst giving evidence to the House of Lords European Union Committee:

'Financial and related professional services pay over £60 billion a year in tax. Of that, banks pay about £31 billion. Of that £31 billion, slightly over half ... is paid by foreign banks based here. It is worth noting that that is bigger than the entire UK net contribution to the EU budget.'

Maintaining a healthy and thriving sector is therefore clearly critical to the UK economy, but the impact beyond our shores should not be underestimated either.

---

1   House of Lords European Union Committee 9th report of Session 2016-17: Brexit: financial services
     https://www.publications.parliament.uk/pa/ld201617/ldselect/ldeucom/81/81.pdf
2   House of Lords European Union Committee 9th report of Session 2016-17: Brexit: financial services
     https://www.publications.parliament.uk/pa/ld201617/ldselect/ldeucom/81/81.pdf

5.2   LONDON – THE LEADING GLOBAL FINANCIAL CENTRE

The Global Financial Centres Index (GFCI) places London ahead of New York, Singapore, Hong Kong and Tokyo.[1] The index takes into account a number of factors including:

*   Business environment
*   Financial services development
*   Infrastructure
*   Human capital
*   Reputation

Essentially, the benefits of London will be hard for any pretender to replicate. Of course, some jobs will be lost as firms decide to create subsidiaries in the EU to retain access to their clients. Prior to the referendum, a number of financial institutions did state that Brexit would more than likely cause them to shift but while EU rivals from Paris, Frankfurt, Madrid and Amsterdam do pose a threat, it will not be easy. So far just the EBA (European Banking Authority) has decided to relocate,[2] alongside announcements from JP Morgan and HSBC that they will move jobs to the continent.[3] As Dr Andreas Dombret, a board member of Germany's central bank, told the BBC at the end of February, although some jobs could be lost, 'London will remain the most important financial centre in Europe'.[4]

The City benefits not only from a trusted and predictable legal system and a strong regulatory framework but also an 'ecosystem' where bankers, brokers, lawyers all the way to FinTech start-ups can co-exist. The closest 'financial cluster' to London is actually New York rather than any other EU country. So although the threat of other EU nations challenging London in the future does exist, the biggest threat will actually come from across the pond.

Giving evidence to the House of Lords European Union Committee, Miles Celic, CEO of the CityUK stated:

> 'It is very difficult to identify another, smaller financial centre in Europe that has anything like the sort of advantages London has. Indeed, in some sectors of the financial and related professional services industry, London has an even stronger advantage than somewhere like New York. London has the creative, regulatory, legislative, funding and technology centres all in one place.'

---

1   Brexit: the United-Kingdom and EU financial services
    http://www.europarl.europa.eu/RegData/etudes/BRIE/2016/587384/IPOL_
    BRI(2016)587384_EN.pdf
2   Briefing Paper: Brexit & financial services by Tim Edmonds
    http://researchbriefings.files.parliament.uk/documents/CBP-7628/CBP-7628.pdf
3   Isaac Wohl, Office of Industries (USITC): The Impact of Brexit on Financial Services
    https://www.usitc.gov/publications/332/executive_briefings/wohl_brexit_and_financial_
    services_final.pdf
4   Germany's Bundesbank plays down Brexit 'punishment'
    http://www.bbc.co.uk/news/business-39095438

This fear has potentially been fuelled following comments from Wilbur Ross (US Secretary of Commerce) that Brexit represented a 'God-given opportunity' for London's financial rivals. The growth of New York would be just as disagreeable to our friends on the continent as it is to us.

The strength of London means its success, albeit critical to the UK economy, is also very important to the EU. According to a briefing by the European parliament, although just over half of the City's turnover was domestic, around a quarter (24%) of EU financial services pass through London.[1]

Of course, during negotiations, there is the danger that the process of leaving the EU becomes highly politicised, as individual countries jostle for position and aim to develop their own financial centres. However, echoing Miles Celic's comments, Axel Weber, UBS Chairman, speaking at an industry conference hosted by German daily Handelsblatt, warns against that approach:

> 'It's too simple of an equation to think that without doing very much, Frankfurt, Madrid and others will profit from London's exit. No European financial centre besides London currently cracks the top-ten globally, but Zurich – which is outside the EU – is ranked sixth. I believe the greater danger is that New York, Mumbai, Dubai or Zurich will benefit if global trade is organised by global financial firms in the most important centres and pass their book from one centre to the next throughout the day, meaning Europe plays a far smaller role.'[2]

5.3   MARKET ACCESS

The challenge for providers who want to deal within the EU face is how they are going to be able to access those markets once the UK leaves the EU. Currently the UK benefits from passporting rights.

Passporting essentially allows firms authorised in one member state (its home base) to conduct business in another member state without the need for separate authorisation. Many international firms have set up a subsidiary in London (in part) for this reason, using London as its home base to access the single market free from any separate regulation and cost.

Currently, around 5,476 UK-based firms are using passports issued by the FCA (Financial Conduct Authority) and the PRA (Prudential Regulation Authority), compared to just over 8,000 firms issued with a passport in the EU or EEA (European Economic Area), enabling it to do business in the UK or other member state.

---

1   Brexit: the United-Kingdom and EU financial services
     http://www.europarl.europa.eu/RegData/etudes/BRIE/2016/587384/IPOL_BRI(2016)587384_
     EN.pdf
2   UBS' Axel Weber Tells Frankfurt Bankers Not to Expect Brexit Business
     http://www.finews.com/news/english-news/24276-ubs-axel-weber-brexit-frankfurt-paris-
     madrid-mumbai-zurich

Passports are issued for different types of services, so a firm can hold more than one passport – and UK based firms hold significantly more passports than firms based on the continent.

5.3.1 Number of inbound and outbound passports[1]

	Total	Inbound	Outbound
Number of passports in total	359,953	23,532	336,421
Number of firms using passporting	13,484	8,008	5,476

One of the strengths of London 'ecosystem' is that it can service the holistic needs of a client. Passporting helps to facilitate that, with both EU and UK clients being beneficiaries. Without the same access to markets and without the ability to provide the same range of services, it is difficult to predict what the final impact will be.

The British government has declared it wants to secure the 'freest access possible' for the sector. The challenge is how it does this whilst also remaining committed to the promises made to the British public. What alternatives exist?

5.4 NORWEGIAN AND SWISS MODELS

There are already a couple of European countries who are outside of the EU but have agreements in place allowing them to trade/work within financial services. The Norway model (EEA) and the Swiss Model (European Free Trade Association – EFTA).

The Norwegian model would mean that the UK Government would have to accept the four freedoms of movement (people, goods, services, capital) alongside the authority of EU law. Given the promises made to the UK public, this seems unlikely.

The Swiss model, through its membership of the EFTA and a series of bilateral agreements (and being deemed equivalent) is able to access the market for financial services. However, its access is limited. A key difference between the two models is Norway enjoys the benefits of passporting, whilst Switzerland does not.

If the UK government were unable to secure similar deals, the UK would have to enter bilateral agreements with the remaining states – otherwise known as Equivalence.

---

1   House of Lords European Union Committee 9th report of Session 2016-17: Brexit: financial services
      https://www.publications.parliament.uk/pa/ld201617/ldselect/ldeucom/81/81.pdf

5.5 NEGOTIATING EQUIVALENCE

Equivalence would mean that the UK would need to negotiate bilateral agreements with the remaining 27 member states to ensure access. This may be conducted by the EU Commission but sometimes separately with each member state, which would be both time consuming and laborious.

Equivalence means that 'equivalent' regulatory standards apply between the two countries. Given that the UK (at the time of separation) will have exactly the same regulatory standards, in theory, this seems the most practical and achievable solution.

But equivalence is not without its problems. Even if all member states reach an agreement, under existing EU regulation, it can be revoked with as little as 30 days' notice.[1] There is also the potential that in the future the EU could force the UK to agree to rules it does not like. The devil is going to be in the detail, as financial services firms in particular do not like instability or uncertainty.

It is only prudent for firms to make contingency plans. If the UK government fails to address these concerns, providers may not only opt for a subsidiary inside the EU, but move more of their operations there. This would come at significant additional cost, both in cash and jobs.

5.6 REGULATION AND INFLUENCE

The UK has historically led the way on financial services regulation, such as the implementation of tougher stress tests for the banks and the Retail Distribution Review (RDR).

The stress tests were designed to make the banks hold enough capital to withstand another financial crisis, whereas the RDR created greater transparency for investors by making the adviser agree their fee upfront (separating the advice fee from the product fee), as well as a drive to improve professional standards.

More recently, following the financial crisis, there has also been a greater trend for greater integration and consistency globally, rather than just within the EU. For example:

- The International Organization of Securities Commissions (IOSCO)
- The Financial Stability Board (FSB)
- The Basel Committee on Banking Supervision (BCBS) i.e. Basel III or the impending Basel IV

The global strength of the UK financial services sector, alongside its membership of the EU, means it currently enjoys the benefit of being able to influence

---

1   EU equivalence rules don't offer post-Brexit equality (https://infacts.org/eu-equivalence-rules-dont-offer-post-brexit-equality/).

decisions to protect UK interests. Not just within the EU but globally. Once Brexit is triggered, the UK's ability to influence these decisions particularly within the EU will be reduced.

The push for tougher regulation has not just impacted the banks either, Solvency II is an EU directive designed to ensure that insurers hold enough capital for the risks they insure, harmonise EU insurance regulation whilst providing greater consumer protection.

Interestingly, an additional benefit of equivalence is that the UK could operate two frameworks: one for those not wanting to trade (eg UK Building Societies) and another for those that do. This could become important as future regulatory standards potentially diverge and as the UK's influence upon the single rulebook and Capital Markets Union (CMU) wanes.

However, the lack of influence and increasing risk of divergence, over time, also involves risk. Especially if it is driven by political manoeuvring, as it could simply become increasingly advantageous for firms to conduct their business elsewhere.

5.7 DOING BUSINESS WITH FINANCIAL SERVICES PROVIDERS

So what does all this mean for those who wish to pursue business relationships with financial services providers? Well it ultimately depends on which part of the sector you are targeting, and for what services.

5.7.1 Domestically

For those businesses targeting domestic providers, the risk of your business being affected is much lower. Remember over half of the turnover generated by financial services firms is domestic. The UK will still have a need for financial products and services, although it can be argued that general market conditions will either be positively or negatively impacted depending upon which side of the debate you reside. Either way, the UK economy will not stop once we are out of the EU.

UK consumers will still have rational and emotional needs which need fulfilling. Financial services providers will still learn, adapt, innovate, develop and introduce new products and services to meet either changing demand or a changing landscape, just as they have always done. Business will carry on.

Of course there will also be the overseeing eye of government, CMA and the FCA to ensure the market is operating as it should – and over the last few years they have certainly taken a more proactive stance towards regulation and intervention.

There has never been a more exciting time to be working within the domestic market, as various parts of the sector learn to adapt and cope with disruption – whether that's political, economic, social, technological, legal or environmental (PESTLE). The sector faces so many challenges that to meet them it will still need the help and support of suppliers.

5.7.2   Technological disruption

Today providers have to deal with a number of initiatives or interventions, either to help ensure customers are treated fairly or to increase competition. A prime example of this is what is happening within retail banking.

By early 2018 customers will be able to share their personal financial data securely via an API (Application Programming Interface) so other banks can tailor their products and services to better meet their needs. Known as 'Open Banking' this will not only be of benefit to other banks, but also credit card providers, mortgage and loan companies as well as saving and investment advisers/providers.

Given that even a bank doesn't necessarily have access to the entire financial dealings of its customers, Fintech[1] companies have already started developing and launching apps which can store all of a customer's accounts in a single place, such as Bud.[2]

Essentially this will give the customer greater control of their own data and rebalance the relationship with the provider, as from within the app a customer will have sight of the most suitable competitive products and services for them, and will also be able to open and close accounts.

Clearly something this radical will take time to bed in, but as society changes and sharing personal information becomes more the norm, it will become reality. In 1994, Bill Gates famously said 'Banking is necessary, Banks are not.' As the years have passed, the statement resonates even more.

From a bank's perspective, when you consider what their needs could potentially be – from consultancy to legal, IT and marketing experts through to customer experience training and even through to companies that will be required to continue to print product literature – you can see banks will still need to rely heavily on their supply chain post Brexit.

Technology is also disrupting the general insurance market with, for example, driverless cars becoming a reality. Not only will this potentially change how

---

1   Financial technology, also known as Fintech, is an industry composed of companies that use new technology and innovation in order to compete in the marketplace of traditional financial institutions and intermediaries. Currently, this could include peer-to-peer lending companies or robo-advice for example. In the future, apps will be developed to help consumers make better financial decisions as retail banks will be forced to share their transactional and account information.

2   www.thisisbud.com.

consumers buy (or rent) cars but it will significantly change the way motor insurance is bought. It is not just motor insurance either; how will SMART homes potentially disrupt the home insurance market and how will PSD2 (The Second Payment Services Directive) change the payments space both domestically and internationally?

5.7.3 Dealing with providers internationally

It is much more difficult to predict how Brexit will impact business which currently comes from within the EU or would be based from the EU in the future. Effectively this is going to depend upon the negotiations and the final deal which is struck.

Clearly if tariffs are introduced, suppliers based in the UK will either be less competitive or it will impact upon margins. Difficult decisions on whether to tender for work will need to be made on a case by case basis.

To some degree, given currency fluctuations, that has already been the case, but imposing tariffs would be an additional, and unhelpful, complication. That does not mean it is impossible. Particularly if contacts and relationships already exist.

If the worst does happen, and parts of the sector do decide to re-locate to inside of the EU, suppliers have to remember that over time they will have built up significant experience and expertise which Brexit cannot take away. More importantly, that experience and expertise will still be valued by providers (maybe by even the same contacts).

Suppliers, just like providers will need to learn to adapt and cope to the changing business landscape, demonstrating how and where they can still add value. It will certainly be more challenging and competitive, but if a supplier knows its clients, has identified and understood their needs and responds in kind, as long as it can remain competitive there is no reason why it can't still be in with a good chance of winning that business.

If tariffs and currency fluctuations are unfavourable then a supplier is always within its right to respectfully decline. It just needs to ensure it maintains strong relationships with potential clients for when market conditions become more favourable.

5.8 SOMETHING WE DO KNOW: CHANGE IS COMING, PREPARATION IS KEY

Change is coming, change is never easy and businesses need to prepare. However, when change happens, opportunity will always present itself.

Irrespective of how and where the change occurs it will be a supplier's ability to react and adapt which will continue to make it successful. Just like with any other disruptive trend. If it fails to do so, other suppliers will be there to take its place.

Looking forward, within the UK financial services sector there is cause for optimism. Of course there are steep challenges and risks, but given the importance of the sector to the UK economy as well as the EU economy, hopefully a common sense approach will prevail. At least in the short term.

Different parts of the sector will certainly be affected differently. The UK domestic retail market should largely remain unaffected whereas areas such as euro clearing business could be significantly impacted, especially if currency nationalism gets in the way.[1]

Some suppliers may prefer to invest in those relationships which effectively will remain unchanged by Brexit, as they are perceived to be more likely to remain more stable. Conversely, there could potentially be even more opportunity amongst those who are impacted the most by Brexit and need to relocate as they need to rely on trusted suppliers.

With the EBA already declaring it will be re-locating once the UK exits the EU, it would be no surprise, given the history of the European Central Bank's 'Eurosystem Oversight Policy Framework' whereby it was essentially trying to force clearing houses dealing in euro-denominated transactions to move to the Eurozone, if in the future, clearing houses trading certain business needed to be based within the EU area.

President Francois Hollande of France has claimed that relocating euro-denominated clearing to the Eurozone should: 'Serve as an example for those who seek the end of Europe … It can serve as a lesson'.[2]

In the longer term, it is already clear that Paris is stepping up its efforts with plans to build seven new skyscrapers in its business district, but it will need to do far more than build infrastructure. It will need to attract talent. That is something that London has in abundance.

---

1   The SWIFT Institute: The Impact of Brexit on the Financial Services Industry
     https://www.swiftinstitute.org/newsletters/the-impact-of-brexit-on-the-financial-services-industry/
2   House of Lords European Union Committee 9th report of Session 2016-17: Brexit: financial services
     https://www.publications.parliament.uk/pa/ld201617/ldselect/ldeucom/81/81.pdf

CHAPTER 6

COMMERCIAL CONTRACTS

Helen Tse, Clarke Willmott LLP

INTRODUCTION

This chapter looks at contracts, commercial agreements and commercial law which might be affected by Brexit. However, this chapter will not look at contracts regarding financial services, employment or intellectual property which will be considered in separate chapters.

Businesses will need to consider the impact of Brexit on contracts and these should be reviewed in light of Brexit to ensure that they are not adversely affected, become uncommercial nor unprofitable. This chapter will give you a practical view point on reviewing commercial contracts so as to avoid financial difficulties.

Some of the laws governing commercial law derive from EU legislation. It is not clear what the transitional and savings arrangements will be implemented but the key laws are set out below. After Brexit, the laws might not change – this is really a wait and see situation.

6.1 CONSUMER RIGHTS ACT 2015

The Consumer Rights Act 2015 is not derived from the EU and therefore Brexit should not affect it. However the Consumer Contracts (Information, Cancellation and Additional Charges) Regulations 2013[1] and the Consumer Protection from Unfair Trading Regulations 2008,[2] as amended in 2014, are from EU law so it remains to be seen if those will be repealed or adopted after Brexit.

6.2 CONTRACTS GOVERNED BY 'ENGLISH LAW'

The choice of law clause will not change but what will need clarity is what constitutes 'English law'.

6.3 TERMS AND CONDITIONS

If you use Terms and Conditions for the EU and UK interchangeably, then this will need to be reviewed and probably two different sets are needed as different legal terms will apply after Brexit.

---

1   SI 2013/3134.
2   SI 2008/1277.

6.4 REFERENCES TO THE EU IN THE CONTRACT

After Brexit, the UK is no longer included in the definition of 'EU', so ensure the UK is expressly included in the contract.

For example in a trade mark licence agreement for the EU, if this is not amended post Brexit, the parties will have to determine whether the UK is covered and they would have to look at the presence of UK trademarks, whether the trade mark was used in the UK and where payments are made. It would be clearer to amend the contract to expressly include the UK as a separate country, whereas before, the term 'EU' would have been sufficient.

6.5 WILL EU LAW REMAIN IN THE UK?

If a 'Hard Brexit' is invoked, the UK will cease to be part of the customs union and EU law will not apply unless the Government adopts such EU laws into the laws of England and Wales. The Government may want to use Brexit as an opportunity to revoke certain laws, eg the Commercial Agents (Council Directive) Regulations 1993[1] (1993 Regulations), which implement the Commercial Agents Directive (86/653/EU), detailed below. This is an area which needs to be monitored on a regular basis as the UK departs the EU.

Cross border enforcement of judgments: Post-Brexit it may become more difficult to enforce an English court judgment in the EU (and vice versa). However, it is hoped that some form of UK/EU harmonised system will be agreed to cover enforcement, jurisdiction and governing law. Without this, the courts of EU member states will apply their own laws when determining questions of enforcement and local law advice will be required. This risk is only of concern for contracts where cross-border enforcement might be needed. Choosing arbitration, rather than court proceedings, may possibly negate this risk (though is not appropriate in every case).

Outsourcing arrangements: These rely heavily on the Transfer of Undertakings (Protection of Employment) Regulations 2006[2] (TUPE) which govern the transfer of employees on the same terms where a business activity transfers from one party to another. Previously, the UK tried to get more flexibility introduced to amend the TUPE laws but this was vetoed by the existing Court of Justice of the European Union case law. Brexit may allow UK judges to relax the instances in which TUPE applies. So in an outsourcing situation, it would be prudent to re- apportion costs and risk allocation accordingly – especially where large numbers of staff are transferred.

Agents: The 1993 Regulations provide protections to commercial agents across the EU and regulates aspects of the legal relationship between a commercial agent and the person appointing it. This law might be abolished after Brexit which is good news for principals who will save money, such termination costs of which are mandatory to be paid out to agents even if an agent voluntarily

1   SI 1993/3053.
2   SI 2016/246.

retires. However, if you are an agent, your position may not be as secure post Brexit so you may want to re-visit your contracts in this regards and include contractual protections especially surrounding termination.

Electronic signatures: The E-Identification and Trust Services Regulations[1] currently in force allows businesses across Europe to use e-signature certification schemes and trust services (certification, timestamps and the like). The regulation provides for evidential weight to be given to electronic signatures. After Brexit, this should remain and the UK Government would merely adopt these regulations into UK law. However, whether an e-signature remains effective for trust services is uncertain.

The EU had a plan to create a Digital Single Market harmonising platforms, geo-blocking and e-commerce but this law has not yet been implemented and may well not occur.

The Audio Visual Media Services Regulations[2] regulate on-demand programmes and rules on television advertising and product placement.

Data: Transferring personal data is key to commercial relationships and within company groups and this is considered in further detail in the Chapter regarding IP and Data.

Late payments legislation[3] provides an implied term giving at least 8% a year interest on the price of goods or services, plus a fixed sum and reasonable costs of recovering the debt in business-to-business contracts.

The Misleading and Comparative Advertising Directive[4] governs business-to-business advertising and comparative advertising.

Consumer Protection Law:[5] protects consumers in relation to the sale of goods, services and digital content.

---

1   The Electronic Identification Regulation, which has direct applicability from 1 July 2016. The regulation repealed the E-Signature Directive. The Electronic Identification and Trust Services for Electronic Transactions Regulations 2016, SI 2016/696 came into force on 22 July 2016 and repeal the laws that implemented the E-Signature Directive, namely, the Electronic Signatures Regulations 2002, SI 2002/318 and the relevant sections of the Electronic Communications Act 2000.

2   Audio Visual Media Services EU Law was introduced into English law by the Audiovisual Media Services Regulations 2009, SI 2009/2979, the Audiovisual Media Services Regulations 2010, SI 2010/419 and the Audiovisual Media Services (Product Placement) Regulations 2010, SI 2010/831.

3   The Late Payments Directive, implemented into English law by various legislation, including the Late Payment of Commercial Debts Regulations 2013, SI 2013/395 (which introduced new provisions in sections 4 and 5A of the Late Payment of Commercial Debts (Interest) Act 1998), the Late Payment of Commercial Debts (No 2) Regulations 2013, SI 2013/908, and the Late Payment of Commercial Debts (Amendment) Regulations 2015, SI 2015/1336.

4   The Misleading and Comparative Advertising Directive, implemented into English law by the Business Protection from Misleading Marketing Regulations 2008, SI 2008/1276.

5   The Unfair Contract Terms Directive, the Consumer Rights Directive (CRD) and the Sales and Guarantees Directive, implemented into English law (in part) by the Consumer Rights Act 2015.

Distance Selling and Doorstep Selling legislation[1] requires consumer contracts to include information and the rules on delivery of goods. Businesses also need to obtain consumers' consent for additional charges and bans charging consumers excessive fees for the use of payment methods.

The Unfair Commercial Practices Directive[2] makes a trader criminally liable for misleading or aggressive sales practices and lists out unfair commercial practices.

The Services Directive[3] applies to the majority of private sector businesses providing services to consumers. A trader must provide consumers with certain information about itself, deal with customer complaints promptly and not discriminate against consumers in the provision of services on the basis of place of residence.

The Equal Treatment Directive[4] prohibits indirect and direct discrimination, harassment and victimisation in the workplace and in the provision of goods, services and facilities.

The Directive on Alternative Dispute Resolution for Consumer Disputes[5] requires traders to provide alternative dispute resolution entities information and the online dispute resolution platform.

The E-Commerce Directive[6] requires traders to provide certain information about their business and determines how contracts are concluded through electronic means.

6.6   WHEN SHOULD YOU REVIEW EXISTING CONTRACTS?

Contracts will not change just because Brexit has come into force. They will still remain legally binding between the parties. Business constantly evolves and therefore contracts should be reviewed on a regular basis especially in times of uncertainty, eg Brexit, or if the economy is in a poor condition. Businesses shouldn't be at the whim of financial hardship and should review contracts to see how to either exit the unfavourable contract or renegotiate the terms or the price.

---

1   The CRD, implemented into English law (in part) by the Consumer Contracts (Information, Cancellation and Additional Charges) Regulations 2013, SI 2013/3134.

2   The Unfair Commercial Practices Directive, implemented into English law by the Consumer Protection from Unfair Trading Regulations 2008, SI 2008/1277.

3   The Services Directive, implemented into English law by the Provision of Services Regulations 2009, SI 2009/2999.

4   The Equal Treatment Directive, implemented into English law by the Equality Act 2010.

5   The Directive on Alternative Dispute Resolution for Consumer Disputes, implemented into English law by the Alternative Dispute Resolution for Consumer Disputes (Competent Authorities and Information) Regulations 2015, SI 2015/542.

6   The E-Commerce Directive, implemented into English law by the Electronic Commerce (EC Directive) Regulations 2002, SI 2002/2013.

With Brexit commercial transactions could be affected in various ways:

- the exchange rate could fluctuate;
- tariffs and customs duties on goods and services provided to and from the EU could vary; and
- relocating a business outside of the UK would mean a contract governed by UK law is no longer needed.

6.7 WHICH CONTRACTS SHOULD BE REVIEWED?

In short, all contracts should be reviewed regularly, especially those which are key contracts and/or may no longer be commercially viable, ie do not make any money or are losing you money. Contracts include supply agreements, purchase agreements, distribution agreements, business contracts, outsourcing agreements, IT agreements, service agreements, maintenance agreements, terms and conditions. If any contracts are up for renewal, this is a perfect time for them to be reviewed.

6.8 WHAT ISSUES SHOULD I BE LOOKING OUT FOR IN A CONTRACT?

The aim is to ensure the contract is still commercially viable and whether any cost savings can be made without needing to resort to litigation.

- Are there any clauses in the contract which look at minimum purchase levels or minimum pricing? Do those minimums still work for your business? If there are no minimums consider buying from another supplier to mitigate any price increases.
- Are there any clauses in the contract which deal with exclusivity? Does that make your contract less commercial in light of Brexit? If there are no exclusivity clauses, consider other sources.
- Could the price be renegotiated? Agreements to agree pricing are just that: if the parties fail to agree then no new price should apply.
- Do rebates or discounts depend on a particular volume of purchases, and if so, have these been met?
- Do you have a clause for anticipating price increases? Does such a clause stipulate a maximum price increase and is this applied correctly and consistently? Failing to comply with such a provision may constitute a waiver if, for example, you allow the supplier to increase the price by a greater amount than the contract allows.
- Is the price linked to the Retail Prices Index? If so, be aware that such prices can fluctuate based on the industry indices. If it is favourable to you, draft the clause in such a way that it can be used to reduce the price.
- Could the products or services being sold or bought be re-negotiated?
- Could the business relationship be terminated?
- How can you exit the contract?
- Can you review credit limits and ensure they are in line with the credit searches against the other party?
- Can you include a retention of title clause so that in the event that the other party goes insolvent, you are covered for the goods or services provided?

- Can a guarantee be given by a parent company or the directors in the event of insolvency?
- Do you specify the currency of the payment and application of exchange rates to avoid huge fluctuations which may be against you?
- Have incoterms been used? If so, these should be reviewed in light of any changes in tariffs and changes to the incoterms.
- Can you request pro-forma invoices, ie payment upfront before delivering goods and/or services? This will help with cash flow.
- Do you have rights for you or your accounting team to access the financial accounts to check royalties, expenses, overheads?
- Can you impose a charge for using credit cards? Most companies are charged say 2% by the credit card company to accept payment by credit card. This cost arguably shouldn't be absorbed and should be passed on to the end customer (if at all possible) and this could fund any loss of funds due to currency exchange or increases in raw material costs.
- Public sector organisations use a best value clause so that they meet best value criteria. Can you use this in your favour?
- Is there a benchmarking clause? If so, check who has to pay to conduct this. Also check whether the supplier has to match a certain quality, price or service.
- Is there a most favoured nations clause which allows a party to benefit from the best terms and conditions from the other party? Ensure this clause complies with competition law.
- Is there a continuous improvement clause where the supplier has to guarantee to their client (ie you) that they will continuously improve the services offered or terms provided? If so, check whether improvements can be requested without additional cost.
- Do you have a change of law clause? Can the risk be born by one party or shared by the parties? See the suggested Brexit clause for drafting notes.
- If Brexit causes a contract to be economically unviable for one party have you got a clause which sets out what happens next eg termination or revision in prices?
- Is the contract assignable in the event that another member of the corporate group should be party to it?
- Have you reviewed where your customers are located geographically? If your customer base is only located in one EU member state, consider whether you should be attracting a wider range of customers from different geographical locations to avoid a risk of say a huge tariff being imposed in that one EU member state making it uncommercial to continue to trade with such customer?
- Data is key. The new General Data Protection Regulation (GDPR) will probably remain and be adopted by UK law post-Brexit. This law requires you to provide the legal 'adequacy' to support the transfer of data to the UK from the EU. Email lists, or any data about customers, clients or contacts needs to comply with the GDPR pre-Brexit as well as post-Brexit.
- Do you outsource staff? TUPE will apply to transferred staff in the event of a business change and post-Brexit the UK is unlikely to revoke TUPE. Nonetheless, consider whether clauses should be included to effect staff transfer and apportion redundancy costs in this eventuality.

- Does Brexit cause force majeure and/or frustration? 'Force majeure' (contract relief and/or termination because of unforeseen events) or 'frustration' (termination because of impossibility of performance) needs to be considered. It would be useful for parties to carve out any Brexit related circumstances from these provisions.
- Cross border enforcement of judgments – will they be recognised after Brexit? To avoid uncertainly, also include an arbitration clause in contracts as this does not rely on court proceedings.
- Have you defined 'European Union' or 'EU'?
- Are there references to EU legislation? If so, is change needed?
- Does your usual events of termination clause need to be modified?
- Will English law be the best law so far as the interpretation of the contract is concerned?
- Is it best that the English courts will determine disputes?

6.9 WHAT CONSTITUTES THE AGREEMENT AND ITS TERMS?

Generally a contract is signed by all parties and this binds the relevant parties to the terms as set out in the contract. However, some agreements can be agreed orally. Alternatively, there are other methods where terms are incorporated, eg in emails and correspondence, implied terms (eg, even if there are no service level agreements or key performance indicators, the Supply of Goods and Services Act 1982 requires the service provider to use reasonable care and skill), schedules, side letters, and the parties' conduct (eg a party accepts payment 90 days instead of 60 days as agreed in the contract) if the parties have been dealing with each other in a certain way, this course of dealing could be tantamount to an agreement.[1]

6.10 HOW CAN I TERMINATE THE CONTRACT?

If you conclude that the contract is no longer favourable or commercial and it would be more prudent to terminate the contract, then look at the contract to see if this is viable without giving rise to any wrongful termination claims.

Termination clauses generally will state when termination can take place, what notice period is required, whether the notice has to be written or oral and what situations trigger termination.

Situations that may trigger a termination clause include where one party breaches its terms of the contract eg doesn't pay on time, does not adhere to marketing or financial levels, where there is a change of control eg a refinancing, where

---

1   *Baird Textile Holdings Ltd v Marks & Spencer plc* [2001] EWCA Civ 274 Any course of dealing between businesses over a period of time. In particular, consider the case of, in which the court held that there were no grounds for implying a contract even though the parties had been in a trading relationship for 30 years, because they had deliberately not entered into an express contract to preserve maximum flexibility in their trading arrangements.

the supplier or purchaser is at risk of becoming insolvent or actually becomes insolvent.

If you have an agency agreement, commercial agents have to receive minimum notice periods and be paid exit payments pursuant to the 1993 Regulations.[1]

6.11 TARIFFS AND TRADE BARRIERS

If the UK failed to agree a free trade deal, the UK would trade with the EU on World Trade Organisation rules, so that tariff-free trade in goods with the EU stops. The UK government would gain greater control over regulatory policy but again there would be regulatory divergence between the UK and the EU over time. This scenario also means that current free trade agreements between the EU and third party countries will no longer apply to the UK so that tariffs and other barriers should be assumed across the board.

6.12 HIGH RISK CONTRACTS

Where there is dependence on EU funding or grants then start to look for other methods of funding.

Where the contract has been awarded under the EU public procurement rules, there is a high chance this will end – so do you have other lines of work?

Where you are trading with the EU ensure your pricing mechanisms reflect tariffs, quotas or other barriers (eg added regulation to trade with EU or compliance with different regulatory standards between the UK and EU, legal costs, transaction costs or currency fluctuations).

Also check whether any clauses could be triggered either against you or in your favour because of Brexit, eg market disruption, illegality or material adverse change.

If the free movement of people is limited after Brexit, long-term contracts will no longer work and employees do not automatically transfer under TUPE. Labour cost increases need to be considered and factored in.

6.13 WOULD BREXIT TRIGGER A FORCE MAJEURE CLAUSE?

A 'force majeure' clause allows the parties of the contract to be free from the liability or obligations of that contact when an extraordinary event or circumstance beyond the control of the parties such as a war, strike, riot or Act of God, eg hurricane, earthquake, flood or volcanic eruption, occurs. However,

---

1   SI 1993/3053.

Brexit would not trigger a force majeure even though Brexit and the run up to Brexit could adversely affect contracts.

Brexit has caused much uncertainly around the markets and impacted the value of sterling against other currencies. For some contracts, this fluctuation in the exchange rate will make contracts uncommercial and unprofitable and ultimately reduce the value of the contract. In this instance, the parties cannot rely on the 'force majeure' clause to exit the contract and this could be potentially detrimental to businesses.

If Brexit resulted in, say, a financial institution being unable to provide financial services either to or from the UK, this could arguably be a force majeure event as these circumstances are beyond the control of the parties. However, it could be argued on the other hand that this is not a force majeure as Brexit was a foreseen event and parties had sufficient time to prepare for it. Therefore the effective date of the contract and the date Brexit is triggered is important when analysing whether a force majeure clause is effective.

It is therefore worth revisiting all contracts and expressly addressing any potential financial hardship implications with an express clause which will, if the situations arise, cover that eventuality and protect the parties.

6.14 WOULD BREXIT TRIGGER A MATERIAL ADVERSE CHANGE?

A material adverse change clause is a legal provision found in merger and acquisition contracts and venture financing agreements that enables the acquirer (or funder) to refuse to complete the acquisition or merger or financing with the party being acquired if the target suffers such a change. This clause protects the acquirer from major changes that make the target less attractive as a purchase. Every definition of material adverse change is different. This clause – if the material adverse change occurs – can allow the acquiring party to refuse to complete a merger or acquisition. Note it is for the acquiring party to prove the material adverse change has occurred.

Whether Brexit can be deemed a material adverse change will very much depend on the definition of the material adverse change clause. Normally economic hardship is not sufficient to claim relief but if drafted widely, Brexit's impact on the financial implications outlined above could trigger this type of clause.

It is worth looking carefully at this clause and ensuring it takes into account the potential impact of Brexit.

6.15 POST-TERMINATION

If the strategy involves terminating an arrangement, then consider the impact on the client's business and the relationship.

- Is an exit plan required? If so, must this be negotiated?
- Who bears the costs of the exit?
- Scrutinise indemnities and cost-underwriting clauses to analyse the impact on termination.
- Consider the impact of employment issues.
- Consider if any intellectual property rights need to be asserted.
- Check any hand-over clauses, for example, for documents or for business processes.
- Consider which clauses survive termination and the impact of these.

6.16 MOBILE PHONE ROAMING CHARGES

EU law will remain in force until repealed or amended. Currently, UK mobile holders benefit from low roaming rates in Europe because there is EU law in place which protects against high costs of roaming. After Brexit, the UK mobile companies will have to negotiate with their EU counterparts. If that proves unproductive, then roaming charges could be increased significantly, although Vittorio Colao, the chief executive of Vodafone has stated as of 1 March 2017 that the roaming charges will not increase. This is once again an area to review on an on-going basis.

6.17 BREXIT CLAUSES

6.17.1 What is a Brexit clause?

A 'Brexit clause' is a clause in the contract which sets out a change in rights or obligations of the parties post Brexit or a Brexit event. It outlines: (a) the definition of Brexit or the Brexit event; and (b) the contractual consequences if Brexit or the Brexit event happens.

6.17.2 Are Brexit clauses fundamentally different from other 'change' clauses (including material adverse change clauses)?

Not really. A Brexit Clause just spells out another material adverse change situation given the topical nature of Brexit. However, some changes are expressly because of Brexit and therefore may indeed widen the definition of a material adverse change clause hence the preference to have a separate Brexit clause.

6.18 WHAT IS 'BREXIT'?

It is unclear at the time of writing – 'Brexit means Brexit'. However, Theresa May has stated that the UK is to leave the EU. It remains to be seen whether all UK laws which have derived from the EU will be repealed and trade between the UK and EU be subject to tariffs and barriers. Note that the UK may well keep many of the laws currently derived from the EU so it is going to be difficult for parties to a contract to agree an effective clause which triggers change just by using the simple phrase 'if Brexit occurs' as 'Brexit' may, in practice, mean different things. It is more likely to be appropriate, and more likely to create an effective clause, to define a specific trigger(s) which is relevant to the contract. For example, if you want the right to terminate if a specific EU law is material to the contract or deal – then expressly include this in the Brexit clause.

6.19 SCHEDULE OF SUGGESTED TEMPLATES

6.19.1 Suggested Brexit clause

(Note this is merely suggestive and should be amended to suit the particular contract.)

1. '**Brexit**': the devolution of the United Kingdom from the European Union;
2. '**Brexit Date**': the date which Brexit occurs;
3. '**Consideration**': the price paid by Party A to Party B;
4. '**Contract**': this contract entered into between Party A and Party B;
5. '**Costs**': the costs that the Parties have undertaken to effect the Contract (excluding each party's legal fees, accountancy fees and other adviser fees);
6. '**Parties**': the parties to the Contract
7. If Brexit results in or is reasonably expected to result in a [X%][X%-Y%] [£x] [£x-£y] [increase/decrease] in costs ('**Adjusted Costs**') to perform the Contract by Party A/B, the Parties will agree on Brexit Date or another date agreed between the parties to [adjust the Consideration as per an agreed formula at Schedule 1] or [bear the Adjusted Costs equally between the Parties] or [Party A/B shall bear the Adjusted Costs solely];
8. If Brexit results in a new or amended permit, licence, consent, approval or similar to be required for the Contract to continue to take effect, the parties/Party A/ Party B will apply for the necessary permit, licence, consent, approval or similar in a timely manner / within [14 days] and bear [their own] [Party A][Party B] costs. [Or this is part of the Adjusted Costs clause above];
9. If Brexit results in any clause of the Contract being invalid, irrelevant or impossible (rather than just difficult to perform), this clause will be amended / deleted.
10. If Brexit results in x, then this Contract will be terminated by giving 30 days' written notice to the other party ('**Brexit Termination**'). Each party will bear its own costs and losses arising from a Brexit Termination, and no party will be liable to any others for any costs, claims, losses or demands of any nature suffered under the Contract due to Brexit. This clause takes precedence over any contrary or conflicting provision elsewhere in this contract.

6.19.2 Letter to vary a contract

1. Pursuant to the agreement dated × between the parties (the '**Agreement**', a copy of which is appended at Schedule 1), the Agreement is varied because of Brexit on the date of this letter (the '**Variation Date**') for consideration [   ] and as a result we will amend the Agreement as follows:

(a)	Clause [x] deleted:	Clause [x] is deleted in its entirety. It will be replaced by 'Not used'.
(b)	Clause [y] added:	Clause [y] is inserted into the Agreement.
(c)	Clause [z] amended:	Clause [z] is amended to read: [Set out the amended clause in its entirety].

2. Except as set out in Paragraph 1, the Agreement shall continue in full force and effect.
3. This letter agreement and any dispute or claim (including non-contractual disputes or claims) arising out of or in connection with it or its subject matter or formation shall be governed by and interpreted in accordance with the law of England and Wales.
4. The parties irrevocably agree that the courts of England and Wales have exclusive jurisdiction to settle any dispute or claim (including non-contractual disputes or claims) that arises out of, or in connection with, this letter agreement or its subject matter or formation.
5. Please sign and return the enclosed copy of this Letter to acknowledge your agreement to the variation of the Agreement.

CHAPTER 7

CONSTRUCTION

John Denis-Smith, 39 Essex Chambers

INTRODUCTION

Any key decision maker in a construction company will face perennial questions. What are the rules covering my market abroad? What are the rules covering my market at home? How do I source my product? On present indications, these three questions are likely to become more intensely pressing as Britain leaves the EU.

The starting point is that construction is seen as a major part of the UK economy. The Office of National Statistics ('ONS') calculates that the construction sector contributed £92.1 billion, 7.9% of the estimated gross value added at basic prices ('aGVA') total of for the UK non-financial business economy in 2015; the House of Commons library stated that, in 2014, the construction industry in the UK contributed £103 billion in economic output, 6.5% of the total.[1] Whatever the overall contours of the UK's disengagement from the EU, those figures are enough to emphasise that construction plays too large a role in the UK economy for it to be overlooked during the negotiations the UK will have with the EU. The good news for the construction sector therefore is that the government will be aware that its needs exist. Against, that background, the three questions above are considered in turn below.

7.1 THE MARKET ABROAD

First, one must consider the EU market. Currently, three public procurement directives set out the EU legal system governing procurement by public authorities and utilities: the Public Contacts Directive 2014; The Concessions Contracts Directive 2014; and the Utilities Directive 2014, brought into the law of England and Wales via the Public Contracts Regulations 2015,[2] the Concession Contracts Regulations 2016[3] and the Utilities Contract Regulations 2016.[4] Space does not allow for detailed consideration here of the rules under those directives: suffice it to say that they are detailed. The first issue for companies hoping to

---

1   See ONS, Annual Business Survey, UK non-financial business economy: 2015 provisional results; House of Commons Library: Research Briefing Number 01432, 6 October 2015: Construction industry: statistics and policy. As a measure, aGVA is equal to GDP at market prices minus taxes plus subsidies on products.
2   SI 2015/102.
3   SI 2016/273.
4   SI 2016/274.

carry out such work in the EU post Brexit is whether those rules will apply and, if not, what the differences might be.

There are various options, simply looking at the relationship with the EU itself.

The 'no change' option would see the UK maintaining the same EU public procurement regime, perhaps by way of the currently envisaged 'Great Repeal' Act, which confirms withdrawal from membership of the EU itself, but not from the various statutes or regulations which EU law has introduced into the UK. This would, in effect, also be achieved were the UK to be a member of the European Economic Area ('EEA'). However, membership of the EEA means acceptance of the EU 'single market' and the single market means acceptance of the rules of free movement which, according to what appears to have become the received wisdom, is a key issue upon which the 'Leave' vote won the Referendum. Much can change between 2017 and 2019 but, unless the 'free movement' issue fades, EEA membership appears relatively unlikely.

There is then the possibility of a bespoke UK-EU trade agreement. Would this cover public procurement at all? The answer is probably yes. EU trade agreements normally cover public procurement. CETA, the Canadian-EU trade agreement provides for Canadian companies to have equal access to EU procurement for processes above the threshold values.[1] The European Neighbourhood and Partnership Instrument is a framework which applies to relations between the EU and countries of the Mediterranean and former Soviet Union. Association Agreements between those countries and the EU typically contain provisions covering mutual access to procurement markets. However, there are various options for whether they do so by repeating and applying to a non-member state the rules applicable to EU member states. These variations can apply in different fields: first, the extent of coverage of the new rules may be different from those under the EU-wide system; and, second, the rules for any procurement within the area covered may be different too. For example, the bilateral agreement between Switzerland and the EU on public procurement which has been in force since 1 June 2002 covers public and private companies in the rail transport, gas and heating supply sectors, as well as procurement by private companies based on special and exclusive rights transferred by a public authority in the sectors of drinking water, electricity and urban transport, airports as well as river and sea transport. This coverage extends beyond the fields covered by what is known as the Government Procurement Agreement ('GPA', discussed further below), but the rules applicable to those sectors are less detailed than EU law would require.

What if the UK chooses not to enter into any specific agreement with the EU at all? At present, the UK is a member of the World Trade Organisation ('WTO'). The GPA is an agreement under the WTO which covers public procurement and sets minimum standards for transparency in award procedures. The EU is

---

1   The rules and thresholds are found in Article 19 and Annex 19 to CETA. As the thresholds are expressed in 'Special Drawing Rights', their precise value in national currencies may fluctuate somewhat but are around 3 million Canadian dollars for services and 7.8 million Canadian dollars for construction projects.

a party to the GPA but the UK is not.[1] It would probably need first to apply to become a member and, then, ensure it has public procurement rules to cover the areas covered by the GPA. Where the rules apply to a sector, the UK would have to apply the same rules there as it applies nationally, if the national award procedures go into more detail. However, there is some flexibility provided by the fact that which areas are covered depends on the party itself and different coverage can be applied by a party to different trading partners. In other words, the procurement regime applied could differ depending on the agreements reached with specific other parties.

It is easy to imagine that, if the UK becomes a party to the GPA, there may be a default trend towards maintaining the same rules in a treaty with the EU as apply at present. Moreover, if the UK wishes to be seen to be 'open for business', there is a case for setting the same regime for all agreements with other parties to the GPA. However, it is very possible that a more complicated agreement may be reached and that different regimes may apply in respect of different countries, at least in terms of coverage (including, possibly, the financial thresholds which determine whether a particular tender process comes within the rules).

Whatever the pressures within the UK, account will have to be taken of the concern within the EU itself that, in the field of public procurement, it is not obtaining a fair balance with non-EU states. In 2012, the European Commission proposed a new Regulation which would meet the concern that third countries were not themselves opening up their markets, by enabling contracting authorities/entities to exclude tenders from tendering procedures where the value of goods and services from such countries exceeds 50% of the total value of goods or services included in the tender for contracts and would have enabled the Commission itself to impose 'restrictive measures' such as a 'mandatory price penalty' on such goods or services.[2] The proposal excited opposition, not least from the UK government. An amended proposal was published in 2016, with the power of the contracting authorities removed and the 'mandatory price penalty' revised in the form of 'price adjustment measures'.[3] Nonetheless, even if the Commission does not seek to revisit the earlier proposals post-Brexit, it is clear that the EU will want to ensure that any agreement with the UK is seen as offering equal access to all parties.

What of the non-EU market outside of the GPA? The questions here are, if anything, less easy to answer than in relation to the EU. If the UK's plan is to engage in bilateral agreements, there could be any number of different

---

1   The Agreement has currently the following Parties: Armenia, Canada, the European Union, Hong Kong, Iceland, Israel, Japan, Korea, Liechtenstein, Moldova, Montenegro, New Zealand, the Netherlands with respect to Aruba, Norway, Singapore, Switzerland, Chinese Taipei, Ukraine and the United States. However, other countries, including China, are in negotiations to become Parties too.

2   See the EU Commission's Proposal for a Regulation 'on the access of third-country goods and services to the Union's internal market in public procurement and procedures supporting negotiations on access of Union goods and services to the public procurement markets of third countries' COM(2012) 124 final, in particular Articles 6 and 9.

3   The Amended proposal is contained in EU Commission document COM(2016) 34 final.

permutations. Perhaps the best way of approaching the question is to imagine the default option. With the EU, currently, there is full integration in policy between the UK and other EU member states, with the ECJ having jurisdiction to give binding decisions on the interpretation of the rules. With other states, the default position is whatever the given country's current arrangements are with the EU itself. The starting point may therefore be different and, if speed of agreement is a key consideration, one could imagine that the resulting treaties with other states may look closer to those other states' agreements with the EU.

7.2   THE RULES GOVERNING THE UK CONSTRUCTION MARKET

Imagine that you do not carry out construction work outside the UK. What is the impact of Brexit on you?

There is much that leaving the EU will not change. Much of construction law rests on the common law principles which cover contract and duties outside contract. Those principles have remained in effect during the UK's membership of the EU and will remain in effect afterwards. Construction law is not an area where the courts are commonly required to pay considerable regard to the effect of EU law – except for two exceptions considered in the following section – and, generally, one cannot identify major decisions which turned on the decisive impact of decisions by the European Court of Justice. There are many standard form construction contracts in the UK market: the NEC and Joint Contracts Tribunal (JCT) forms of agreement among them. These rest on common law principles and we are unlikely to see a major transformation in them because of Brexit. There is also statute law passed by Parliament which affects the construction market. The Sale of Goods Act 1979 and Supply of Goods and Services Act 1982 impact on contracts for the sale of materials to a construction company and to the quality of work expected of that company. There are specific measures designed to meet the needs of the construction business in the Housing Grants, Construction and Regeneration Act 1996 (amended significantly from 2011 onwards), designed to ensure cash flow in the industry. Such legislation does not rest on EU legislation and shall be unaffected by Brexit.

However, it would be a mistake to assume that, if one only trades in the UK itself, the construction industry will be unaffected by Brexit or that, going forward, European Union law shall become irrelevant to one's day to day business. In three areas at least, EU law has been highly important: state aid; public procurement and jurisdiction of the Courts determining disputes.

State aid is one area in which companies in the UK construction sector may be affected by any agreement reached with the EU post Brexit. EU trade agreements with non-Member states also include rules prohibiting state aid. As this includes tax incentives, it will remain the case that agreements between the UK and others, including the EU, will impose some limits on the steps contracting authorities, or the tax authorities may take. Similar points apply because the UK is a member of the WTO and of the WTO Agreement on Countervailing Measures and Subsidies, which prohibits subsidies, defined as: (i) a financial contribution; (ii) by a government or any public body within the territory of a Member; and (iii) which confers a benefit.[1] Financial contributions covered include grants, loans, equity infusions, loan guarantees, fiscal incentives – including tax – the provision of goods or services and the purchase of goods. For this reason, care will need to be taken by the relevant authorities. In its Autumn Statement of November 2016, the government has announced an intention to invest considerable sums in infrastructure, including a new National Productivity Investment Fund to provide £23 billion of additional spending, including £1.1 billion to reduce congestion and upgrade local roads and public transport, £220 million to tackle road safety and congestion on Highways England roads and £27 million to develop an expressway connecting Oxford and Cambridge. The government also announced £2.3 billion for a new Housing Infrastructure Fund, to secure the construction of up to 100,000 new homes. If, following the June 2017 election the Government proceeds with such plans, this infrastructure investment however would need to be carried out in a way which is not treated as 'State aid'.

Public procurement law is another area in which individual construction companies will still be affected, even if they only take part in procurement exercises in the UK itself. Public procurement law is an area which, in the United Kingdom, had showed little development before the impact of EU law. The common law placed no requirement on a person putting work out to tender, including public authorities, to accept the lowest tender. Indeed there were few requirements of any kind. If the public authority published tender rules and a bid was made in good time and in the appropriate form, the authority was obliged by an implied contract to open and consider the tender.[2] If an authority has a shortlist of tenderers, it has to consider them honestly.[3] Where several tenderers have been invited to bid for a contract, there is an obligation to treat them fairly and equally.[4] These are, in substance, limited obligations to act in good faith and they do not import a full-scale obligation to carry out intensive reviews of tenderers. Beyond these common law rules, there are various Acts of Parliament which impose obligations on local authorities and other organisations providing public services. The requirement to have formal contracting procedures for the performance of works or the supply of goods or services was imposed by the Local Government Act 1972.[5] The requirement on local authorities to provide reasons for rejection or acceptance of a tender was imposed by the Local Government Act 1988, which also prohibits the award of contracts on non-commercial grounds.[6] This last change was the product of the politics of the time. Local authorities were seen by central government as making expressly political decisions (as opposed to decisions based on any personal, financial conflict of interest) in the award of contracts. More recently, it was felt that these

---

1   Article 1 of the Agreement on Subsidies and Countervailing Measures.
2   *Blackpool and Fylde Aero Club Ltd v Blackpool Borough Council* [1990] 3 All ER 25.
3   *Fairclough Building Ltd v Port Talbot Borough Council* [1992] 62 BLR 86.
4   *Central Tenders Board v White* [2015] UKPC 39; [2015] B.L.R. 727. Technically, this was a Privy Council decision, not binding within the UK itself but it relied upon English case law and was a Judgment of three members of the Supreme Court of the United Kingdom.
5   See section 135.
6   See sections 17 to 22: see also Schedule 2.

rules were not going far enough to achieve continuous efforts to improve the value obtained by authorities. The Local Government Act 1999 which, despite its title, also applies to other bodies,[1] requires such 'best value authorities' to make arrangements to bring out improvements in the way they carry out their functions generally, including in relation to procurement, to:

> 'make arrangements to secure continuous improvement in the way in which its functions are exercised, having regard to a combination of economy, efficiency and effectiveness.'[2]

These rules apply to all tenderers. They also apply equally to the tenderer from outside the UK, including tenderers from other EU member states. A contractor based in and only trading in the UK therefore is going to be trading against EU-based competitors.

All this suggests that the government will face a key decision. What public procurement rules does it want to have? Does it want to focus on 'best value' and how much detail will it impose on the authorities and the contractors who want to supply them? The coalition Government in power between 2010 and 2015 stated an intention 'to remove barriers to more open and efficient local public services by freeing local authorities from targets, prescription and duties' and revoked in its entirety the then current statutory guidance 'Creating Strong, Safe and Prosperous Communities', dating from 2008, which had included general Best Value guidance on commissioning. Paragraph 6.12 of that 2008 Guidance had stated that:

> 'Local authorities should represent the interests of citizens, service users, and their communities by ... ensuring that any procurement decision, including retaining services in-house, is undertaken and justified in an open and transparent way regardless of whether a full European Union (EU) Procurement exercise is involved.'

Now that such Guidance has been revoked, does the government wish to return to more detailed guidance or not?

How that question is to be answered has to be informed by three factors. First, commissioning bodies and tenderers need to understand the rules and be able to apply them. Second, there is a political issue at stake. Does the government focus on British work for British companies or adopt a 'free-trade' outlook? Third, if 'no agreement' is reached with the EU, what is the default position?

---

1   See section 1 of the Local Government Act 1999. The list is long: a local authority; a National Parks authority; the Broads Authority; police and fires authorities, the London Fire and Emergency Planning Authority; a Waste Disposal Authority, Joint Waste Authority, an Integrated Transport Authority; Transport for London; the London Development Agency. It also covers economic prosperity boards established under section 88 of that Act and combined authorities established under section 103 of the Local Democracy, Economic Development and Construction Act 2009. Section 1 was amended by the Local Government and Public Involvement Act 2007, Part 7.

2   See section 3(1).

If understanding the commissioning rules is the key standard, one might expect the government, in the immediate post Brexit period, to wish to continue the same rules as previously applied. EU procurement law would apply in the same way as it did before. Court decisions in respect of those rules may go no higher than the Supreme Court and may, unless agreement is reached with the EU, not be the subject of reference to the European Court of Justice – the 'ECJ' – for decision on issues where the law does not appear to be clear. However, the English courts would be likely still to take account of decisions of the ECJ in deciding how the rules work.

As to the future trend of procurement law in the UK, the outcome depends on the UK's internal politics. The pressure to focus on 'buying British' may become strong. Even at a time when there was a consensus between the major political parties in favour of free trade (and membership of the EU), that pressure existed. The procurement of the new Parliament building (now called 'Portcullis House') in the 1990s was marked by what the courts decided was a deliberate or reckless breach of EU procurement law and, consequently the tort of misfeasance in public office, when the lowest priced (compliant) tender by a French company was passed over in favour of another contractor with a stronger British presence. Evidence in the case suggested that what was referred to in terms as a 'Buy British' campaign had been underway.[1] For as long as the UK is a member of the EU, such a procurement policy would render the authority liable to a claim for damages. Post Brexit, there is a political question for the government whether to move in a more overtly 'Buy British' direction, assuming the country's obligations under treaty with the EU and other states permit.

Companies trading within the UK alone need to know what the rules of engagement with other states will be going forward. As discussed in the previous section, the extent to which the UK market will be open to the EU will depend on the terms of the new arrangements between the UK and the EU. Therefore, the extent to which a company which only builds in the UK is likely to face competition from companies from EU member states turns on the outcome of that process.

Finally, one must consider both jurisdiction, which concerns where disputes are to be decided and governing law, which concerns the law relating to parties' obligations in contract or other legal duties. For several decades, there has been an agreement in place between the UK and other EU member states (and some non-EU states too) concerning how to resolve the question of which court should be hearing disputes between parties based in different states. The agreement governing which court has jurisdiction was found in the 1968 Brussels convention and, from 2015, in an updated version embodied in an EU Regulation.[2] There are also related Conventions which apply to other non-EU states. Broadly, these

---

1   See *Harmon CFEM Façades (UK) Ltd v Corporate Officer of the House of Commons* (1999) 67 ConLR 1. References to 'Buy British' (or 'Buy British!') can be found at paragraphs [40], [45], [90] to [91].
2   Article 81 Regulation (EU) No. 1215/2012 ('the Regulation').

rules provide that parties to a dispute should be sued in their state of domicile and provide for the recognition of court judgments made in other countries.

Similarly, under the Rome Conventions, EU member states are party to agreement concerning how the court which has jurisdiction should determine which legal system applies to the dispute itself, a point relevant to construction disputes because such disputes may give rise both to issues concerning contractual obligations and to duties outside contract (in tort or restitution).[1]

If the UK leaves the EU without entering into the same commitments, the consequences may be significant. English 'conflict of law' rules about how to determine the governing law are complex. So may be the rules of the EU member states. Jurisdiction may be no less straightforward. How a Court, including the court here in the United Kingdom (England and Wales, Scotland and Northern Ireland form three separate jurisdictions) and the court in a given EU member state, decides who has jurisdiction will depend on the jurisdictional rules of the law where that court is to be found. At present, a German supplier who claims to be owed money by a construction company based in London must, under the EU wide regime, sue the company in England and Wales. Post-Brexit, the answer may change: if the German court considers the claim can be brought in Germany, the construction company may find itself being sued there. There is also the possibility of a serious conflict between courts of different states, each claiming that, under its law, it should be hearing the case. At the same time, the Judgment obtained from the court in one jurisdiction, say England and Wales, would not be automatically enforceable in the other EU states if the regime is no longer applicable.

One does not at present know what the new regime will be. There is however a way to mitigate the risk of being sued abroad. The current EU-wide regime provides that clauses which identify a particular place as having jurisdiction will be respected.[2] It may be, post-Brexit, that a similar approach will apply. At the very least, parties who hope to have their disputes resolved in England and Wales should ensure that their contracts contain a clause giving the courts in England and Wales exclusive jurisdiction to determine any dispute which may arise and providing that the law of England and Wales covers all aspects of their relationship. As for enforcement of court judgments, there may be a stronger case for a return to arbitration since most EU member states would continue to enforce arbitration awards, under what is known as the New York Convention.

7.3   SOURCING THE PRODUCT

Sourcing of materials is unlikely to be the major issue of contention or change post-Brexit. Labour is a different matter. Estimates differ as to how large the construction based workforce is: the ONS in its 2011 Annual Business Survey

---

1   See Regulation (EC) No. 593/2008 and Regulation (EC) No. 864/2007.
2   See Article 25 of the Regulation, although this does not necessarily apply to consumer contracts: see Article 19.

calculated that around 3 million jobs are based in construction,[1] 10% of total UK's employment; another estimate is that 2.1 million jobs or 6.2% of the UK total were in the construction industry in 2015.[2] On any view, the key issue is that it is very large, sufficiently so for government to have construction clearly in its sights as a key employment issue. Whatever the understanding (or misunderstandings) as to what the UK voted for in the EU Referendum, the result has been understood to be a clear indication that the country was voting against the free movement of labour into the UK. Moreover, indications from the government to date are that it reads the result in that way. This gives rise to the following questions: how open will the UK's borders be for the free flow of construction labour and how will that process be managed?

We are likely to hear much about work permits. However, there is much we do not know about the approach the UK government will take. Would there be caps and, if so, how would they be applied? What would the timetable be between an application for a permit and the time the permit would be issued? Would there be a burden of proof on the employer to show that it cannot source the workforce using UK labour? If so, how heavy would that burden be to shift? Security may also be an issue. It appears that Home Office officials are also working on the idea of an electronic visa-waiver scheme for EU citizens visiting Britain, similar to the US Electronic System for Travel Authorisation ('Esta'), to allow for pre-travel security screening. Presumably that regime would apply to workers too. Whether the new system will provide enough flexibility to allow companies to obtain the labour they need in a short timescale is going to be a serious question.

7.4 CONCLUSIONS

The legal framework affecting UK construction companies' access to other markets could be about to become very complicated. Whether it does so shall depend in large part on the political decisions of the UK government. Put another way, the construction industry has an important role to play in communicating its needs to decision-makers in government. Part of the rhetoric heard post Brexit is that of a desire for flexibility and a reduction in complex regimes which are seen to be a barrier to doing business. Where public procurement is concerned, however, some agreed rules do need to be in place. Moreover, there may need to be a sustained dialogue concerning how the construction workforce can be effectively sourced, if new burdens are to be managed successfully. In the meantime, those in the industry would do well to ensure their supply chains are robust and able to manage the imposition of new requirements or restrictions. Finally, if disputes do arise with suppliers or clients outside the UK itself, there is greater reason than ever for ensuring in advance that agreements are in place to explain where those disputes should be decided and under which system of law.

---

1   ONS Annual Business Survey 2011.
2   See House of Commons Library: Research Briefing Number 01432, 6 October 2015: Construction industry: statistics and policy.

CHAPTER 8

IMMIGRATION

Gary McIndoe, Shara Pledger and Alex Wright, Latitude Law

INTRODUCTION

Domestic laws have always been used to regulate entry and residence in the UK. Original powers under Royal Prerogative were later codified into Acts of Parliament, starting with the Aliens Act 1905. That Act was a reaction to perceived high levels of migration into the UK by eastern European Jews. Subsequent legislation enacted during the 20th Century had another target: migrants from Britain's former colonies and protectorates around the world. The one notable exception was the European Communities Act 1972; although not of course entirely about migration, this Act codified the UK's acceptance of a new, supra-national system for regulating entry and residence for citizens of the EC, and their families.

Numerous amendments to the European treaties have followed, all firmly predicated on the UK's acceptance of the principle of free movement of citizens of EU – later EEA – member states. Through these international agreements we have accessed tariff-free trade, and later the single European market. These trading advantages have served the country well over the years; non-EEA car manufacturers have for example chosen sites here for production of vehicles bound for the European market. With economic success, however, has come an inevitable rise in the numbers or EU workers seeking to relocate to the UK in search of job opportunities.

Migration into big cities has caused relatively little friction, beyond EU migrant communities which have grown in usually poorer suburbs. In market towns, however, the impact of such migration on schools, health services and even the ethnic balance of a community has led to widespread discontent with the European model for free movement. Immigration was reportedly a major – if not the most significant – factor in many people's decision to vote to leave the EU. The government has been very clear since the Referendum that it sees taking back control of our borders as the most important task at hand, to be implemented at the expense of the UK's access to the single European market for trade in goods and services.

In this chapter we outline how EU laws, and the UK's domestic transposition of those laws, have regulated entry and residence for EU citizens and their families since the UK acceded to the European Economic Community on 1 January 1973.

How immediate freedom of movement was first welcomed by employers and the public alike, as tens of thousands of British citizens took advantage of moving in the opposite direction, forging careers and lives across the continent.

How, beginning in the 1990s, the government's decision to give similar free rights to enter and work to nationals of the new Accession States of eastern Europe led to a backlash, presaging restrictions on rights to work for citizens of subsequent EU joiners such as Bulgaria, Romania and most recently Croatia.

We consider the rights of EU citizens already living and working here, and how these might be preserved in the future.

We then go on to consider how a new migration regime might look after the UK has left the European Union, postulating two scenarios: one reflective of a hard Brexit, where EU citizens are subject to the same rules on entry as every other foreign national, and a softer position, where EU citizens enjoy – perhaps for a limited or transitional period – a preferential migration regime into the UK.

We examine the particular issues facing citizens of the Republic of Ireland, and how the UK's new immigration regime might affect the concept of the Common Travel Area, an entity that has existed for much longer that the European Union.

And how, finally, might either approach affect the rights of British citizens to continue – or begin – new lives in an EU to which the UK no longer belongs.

8.1 THE PRINCIPLE OF FREEDOM OF MOVEMENT

Every EU citizen has a right to enter another member state, without restriction, subject to being able to prove their identity and nationality. This right last for an initial three month period. The right to enter also extends to non-EU family members, who in practical terms are best advised to obtain a visa (more accurately a Family Permit) before travel, to avoid problems at border immigration control.

The right to live, or reside, in another member state is understandably subject to more regulation. It is important to note at the outset that – contrary to some politicians' beliefs – the EU treaties enshrine the notion of free movement of individuals – not of workers, nor of labour – within Europe's borders. For this reason, European free movement law in its most recent incarnation – Council Directive 2004/38/EC – sets out various categories of individual who are entitled to reside in another EEA Member State by virtue of being a 'qualified person', falling into one of the following categories:

(a) Worker
(b) Self-employed person
(c) Self-sufficient person
(d) Student
(e) Job seeker

8.2 EU NATIONALS ALREADY LIVING AND WORKING IN THE UK

It is not only necessary to consider the position of those who wish to come to the UK post-Brexit, but also of those EU nationals who are currently present, their family members (whether EU or non-EU nationals) and what likelihood they have of being able to secure further residence in the UK. As there are an estimated 2.9 million EU nationals living in the UK, their rights will form a significant part of the upcoming negotiation. The Prime Minister has indicated that they can expect a fair deal, should the same be offered to the 900,000 British nationals living elsewhere in the EU.

As detailed above, the current form of EU nationals' right to reside in the UK is governed by the Free Movement Directive (Directive 2004/38/EC) which were first transposed into domestic legislation by the Immigration (European Economic Area) Regulations 2006[1] and, in force from 1 February 2017, the Immigration (European Economic Area) Regulations 2016.[2]

At present, any EU national has the right to enter the UK for a period of three months and the only requirement for this is that they hold a valid, government-issued form of ID. Most commonly EU nationals use this right for the purposes of visits and holidays to other EU member states but, for those who wish to relocate, this initial period allows them an opportunity to experience living in the UK, seek employment and locate accommodation without the pressure of having to commence other activity to support their continued residence. Their immediate family members, which for EU law purposes includes spouses (but not necessarily unmarried partners) and children up to the age of 21, regardless of nationality, are also able to join them.

Continued residence after this period has been reliant on the EU national undertaking one of the above qualifying activities. As long as such an activity is being undertaken, the EU national and their immediate family can remain in the UK indefinitely. After five years of continuous activity, their right to reside becomes permanent and they no longer need to work, study etc in order to continue their lives here. Whilst documents can be applied for to confirm these rights, they are not compulsory. This documentation may be summarised as follows:

1. Registration Certificate – A five-year document issued to an EU national upon evidence being provided to the Home Office that they are: (a) an EU national; and (b) undertaking a qualifying activity.
2. Residence Card – A five-year document issued to non-EU family members of an EU national upon evidence that they are: (a) the immediate family member of an EU national; and (b) the relevant EU national is undertaking a qualifying activity. This document is sufficient evidence of a right to work in the UK.
3. Document Certifying Permanent Residence – A one-off document issued to an EU national upon evidence of a five-year, continuous period of qualifying activity. That individual can be said to be 'settled' in the UK.
4. Permanent Residence Card – A one-off document issued to an EU family member upon evidence that their relevant EU sponsor has undertaken

---

1   SI 2006/1003.
2   SI 2016/1052.

a five-year, continuous period of qualifying activity. Also results in the individual being considered 'settled' in the UK for immigration purposes, which is a necessary first step for that person should they later choose to naturalise as a British citizen.

For British companies this system has been broadly beneficial and opened a wider skills market, allowing EU nationals to accept offers of employment in a straightforward manner. Until now, offering EU nationals employment has been simple, and proof of nationality has been sufficient evidence of a right to work alone. An EU national's family members also have the right to work by dint of their relationship to a qualified person but, unlike their 'sponsor', must be able to provide additional evidence of their right to work. This must be in the form of a Residence or Permanent Residence card or, in some cases, a letter from the Home Office confirming such a document has been applied for called a 'Certificate of Application' which will explicitly state whether that person can work whilst they await a decision.

8.2.1   Protecting your business

In order to employ an EU national, according to Home Office guidance, an employer must have had sight of one of the following:

1. A passport issued to a national of an EU or EEA member state, or Switzerland.
2. A Registration Certificate or Document Certifying Permanent Residence issued by the Home Office to a national of an EU or EEA member state, or Switzerland.
3. A Permanent Residence Card issued by the Home Office to the family member of a national of an EU or EEA member state, or Switzerland.
4. A five-year Residence Card issued by the Home Office to the family member of a national of an EU or EEA member state or Switzerland.
5. A Certificate of Application issued by the Home Office to a family member of a national of an EU or EEA member state, or Switzerland, stating that the holder is permitted to take employment which is less than six months old together with a Positive Verification Notice from the Home Office Employer Checking Service. Please note that a Certificate of Application takes the form of a letter from the Home Office whilst a Verification Notice is an email.

Sight of, and a copy taken of, the first three documents will permanently protect an employer against any allegation of employing someone illegally. Whilst Registration Certificates and Documents Certifying Permanent Residence tend to be either endorsements in passports or on blue cardboard documents, the Home Office have recently been issuing documents for EU family members (Residence and Permanent Residence Cards) on credit-card style Biometric Residence Permits. These are also acceptable documents.

A Certificate of Application also protects an employer against liability but only for a maximum of six months. This should also be coupled with an online check with the Home Office at https://www.gov.uk/employee-immigration-employment-status. These checks can take up to five days for results to be produced and are emailed to the employer. Employers will need assistance from their employees to help complete these checks and should ask for date/method of postage, as well as any Home Office reference or case ID numbers. This should speed up the checking process.

It is important to stress the value that such document checks have for a company. Having had sight of such documents protects against significant potential fines for employing workers illegally, or of failing to keep adequate HR records. For those who also hold sponsor licences for non-EU migrants under the Points Based System, compliance with illegal worker rules is all the more important, as the loss of your licence can follow if you fail to maintain adequate records of all your employees.

8.2.2   Protecting your employees

Whilst the future status of EU nationals in the UK remains uncertain (although transitional provisions of some kind to move people over from free movement to the British immigration rules seem likely), it would be wise for employers to discuss how they best support EU national employees or third-country nationals holding Residence Cards as Britain negotiates its exit from the Union. Regardless of what occurs during Article 50 negotiations, it would seem prudent that those who can demonstrate their lawful residence in the UK will be better prepared to handle future developments.

It is certainly not expected that those who hold Permanent Residence would be asked to depart the UK. The situation is more fluid for those who are lawfully in the UK but have yet to reach the five-year milestone. Employers have a role to play in all applications for Registration Certificates and Residence Cards where employment is relied upon as a qualified activity. They are obliged to either complete a section of the employee's application form or, in the alternative, provide a letter confirming the terms of employment. Employers could consider publicising their willingness to assist with such applications to their workforce to encourage them to apply for documents. You may be in a position to assist employees with key supporting documents such as P60s, wage slips and contracts.

Once permanent residence is obtained, an EU national may go on to consider naturalising as a British citizen. This may be seen as the ultimate act of integration into British life, and many EU citizens are already eligible to apply, subject to obtaining confirmation of their permanent residence. An applicant must demonstrate the following:

- five years' continuous lawful residence in the UK, the last 12 months of which must have been as a 'settled' or permanently resident person; unless married to a British citizen, in which case the five years reduces to three, and there is no requirement to complete 12 months as a settled person.
- Good character.
- Ability in the English language and knowledge of life in the UK.

The application fee is significant compared to the low fees applicable to EU residence applications, so individuals are best advised to check their eligibility carefully before applying. Since 2015 the Home Office has instigated checks into the lawfulness of an individual's residence going back beyond the usual three or five-year qualifying period, to a point ten years prior to date of application if the individual has been in the UK so long. If there was, before that time, any unlawful residence, or failure to comply with immigration laws, then expect your application to be refused.

Naturalisation as a British citizen means freedom from UK immigration control. It guarantees future residence, and can only be lost if an individual commits a serious criminal offence, or is found to have obtained citizenship by deception or fraud. All EU countries – like the UK – are happy for their citizens to hold more than one nationality, so existing citizenship is not put in jeopardy. Note however that EU family members who are nationals of other countries should check before proceeding to naturalise, as their own government may not allow dual citizenship.

One final, practical point on naturalisation. An EU national who has until now been able to sponsor the entry and residence of non-EU family members should consider very carefully whether to become British, because as soon as they do, they lose the ability to sponsor their family under EU regulations. Rather, they put themselves in the same position as British nationals seeking to sponsor spouses, children etc: they must meet the far more onerous requirements of our domestic Immigration Rules. For spouses, as well as proving a genuine and subsisting relationship, and a future intention to live together, they must address the minimum income threshold (currently £18,600 pa) and their family member's ability to pass a specified English language test. For children, the age threshold is lowered from 21 to 18.

As we have discussed, the ongoing right of EU nationals to reside in the UK is one the biggest unknowns in the Brexit process. It is felt that the continued residence of EU nationals currently residing in the UK is a 'bargaining chip' on which the government will seek to rely going into negotiations, when seeking to secure the rights of UK nationals living elsewhere in the EU. At time of writing, the only significant indication as to the principles behind this are to be found in the White Paper on Brexit:

> 'The UK remains ready to give people the certainty they want and reach a reciprocal deal with our European partners at the earliest opportunity. It is the right and fair thing to do.'

The preferred option of many interested groups, including the UK's Immigration Law Practitioner's Association (ILPA), is a 'Standstill' clause. This would, broadly, involve creating a cut-off date. At this point, the following would occur:

(a) Those who hold Permanent Residence would retain this right. Practically this could mean accepting Permanent Residence as the equivalent of 'Indefinite Leave to Remain' under the UK's domestic Immigration Rules. The two statuses are broadly equivalent. The Home Office could potentially still allow people to make applications for Permanent Residence following the cut-off date but they would have to rely on a five-year period preceding it in order to qualify for confirmation of their status.

(b) Those without Permanent Residence could be allowed to continue residing in the UK and apply for it once they meet the current conditions (ie the government could seek to preserve the existing law under domestic law for a stated period of time).

This would be a logical and pragmatic approach to what is undoubtedly going to be a challenging issue which will be the subject of significant public debate. This, at present, appears to be the preferred choice of the British government whilst they decide what might replace current EU Regulations governing free movement. The Home Secretary, Amber Rudd MP, wrote in a letter to a colleague on 06/02/2017 on this issue:

'...I'd also like to reassure colleagues that Parliament will have a clear opportunity to debate and vote on this issue in the future. The Great Repeal Bill will not change our immigration system. This will be done through a separate Immigration Bill and subsequent secondary legislation so nothing will change for any EU citizen, whether already resident in the UK or moving from the EU, without Parliament's approval.'

Regardless of the chosen solution, this will need to be clearly advertised to both employers and the general public so that there is ample opportunity for EU nationals and their family members to take appropriate steps to secure their status or make arrangements to depart the UK.

8.3 FUTURE ARRIVALS – HOW WILL THE UK REGULATE ENTRY AND RESIDENCE?

8.3.1 EU visitors

EU nationals are entitled, further to regulation 13 of the Immigration (European Economic Area) Regulations 2016, to reside in the UK for 90 days. This right of residence can be extended once they start a qualified activity, such as work or study. EU nationals who 'an unreasonable burden on the social assistance system of the United Kingdom' do not enjoy this initial right. As well as being the main method by which EU nationals commence their residence here it is commonly the method used for holidays, business visits etc. Pragmatically, whatever the terms of Brexit, it is highly likely that terms for visits to the UK would remain favourable for EU nationals.

Under domestic law regarding visitors, the UK differentiates between visa and non-visa nationals. Visa nationals are those who need to apply for a document prior to entry, while non-visa nationals can simply deal with this on arrival at the UK border by filling in a landing card (although they can still be refused if not considered to be a genuine visitor). It would seem likely that citizens of EU member states would become non-visa nationals if visiting the UK, and would be able to obtain standard 6 month visit entry with relative ease.

The UK does have a third category of visitor which are those from non-visa national countries who are eligible to apply for an Electronic Visa Waiver (EVW), similar to the US ESTA scheme. This has been in place since 2014. Currently, nationals of Kuwait, Oman, Qatar or the United Arab Emirates, all visa national countries, may pay £15 and complete a brief online process in order to have a 6 month visa (for the purposes of tourism only) approved prior to travel. In the past the Home Office has indicated that they may consider extending this model to other countries in order to both improve record keeping and due to the additional income it would provide. It is possible that the Home Office may extend this scheme to EU member states but this of itself would not provide much of a barrier to entering the UK.

8.3.2   Future students and workers: the current points-based system

After Brexit, what happens to European economic migrants and those travelling to the UK to study? As explained in the preceding section of this chapter, under current rule and regulations the UK has two very distinct schemes operating in tandem:

- European nationals have freedom of movement to travel to the UK for the purposes of work, study or self-sufficiency, with few restrictions placed on their activities or UK residence;
- Non-European nationals are instead subject to a points-based system, or in limited cases to alternative routes, which more closely regulate individuals, and in some instances mandatorily restricts their numbers.

The scheme applicable to European nationals is far simpler than that applied to others; almost all European citizens may seek employment or self-employment in the UK without any prior permission from the Home Office or formal sponsorship from an employer. There are equally no minimum requirements for personal finances, so European nationals do not need to submit evidence of money in the bank in the way that non-European applicants do. Individuals travelling to the UK to study are similarly welcome, but are subject to an additional requirement to hold comprehensive health insurance for the duration of their residence. The same is true for the financially self-sufficient, who do not undertake economic activity as they have no financial need to do so.

As the UK leaves the EU, more restrictions on entry and residence will be introduced for European nationals, of that the government has already been clear. The White Paper published in February 2017 unequivocally states that upon Brexit:

'the Free Movement Directive [the European provisions confirming an EU national's right to travel through EU countries] will no longer apply and the migration of EU nationals will be subject to UK law.'

What it still not known, is what UK law applicable to new EU arrivals will look like. With no information yet known about the specific measures that will be introduced, in this section we review the existing schemes for non-European nationals, which can help to inform us as to the options which are available to the government, and what may be under consideration. Business owners would be well advised to contemplate how changes may affect their HR and recruitment practices in relation to new EU hires.

8.3.3   A hard Brexit: a points-based system for managed migration

The points-based system (PBS) is applicable to almost all non-European nationals wishing to enter the UK for anything other than a 'family' route. It seems likely that this will form the basis for future regulation of entry for prospective EU citizens seeking to work or study in the UK. The PBS is split into five Tiers which are applicable to different categories of applicant:

- Tier 1 is reserved for those with high-net-worth (called investors), those who seek to establish their own business (called entrepreneurs) and individuals with exceptional talent in a few key industry sectors;
- Tier 2 is for skilled workers holding sponsored employment with a UK-registered business;
- Tier 3 was never implemented. It was planned for low-skilled work at times of specific shortage;
- Tier 4 covers students, both child and adult; and
- Tier 5 is a wide category applicable to several temporary work options, including internships and young people (from a few selected countries) seeking work experience in the UK.

If Tier 3 were reinstated and opened, the PBS could theoretically cover every category of European national currently migrating to the UK. However, due to limitations of the PBS (discussed below), that is almost certainly not the route that will be taken once the UK leaves the EU. Nonetheless, an assessment of the shortcomings of the existing system may help to inform British companies of issues that should be considered now, before any changes are made.

8.3.4   Economic routes – Tiers 1 and 2

More than two thirds of European Economic Area nationals currently resident in the UK have some form of employment here. The nature of their work covers many different sectors, but some – such as hospitality and healthcare – see a particular concentration of the European workforce. For example, European workers make up 5% of NHS staff (including 10% of the UK's NHS doctors) and the total number of European nationals working for the NHS is almost 60,000.

The number of European nationals who continue to migrate to the UK poses a problem for expanding the PBS to encompass them. Tier 2 of the PBS restricts migration to the UK by limiting the number of places available to new economic migrants. The current maximum is set at 20,700 new migrants per year, split into individual monthly allocations. For many months, these individual allocations have not been fully utilised, and in fact it is common for leftover spaces to be added to the following month's allocation (over 1,200 spaces were carried over to add to the February 2017 limit). However, if European nationals were added to Tier 2, it is highly likely that that the monthly allocations available would soon be met and exceeded.

In addition to the monthly limit imposed on new migration, all Tier 2 sponsors have a finite number of sponsorship places available to offer to a foreign worker. If European nationals were added to Tier 2, those available allocations would need to be revised and expanded for a UK business to continue to offer employment to new individuals it has identified as being best for a particular role.

Tier 1 is unlikely to alleviate these pressures. The route is already relatively restricted, limiting applications to investors bringing at least £2 million to the UK, and entrepreneurs willing to invest at least £200,000 in their UK business, so there is little prospect of many existing employees changing their status to becoming self-employed. In fact, many of the existing self-employed or self-sufficient European nationals who would otherwise migrate to the UK may discover that they are no longer eligible to do so upon Brexit. There is no natural replacement route for individuals in these categories, and it is unlikely that any new option would be created for them.

As existing sponsors will already be aware, holding an active Tier 2 licence is a significant undertaking, requiring the investment of both time and money. There is a fee for the licence itself, a charge for each certificate of sponsorship (CoS) allocated to a migrant worker, and from April 2017 all Tier 2 sponsors will be required to pay an 'immigration skills charge' of up to £1,000 (reduced to £364 for small businesses and charities) per migrant, per year. In addition to the monetary cost, Tier 2 sponsorship is subject to complicated restrictions and guidance, which if breached can lead to revocation of the licence and illegal working (resulting in fines or even criminal prosecution). Employers of European nationals have thus far avoided many of these concerns, due to the straightforward nature of right to work checks for Europeans and their families. As more restrictions are introduced, employers would be well advised to ensure that they understand any new requirements they must satisfy, as well as the implications of failing to comply.

In its present state, Tier 2 is not fit for purpose to cater for every skilled worker entering the UK. One option to address the shortcomings would be to simply make the route more flexible. Relaxing the annual limit from the 20,700 maximum and offering larger allocations to individual sponsors would ease the pressures on numbers, but it is perhaps unlikely that this is an option the government would seriously consider. Reducing net migration figures has been a target of the government for several years, and Tier 2 is one of only a small number of immigration routes whose numbers can be strictly limited.

Even if the limit on numbers could be relaxed, another limitation of Tier 2 indicates that this route will not be the option to which European workers are directed. Tier 2 is suitable for skilled migrants only, meaning that a very high proportion of the current European workforce would have no continued access to the labour market if required to qualify under the Tier 2. An example of this is the hospitality and tourism industry; many of the jobs it provides are too low skilled and too low paid for Tier 2 sponsorship, but the sector is the UK's fourth largest industry (representing 10% of GDP) and it employs an estimated 700,000 European nationals. If Tier 2 cannot cater for those people, could another area of the PBS fill the gap? Currently, the answer would have to be 'no'. Tier 3 was never opened, and it has been fully deleted from the Immigration Rules, so there would need to be significant re-drafting to the rules for low skilled workers to have access to the PBS.

The UK has previously used 'sector based schemes' to fill temporary demands for low-skilled work. One example is the Seasonal Agricultural Workers Scheme (SAWS), which closed in 2012, but before this allowed for more than 20,000 people per year to work in UK farming. The scheme's phasing out was broadly in response to the admission to the EU of countries such as Romania and Bulgaria (whose nationals then no longer needed admission under the SAWS), and it is estimated that 65% of the UK's current agricultural workforce are European nationals. According to research conducted by Oxford's Migration Observatory for the Financial Times, up to 96% of current European workers would most likely fail existing UK visa requirements, indicating that some form of action is needed to protect industries like farming which are reliant on a migrant workforce.

As there are currently no specific arrangements in place for skilled or unskilled European labour post-Brexit, British business must for now remain alert to the ongoing debate. The government's White Paper has suggested that immigration law is likely to receive its own bill to be debated in parliament, and also that significant changes may be phased in gradually to allow businesses adequate time to prepare for the post-Brexit world. Ultimately, making robust and adequate arrangements for workers is a significant undertaking for the government as Brexit negotiations begin. There are options under existing and former schemes, but it is unclear whether these will fully cover the diverse requirements of the UK labour market. It is even possible that a completely new approach may be taken to governing migrant workers, with a specific registration scheme for European workers covering both those already present in the UK and those seeking to migrate in future. For now, British businesses must watch and wait.

8.3.5   Students – Tier 4

Unlike the PBS economic routes, the existing Tier 4 scheme for students is better placed to accommodate European students in addition to the non-European nationals it currently covers. Annual numbers for Tier 4 are not fixed under the Immigration Rules, although individual allocations are set for each sponsor (education provider), limiting the number of students they may enrol. To cope with the high increase in applications to Tier 4, each sponsor's annual application would need to be increased. Whether the government would allow such a response is unclear; student numbers are currently included in net migration figures, and so a significant increase of Tier 4 students would also cause the overall figures to swell, which is an issue that remains politically sensitive.

Tier 4 has more detailed requirements than those European students are currently used to. Specifically, a Tier 4 student's ability to work part-time while studying is limited, and there is a much more onerous requirement for a Tier 4 student to show financial independence than that applicable to their European counterparts. By bringing European students under Tier 4, it may be the case that a proportion of them are simply 'priced out' of UK study. The education sector is keen to avoid this; whether European or otherwise, foreign students bring an important stream of revenue to UK institutions, and they also fill a high number of research and other post-graduate posts upon which institutions rely. In addition, a great many Tier 4 students complete higher education in the UK and then join the graduate job market. British businesses should be alert to the possibility that the graduate talent point will shrink as a result of Brexit, either due to European students turning away from UK education, or to a restriction on numbers applicable to students overall.

Alternatives to Tier 4 are difficult to predict. There is no real incentive for the government to prioritise European students above any other, and a scheme totally separate to the existing Tier 4 offering could cause confusion. Further guidance from government is awaited to confirm how this issue will be addressed.

8.3.6 Temporary routes – Tier 5

EU free movement offers flexibility which the Immigration Rules cannot replicate. If a young European person wishes to travel to the UK for work experience, internship or volunteering, their route is simple and there are no prior conditions to satisfy beyond holding a valid form of identification. Tier 5 of the PBS is not so open. There are opportunities in the UK, but they are usually limited to pre-approved schemes or sponsors, and are limited in number. The Tier 5 Youth Mobility scheme more closely resembles EU free movement, and allows for virtually unimpeded access to the UK based on a person's nationality (visa permitting). As the route is so accessible, it is restricted to just a few nations (Australia, Canada, Japan, Monaco, New Zealand, Hong Kong, Republic of Korea and Taiwan) and only where the applicant is aged between 18 and 30.

It is possible that a similar Youth Mobility scheme may be opened to European nationals after Brexit, and a more straightforward route to temporary work (which would generally be lower paid and lower skilled) would alleviate pressure that would otherwise fall on Tier 2 or its alternative. The government has made no firm announcements at the time of writing, but this is one option that may be under consideration. For employers not currently familiar with Tier 5, this route could present an opportunity. Existing available internship/work experience schemes may compliment your business, allowing continued access to a pool of talent which would otherwise be shut off after Brexit. As with all immigration options, developments to Tier 5 or the introduction of similar schemes should be closely monitored.

8.4 A SOFTER BREXIT?

The imposition of existing domestic Immigration Rules on future EU arrivals is unlikely to meet the British economy's employment needs, at least in the short term. So what alternatives might the government consider?

8.4.1 A worker registration scheme

The British government has indicated that it does not want EU nationals coming to the UK without already securing employment. Over the years, treaties signed by the British government in connection with EU enlargement have included an option to derogate from normal free movement principles for a limited period. It is instructive to consider what has happened when the UK has sought to limit access to its labour market for newly-acceded Member States and their nationals.

At the commencement of the 'A8' enlargement of the EU on 1 May 2004, which brought countries such as Poland and the Czech Republic into the Union, the first Accession State Workers Registration Scheme was implemented as a way of monitoring EU migrants from new member states and allowing them to work in the UK at a time when they did not have full rights of free movement. Whilst students, the self-sufficient and the self-employed were exempted, employed EU nationals had to register with the scheme within a month of beginning employment. If they stayed with the same employer for over 12 months they would automatically gain full access to the labour market in the UK. Experience showed that such a 'light touch' scheme did nothing to deter A8 nationals from relocating to the UK in search of employment. The numbers of eastern European migrants who have made the UK their home since 2004, changing the ethnic make-up of certain regions such as the farming areas of Lincolnshire, is often cited as a reason people voted to leave the EU.

The time limit on the UK's A8 derogation ended on 30 April 2011, meaning that citizens of this first round of accession states have enjoyed full freedom of movement since then.

A similar, although more bureaucratic, accession model was adopted when Romania and Bulgaria joined the EU on 1 January 2007. For citizens of those countries seeking employment in the UK, processes were introduced requiring application for an 'accession worker card', akin to a work permit in that it ties the particular individual to their sponsored employment. Unlike A8 nationals, this employment authorisation did not come to an end after 12 months with the same employer. Once again, students and the self-employed were not covered. The scheme covering Romania and Bulgaria came to an end, in line with the UK's derogation from the relevant accession treaty, on 1 January 2014.

8.4.2 The Croatia model

Tier 2 of the Points Based System, as mentioned above, is the main method by which non-EU skilled workers are allowed to work in the UK. It involves having an offer of employment at degree level or above, there are minimum salary thresholds and the employer must have an appropriate sponsor license, to demonstrate they are a genuine business and understand their responsibilities to the Home Office when it comes to employing foreign nationals.

Croatia is the most recent member state of the EU and, like the other accession states before it, has been subject to transitional provisions as to how nationals can access the labour market in the UK. This time there was a move away from a simple 'worker registration scheme', in favour of something similar in structure to Tier 2 (ie employers must hold a sponsor licence and employees must be sponsored) but with significantly more lenient provisions. This implies a more rigid framework than mere registration, and puts a more significant burden on employers to ensure employee records are up to date. Briefly the main differences for Croatian nationals are as follows:

- They are allowed to work at jobs from RQF level 4 and above, rather than RQF level 6 (degree level).
- They do not need to demonstrate access to sufficient maintenance.
- They are not banned from returning to Tier 2 for 12 months if they leave it, aka the 'cooling off period'.
- There is no English language requirement.

Once they have been with their employer for a year, Croatians become able to access the labour market without restriction and, crucially, without the need for further sponsorship.

Both worker registration schemes and the Croatian model could be said to be a balance of the government's wish to ensure that EU migrants have come here for genuine economic opportunity as well as being sufficiently lenient to continue to attract EU workers without being seen to 'pull up the drawbridge'. The issue with these approaches are that they would not provide any realistic protection for the self-employed, students or self-sufficient EU migrants who, under the worker registration scheme, were exempted from regulation. It is highly unlikely that this would continue outside of free movement. Whilst not necessarily an issue for those whose businesses rely on employees who would theoretically be able to sponsor them, it does create some ambiguity in terms of using specialist contractors, offering paid internships to EU national students etc.

The clear disparity between the EU and domestic legal systems for authorised work demonstrates that it would be in the interests of all parties to come to an agreement that makes the rights of those currently in the UK clear, to set out who is lawfully present, who is not and how settled status in the UK might be achieved. The Immigration Acts 2014–2016 created a number of restrictions for those without the ability to prove their status. This means that there could be a situation where those who should be lawfully resident in the UK lose access to, amongst other things, public funds (where entitled), ability to rent, opening bank accounts or holding a driving licence. Clear transitional provisions should avoid such consequences.

8.4.3   Dependants

The dependent family member of a European national may be European themselves or from a third country which would ordinarily be subject to the PBS (or alternatives under the Immigration Rules). As free movement rights end, the rights of those individuals will also be altered.

Once final immigration arrangements are confirmed, British businesses must ensure that they understand the provisions applicable to European nationals and to their family members, and also understand that there may be separate schemes applicable dependent on whether an individual is European or not. Regardless of the measures introduced for European workers, a family member who is not themselves from Europe may need to satisfy the provisions of the PBS, and may be unable to do so.

What is likely, is that the dependants of a European national who retains the ability to reside and work in the UK after Brexit, will also have freedom to live and work here. This would mirror the existing PBS, which makes provision for family members and affords those individuals the right to work with very few restrictions. British business should consider however that the definition of a 'dependant' is more restrictive under the PBS than it is under European law. As a result, a full review of all migrant workers is advisable, to ensure that employers understand who will be affected by Brexit and whether any arrangements can currently be made for those people. Many European nationals and/or their family members will already qualify for residence documents, and it is to the benefit of both employee and employer that existing rights are confirmed in formal documentation where possible.

8.5   THE IRISH QUESTION

The history of British-Irish immigration is a long and complex one, which began when the Irish Free State was formed in 1922. The Common Travel Area is an administrative agreement between the two countries, which has evolved over the years to reflect changes to our respective countries' immigration legislation, and since the 1970s membership of the EU.

Irish citizens are of course also EU nationals, and their ability to travel to, live and work in the UK now derives from EU membership, rather than from bilateral agreement between the two countries. They remain technically 'subject to immigration control', but only in the limited sense that EU nationals are subject to such control. This will technically change when British leaves the EU, probably requiring a return to the position under the Immigration Act 1971, whereby Irish citizens' entry and residence was not regulated in practice.

Under section 1(3) of the 1971 Act, arrival from and departures to any of the Channel Islands, the Isle of Man and Republic of Ireland were deemed to be local journeys and 'shall not be subject to control under this Act'. From the 1990s, changes were introduced which led, among other things, to active immigration enforcement on routes between the two countries. There is still today no border control as such, but at ports such as Holyhead British immigration officials may check arriving passengers if they consider there is reason to do so.

For such non-citizens travelling from Ireland, entry is governed by the Immigration (Control of Entry through Republic of Ireland) Order 1972.[1] Those who are visa nationals in the UK are required to obtain a British visa before travelling here, despite entering from the Republic. They risk refusal of leave to enter if they fail to comply and are challenged by immigration enforcement officials when entering the UK.

Those who are not subject to a visa requirement for short-term entry are deemed to be granted three months' leave to enter the UK if they travel via Ireland.

The position for Irish citizens and their family members will, according to the government, remain the same post-Brexit. They will retain the ability to travel and reside in the UK.

The position for non-Irish citizens, including EU nationals, travelling from the Republic will, however, change. There have already been talks about the nature of border control with Ireland after Britain leaves the EU. There is political support for a 'soft border' between Northern Ireland and the Republic. Neither country signed up to the Schengen acquis relating to visa-free travel within participating parts of the EU. Importantly, Protocol 20, Article 2 of the current EU treaty provides that 'the UK and Ireland may continue to make arrangements between themselves relating to the movement of persons between their territories (the Common Travel Area)'. There is no similarly legal obligation on Ireland to join the Schengen zone or to give up its CTA arrangements.

Subject to negotiation, we would expect the border between North and South to remain free of immigration control, for the practical reason that such a border would be too difficult to police. Third country nationals, including EU citizens, entering the UK via that land border can expect to face immigration controls if going on to travel to the British mainland, despite the domestic nature of such travel.

8.6 BRITS ABROAD – RECIPROCAL RESTRICTIONS FOR UK NATIONALS

Free movement does of course work both ways. At present, British citizens can travel to EU Member States in much the same manner as EU nationals can here. After Brexit, EU member states will be able to consider individually how they wish to admit them. The favourableness of these conditions will inevitably depend on the extent to which the UK seeks to protect or guarantee the rights

---

1   SI 1972/1610.

of EU nationals present in the UK, and how it proposes to regulate entry and residence of future arrivals.

In the worst-case scenario – assuming a hard Brexit where negotiations between Member States and the UK do not go well – British citizens become like any other non-EU nationals. Many so-called third-country entrants and potential residents to the EU are subject to limited visa requirements, often only required for long-term residence, study and work.

8.6.1 Visits

Visits to our former EU colleagues are unlikely to require prior entry clearance, in the form of visit visas; the Schengen visa model would suggest admission without prior formality for up to 90 days, possibly subject to a limit of 90 out of every 180 days' residence inside the EU.

The European Commission has, in recent years, considered an ESTA or online pre-authorisation scheme for non-visa national visitors to EU Member States. If this were rolled out to all non-visa countries, the UK could expect to be included. The US ESTA scheme, as many will know, is a quick, cheap online process which returns a result within a few days.

Unless a new channel for 'former EU members' is introduced, at air and sea ports, British citizens can expect to use the non-EU immigration line, and to have a longer wait than previously at passport control.

In the event that the UK sought to impose a visit visa requirement on certain EU nationals, the principle of visa reciprocity could lead to similar requirements being placed on British travellers to certain parts of the EU, unless an exception were negotiated as part of the Brexit deal.

8.6.2 Study

It is of course those seeking long-term residence in the EU who face the biggest upheaval. Students, school pupils, voluntary workers and researchers will be covered by an EU Directive which imposes requirements similar to those contained in our domestic Immigration Rules. For students, for example, the conditions are:

- Acceptance at a higher education establishment.
- Sufficient resources to cover study fees (which must be paid in advance is some instances), subsistence and return travel.
- Knowledge of the language of the course taken.
- Maximum of 15 hours' work while studying.

This form of residence may be extended upon completion of a course for the purpose of seeking employment or setting up a business. Family members will be permitted to accompany, and it will be possible to secure status akin to permanent residence after five years.

8.6.3 Work

British workers seeking to take up opportunities within the EU will face a complex set of rules, adopted by all member states except Ireland and Denmark (and of course, until now, the UK) far removed from the current position. The underlying principle is that EU workers are given preference: if a Czech applicant can do a job in Paris that a British person has also applied for, the Czech worker must be employed. There are sanctions for employers who flaunt this principle.

A British citizen seeking to work in the EU will need to apply for a work and residence permit prior to travel. The employer is key to that process: an individual will not be able simply to travel to Europe and seek work.

(a) *The Blue Card Scheme for highly skilled workers*

This kind of EU work permit requires a valid work contract or binding job offer of at least 12 months' duration, offering a salary that is at least 1.5 times the average gross salary in that EU Member State. Proof of qualifications and comprehensive sickness insurance are also necessary. This category leads to permanent residence after five years. Family members may accompany the sponsored worker. Individual member states are permitted to have their own work permit schemes which relax – but importantly do not restrict – the Blue Card scheme.

(b) *Intra-corporate transfers*

A British citizen employed by a business in the UK or anywhere outside the EU (excluding Denmark and Ireland) will require prior authorisation in accordance with the relevant Directive. The individual must have a minimum length of service with the company before relocating to the EU; family members may accompany.

(c) *Seasonal workers*

Specific rules cover agricultural workers, ski instructors, tour guides etc, permitting short term residence with prior entry clearance. These workers are limited to between five and nine months' residence in any 12-month period, and may switch employers.

(d) *Long term residents*

British citizens may, like their EU counterparts living in the UK, have acquired permanent resident status after five years' continuous lawful residence while exercising free movement rights under current rules. Once we leave the EU, British citizens seeking to assert permanent residence will have to meet additional requirements:

o   Stable and regular resources sufficient to support yourself and your family.

o   Comprehensive sickness insurance.

o   Ability to pass an integration – including language – test.

CHAPTER 9

COMMERCIAL DISPUTES

Anna Pertoldi and Maura McIntosh, Herbert Smith Freehills LLP

INTRODUCTION

There are a number of themes for discussion when it comes to commercial disputes and Brexit. This chapter focuses on three:

- Will there be any changes to how disputes are or should be resolved?
- Will Brexit mean an increase in the number of commercial disputes?
- What are the legal issues which are likely to arise in commercial disputes?

Each is considered in turn, with the aim of giving practical guidance on what commercial parties need to consider.

9.1 HOW COMMERCIAL DISPUTES ARE RESOLVED

9.1.1 The role of English law

Many commercial disputes are resolved applying English law. Will that change post-Brexit? For the reasons explained below, that seems unlikely, although businesses will need to give more detailed consideration to the appropriate dispute resolution clause in some cases.

9.1.2 English law – key attractions will not be diminished as a result of Brexit

English law has long been a popular choice in commercial contracts. It has been developed over many centuries. It is stable and predictable whilst also being flexible enough to adapt to new developments in commercial practice. It respects 'freedom of contract' thereby generally giving effect to the parties' contractual bargain with only limited scope for implied terms or the influence of public policy. It is the market-standard in a number of industries and commercial parties globally have extensive experience in applying it.

None of these key attractions will be diminished as a result of Brexit. The core principles of English contract law come from the common law (ie judge-made case law) and as such are unaffected by Brexit. Only in specific areas such as consumer and employment contracts has English contract law been significantly affected by EU law.

9.1.3   Choice of English law – will still be respected by EU courts post-Brexit

Brexit will not have any impact on the effectiveness of a choice of English law to govern commercial contracts.

The rules which determine which law applies to a contractual dispute brought before the courts of an EU member state are contained in Regulation (EC) No 593/2008, commonly referred to as Rome I. There are similar provisions in respect of non- contractual obligations in Regulation (EC) No 864/2007, referred to as Rome II.

Rome I and II require member states to respect a choice of law regardless of where the contracting parties are from and whether or not the chosen law is that of an EU member state.

So, post-Brexit, if a contract contains an English choice of law clause and the dispute is being heard before, say, the German, courts, those courts will be obliged to apply English law to determine the dispute.

There are exceptions in some areas, such as the financial services sector, where EU legislation constrains the parties' choice of law (and jurisdiction) in relation to certain activities. But as a general rule in a commercial context party autonomy will prevail.

9.1.4   Arbitration – no change: arbitration clauses and awards will still be respected post-Brexit

Many commercial contracts provide for arbitration. There are a number of reasons arbitration may be chosen by the parties – ease of enforcement, greater privacy and choice of arbitrator being key amongst them.

Brexit will not have any impact on arbitration clauses or enforcement of arbitral awards. The regime for the recognition of an agreement to arbitrate and enforcement of an arbitral award is the 1958 New York Convention, an international treaty to which 156 states worldwide are party, including the UK and all other EU member states. The New York Convention will not be affected by Brexit.

9.1.5   English judgments – will still be enforced by EU courts post-Brexit, but enforcement may be subject to different rules

The position in respect of English judgments is more complex, in large part because of the uncertainty over whether any arrangements will be put in place to replace the current regime.

The regime which applies throughout the EU to enforce a judgment from another member state is contained in the Brussels I Regulation (Regulation

(EC) No 44/2001) in respect of proceedings begun before 10 January 2015 and the recast Brussels Regulation (Regulation (EU) 1215/2012) in respect of proceedings begun on or after that date. Broadly speaking, effect is given to a wide range of judgments with limited grounds to object and in a relatively straightforward and cost effective way.

Those Regulations will no longer apply between the UK and the EU post Brexit[1] and it is not known what if anything will replace them. There are a number of possibilities:

- *An agreement with the EU on similar lines to the recast Brussels Regulation.* Sometimes referred to as the Danish option. This is the outcome favoured by most legal commentators. It may well not be possible to achieve in the event of a 'hard' Brexit as it would likely require the UK to agree to be bound by decisions of the European Court of Justice (CJEU). All the indications to date are that this will not be an acceptable outcome for the British government.

- *An agreement to join the Lugano Convention 2007.* In this case the position would be as it was before the recast Brussels Regulation took effect, so without certain improvements introduced in that Regulation in 2015. It is the regime which currently applies between EU member states and Norway, Switzerland and Iceland. It would require the UK to have regard to, rather than be bound by, decisions of the CJEU, which may be more palatable to the government in the event of a hard Brexit. Even if achievable it may take some time as, unless we become a member of the European Free Trade Association (EFTA) which is looking unlikely, it would require agreement from all parties, including all EU member states. In due course it is likely that the Lugano Convention will be updated to include the improvements introduced in the recast Brussels Regulation.

- *Joining the 2005 Hague Convention on Choice of Court Agreements* (the UK is currently a party by reason of its membership of the EU). In this case there would probably be relatively little change where an exclusive English jurisdiction clause has been agreed. It would be possible to join this Convention without needing the agreement of the EU. Legal commentators are urging the government to join Hague as soon as possible post-Brexit and to make its intention to do so clear as soon as possible during the pre-Brexit negotiation period so commercial parties have some certainty. There will however be some remaining uncertainty over whether the Convention will continue to apply to jurisdiction agreements entered into on or after 1 October 2015 when the Convention came into force for the EU (including the UK) but before the UK joins in its own right.

---

1   Subject to any transitional arrangements put in place. The European Commission's Position Paper on Judicial Cooperation in Civil and Commercial Matters, published on 29 June 2017, sets out the EU's position that current provisions on recognition and enforcement of judgments under the recast Brussels Regulation should continue to govern judgments given before the date of the UK's withdrawal from the EU.

- *A bespoke agreement* with the EU or particular member states. This would be likely to take some considerable time to achieve, even assuming the political will existed within the EU to make it happen.
- *No agreement or convention.* Whether an EU member state would enforce an English judgment if there is no agreement would depend on the domestic rules on enforcement in each member state. It would mean that an English judgment would generally be in no better (or worse) position than a judgment from, eg, New York.

Enforcement of an English judgment in another EU member state may not be a major concern for a business. This may be because there are assets in England to enforce against, or because it is very unlikely to become necessary to force the counterparty to comply with any judgment given. If it will or may be necessary to enforce in the EU then an exclusive English jurisdiction clause may be the best option in the long run – to take advantage of the UK's likely accession to the Hague Convention.

If exclusive jurisdiction is considered too inflexible, or there are concerns over the transitional position, then it may be worth checking what the position is on enforcement in those countries most likely to be relevant in the case of a dispute. So for example, if there is a Spanish counterparty to a contract, check what the likely position would be on enforcement of an English judgment in Spain (at present, there are wide enforcement rights in Spain).

9.1.6 English jurisdiction clauses are likely to still be effective post-Brexit

At present the approach taken by EU member state courts to jurisdiction agreements in favour of another member state is also governed by the Brussels regime – the recast Brussels Regulation in respect of proceedings begun on or after 10 January 2015.

Where proceedings are commenced in a different member state to that chosen in the contract, the other party can start proceedings in the chosen court. So in the case of an exclusive English jurisdiction clause where proceedings are started in, say, Italy, proceedings can also be started in England. The Italian court is then obliged to stay its proceedings until the chosen court, the English court, has determined whether it has jurisdiction. When it decides it does have jurisdiction, the Italian court must dismiss its proceedings.

Post-Brexit these rules will not apply to the UK.[1] Very similar rules are contained however in the Hague Convention so there is unlikely to be any material change if

---

1   Again, subject to any transitional arrangements put in place. The European Commission's Position Paper on Judicial Cooperation in Civil and Commercial Matters, published on 29 June 2017, sets out the EU's position that current rules on jurisdiction under the recast Brussels Regulation should continue to apply to proceedings instituted before the date of the UK's withdrawal from the EU, and to choices of jurisdiction in contracts entered into before the withdrawal date.

we sign up to that convention, at least where one of the parties is UK resident and there is an exclusive jurisdiction agreement. In the unlikely event that we do not, the position is more uncertain and complex, but there are cases where the CJEU has given effect to exclusive jurisdiction clauses in favour of non-EU countries.

9.1.7 Arbitration versus litigation post-Brexit

Given there is uncertainty over what, if anything, will be agreed to replace the Brussels regime, some commentators have argued that commercial parties should include an arbitration clause in their contracts, given there will be no changes to the arbitration rules.

Arbitration has many advantages, but so does English litigation, including the expertise of the judiciary, the availability of summary procedures and appeals and the ability to deal with multiple parties and issues.

Brexit does not mean that a business which normally favours litigation as a dispute mechanism should now adopt an arbitration clause. What it does mean is that more thought needs to be given to what is the best dispute resolution clause in all the circumstances. This might result in a jurisdiction clause being chosen, an arbitration clause or possibly an optional clause – jurisdiction with an option to arbitrate or arbitration with an option to litigate.

Jurisdiction and choice of law clauses should never be treated as boiler plate. That is truer with the uncertainties Brexit brings than perhaps ever before.

9.2 WILL COMMERCIAL DISPUTES INCREASE?

This isn't so much a legal question as a practical and commercial question. When there are major unforeseen events or periods of uncertainty, there are winners and losers. What looked like a good deal or a risk worth taking turns out to be a mistake and parties start looking to see if there are ways of exiting contracts or passing on losses to third parties.

So since the financial crisis in 2008 there have been many cases, some of which are still working their way through the courts, where parties have tried to escape the effects of their contracts on the basis they were misinformed or that they are entitled to terminate the contract. When property prices drop, valuers (and their insurers) often find themselves in the firing line and when companies and individuals become insolvent, there are disputes about who has priority over limited assets.

It is early days in terms of what the effects of Brexit will be and whether British business will in the long term be the winner or loser. Issues which are likely to arise will concern matters such as:

- *Profitability and pricing* – changes in exchange rates may mean the parties' profit margins have changed. The introduction of tariffs and tariff barriers may affect the pricing of goods.

- *Territories* – is the UK included or excluded in a contract.
- *Intellectual property rights* – there will need to be new provisions put in place to replicate rights held pre Brexit on an EU wide basis. There may be disputes over the effect of those rights.
- *Insolvency* – given the increased risk of competing insolvencies in different jurisdictions, there may be more disputes over the rights to a company's assets.

9.3 HOW WILL COMMERCIAL DISPUTES ARISE?

It is very difficult to predict how commercial disputes will arise – each case will of course be very fact specific. This section therefore focuses on the law in two general areas which are likely to feature in many disputes: interpretation and termination of contracts.

So far as interpretation is concerned, issues may arise for example over how references to the EU should be interpreted. There is also the question of how references to EU legislation should be treated and how UK legislation which replicates former EU legislation should be interpreted.

So far as termination is concerned, parties faced with uneconomic contracts will be looking for ways of exiting those contracts. This section therefore considers ways in which commercial contracts might be brought to an end, whether directly as a result of Brexit or indirectly relying on rights under the contract. Consideration is also given to the arguments which will be put forward to resist termination.

9.3.1 Interpretation

How will the court interpret a reference to the 'EU' in a contract? Will it include the UK, as it was a member state at the time the contract was entered into, or will it mean the EU from time to time so that the UK is not included?

There is no hard and fast answer to this as it depends upon the particular contract. Whilst this is unhelpful in terms of certainty, it means the court can give effect to the parties' intentions.

Under English law, the court's aim in interpreting a contract term is to determine the meaning it would convey to a reasonable person with all the background knowledge available to the parties at the time the contract was made. As well as the words used and the relevant background, the court will take into account how the clause fits within the contract as a whole and considerations of commercial common sense.

It may be clear from the wording and context that the members of the EU from time to time were intended. Conversely, it may be clear that the UK was intended to be included come what may, perhaps where the main focus of the contract concerned the UK in some way. So for example in the context of an ongoing distribution agreement, if the UK forms an important part of the distributor's operation, a court might readily conclude that the territory was not intended to change in the event of the UK's exit from the EU. All will depend on the facts and circumstances of the contract.

Alongside arguments regarding interpretation, a party may seek to argue that a term should be implied into the contract. For example, that in the event the UK were no longer a member of the EU, the contract would continue with adapted terms.

The bar for implying a term is however set high. The test has been considered recently by the Supreme Court in *Marks and Spencer plc v BNP Paribas Securities Services Trust Company (Jersey) Limited and another*.[1] In general, the term either must be so obvious as to go without saying or must be necessary to give business efficacy to the contract. These are not easy hurdles to meet.

Where a contract refers to directly applicable EU legislation which no longer applies to the UK following Brexit (ie treaty provisions or EU Regulations) questions may arise as to whether this means the relevant legislation as it existed at the time or any legislation enacted to replace it. Hopefully the Great Repeal Bill[2] or other legislation will address this issue as the position as a matter of general law and under the Interpretation Act 1978 is not straightforward.

The intention is that the Great Repeal Bill, announced to Parliament on 10 October 2016, will preserve EU law where it stands at the moment, before we leave the EU, by 'converting' EU law into domestic law as required. Parliament will then decide which elements of that law to keep, amend or repeal. So all EU laws which are directly applicable in the UK and all laws which have been made in the UK, in order to implement our obligations as a member of the EU will, so far as possible, remain part of domestic law on the day we leave.

How will those laws be interpreted? The government's White Paper published in March 2017 makes clear, echoing political statements made beforehand, that decisions of the CJEU will not be binding on UK courts going forward. It also says however that, to provide continuity and maximise certainty, the Bill will provide that any question as to the meaning of EU-derived law will be determined in the UK courts by reference to the CJEU's case law as it exists on the day we leave the EU. To achieve this, the Bill will provide that historic CJEU case law be given the same precedent status as decisions of the Supreme Court.

Given the uncertainties, it clearly would be advisable for businesses to review significant contracts for obvious questions of interpretation, with a view to resolving any ambiguities by amendment wherever possible.

---

1   [2015] UKSC 72.
2   Referred to simply as the 'Repeal Bill' in the legislative programme introduced in the Queen's Speech delivered to Parliament on 21 June 2017. The Government's policy paper Policy paper 'Queen's Speech 2017: what it means for you' states that the Bill will 'allow for a smooth and orderly transition as the UK leaves the EU, ensuring that, wherever practical, the same rules and laws apply after exit and therefore maximising certainty for individuals and businesses'.

9.3.2   Termination

Where a contract has turned into a bad bargain a party will want to get out of it. A bad bargain for one party is generally a good bargain for the other party, so it is unlikely this can be achieved by agreement unless compensation is paid.

That is likely to lead a party to consider how it might be able to bring the contract to an end unilaterally. This might be by seeking to rely on Brexit issues directly, or looking to see if there are any rights to terminate generally, based on express terms or breaches of contract.

9.3.3   Termination because of Brexit – may be possible in some circumstances but difficult

There are three main routes a business wishing to end its contractual obligations as a direct result of Brexit may try to rely on:

Frustration

This common law doctrine excuses the parties from performance where something has happened to make performance impossible or illegal or to render the obligation radically different from what was contracted for.

The courts have however tended to apply the doctrine narrowly, emphasising that it is not lightly to be invoked to allow a contracting party to escape from what has turned out to be a bad bargain. So events which make performance more onerous or more expensive will not of themselves be sufficient to frustrate the contract. Whilst the doctrine might apply because of Brexit related events, cases are likely to be rare.

Force majeure

This is a contract term which excuses one or both parties from performing the contract if prevented by circumstances outside the party's control.

Whether Brexit-related events might constitute force majeure will depend on how the particular clause is drafted. In most clauses, force majeure is defined by reference to a non-exhaustive list of events, together with a general 'wrap up' provision to include other events which are not within a party's reasonable control. The clause may also exclude specific categories of event which the parties agree will not constitute force majeure.

Absent any express consideration of Brexit, categories of event which are commonly included in the definition and which might occur in connection with Brexit include: acts of government; restriction, suspension or withdrawal of any licenses etc and changes in law or regulation.

However, it is not enough to have an event falling within the definition of force majeure. The clause will generally be triggered only if the event prevents, hinders or delays a party performing its obligations. Typically, in that event, the obligations are suspended without liability while the impact of the force majeure event continues (subject to obligations to notify the counterparty of the force majeure event and to seek to mitigate its effects). Most force majeure clauses will also give a right to terminate the contract if the force majeure event continues for a specified period of time.

As with frustration, a change in economic or market circumstances which makes the contract less profitable or performance more onerous is not generally regarded as sufficient to trigger a force majeure clause. So again it may well be difficult to rely on this clause to terminate.

Material adverse change (MAC) clause

This is a term found in some agreements which allows a party, for example a buyer or lender, to refuse to proceed if certain events occur after the contract date.

The drafting of MAC clauses varies greatly. They may be drafted widely, subject to specific carve outs of events that will not qualify, or they may be drafted more narrowly to specify particular events that will qualify as a MAC.

The party seeking to terminate the contract under a MAC clause has the burden of proving that MAC has occurred. In general, a court will not be easily persuaded that a party should be released from its obligations under a contract, so there is a heavy evidential burden on the party seeking to rely on the clause.

A MAC clause cannot be triggered on the basis of circumstances known to the relevant party on entering into the agreement, although it may be possible to invoke the clause where conditions worsen in a way that makes them materially different in nature. The change relied on must also be material in the sense that it must be sufficiently significant or substantial and it must not be merely a temporary blip.

Whether Brexit-related events may amount to a MAC will depend on the terms of the clause and the specific circumstances. In general, however, it will once again not be a straightforward argument.

9.3.4 Express termination provisions in the contract

Contracts will often contain express termination provisions, allowing for termination in particular circumstances. It may be possible to take advantage of these provisions to exit the contract.

Termination for convenience

The best scenario from the perspective of the party seeking to terminate is that the contract contains a right to terminate for convenience, so either party can bring the contract to an end without having to establish particular grounds. This is unlikely to lead to disputes in most cases as the court will respect the parties' agreement. It is very unlikely, for example, that a court will fetter such a right by requiring that it is exercised only for good cause or in good faith.

So for example in *TSG Building Services PLC v South Anglia Housing Limited*[1] a gas servicing contract contained a term providing for the parties to 'work together and individually in the spirit of trust, fairness and mutual co-operation'. A separate clause gave a right to terminate for convenience. The court held that the obligations to co-operate and act reasonably related only to the provision of gas-related works, not to the right to terminate. The court also refused to imply a term. Even if there was some implied term of good faith, it could not circumscribe what the parties had expressly agreed, which was a right to terminate at any time for no, good or bad reason.

A contract may also be for a set period of time, possibly with the option to renew, so in that case it is just a matter of waiting for the contract to expire and not renewing it.

Termination in specified circumstances

The contract may provide for a right to terminate in particular circumstances. A common example is where there has been a change of ownership or control of the counterparty. It will be possible to terminate in these circumstances even if the circumstance does not materially affect the contract – so for example even if the change in control does not prejudice the terminating party. It will only be possible to take advantage of such rights however for a short period after the event. If you continue to perform the contract after the event has taken place then you may be taken to have waived your rights or be estopped from relying on them.

Termination for 'any breach'

If there are no 'no fault' grounds on which to terminate, a party may turn its attention to whether there are any breaches of contract which it may be possible to rely on, under the terms of the contract, the common law or on occasions both.

Contracts sometimes contain a provision giving a right to terminate for 'any breach'. On the face of it this is very broad and a party seeking to exit a contract may think it confers wide rights. Caution is however needed – the courts have on a number of occasions interpreted such a term restrictively.

In *Antaios Compania SA v Salen Rederierna AB*[2] for example the House of Lords held that a right to terminate a time charter 'on any breach' had to be read as meaning 'any repudiatory breach.' A similar conclusion was reached by the

---

1   [2013] EWHC 1151 (TCC).
2   [1985] 1 AC 191.

Court of Appeal in *Rice v Great Yarmouth Borough Council*[1] which concerned a right to terminate if a contractor committed 'a breach of any of its obligations.'

In *Dominion Corporate Trustees Ltd v Debenhams Properties Ltd*[2] an agreement for lease allowed termination if 'either party shall in any respect fail or neglect to observe or perform any of the provisions of this Agreement.' The High Court held that the clause did not allow termination for just any breach, however minor.

More recently, in *Vivienne Westwood Limited v Conduit Street Development Limited*,[3] the High Court found that a reference to 'any breach' did not include a trivial breach, but it was not necessary that a breach would have to be 'material' or 'substantial' in the colloquial sense.

Termination for 'material breach'

Some contracts permit termination where there has been a 'material breach' of contract. What amounts to a 'material breach' will be a matter of interpretation in each case.

In *Mid Essex Hospital Services NHS Trust v Compass Group UK and Ireland Ltd*[4] Lord Justice Jackson put it like this:

> 'In my view this phrase connotes a breach of contract which is more than trivial, but need not be repudiatory .... Having regard to the context of this provision, I think that 'material breach' means a breach which is substantial. The breach must be a serious matter, rather than a matter of little consequence.'

In *Vivienne Westwood*, referred to above, the High Court took the view that the test of materiality is 'fraught with conceptual uncertainty'. The court in that case was considering a clause allowing termination for 'any breach'. It declined to imply a requirement that such a breach should be material.

Strict compliance with contract terms

If a party wishes to take advantage of express termination provisions, it is important to comply to the letter with the requirements set out. If notice can only be given on an anniversary or by a particular method, it is important to comply with the requirements, or risk losing the opportunity.

9.3.5 Termination for breach where there are no express terms

Regardless of any express right to terminate, a party may be entitled to terminate under the general law (or common law) as a result of a counterparty's breach. Not just any breach will give rise to a right to terminate. In summary, it must

---

1   [2003] TCLR 1.
2   [2010] EWHC 1193 (Ch).
3   [2017] EWHC 350 (Ch).
4   [2013] EWCA Civ 200.

be a breach of a particular type of term (known as a condition), or it must be a sufficiently serious breach of some other term or the counterparty must have made it clear that it is unwilling or unable to perform the contract in some essential respect. In addition there will be a right of termination if the counterparty's conduct has made performance impossible.

Breach of a condition

A term will be a condition of the contract if:

- The parties have agreed in the contract that it will be a condition eg by stipulating expressly that 'time is of the essence' of the particular obligation.
- The term is so important that any breach of it will deprive the innocent party of substantially the whole benefit of the contract; or
- It is designated as such by statute eg under the Sale of Goods Act 1979.

These principles are not straightforward to apply and can therefore readily lead to disputes. Referring to a term as a 'condition' will not necessarily make it so, for example – as the word has a number of different meanings. It is a matter of interpretation in each case.

Breach of an intermediate term

Breach of a condition allows a party to terminate. Breach of a warranty only entitles a party to damages for the breach. There is however a third type of term, an intermediate term. Whether the innocent party is entitled to terminate for breach of an intermediate term will depend on the consequences of the breach – so whether the breach goes to the root of the contract or deprives the innocent party of substantially the whole benefit of the contract.

It is difficult to be certain whether the test is met in any given case so the scope for disputes is clear.

Continued failure to pay on time under a time charter of a ship was considered sufficient by the Court of Appeal in *Grand China Logistics v Spar Shipping AS*.[1] In contrast in *Valilas v Januzaj*[2] the Court of Appeal held that the deliberate withholding of payments under a contract in circumstances where the counterparty could expect to receive payment eventually was not sufficient.

9.3.6   The risks of terminating where no good cause – repudiation

Terminating a contract for breach is not without its risks.

---

1   [2016] EWCA Civ 982.
2   [2014] EWCA Civ 436.

If the court decides that the party was not entitled to terminate then it will itself be in repudiatory breach of contract and liable to pay damages to the other party. The basic rule in a breach of contract claim is that the innocent party is entitled to be put into the position it would have been if the contract had been performed. This is subject to the express provisions in the contract and the duty to mitigate.

The party may not have been entitled to terminate for a range of reasons. For example the court may decide the contract has not been frustrated or a breach of contract was not so serious so as to permit termination. Alternatively, a party may have lost the right to terminate because it has affirmed the contract or is estopped from relying on the breach. There are detailed rules and cases explaining each of the circumstances in which a right to terminate has been lost, but in general terms these all involve continuing to perform the contract once the right to terminate has arisen.

9.3.7 Negotiated deal?

It will always be very fact dependant, but consideration should be given at the outset to whether the best option is to seek to negotiate a new contract which ameliorates the worst effects of the changed position or to negotiate an exit – at a price – from the contract.

9.3.8 New contracts – consider whether to 'Brexit proof'

When entering into new contracts, businesses should consider whether to provide expressly for a right to terminate the agreement when the UK leaves the EU. If the contract becomes less profitable, or it no longer fits in with the core business, it will then be possible to exit the contract relatively easily. It might also be possible to agree to amend existing contracts to provide similar rights.

Depending on the negotiating strength of the parties, this is likely only to be achievable on a mutual basis, so will not be appropriate where a business does not want the other party to have a similar right.

9.4 CHECKLIST FOR BUSINESSES

Every business is of course different and there are considerable uncertainties over what the UK's exit from the EU will entail. Drawing the threads above together, however, sensible steps to take now include:

9.4.1 New contracts

- Consider whether to Brexit proof – for example include an express right to amend or terminate post Brexit
- Consider whether a termination for convenience clause is desirable and, if so, achievable
- Consider the length of the contract and whether to include break clauses

- Choose an appropriate dispute resolution clause – it is not just boiler plate
- Be careful how you define territories
- Be careful with references to EU legislation – may lead to uncertainty when that legislation is replaced, so make your intentions clear
- Consider possible impact of currency fluctuation in pricing the contract
- Consider possible impact of changes in the tariff regime on goods
- Consider possible impact of changes in Intellectual Property Law
- Consider possible impact of changes in tax law

9.4.2   Existing contracts

- Review for possible uncertainties post Brexit – territories, references to EU legislation for example
- Review termination provisions available to you and other parties
- Make sure you have the right to terminate before pressing the trigger – wrongful termination will mean you are in breach of contract
- Consider approaching counterparties with a view to amendment/ clarification before a possible dispute arises

CHAPTER 10

IP AND DATA PROTECTION

Jane Lambert, 4–5 Gray's Inn Square[1]

INTRODUCTION

It is important to start this discussion by defining the terminology because *intellectual property* is often used interchangeably with the term *intellectual assets* which can lead to confusion. Similarly, *data protection* is often confused with *privacy* which is a much broader concept.

10.1 INTELLECTUAL PROPERTY

Intellectual property (usually abbreviated to 'IP') is the shorthand term for the bundle of rights that protect investment in *intellectual assets*. Examples of those rights include copyrights, patents and trade marks. The objects of their protection, examples of which include novels, inventions and brand names, are intellectual assets. They are creations of the mind that give (or are at least intended to give) a business a competitive edge over others. They are just as much assets of a business as a factory, machinery or bank deposits. They are called 'intellectual' because they are generated by mental as opposed to physical labour.

10.2 DATA PROTECTION

Data protection refers to the legislation that regulates the collection and use of *personal data*. At present the relevant legislation in the UK is the Data Protection 1998[2] and the secondary legislation made under its provisions. Section 1(1) of the Act defines 'personal data' as:

'data which relate to a living individual who can be identified—

(a) from those data, or

(b) from those data and other information which is in the possession of, or is likely to come into the possession of, the data controller,

and includes any expression of opinion about the individual and any indication of the intentions of the data controller or any other person in respect of the individual.'

There is a rather complex definition of *data* but the definition covers information processed by computer or manually using card index systems. Those holding

---

1   Barrister, 4-5 Gray's Inn Square, London WC1R 5AH, jane.lambert@niclaw.com, http://nipclaw.blogspot.com, Tel +44 (-0)20 7404 5252
2   1998 c. 29, http://www.legislation.gov.uk/ukpga/1998/29/contents

personal data ('data controllers') have a duty to collect it, process it and hold it in accordance with a number of statutory principles known as 'the data protection principles' which are set out in Part I of Sch 1.[1] They must also notify an official known as 'the Information Commissioner'[2] of the type of data they hold and how they use it.[3] The Commissioner enters such notifications into a register of notifications[4] which may be inspected by the public. It is an offence to process personal data without notifying the Commissioner. Individuals who believe they may be the subject of data processing ('data subjects') can ask data controllers whether they are data subjects and, if they are, for particulars of the data held on them.[5] Data controllers who fail to comply with such requests can be sued by the data subjects for breach of statutory duty. They can also be sued for any damage caused by their failure to comply with the data protection principles.

10.3 IP POLICY

Ever since the Statute of Monopolies 1623[6] Parliament and the courts have tried to strike a balance between three conflicting public interests:

- abolishing monopolies and restraints of trade except where they serve another public interest;
- incentivizing innovation, creativity and the efficient distribution of goods and services; and
- encouraging competition in the market.

Legislators and judges have pursued that task in different ways in respect of different intellectual assets but, in general, IP rights ('IPR') are granted upon stringent conditions. IPR can be revoked or invalidated if it is found that the conditions were not, or have ceased to be, complied with. Most IPR are granted for a fixed term. They are subject to licences and exceptions. In some circumstances, threatening to enforce IPR can be actionable if such threats prove to be groundless.[7]

An IPR confers the following benefits on the owner of the right. First, the IPR enables the owner to restrict the supply of competing products or services. By so doing it affords an opportunity for the owner to establish him or herself in the market and thereby recoup his or her investment in the intellectual asset and possibly even make a profit. Secondly, the restriction of competition and the opportunity to recoup investment and make a profit encourages investment in the intellectual asset or the business that possesses the asset. Thirdly, it provides

---

1   Data Protection 1998, s 4(1).
2   Data Protection 1998, s .6(1).
3   Data Protection 1998, s 16(1).
4   Data Protection 1998, s 19(1).
5   Data Protection 1998, s 7(1).
6   21 Jac. 1, c. 3, http://www.ipmall.info/sites/default/files/hosted_resources/lipa/patents/English_Statute1623.pdf
7   For example, Patents Act 1977, s 70. There are similar provisions in the Registered Designs Act 1949, the Copyright, Designs and Patents Act 1988, the Trade Marks Act 1994 and several statutory instruments.

an opportunity to earn royalties or licence fees from those who wish to make or use the intellectual asset.

10.4 HOW IP LAWS WORK

Some laws, such as copyright and unregistered design right, grant a right to prevent others from doing certain acts such as copying a copyright work or making an article to an original design. However, copyright does not prevent the creation of a similar or even identical work, and design right does not prevent the making of a similar article, so long as there is no copying of, or reference to, the copyright work or original design. Thus, two photographers standing side by side at the same time may take pictures of the same scene. Their pictures may be identical but neither is a copy of the other and neither photographer infringes the copyright of the other. On the other hand, if a third party obtains the negative or – more likely nowadays – the jpeg file of one of the photographers, manipulates it and reproduces the manipulated image without the photographer's permission, that third party will have infringed the photographer's copyright even though the end result may look quite different from the original. That is because there will have been copying without the copyright owner's licence. By contrast, patents grant monopolies of new inventions which may be infringed by making or selling products that fall within any of the claims[1] of the patent even if there has been no copying or indeed even if the person making the infringing product had been unaware of the existence of the patent.

As a general rule, IPR that confer monopolies are obtained upon registration with a national or regional intellectual property office such as the Intellectual Property Office ('IPO') at Newport[2] which registers patents, designs and trade marks for the UK. IPR that confer the right to prevent others from doing certain

---

1   Numbered paragraphs at the end of a patent specification that set out the scope of the invention. Patents Act 1977, s 14(2) provides:
'Every application for a patent shall contain –
(a) a request for the grant of a patent;
(b) a specification containing a description of the invention, a claim or claims and any drawing referred to in the description or any claim; and
(c) an abstract;
..............'
Patents Act 1977, s 14(5) provides:
'The claim or claims shall –
(a) define the matter for which the applicant seeks protection;
(b) be clear and concise;
(c) be supported by the description; and
(d) relate to one invention or to a group of inventions which are so linked as to form a single inventive concept.'
Patents Act 1977, s 125(1) further provides:
'For the purposes of this Act an invention for a patent for which an application has been made or for which a patent has been granted shall, unless the context otherwise requires, be taken to be that specified in a claim of the specification of the application or patent, as the case may be, as interpreted by the description and any drawings contained in that specification, and the extent of the protection conferred by a patent or application for a patent shall be determined accordingly.'
2   https://www.gov.uk/government/organisations/intellectual-property-office

acts, such as copyright, unregistered design right and rights in performances, come into being automatically when specified conditions are met. Most IPR are statutory but the action for passing off[1] and the obligation of confidence[2] have been developed over the years by the judges.

IPR are enforced primarily by actions for injunctions[3] and damages[4] brought by the owners of those rights in the civil courts. However, some IPR infringements such as counterfeiting[5] and piracy[6] are also criminal offences which are punishable by fines or imprisonment. In some countries, customs officials will look out for goods that are believed to infringe an IPR at a border, port or airport and impound them until a court has an opportunity to decide what should be done with them.

10.5 IP LAW IN THE UK BEFORE 1973

As the first country to industrialise, the UK developed a comprehensive system of IP laws early in its history. Although ostensibly an Act to abolish monopolies, the Statute of Monopolies 1623 laid the foundations of modern patent law. Section 6 provided that the provisions abolishing monopolies

> 'shall not extend to any letters patents (b) and grants of privilege for the term of fourteen years or under, hereafter to be made, of the sole working or making of any manner of new manufactures within this realm (c) to the true and first inventor (d) and inventors of such manufactures, which others at the time of making such letters patents and grants shall not use (e), so as also they be not contrary to the law nor mischievous to the state by raising prices of commodities at home, or hurt of trade, or generally inconvenient (f): the same fourteen years to be accounted from the date of the first letters patents or grant of such privilege hereafter to be made, but that the same shall be of such force as they should be if this act had never been made, and of none other (g).'

Similarly, the Statute of Anne 1710[7] established modern copyright law. An office for the registration of patents which is now known as the Intellectual Property Office was opened in 1852. It began to register trade marks under the Trade Marks Registration Act 1875 and designs under The Patents, Trade Marks and Designs Act 1883. Over the same period, the courts developed the law of confidence and the action for passing off. Immediately before the UK joined

---

1   The right of a trader with a reputation or goodwill in relation to a trade name, logo, get-up or some other indicia to prevent another trader from filching his or her customers by using the same or similar sign or indicia.
2   The duty of a person who receives information that is secret or not generally known in confidence neither to use that information otherwise than the purpose for which it was entrusted nor to disclose that information to a third party.
3   Orders by a judge to do or refrain from doing something disobedience to which can be punished by fine or imprisonment.
4   Compensation for injury, loss or damage caused by wrongdoing.
5   Trade mark infringement on an industrial scale
6   Copyright infringement on an industrial scale
7   8 Anne, c. 19 (http://avalon.law.yale.edu/18th_century/anne_1710.asp)

the European Communities patent law was codified by the Patents Act 1949,[1] trade marks law by the Trade Marks Act 1938,[2] registered designs law by the Registered Designs Act 1949[3] and copyright law by the Copyright Act 1956.[4] The UK was party to a number of international agreements on IP including the Paris,[5] Berne,[6] the Universal Copyright[7] and Rome Conventions.[8] Those treaties imposed requirements on contracting parties which Parliament took into account when legislating and, occasionally, the courts when interpreting a provision that was intended to give effect to a treaty but they formed no part of the law of any the jurisdictions of the UK.

10.6 ACCESSION TO THE EUROPEAN TREATIES

On 1 January 1973 the United Kingdom acceded to the treaties establishing the European Economic Community ('EEC'), the European Coal and Steel Community and the European Atomic Energy Community. The Treaty of Rome[9] which established the EEC[10] set out the EEC's task in art 2:

'The Community shall have as its task, by establishing a common market and progressively approximating the economic policies of Member States, to promote throughout the Community a harmonious development of economic activities, a continuous and balanced expansion, an increase in stability, an accelerated raising of the standard of living and closer relations between the States belonging to it.'

Article 3 included within those economic activities:

'the elimination, as between Member States, of customs duties and of quantitative restrictions on the import and export of goods, and of all other measures having equivalent effect;'[11]

....

'the abolition, as between Member States, of obstacles to freedom of movement for persons, services and capital;'[12] and

...

---

1   12, 13 & 14 GEO. 6 CH. 87 (http://www.legislation.gov.uk/ukpga/1949/87/pdfs/ ukpga_19490087_en.pdf)
2   1 & 2 GEO. 6. CH. 22.(http://www.legislation.gov.uk/ukpga/1938/22/pdfs/ukpga_19380022_ en.pdf)
3   12 13 and 14 Geo 6 (http://www.legislation.gov.uk/ukpga/Geo6/12-13-14/88/contents)
4   4- 5 Eliz 2 Ch 74 http://www.legislation.gov.uk/ukpga/1956/74/pdfs/ukpga_19560074_en.pdf
5   Paris Convention for the Protection of Industrial Property http://www.wipo.int/wipolex/en/ treaties/text.jsp?file_id=288514
6   The Berne Convention for the Protection of Literary and Artistic Works http://www.wipo.int/ wipolex/en/treaties/text.jsp?file_id=283698
7   http://www.wipo.int/wipolex/en/other_treaties/text.jsp?file_id=172836
8   Convention for the Protection of Performers, Producers of Phonograms and Broadcasting Organizations. http://www.wipo.int/wipolex/en/treaties/text.jsp?file_id=289757
9   http://www.gleichstellung.uni-freiburg.de/dokumente/treaty-of-rome
10   Art 1
11   Art 3 (a)
12   Art 3 (c)

the institution of a system ensuring that competition in the common market is not distorted.'[1]

The EEC's objectives were to be achieved by 'the approximation of the laws of member states to the extent required for the proper functioning of the common market'.[2] Member states also agreed to establish a common commercial policy with third countries.[3]

The Treaty created new institutions to carry out its tasks, namely the Council consisting of representatives of the governments of the member states, a civil service known as the Commission and a Court of Justice. Both the Council and Commission had power to legislate. Legislation could take the form either of a *directive* requiring member states to bring their laws into line with its provisions by a specified date or a *regulation* which became law in each and every member state automatically.

The Treaty of Rome together with the treaties establishing the other Communities and all other laws made under those treaties were incorporated into the laws of England and Wales, Scotland and Northern Ireland by the European Communities Act 1972.[4] In each member state, including the United Kingdom, Community law prevailed over national law.[5] The Court of Justice was the final authority on all issues relating to Community law and its decisions bound all national courts.

10.7 CHANGES TO IP LAW SINCE 1973

It will be no surprise that there have been considerable changes to the IP laws of the UK since 1973 though some of those changes would have occurred even if the country had never joined the EU.

The changes that have arisen directly from membership of the EU are as follow. First, an IPR granted under national law could not be relied upon if conflicted with a treaty objective such as the free movement of goods or European competition policy. In *Case 15-74, Centrafarm BV et Adriaan de Peijper v Sterling Drug Inc*[6] a Dutch patentee was not allowed to rely on its patent to prevent the importation into the Netherlands of a product that it had sold at a lower price in another member state. In *C-241/91 P and C-242/91 P Radio Telefís Eireann (RTE); and*

---

1 Art 3 (f)
2 Art 3 (h)
3 Art 3 (b)
4 1972 c. 68 http://www.legislation.gov.uk/ukpga/1972/68/contents
5 Case 6/64. *Flaminio Costa v ENEL* http://eur-lex.europa.eu/legal-content/EN/TXT/HTML/? uri=CELEX:61964CJ0006&from=EN
6 ECLI:EU:C:1974:114, [1974] EUECJ R-15/74, EU:C:1974:114 ECLI:EU:C:1974:114, [1974] EUECJ R-15/74, EU:C:1974:114, http://www.bailii.org/eu/cases/EUECJ/1974/ R1574.html

Independent Television Publications Ltd[1] the national broadcasters of the Republic of Ireland and the United Kingdom were not allowed to exercise their copyrights in programming schedules to prevent the publication of an independent TV guide on the ground that such exercise would amount to an abuse of a dominant position.[2] Secondly, the Council has used its power to approximate the laws of member states to adopt directives on trade marks, registered designs, copyright and related rights and, to a lesser extent, patents and trade secrets which required far reaching changes to the existing legislation. Thus, Parliament had to repeal the Trade Marks Act 1938 Act and replace it with a new Trade Marks Act 1994[3] to give effect to the First Trade Mark Directive.[4] The Design Directive[5] was implemented by a statutory instrument[6] that made substantial amendments to the Registered Designs Act 1949. Although the Copyright Designs and Patents Act 1988[7] did not implement Community legislation, it was amended substantially to give effect to directives on the protection of computer programs,[8] copyright

---

1   [1995] 4 CMLR 718, [1995] EUECJ C-241/91P, [1995] ECR I-743, [1995] FSR 530, [1995] EMLR 337, [1995] All ER (EC) 416, [1998] Masons CLR Rep http://www.bailii.org/eu/cases/EUECJ/1995/C24191.html

2   The prohibition of abuses of a dominant positon are now contained in art 102 of the Treaty on the Functioning of the European Union ('TFEU'):
'Any abuse by one or more undertakings of a dominant position within the internal market or in a substantial part of it shall be prohibited as incompatible with the internal market in so far as it may affect trade between Member States.
Such abuse may, in particular, consist in:
(a) directly or indirectly imposing unfair purchase or selling prices or other unfair trading conditions;
(b) limiting production, markets or technical development to the prejudice of consumers;
(c) applying dissimilar conditions to equivalent transactions with other trading parties, thereby placing them at a competitive disadvantage;
(d) making the conclusion of contracts subject to acceptance by the other parties of supplementary obligations which, by their nature or according to commercial usage, have no connection with the subject of such contracts.' http://eur-lex.europa.eu/legal-content/EN/ALL/?uri=CELEX:12008E102

3   An unofficial consolidated version of the Trade Mark Act 1994 as amended appears at https://www.gov.uk/government/uploads/system/uploads/attachment_data/file/476173/Unofficial_consolidated_version_Trade_Marks_Act_1994_as_amended.pdf

4   First Council Directive 89/104/EEC of 21 December 1988 to approximate the laws of the Member States relating to trade marks OJ L 040 , 11/02/1989 P. 1 – 7 http://eur-lex.europa.eu/LexUriServ/LexUriServ.do?uri=CELEX:31989L0104:en:HTML

5   Directive 98/71/EC of the European Parliament and of the Council of 13 October 1998 on the legal protection of designs OJ L 289 28/10/1998 P. 28 – 35 https://euipo.europa.eu/tunnel-web/secure/webdav/guest/document_library/contentPdfs/law_and_practice/cdr_legal_basis/EUR-Lex%20-%2031998L0071_en.htm.

6   The Registered Designs Regulations 2001 S! 2001 No 3949 http://www.legislation.gov.uk/uksi/2001/3949/introduction/made An unofficial consolidated version of the Registered Designs Act 1949 as amended appears at https://www.gov.uk/government/uploads/system/uploads/attachment_data/file/498821/Registered_Designs_Act_1949.pdf

7   An unofficial consolidated version of Parts I and II of Copyright, Designs and Patents Act 1988 as amended appears at https://www.gov.uk/government/uploads/system/uploads/attachment_data/file/462194/Copyright_Designs_and_Patents_Act_1988.pdf and an unofficial consolidation of Part III at https://www.gov.uk/government/uploads/system/uploads/attachment_data/file/406766/Copyright_Designs_and_Patents_Act_1988.pdf

8   Council Directive 91/250/EEC of 14 May 1991 on the legal protection of computer programs OJ L 122 , 17/05/1991 P. 42 – 46, http://eur-lex.europa.eu/LexUriServ/LexUriServ.do?uri=CELEX:31991L0250:EN:HTML

duration[1], protection of databases;[2] conditional access,[3] the information society,[4] resale rights[5] and orphan works.[6] Thirdly, the Council adopted regulations that establish an EU Intellectual Property Office in Alicante to grant EU trade marks[7] and Community designs[8] and which apply throughout the EU including the UK. Similarly, the Council has adopted the Community plant varieties regulation[9] which establishes the Community Plant Varieties Office in Angers to grant Community plant variety rights.

Fourthly, the Council has enacted legislation to implement member states' obligations under multilateral IP treaties pursuant to the mandate to establish a common commercial policy with third countries. Examples include the semiconductor topography directive[10] and the regulation on quality schemes for agricultural products and foodstuffs.[11] Fifthly, the court's case law has moulded the development of national as well as EU law. Thus, IPO hearing officers routinely apply rules developed by the Court of Justice when determining whether an application for a trade mark conflicts with an earlier mark and the courts of England and Wales refer to the same rules when determining whether a mark has been infringed.

Changes that would have occurred anyway include the Patents Act 1977 and amendments to the IP statutes to comply with TRIPS (the Agreement on Trade-

1   Directive 2006/116/EC of the European Parliament and of the Council of 12 December 2006 on the term of protection of copyright and certain related rights (codified version)
2   Directive 96/9/EC of the European Parliament and of the Council of 11 March 1996 on the legal protection of databases http://eur-lex.europa.eu/legal-content/EN/TXT/?uri=CELEX%3A31996L0009
3   Directive 98/84/EC of the European Parliament and of The Council of 20 November 1998 on the legal protection of services based on, or consisting of, conditional access (http://eur-lex.europa.eu/LexUriServ/LexUriServ.do?uri=CELEX:31998L0084:EN:HTML)
4   Directive 2001/29/EC of the European Parliament and of the Council of 22 May 2001 on the harmonisation of certain aspects of copyright and related rights in the information society OJ L 167 , 22/06/2001 P. 10 – 19 http://eur-lex.europa.eu/LexUriServ/LexUriServ.do?uri=CELEX:32001L0029:EN:HTML
5   Directive 2001/84/EC of the European Parliament and of the Council of 27 September 2001 on the resale right for the benefit of the author of an original work of art OJ L 272 , 13/10/2001 P. 32-36 http://eur-lex.europa.eu/LexUriServ/LexUriServ.do?uri=CELEX:32001L0084:EN:HTML
6   Directive 2012/28/EU of the European Parliament and of the Council of 25 October 2012 on certain permitted uses of orphan works Text with EEA relevance OJ L 299, 27.10.2012, p. 5–12 http://eur-lex.europa.eu/legal-content/EN/TXT/?uri=CELEX%3A32012L0028
7   Council Regulation (EC) No 207/2009 of 26 February 2009 on the European Union trade mark (http://eur-lex.europa.eu/legal-content/EN/TXT/?qid=1461325727753&uri=CELEX:02009R0207-20160323)
8   Council Regulation (EC) No 6/2002 of 12 December 2001 on Community designs (OJ EC No L 3 of 5.1.2002, p. 1) https://euipo.europa.eu/tunnel-web/secure/webdav/guest/document_library/contentPdfs/law_and_practice/cdr_legal_basis/62002_cv_en.pdf
9   Council Regulation (EC) No 2100/94 of 27 July 1994 on Community plant variety rights (OJ L 227 of 01.09.94 p.1).
10   Council Directive 87/54/EEC of 16 December 1986 on the legal protection of topographies of semiconductor products http://eur-lex.europa.eu/legal-content/EN/TXT/?uri=CELEX%3A31987L0054
11   Regulation (EU) No. 1151/2012 of the European Parliament and of the Council of 21 November 2012 on quality schemes for agricultural products and foodstuffs http://www.wipo.int/wipolex/en/text.jsp?file_id=309789

Related Aspects of Intellectual Property Rights).[1] A new Patents Act would have been required to implement the Patent Co-operation Treaty ('PCT')[2] which facilitates multiple patent applications and to allow the UK to accede to the European Patent Convention ('EPC').[3] Neither of those international agreements are EU treaties even though all EU Member States are party to them. The reason why it was necessary to comply with TRIPS is that the agreement is annexed to the Agreement to establish the World Trade Organization ('WTO') which the UK would almost certainly have wished to join as the WTO facilitates access to the world's largest and richest markets.

10.8 THE DATA PROTECTION DIRECTIVE

Parliament passed the Data Protection Act 1998 in order to implement the Data Protection Directive[4] but it ls important to note that the UK would almost certainly have enacted some sort of data protection legislation even if it had never joined the EU. It would have needed such legislation to comply with the Council of Europe Convention for the Protection of Individuals with regard to Automatic Processing of Personal Data[5] and the OECD Guidelines on the Protection of Privacy and Transborder Flows of Personal Data.[6] Such compliance would have enabled the UK to continue to exchange personal data with countries like Sweden and Germany which enacted data protection legislation before the rest of the world. Moreover, there had been calls within the UK for the regulation of the processing of personal data by the Younger Committee on Privacy as long ago as 1972[7] and for legislation to regulate such processing in 1978.[8]

10.9 ARTICLE 50 OF THE TREATY ON EUROPEAN UNION

The procedure for leaving the EU is set out in art 50 of the Treaty on European Union:

'1. Any Member State may decide to withdraw from the Union in accordance with its own constitutional requirements.

2. A Member State which decides to withdraw shall notify the European Council of its intention. In the light of the guidelines provided by the European Council, the Union shall negotiate and conclude an agreement with that State, setting out the arrangements for its withdrawal, taking

---

1   https://www.wto.org/english/docs_e/legal_e/27-trips_01_e.htm
2   http://www.wipo.int/wipolex/en/treaties/text.jsp?file_id=288637
3   http://www.epo.org/law-practice/legal-texts/html/epc/2016/e/index.html
4   Directive 95/46/EC of the European Parliament and of the Council of 24 October 1995 on the protection of individuals with regard to the processing of personal data and on the free movement of such data OJ L 281 , 23/11/1995 P. 31 – 50, http://eur-lex.europa.eu/ LexUriServ/LexUriServ.do?uri=CELEX:31995L0046:en:HTML
5   https://www.coe.int/en/web/conventions/full-list/-/conventions/rms/0900001680078b37
6   https://www.oecd.org/sti/ieconomy/oecdguidelinesontheprotectionofprivacyandtransborder flowsofpersonaldata.htm
7   Report of the Committee on Privacy (Cmnd 5012)
8   Lindop report of the Committee on Data Protection (Cmnd 7341)

account of the framework for its future relationship with the Union. That agreement shall be negotiated in accordance with Article 218 (3) of the Treaty on the Functioning of the European Union. It shall be concluded on behalf of the Union by the Council, acting by a qualified majority, after obtaining the consent of the European Parliament.

3.   The Treaties shall cease to apply to the State in question from the date of entry into force of the withdrawal agreement or, failing that, two years after the notification referred to in paragraph 2, unless the European Council, in agreement with the Member State concerned, unanimously decides to extend this period.

4.   For the purposes of paragraphs 2 and 3, the member of the European Council or of the Council representing the withdrawing Member State shall not participate in the discussions of the European Council or Council or in decisions concerning it.

A qualified majority shall be defined in accordance with Article 238(3)(b) of the Treaty on the Functioning of the European Union.'[1]

The Prime Minister has now given the President of the Council notice of HM Government's intention to leave the European Union pursuant to Article 50 of the Lisbon Treaty. It is impossible at the time of writing to forecast how smoothly the withdrawal negotiations will run, whether agreement will be reached and, if it is, whether the withdrawal agreement will be ratified on time by the legislatures of all the member states including that of the United Kingdom. There is at least a possibility that no agreement will be reached and that the EU treaties will cease to apply to the UK from the second anniversary of notification at the end of March 2019.

10.10 CONSEQUENCES OF WITHDRAWAL

Since all the directives and regulations that have ever been adopted were founded on the EU treaties it follows that that enormous body of legislation will simply fall away with those treaties. That should not affect legislation that implements directives such as the Trade Marks Act 1994 or the amended Registered Designs Act 1949 since the implementing statutes and statutory instruments are UK enactments, but the lapse of the treaties will affect EU regulations. The Prime Minister has proposed a Great Reform Bill that will adopt all EU regulations and transpose them into national law from the date of withdrawal. That should ensure some continuity in the UK but it is important to note that such transposition will have no effect outside the UK. [2]

---

1   http://eur-lex.europa.eu/legal-content/EN/TXT/HTML/?uri=CELEX:12012M/ TXT&from=EN

2   See' *Theresa May's 'great repeal bill': what's going to happen and when?'* 2 October 2016   (https://www.theguardian.com/politics/2016/oct/02/theresa-may-great-repeal-bill-eu-british-law).

There are four regulations of particular importance to businesses in this country:

- the Recast Brussels regulation;[1]
- the EU trade mark regulation;[2]
- the Community design regulation;[3] and
- the General Data Protection Regulation ('GDPR').[4]

The importance of the Recast Brussels regulation was summarised by the Bar Council's Brexit working party in paragraph 4 of its Paper on Jurisdiction and Enforcement of Judgments:

'4.1. Judgments of the courts of EU Member States are to be enforced throughout the EU as if they were judgments of a court of the Member State in which enforcement is sought. This includes 'protective measures' such as injunctions freezing assets.

4.2. The courts of one Member State may apply 'protective measures' to assist with proceedings in another Member State.

4.3. Subject to a number of notable exceptions, persons domiciled in an EU Member State should be sued in that Member State and where this is not what has happened courts are required to decline jurisdiction.

4.4. Where the parties have specified in their contract that disputes should be heard in a particular jurisdiction (an exclusive jurisdiction clause), the courts of other Member States are required to abide by the terms of that jurisdiction clause and to decline jurisdiction.

4.5. Where a person is one of a number of Defendants, he may be joined to proceedings which are commenced in another Member State where he is not domiciled if those proceedings are 'so closely connected that it is expedient to hear and determine them together to avoid the risk of irreconcilable judgments'.

4.6. Where proceedings have already been commenced in one Member State, the courts of other Member States are required to stay any subsequent proceedings dealing with the same subject matter until jurisdiction has been decided by the court first seized of the matter (the *lis alibi pedens* principle).

4.7. Clarifies the scope of the exclusion of arbitral proceedings from the jurisdiction rules.'

---

1   Regulation (EU) No 1215/2012 of the European Parliament and of the Council of 12 December 2012 on jurisdiction and the recognition and enforcement of judgments in civil and commercial matters (http://eur-lex.europa.eu/legal-content/EN/TXT/HTML/?uri=CEL EX:32012R1215&from=EN)

2   Council Regulation (EC) No 207/2009 of 26 February 2009 on the European Union trade mark (http://eur-lex.europa.eu/legal-content/EN/TXT/?qid=1461325727753&uri=CELEX: 02009R0207-20160323)

3   Council Regulation (EC) No 6/2002 of 12 December 2001 on Community designs (OJ EC No L 3 of 5.1.2002, p. 1) https://euipo.europa.eu/tunnel-web/secure/webdav/guest/document_library/contentPdfs/law_and_practice/cdr_legal_basis/62002_cv_en.pdf

4   Regulation (EU) 2016/679 of the European Parliament and of the Council of 27 April 2016 on the protection of natural persons with regard to the processing of personal data and on the free movement of such data, and repealing Directive 95/46/EC (http://ec.europa.eu/justice/data-protection/reform/files/regulation_oj_en.pdf)

The working party warns that unless HM government makes special arrangements with the remaining states of the EU, the enforcement of judgments of British courts (and the judgments of courts of the remaining member states in the UK) will become considerably less certain and proceedings for the enforcement of such judgments more expensive.

As mentioned briefly above, the EU trade mark regulation established the EU IPO[1] and provided for

'A trade mark for goods or services which is registered in accordance with the conditions contained in this Regulation and in the manner herein provided is hereinafter referred to as a 'European Union trade mark ('EU trade mark').' [2]

The characteristics of such trade mark will be as follows:

'An EU trade mark shall have a unitary character. It shall have equal effect throughout the Union: it shall not be registered, transferred or surrendered or be the subject of a decision revoking the rights of the proprietor or declaring it invalid, nor shall its use be prohibited, save in respect of the whole Union. This principle shall apply unless otherwise provided in this Regulation.'[3]

Each member state is required by art 95(1) of the regulation to designate in their territories as limited a number as possible of national courts and tribunals of first and second instance EU trade mark courts to resolve infringement and other disputes relating to EU trade marks. Each of those courts has jurisdiction beyond its borders. The UK has designated the senior courts and county court of England and Wales, the Court of Session in Scotland and the Court of Judicature of Northern Ireland as EU trade mark courts. Except to the extent that its provisions may be transposed into a UK enactment by the proposed Great Repeal Bill, the EU trade mark regulation will cease to apply to the UK after Brexit. That should be enough to preserve the registrations of EU trade mark proprietors in the UK but it will not save the jurisdiction of the courts that have been designated as EU trade mark courts beyond the UK's shores. Nor will the EU trade mark courts of other countries enjoy any standing in the UK. After Brexit, businesses that wish to register their marks in both the UK and EU will have to file separate applications. If their marks are infringed in the UK and any of the remaining states of the EU they will have to bring two sets of proceedings.

The Community design regulation created two IPR:

- a right in a registered Community design whereby new designs having individual character can be registered with the EU IPO; and
- a right in an unregistered Community design whereby new designs having individual character can be protected automatically from copying for up to three years after first being made available to the public.[4]

---

1   Art 2
2   Art 1 (1)
3   Art 1 (2)
4   Art 1 (2)

Both registered and unregistered Community designs have unitary character with equal effect throughout the EU. As in the EU trade mark regulation, member states are required to designate Community design courts and the UK government has designated the superior courts of each of the jurisdictions of the UK for that purpose. The consequences of the disappearance of this regulation will be similar to the consequences that will result from the disappearance of the EU trade mark regulation that are discussed above. However, there is one big difference in that there is no equivalent to unregistered Community design in national law. Unregistered Community design is relied upon mainly by the fashion industry and its appeal lies in its unitary character and subsistence throughout the EU. Even if the right is preserved within the UK by the proposed Great Repeal Bill it will be a short term right that applies only in one country. Considering that it is necessary to prove both novelty and individual character as well as copying in any enforcement proceedings, the utility and value of this IPR is far from obvious.

The exchange of personal data between the UK and the rest of the EU is vital for the financial services industry. It is also essential for the creative, information and communications technology and information services industries of the United Kingdom to continue to do business in the digital single market. On 27 April 2016 the Council adopted the GDPR which will repeal the Data Protection Directive and introduce a new data protection regime that will apply throughout the EU from 25 May 2018. The GDPR will, of course, fall away with the treaties when the UK leaves the EU, but the Secretary of State for Culture Media and Sport has confirmed to the Parliamentary Committee on Culture Media and Sport that the government will implement it notwithstanding the UK's intended departure from the EU.[1] As the GDPR is a regulation and not a directive it will come into force automatically in the UK but the Secretary of State's remarks can be taken as an indication that she plans to prepare for the regulation and will preserve its provisions after the UK's departure from the EU. Writing in the *Information Commissioner's Office Blog* shortly after the announcement.[2] Elizabeth Denham, the recently appointed Information Commissioner greeted the Secretary of State's remarks as 'good news for the UK.'

One further consequence of British withdrawal from the EU is that the European Court of Justice will cease to have any jurisdiction in the UK. Consequently, it will no longer be possible for courts in the UK to refer issues concerning the interpretation of implementing legislation such as the Trade Marks Act 1994 to the court under art 267 of the TFEU. Although decisions of the Court of Justice and the superior courts of the remaining member states are likely to have persuasive authority after withdrawal, the IP laws of the UK are likely to diverge

---

1   Oral evidence: Responsibilities of the Secretary of State for Culture, Media and Sport, HC 764 Monday 24 October 2016, http://data.parliament.uk/writtenevidence/committeeevidence. svc/evidencedocument/culture-media-and-sport-committee/responsibilities-of-the-secretary-of-state-for-culture-media-and-sport/oral/42119.html

2   31 October 2016 https://iconewsblog.wordpress.com/2016/10/31/how-the-ico-will-be-supporting-the-implementation-of-the-gdpr/

from those of the rest of Europe,[1] especially after the EU directives and the UK statutes are repealed or amended.

10.11 THE UNITARY PATENT AND THE UNIFIED PATENT COURT

In November 2003 the Intellectual Property Advisory Committee published a paper entitled *The Enforcement of Patent Rights*.[2] In a table on p 50, the Committee compared the cost of patent infringement proceedings in the UK with the costs in France, Germany, the Netherlands and the USA. In the UK a patent action in the Patents County Court[3] could cost between £150,000 and £250,000 and an action in the Patents Court £1 million. By contrast, an infringement action in France could cost between €30,000 and €50,000, it Germany it could cost between €25,000 and €50,000 and in the Netherlands €10,000 for summary proceedings and €40,000 for a simple action. Only in the USA were costs comparable to those in England but in that country it is rare for costs to follow the event and lawyers are entitled to accept instructions on a contingency fee, that is to say the promise of a share of any damages that may be awarded. The high cost of enforcement in the UK is thought to be one of the reasons why the UK consistently trails not just countries of similar size such as France and Germany in the number of European patent applications but also the Netherlands with a third of the UK's population and Switzerland with one eighth despite having some of the world's finest research universities and until the recent slump in the value of sterling the 5th largest economy in the world. In recent years it has been overtaken by China and South Korea. The latest figures are as follows:

European Patent Applications 2015	
Country	Number
USA	65,754
Japan	50,597
Germany	31,670
China	31,504
South Korea	18,215
France	13,370
Netherlands	8,451
Switzerland	8,354
UK	7,095

Source: European Patent Office

---

1   The IP Bar Association considers there is only 'a real risk of jurisprudential divergence' (page 48 of the Brexit papers http://www.barcouncil.org.uk/media/508513/the_brexit_papers.pdf).
2   http://webarchive.nationalarchives.gov.uk/+/http:/www.hm-treasury.gov.uk/d/contra_vision_ltd_336_p4_163kb.pdf
3   The forerunner of the Intellectual Property Enterprise Court

One reason why costs appear to be higher in the UK and USA than in France, Germany or the Netherlands is that litigation under the adversarial system where the parties choose the issues and decide the evidence that they wish to present to the court requires considerably resources than litigation under the inquisitorial system where the issues and evidence to be heard are determined by the judge. As it is not politically feasible for the UK to abandon the adversarial system for the inquisitorial system simply to reduce the costs of patent litigation the UK has consistently supported efforts to establish a European patent court within the framework either of the EU or the EPO. [1]

In his report Digital Opportunity, A Review of Intellectual Property and Growth;[2] Professor Ian Hargreaves wrote, at para 3.24:

> 'This lack of a single unified patent system creates self evident problems for innovative firms attempting to operate in the European market compared with the unified markets of the US, India and China. It causes wasteful duplication in terms of litigation in each jurisdiction – projected private annual savings on duplicated litigation alone are estimated at between €120 million and €240 million. Furthermore, it increases the cost of cross border commerce. Removal of inter EU country barriers in IP could increase UK national income by over £2billion a year by 2020.'

In his recommendations he urged the government to 'attach the highest immediate priority to achieving a unified EU patent court and EU patent system, which promises significant economic benefits to UK business.'

It was not possible to establish such a court or patent in 2011 when the report was published because of objections from Italy and Spain. The remaining member states agreed to authorise the EPO to issue a patent for all their territories to be known as a 'unitary patent' and to establish a Unified Patent Court to determine disputes relating to unitary and other European patents. The Agreement on a Unified Patent Court[3] was signed on 19 February 2013 and is due to come into force four months after 13 member states including France, Germany and the UK ratify the instrument. So far, ten member states have ratified the agreement including France. Section 17 of the Intellectual Property Act 2014[4] enables the UK to ratify the agreement and the statutory instrument to give effect to such ratification was drafted shortly after that Act received Royal Assent.

---

1   The UK was one of the few countries to ratify the Community Patent Convention of 15 December 1975 and one of the reasons for the Patents Act 1977 was to enable the UK to ratify that Convention. The Convention would have established a Community patent but it would have been enforced by the national courts. Concern over the quality of the tribunals of some of the member states was one of the reasons why an insufficient number of countries ratified the Convention. See http://eur-lex.europa.eu/LexUriServ/LexUriServ.do?uri=OJ:L:1 976:017:0001:0028:EN:PDF

2   https://www.gov.uk/government/uploads/system/uploads/attachment_data/file/32563/ipreview-finalreport.pdf

3   https://www.unified-patent-court.org/sites/default/files/upc-agreement.pdf

4   2014 c 18 http://www.legislation.gov.uk/ukpga/2014/18

In a press release dated 28 Nov 2016;[1] Baroness Neville Rolfe, the Minister for Intellectual Property said:

'The new system will provide an option for businesses that need to protect their inventions across Europe. The UK has been working with partners in Europe to develop this option.

As the Prime Minister has said, for as long as we are members of the EU, the UK will continue to play a full and active role. We will seek the best deal possible as we negotiate a new agreement with the European Union. We want that deal to reflect the kind of mature, cooperative relationship that close friends and allies enjoy. We want it to involve free trade, in goods and services. We want it to give British companies the maximum freedom to trade with and operate in the Single Market – and let European businesses do the same in the UK.

But the decision to proceed with ratification should not be seen as pre-empting the UK's objectives or position in the forthcoming negotiations with the EU.'

The Minister's announcement is welcome as a unitary patent and a Unified Patent Court for the remaining member states is in British interests whether the UK participates in the project or not, but it should be treated with considerable caution since it seems likely that the UK would have to withdraw from the Agreement after it ceases to be a member of the EU. The Chartered Institute of Patent Attorneys and the Intellectual Property Lawyers Association have consulted Richard Gordon QC and Tom Pascoe on whether it will be possible for the UK to continue to participate in the project after Brexit. Counsel have advised that continued British participation after Brexit is not possible without an amendment to the agreement. As such amendment would require the UK to accept the jurisdiction of the Court of Justice in matters arising out of the agreement it is hard to see how such an agreement can be achieved, particularly in a two-year time frame.

10.12 CONCLUSION

In an interview on the Today programme on 26 December 2016, Lord King, the former governor of the Bank of England, remarked that leaving the EU would not be a bed of roses but neither would it be the end of the world.[2] That is probably as fair and as accurate a forecast of the next few years as can be given in present circumstances. There are many uncertainties at the time of writing as negotiations for a withdrawal agreement have yet to begin and the parties' negotiating objectives are unknown. Looking on the positive side the UK's geographic proximity to the rest of the EU including a land border with one of its members should ensure that trade, investment and further economic integration

---

1   'UK signals green light to Unified Patent Court Agreement' https://www.gov.uk/government/news/uk-signals-green-light-to-unified-patent-court-agreement
2   Rowena Mason *Mervyn King: Britain better off going for hard Brexit* 26 December 2016 The Guardian https://www.theguardian.com/business/2016/dec/26/mervyn-king-britain-should-be-more-upbeat-about-brexit

will continue at some level regardless of the referendum result. There is no call for the UK to leave other multilateral treaty organisations such as the European Patent Convention, the World Trade Organization or the Council of Europe all of which promote some degree of political and economic co-operation between members. However, it is impossible to ignore the negatives. The IP laws of the UK and its former partners are likely to diverge which will become in time a non-tariff barrier to trade. It is hard to see how the UK can continue to participate in such projects as the digital single market or the unitary patent and that, too, is likely to affect trade and investment. It is possible that the UK will do more trade outside Europe but its industries will have to become considerably more efficient and productive to do so.

CHAPTER 11

TECHNOLOGY

Steve Kuncewicz, Slater & Gordon

INTRODUCTION

The Technology, Media and Telecoms Sector, as well as the more broadly-defined 'creative industries', have for some time suggested (and often complained) that legal regulation simply can't keep pace with the evolution of technology and the habits of its users; it's worth bearing in mind that copyright law in particular has struggled to keep pace with the 'sharing' economy, and monopoly rights over the control of content have never been less popular.

That said, if the UK intends to remain a world leader in these sectors and a good location to either relocate or establish the next Netflix, Facebook or Uber, it will need to reassure that whatever form its legal system takes after the Article 50 process is complete is fit for purpose in a globalised market, where geographical boundaries are becoming increasingly meaningless. Whatever format we choose to adopt, it needs to be compatible with other national 'platforms' across the EU and the wider world.

11.1 ADVERTISING LAW

The majority of UK law governing marketing communications originates from the EU. Specifically, the Consumer Protection From Unfair Trading Regulations 2008[1] brought into UK law the provisions of the EU Unfair Commercial Practices Directive 2005/29[2] and the Business Protection From Misleading Advertising Regulations 2008[3] implemented EU Directive 2006/114/EC Concerning Misleading And Comparative Advertising;[4] amongst a litany of others have, alongside existing intellectual property, wider media and communications and consumer law, given rise to the 'patchwork' of legislation, codes of conduct, industry guidance and common law which governs the dissemination of 'marketing communications' in the UK. .

---

1   SI 2008/1277.
2   Directive 2005/29/EC of 11 May 2005 concerning unfair business-to-consumer commercial practices in the internal market and amending Directives 84/450/EEC, 97/7/EC, 98/27/EC and 2002/65/EC and Regulation (EC) No 2006/2004 (Unfair Commercial Practices Directive).
3   SI 2008/1276.
4   Directive 2006/114/EC concerning misleading and comparative advertising, codifying and repealing Directive 84/450/EEC

The key legal concepts which this patchwork introduced lead to the introduction of the UK's system of self-regulation designed to police the marketing and advertising industry, set out in the Code of Non-Broadcast Advertising, Sales Promotion and Direct Marketing ('the CAP Code'), created, revised and enforced by the Committee of Advertising Practice ('CAP') which in turn is endorsed and administered by the Advertising Standards Authority ('ASA').

Self-regulation derived from a statutory framework which it supplements, clarifies and makes more accessible has long been recognised as an effective alternative to direct statutory control, even in the EU Directives referred to above, and is recognised by the Government as a valuable 'first line of control in protecting consumers and the industry';[1] and specialist sectors within the marketing industry (such as the Direct Marketing Association) have also adopted their own specific codes of practice to plug perceived gaps and attempt to deal with a changing industry more effectively and quickly than any Government, let alone one dealing with the fallout of the Brexit Referendum, may be able to accomplish.

Compliance with the CAP Code is seen as 'going a long way to ensuring compliance with the law' to produce marketing communications which are, as is CAP and the ASA's (which endorses and administers the CAP code) primary objective, 'legal, decent, honest, and truthful.'

However, legislative gaps can also expose gaps in capability and the enforcement of any breach of advertising codes. Much as the Competition and Markets Authority ('CMA') sits behind the ASA and CAP and can (and increasingly does) in certain circumstances, threaten direct enforcement action including civil injunctions and criminal prosecutions for breach of the regulations referred to above, the ASA's existing regime allows it to request that a marketing communication be amended or withdrawn, to deny advertising space, to publish adjudications on complaints (which can be made without the payment of any fee, without any need for a baseline number of complaints – one is sometimes enough – and by competitors, other stakeholders such as the press and members of the public) and attendant publicity through the press and, in the online space, to remove sponsored links displayed by search engines to non-compliant material and introduction of banner ads to 'name and shame' repeat offenders. By and large, the current system works and it is unlikely that any change in underlying law would diminish the CAP Code's position in the eyes of those to whom it applies.

As is the case with many other beneficial legal concepts introduced and clarified by the EU, it may well be that the legal framework behind marketing in the UK will remain undisturbed by Brexit. Self-regulation has proved very successful, and the ASA has been viewed for many years as a valued partner to Government in ensuring, as its primary goal, that consumers are not misled by unfair commercial practices designed to distort their decision-making process when

---

1   Introduction, UK Code Of Non-Broadcast Advertising and Direct & Promotional Marketing, 12th Edition

looking to make a purchase, or by unfair comparisons with competitors which aren't made on a 'like for like' basis or which take advantage or (or denigrate) existing businesses or brands.

The fact remains that in this, as in many other areas of law due to be recast in the wake of the UK's departure from the EU, consumer protection is no bad thing and that retaining key concepts may not only be desirable but essential where UK businesses may be forced to live with equivalent protections and regulations if they want to continue to trade with the remaining members of the EU.

Harmonisation in the new world may not lead to exact 'like for like' protections, but will almost certainly lead to the introduction of very legal familiar systems even if more contentious and uncelebrated obligations are done away with.

Of course, this may bring with it the risk of a 'two-tier system' which is less stringent than any new equivalent, although without knowing what the new system will look like save for the desire of many UK legislators to loosen the EU's perceived restrictions on the operations of our businesses, it is currently impossible to predict (save in relation to Data Protection, a topic addressed elsewhere in this publication and consequentially below) what obligations the 'new' tier may impose. It may be considerable more liberal and creative, or may go the other way – either may lead to brands having to make their campaigns bespoke for the requirements of UK market and making it less attractive for global brands.

From the ASA's point of view, as per its article 'The potential impact of Brexit on advertising regulation';[1] until a new and different legal framework is introduced, their work as the arbiter of self-regulation is likely to continue without any real disruption in terms of standards (kept high by the requirements of the CAP Code) or available sanctions (observed by the vast majority of the industry without the need for regular intervention by the CMA, even where it is becoming more willing to take action in relation to marketing communications and seek assurances in relation to future conduct, notably in the online and social media environment). In its view, the CAP Code's principles will continue to reply in spite of Brexit, at the very least for the next few years whilst the UK is extricated from its membership of the EU.

The message from the ASA is, therefore, clear – it continues to act based upon its own standards and historical decisions and until the CAP Code changes, (the industry will be the first to know when this takes place) then it continues to apply and should be complied with. We're telling our clients to do so, especially in the online and social media environment, where the challenge of convergence and need, as per Rule 2 of the CAP Code, to clearly identify advertising content when disseminated through evolving platforms (whether by businesses, brands or celebrity ambassadors) will be of the utmost importance in a digital world of which the EU forms part.

---

1   https://www.cap.org.uk/News-reports/Media-Centre/2016/Insight-The-potential-impact-of-Brexit-on-advertising-regulation.aspx#.WJd67rGcZcA

11.2 INTELLECTUAL PROPERTY IN CONTENT AND BRANDING

Heading away from advertising and marketing, the importance of content, brands and their exploitation to the TMT and wider creative industries is and will remain hugely important to their continued success. This being the case, any change to copyright and trade mark law (especially in light of the recent introduction of the proposed EU 'Digital Single Market') may have far-reaching consequences for businesses which are part of one of the main pillars of the Prime Minister's 'modern industrial strategy', even where they could benefit for new 'sector deals' designed to support them and where 'Britain has the potential to lead the world'.[1]

The impact of Brexit upon IP rights is covered in further, more extensive detail, elsewhere in this publication. However, for the sake of this chapter it is enough to remind readers that IP rights do not protect an *idea*, but the expression of that idea through a set of rights including patents, design rights, trade marks and copyright, all of which are designed to confer a limited monopoly right upon their creators (or their employers, dependent upon whether or not a 'work' is created during the course of employment) as their owner for a set period of time. In short, IP rights largely guarantee that their owners are the only party who can exploit them, subject to some very narrow exceptions.

IP rights have arguably become as important to their owners as physical assets such as plant or machinery, and in the knowledge and brand economies with which this chapter deals, the ability to exploit and defend them with a sense of certainty across geographical boundaries raises its own challenges given that IP is largely 'territorial', with each legal system dealing with its subsistence and enforcement slightly differently. However, the introduction of international agreements such as the Berne Convention[2] have long given comfort to content owners as Berne in particular requires member countries (including the US and many others) to give the same protection to copyright 'works' as those of its own nationals, without much formality.

11.2.1 Copyright

However, and much more recently, the EU has sought to harmonise copyright law across the union. Copyright according to UK law is an unregistered intellectual property right, meaning that it does not require registration or examination to come into being or to exploit or protect it, and its protection begins on the date upon which an idea is 'fixated' or recorded in a permanent form, provided that it is sufficiently 'original' (a relatively low hurdle to overcome) and created by a 'qualifying person'. Effectively, provided that its creation involves skill,

---

1   https://www.marketingweek.com/2017/01/27/theresa-mays-industrial-strategy-major-step-forward/
2   The Berne Convention for The Protection of Literary and Artistic Works

judgement and independent effort, the issue of whether or not that creation involves artistic merit or new and inventive thought (protected, as that is, by patent law) then a 'work' is of value and can be protected by copyright.

UK copyright law has been modernised to take into account various EU directives (including in relation to the protection of software and database rights) over the course of the UK's membership of the EU, however there has for some time been a drive towards greater harmonisation across the union. This arose from the fact that, even within its own borders, copyright has long been treated very differently by its various member states. The concept of 'originality' in particular is far lower in UK law than it is in others, even though the importance of 'intellectual creation' to copyright subsistence and protections is widely recognised across the EU.

Post-Brexit, it is easy to see how UK copyright law would be relatively unaffected, save in relation to the effect that any derogation from the E-Commerce Regulations would have upon intermediary liability for copyright infringement (see below), although given the continuing rise of tech and content businesses, of which the UK is a key exporter, the need for those businesses to continue to trade and collaborate with other innovative EU-based tech platforms may force the government to meet the challenge which they create by comping up with a system of copyright protection arguably more fit for the digital age, and which is still largely compatible with its nearest neighbours.

It is worth noting, however, that recent EU legislation recently saw the introduction of the 'private copying exemption', finally allowing members of the public to copy musical and other works for their own personal use, notably CDs onto digital music players. That exemption was qualified by the need for rights holders (such as record companies and other content providers) to receive 'fair compensation', however when introduced into UK law that compensatory element was conspicuous in its absence from our own equivalent legislation, leading to a High Court challenge through judicial review by the music industry, and to the exemption being cancelled for the foreseeable future on the basis that the government had failed to demonstrate that no real 'harm' would done to the music industry by such permitted private copying. We are left, therefore, with an unenviable and yet unenforced legal position in that it remains technically unlawful to 'burn' a CD to an iPod.

Ultimately, overarching obligations under conventions such as Berne and the largely inward focus of previous UK legislation, largely untroubled by attempts to harmonise it may serve to deter any radical overhaul of UK copyright law for the foreseeable future. However, the developing EU Digital Single Market strategy may yet lead to further complications. Whilst its various proposals to remove barriers to online cross-border trade are still subject to intense debate and negotiation, including allowing EU consumers to access online content from portable devices across the Union when outside their member state, and so unlikely to force any real change in UK law before they are finally formalized, whatever form they finally take may lead to the creation of a 'two-tier' content ecosystem from which the UK may be effectively excluded.

Of course, content platforms will likely welcome increased portability of content across the EU given that it would do away with the need to negotiate licenses across various geographical restrictions. From the content owners' point of view, this may of course have a significant effect upon their commercial models and upon the way in which they deal with licensing arrangements.

In terms of what we are telling clients, keeping a close eye on the progress of the Digital Single Market is our best advice for the time being. As of February 2017, the final terms of the 'Portability Regulation' have largely been agreed, meaning that it is likely to become law in the UK prior to the Article 50 process being completed. Of course, it may not remain in force for long after that, although preparing for its immediate impact by planning for a pan-European approach (both technically and legally) to access to content and services in the short-term is the best policy. Failing that, UK copyright law is likely to remain stubbornly individual, if brought at least partly into line by the demands of technological change.

11.2.2 Trade marks

Whilst restraining the infringement of 'unregistered' trade marks and the misuse of their attendant goodwill within the UK is unlikely to be affected by Brexit as the concept itself was developed through decisions of the UK courts, UK law surrounding registered Trade Marks is based largely upon EU regulations. UK registered marks will remain unaffected, however EU registered marks may need to be re-registered in the UK wherever possible to ensure protection within our borders. This may well have an impact, at least in the short-term, upon any anti-counterfeiting strategies. However, the rules around intermediary liability and continuing operation of the E-Commerce Regulations (for the time being) alongside the deployment of 'blocking' injunctions against ISPs should help to maintain the 'take-down culture'.

However, re-registering each and every EU registered trade mark in the UK may yet be a bridge too far, and current uncertainty may well present an opportunity to review portfolios of registered marks in the EU and consider which registrations are truly indispensable to clients' ongoing business whilst the dust settles on the form of any new registration regime, which may include the option of 'converting' EU registrations into UK versions.

In an environment where brands are more valuable than ever, defending them will be increasingly important regardless of Brexit, and many EU-based brand owners will need to keep a close eye on whatever new registration system the UK eventually adopts; certainly the idea of 'successor' registrations may help to promote the UK's current position as one of the world's, let alone Europe's, leading IP enforcement regimes.[1]

---

1   https://www.verdict.co.uk/uk-and-us-leading-the-world-in-intellectual-property-whilst-pakistan-and-india-lag-behind/

11.3 E-COMMERCE REGULATIONS

Amongst the chorus of concern and demands for online platforms and other intermediaries to do more when they become unwittingly involved in the dissemination of content or amplification (often encouraged by its users) of behaviour which is either abusive, hateful or otherwise unlawful, many take comfort from the current, largely favourable framework of existing legislation. One of the most important sources of protection for online intermediaries came into being before the rise of social media came from Brussels, and has helped to secure the continent's reputation as a good place for tech platforms to either do business or set up shop.

The Electronic Commerce (EC) Regulations 2002[1] were introduced with the intent to harmonise regulations for online business across the EU, and to boost consumer confidence against the rise of the still-developing online retail market. Covering virtually any commercial website or platform, these Regulations deal with 'Information Society Services' (whether supported by transactions or paid subscriptions or otherwise) which involve either the sale of goods or provision of communications and information services (subject to a number of exceptions around gambling and other sectors).

Most significantly, apart from setting out certain minimum information disclosure requirements and the 'country of origin' principle which avoids the need for online retailers to roll out legal terms which comply with *every* member state's e-commerce legislation and rely mainly on the laws of the state in which their operation is based, (although consumer terms of purchase *do* need to comply with local laws of every state into which they sell) the Regulations also contain some of the most important exemptions from liability for any service provider acting as a 'web host' or 'mere conduit' or simply caches or hosts material.

Provided that the Regulations are complied with, intermediaries are not liable in most civil or criminal proceedings relating to material posted or disseminated by their users via their platforms. To fall under the Regulations' 'mere conduit' defence;[2] any intermediary which doesn't initiate the transmission of content, select its receiver or modify it in transit can defend any damages claim or other pecuniary remedy relating to it. Similarly, automatic, intermediate and temporary caching to provide an efficient service without modification of content is also a defence, as is hosting;[3] where recipients of or subscribers to a service are not acting under its authority or control and where that service has no knowledge or control over the nature of any data or content which its users post on it that supports unlawful activity, nor provides any assistance to any such unlawful activity (through promotion or otherwise).

These defences are usually lost, however, where intermediary services are put on notice of any claim relating to content, data or the activities of their users

---

1   SI 2002/2013, implementing Directive 2000/31 On Certain Legal Aspects of Information Society Services, In Particular Electronic Commerce, in the Internal Market [2000]
2   Regulation 17, SI 2002/2013
3   Regulation 19, SI 2002/2013

(at which point they gain actual knowledge of the unlawful activity or content in dispute) and fail to act 'expeditiously' to remove or disable access to the links or data in issue. The level of knowledge required to render an intermediary service liable varies dependent upon the defence relied upon, along with the quality of information provided when that notice is given. Most importantly, the Regulations also confirm that service providers are not under a general obligation to monitor data or content on their services. They can't, however, turn a 'blind eye' to unlawful activity although active monitoring would also potentially displace these defences by making them a less-passive 'publisher'. Of course, operating a suitable 'take-down' procedure and user complaint/abuse policies will help to mitigate that risk, hence why platforms tend to respond to complaints quickly and remove content or links when doing so first before resolving the issue later.

This of course counts not only for content which may infringe intellectual property rights, but also applies to defamatory comments. Although the recently-reformed UK law of defamation has its own set of statutory protections for intermediaries who are not responsible for the creation or editing of, or aware of, the content of user-generated comments posted on their sites and took 'reasonable care' in relation to their publication via the existing 'intermediary' or 'internet defences' set out in section 1 of the Defamation Act 1996 and the Defamation Act 2013's 'section 5' defence. Similarly, section 10 of the 2013 Act places an emphasis on actions being brought against authors, editors and publishers of defamatory statements rather than platforms, adding a further layer of protection.

However, being able to rely upon the section 5 defence in particular involves complying with strict timetables and what can be seen as an unwieldy process, dependent largely upon the quality of information held about the users which claimants are encourages to pursue, rather than the platform. Regulation 19's 'hosting' defence provides a great deal of comfort to secondary publishers and online fora, however that protection has been under attack as a result of several decisions of the European Convention Of Human Rights, notably *Delfi v Estonia;*[1] which saw an Estonian news site found liable for defamatory comments even after they were removed 'expeditiously'. As the European Commission's 2015 review of the regulations saw the possibility of a 'duty of care' being imposed upon website operators, the UK's existing defamation framework may, if taken alongside equivalent new legislation to the regulations, only serve to maintain the current 'shield' around platforms which allow the posting of user comments and make the UK legal approach more appealing to content providers.

The extent to which Brexit may change this regime, as in every other based on EU legislation, remains unclear. However, platform operators will doubtless make their own opinion known if and when the government looks to come up with a new equivalent to the permissive and protective Regulations, which they again had a hand in influencing when they originally became law. For the sake of continuing to attract tech giants who depend upon these protections and wanting

---

1   Delfi AS v. Estonia (2015) ECtHR 64669/09

to avoid a flood of further speculative litigation against them, we expect any new legislation to be largely equivalent to the current regime. Much as technology and user behaviour may change, the sector will need the law which regulates it to remain the same, and for certainty to come very quickly.

Whilst the protectionist approach taken by many UK content providers and interest groups may see lobbying for a far harsher regime of intermediary liability amidst claims that content is already being shared too widely without payment, the more recent deployment of the 'internet blocking injunction' to choke off access to peer-to-peer downloading sites[1] or to ISPs providing access to sites promoting the sale of counterfeit copy goods[2] may help the Government to resist calls for new civil or even criminal penalties to be brought to bear against mere 'links in the chain'. The Digital Single Market's own proposals around greater responsibility for intermediaries to monitor and filter for infringing content may however take the decision out of their hands if it does proceed as threatened and become law prior to the completion of Brexit, however, although this is far from certain.

Given the EU's own approach to intermediary liability is currently under review in its own right, we expect to see any new UK versions of the E-Commerce Regulations to adopt many of the key principles of the existing legislation, at least for the time being. The pace of change in law at the EU level is slow, one of the many reasons behind the 'Leave' campaign, and the response to that change at a UK level likely to be slower still if the UK intends to break away from the E-Commerce Regulations' approach given that great care will need to be taken to ensure ongoing trade with EU businesses and to avoid placing a higher level of responsibility upon tech platforms to monitor and deter the unlawful activities of their users.

11.4 DATA PROTECTION AND PRIVACY REGULATION

Without wanting to cover similar ground as other chapters, the creative and tech industries have for some time been grappling with their responsibilities to their users as imposed by Data Protection Law, if for no other reason than the fact that they have served to focus attention upon the 'sharing' of user data and content in the wake of consolidation in the sector (such as Facebook's acquisition of WhatsApp, which saw data protection regulations forced both to provide undertakings which committed them to better explaining to users of both platforms how their data would be used by the other and to allow them to retain control over the process[3]) and, in the wake of Edward Snowden's revelations on regular monitoring of the personal data of EU nationals which led to the dismantling of the US's position as a 'safe harbor' for data and several high-profile hacks such as that which paralysed the PlayStation Network during 2011

---

1   Via S.97 A of the Copyright, Designs & Patents Act 1988 in relation to copyright-protected 'works'
2   As in the case of Cartier & Ors v BskyB & Ors EWHC 3354 (CH)
3   https://iconewsblog.wordpress.com/2016/11/07/information-commissioner-updates-on-whatsapp-facebook-investigation/

and saw TalkTalk receive a record fine of £400,000 from the UK Information Commissioner's Office for failing to prevent user data being accessed by hackers levied in October 2016[1], data privacy, exploitation and security has well and truly gone mainstream.

Current UK data protection law contains a very wide definition of 'personal data' (effectively any data which can, individually or when combined, identify a living individual), and ensures the safe, fair, secure and lawful 'processing' of that data by businesses (and, in certain instances individuals), with various obligations imposed upon 'controllers' and rights conferred upon 'data subjects', not least in relation to their ability to object to the processing of their data for marketing purposes, to request access to it and to pursue compensation for its misuse, including more recently damages for 'distress' rather than merely for specific financial loss.[2]

As if the current legal position did not make the effective use and exploitation of personal data difficult enough, even where consent appears to have been validly obtained from users in circumstances where use of their data is justifiable and transparent, what is coming next will only require further attention and a shift towards the new maxim of 'privacy by design'.

The EU's General Data Protection Regulation (GDPR) will come into force by May 2018, and the UK government has already indicated that it will 'opt into' its new requirements, at least in the short-to-medium term. Effectively, the UK had no choice in the matter even if Article 50 only sees the new regime in place for a short period of time. This being the cases, businesses need to prepare for the worst and hope for the best.

The GDPR will set a higher standard for obtaining consent before processing data, mandatory breach notification to local Data Protection Regulators and potentially to affected data subjects in serious cases where individuals and their rights are likely to be prejudiced (a departure from the current position, where breach notification is optional, if recommended by ICO best practice in certain circumstances), the introduction of the fabled 'right to be forgotten' (or, more accurately, a 'right to erasure', based on the celebrated, at least in some quarters, case of *Google Spain v Costeja*[3]) in specific instances (rather than on a carte blanche basis) and most significantly increase the upper limit for monetary penalties for controllers in breach of its terms to up to 4% of annual global turnover from the ICO's current limit of £500,000.

The UK may, if it seeks to water down the GDPR's new protections over time, also lose its position as a 'safe harbor' for user data, which may lead to further uncertainty over any new system whilst the GDPR's more punitive provisions

---

1   https://ico.org.uk/about-the-ico/news-and-events/news-and-blogs/2016/10/talktalk-gets-record-400-000-fine-for-failing-to-prevent-october-2015-attack/

2   Google v Vidal-Hall [2015] EWCA Civ 311

3   Google Spain SL, Google Inc. V Agencia Espanola De Proteccion de Datos, Mario Costeja Gonzalez Case C-131/12

remained in force for the foreseeable future. Equally, the Privacy & Electronic Communications Regulations 2003;[1] which implemented the EU E-Privacy Directive[2] are also likely to remain in force pending the fallout from the Great Repeal Bill, leaving the controversial 'cookie law' unchanged to the chagrin of website operators and User Experience Specialists everywhere. That may, however, change in time and lead to an end to the ubiquity of 'consent boxes'.

Currently, the ICO's own guidance on Consent in a post-GDPR world and the suggestion that databases which do not evidence consent to the same standard as proscribed by the GDPR has caused no small amount of consternation amongst the marketing community. Much has been made of the stringent expectations of the ICO in terms of being able to demonstrate consent to processing through an informed, unequivocal choice to receive marketing communications, being very clear about who and why data may be shared for onward marketing purposes and not making consent a prerequisite before making even the most elementary use of a product or service. The initial guidance is still to be clarified, and many fear that such clarity will not come in time to allow businesses to be compliant with the new rules by May 2018.

Whilst some in the marketing community may seek to rely on the usual 'legitimate purpose' or other legal justification for the processing of personal data (in most cases, the right to do business in the first place), guidance on those expectations is in very short supply even if direct marketing is explicitly stated as a 'legitimate purpose' in the GDPR's text. Reliance upon those purposes will involve a balancing of the commercial interests of businesses against the rights of data subjects, which in most instances tend to win out in both the hearings of regulatory bodies and the court of public opinion. It's expected that direct marketing will only likely be viewed as a legitimate interest capable of justifying processing without consent when absolutely necessary – currently, many marketers may be looking to run reactivation campaigns to refresh consents, even if the ICO may frown upon them doing so without having provided for being able to run such an exercise when the data was first obtained. Morrisons recently fell foul of the ICO after running such a campaign and clarity on the point remains in short supply save for the general demand to get compliant all over again rather than rely on consents which may simply not be up to scratch.

Of some comfort is the fact that the 'soft opt-in' remains a viable justification for direct e-mail marketing in the case of data subjects who have either bought or enquired about a product or service, and the revised EU ePrivacy Regulation, due to come into force on the same date as the GDPR retains the concept of the soft opt-in although only in relation to data subjects who have purchased a product or service, rather than merely enquire about them. It's of note that the ePrivacy Regulation contains similar punitive fines as the GDPR, and is of equal importance as the other side of the privacy coin, especially as it requires marketers to be transparent and avoid concealing their true identity.

---

1   SI 2426/2003
2   Directive 2002/58/EC

Much as the Data Protection Act 1998 has not been the source of a flood of litigation since its introduction, the availability of distress damages as a result of the *Vidal-Hall* case and various pending class actions against data controllers may see a change in the public appetite for such claims where the tipping point in awareness around the trade in their personal data may not have already been reached, if it is not just around the corner.

Notably, the GPDR's own enshrinement of the right of data subjects to avail themselves of an 'effective judicial remedy' for material and non-material damage arising from breaches of its terms will only serve to remind individuals that they can now effectively and directly hold data controllers to account when their personal data is misused. Whilst regulation and enforcement has always lurked in the background, privacy activism is a very real item on the corporate risk agenda as privacy claims become more mainstream and less the preserve of the rich and famous, based largely on human rights law. The rights and entitlements of data subjects can no longer be ignored or damages flowing from their breaches undervalued, even if current case law has only seen relatively minor damages awarded for comparatively serious breaches of the 1998 Act. We are only a few decisions away from the bar being raised considerably.

A similarly under-argued section of the 1998 Act has been the 'journalistic exemption' set out in section 32. Currently, there have been very few claims that dispute the public interest justifying the extent of journalistic intrusion into a data subject's private life. As that exemption is enshrined in the GDPR, the continued deployment of data protection claims where defamation or other claims are harder to pursue successfully may lead to some landmark judgments and significant payouts as a result of intrusive media commentary.

At least in the field of Data Protection, we can provide some useful preparatory advice for businesses looking to prepare for the impact of the GDPR, as set out by the ICO:[1]

- Identify a legal basis for processing personal data and document it, which will be especially important where that processing will affect individuals' rights – If consent is relied upon for processing, there will be a stronger right to ask for that processing to be stopped;
- 'Consent' remains important, but must now involve clear, affirmative action and must be verifiable – pre-ticked boxes and poor record-keeping will not be tolerated, and consent can be withdrawn at *any time* – 'fresh' consent, however, may not be necessary if already obtained but consent from parents or guardians will need to be obtained where children under the age of 16 access online services;
- Protection of personal data relating to children will be enhanced, and privacy notices will need to be clear and understandable for that audience;
- Data subjects will enjoy new rights to 'be informed' (through privacy notices provided when the data is obtained, which must be transparent

---

1   https://ico.org.uk/for-organisations/data-protection-reform/overview-of-the-gdpr/key-areas-to-consider/

and in plain English), to access (subject to payment of a fee and within strict timescales, unless the request is manifestly unfounded or excessive), rectification (if personal data is inaccurate or incomplete, and details provided of any third parties to whom data has been provided), erasure (if consent to processing has been withdrawn, where use of the data is no longer necessary for the purposes for which it was originally collected or processed, where there is no overriding legitimate interest in continued processing, or where unlawfully processed), to restrict processing (on objection, where its accuracy is disputed or where the processing is unlawful and reassure is not requested, which is likely to be rare), for their data to be portable (meaning that it must be provided in a structured and easily compatible form to third parties on request), to object to processing (including, for example, for marketing purposes) and in relation to automated decision-making;

- Accountability and Governance are at the heart of the GDPR, alongside transparency. Comprehensive, but proportionate, governance is a hallmark of the new regime and privacy impact assessments alongside other policies, codes of conduct and procedures will be essential, along with detailed records of consent and details of processing, retention and transfer – data protection now needs to be considered and integrated into all processing activity;

- Data Protection Officers must be appointed in certain circumstances, although they may be optional for many businesses. However, unless a business has sufficient staff and skills to discharge its new obligations under the GDPR, their appointment may become the rule rather than the exception to ensure compliance and act as a first point of contact for data subjects and the ICO. Remember, however, that a 'DPO' can be an existing member of staff provided that there is no conflict of interest and that there is no set level of qualification save for proportionate experience and knowledge of data protection law;

- Certain data breaches will require mandatory notification to both the ICO and to data subjects, specifically where it is likely to result in a risk to the rights and freedoms of individuals and notification must take place within 72 hours of the event to avoid a monetary penalty of up to 2% of annual global turnover – preparing for breaches ahead of time as part of an overall disaster recovery plan is now essential for regulatory, liability and public perception purposes.

Data protection is, Brexit aside, here to stay and should be at the top of your corporate agenda. Planning now is likely to mitigate significant known and unknown risks, and will have a major impact upon your future data governance and wider operations, especially where transfer outside of the EU will only be possible with an individual's informed consent and for specific purposes. Certainly, any business which harvests data across multiple platforms, let alone few, will need to develop sophisticated systems to allow for the exercise of the new rights of data subjects and new and improved security measures to both deter hacking and large-scale litigation for when the worst does, rather than may happen. Investing in infrastructure and compliance by default will pay off well off way past May 2018.

Thankfully, further guidance from the ICO will arrive in due course and there shouldn't be any shortage of opinion and advice available in the run-up to May 2018, and as of August 2017, we now have a much better idea of how the GDPR is likely to be implemented in the UK through the introduction of the Data Protection Bill, which mirrors the majority of the GDPR's requirements. As the regulation would not have needed enacting legislation to become law in the UK, the introduction of the new Bill is likely a statement of intent and a commitment to privacy rather than a necessary step, but privacy, transparency and the primacy of the rights and interests of data subjects are very much here to stay after May 2018 and beyond.

11.5 CONCLUSION

Heading back to China for a moment, Western motivational speakers often refer to John F Kennedy's claim that their word for 'crisis' is made up of characters representing 'danger' and 'opportunity'. That's since been proven wrong, however the potential knock-on impacts of Brexit on our clients and their changing needs may be seen as an exercise in crisis planning in the short term, but their changing needs, however, also present opportunities to get to grips with their ongoing and future legal obligations in a changing world and help to equip themselves for what may come once the UK becomes a political island once again, albeit one that is part of an increasing globalised and technologically-sophisticated world.

CHAPTER 12

EMPLOYMENT

Kevin Poulter & Amanda Trewhella, Child & Child

INTRODUCTION

In this chapter, we will look at what being a member of the EU has meant to employment law and employee rights in the United Kingdom over the past 40 years or so and make some predictions as to what may change in the months following Brexit.

It should be noted that the legislative provisions referred to are from employment law in England and Wales only. Local advice should be sought if necessary.

12.1 THE CURRENT STATUS OF UK EMPLOYMENT LAW

A significant amount of employment law in the UK derives from EU law. As a member state of the EU, the UK is currently obliged to ensure a number of minimum rights for its workers.

In order to forecast what might happen to UK employment law, it is necessary to consider how we have arrived at where we are today, with the help of Europe.

From the earliest stages of the EU, social objectives were an important part of the Union. As far back as the European Coal and Steel Community, established in 1951 (which was the model for the European Economic Community) this included an objective that:

> 'the institutions of the Community shall, within the limits of their respective powers, in the common interest [...] promote improved working conditions and an improved standard of living for the workers in each of the industries for which it is responsible, so as to make possible their harmonisation while the improvement is being maintained'.

The Treaty of the European Union, known as the Maastricht Treaty 1992, contains a number of employment directives which applied to all member states, including the UK. However, the Maastricht Treaty was highly controversial in the UK. Initially John Major's Conservative Government chose to opt out of the Social Chapter, arguing that 'there is no doubt that Britain – with low interest rates, competitive labour costs and competitive interest rates – has the leading edge in the marketplace in Europe. The government has no intention of throwing away those hard won advantages, as the Social Chapter would compel us to do'. The Opposition was strongly against the opt-out; John Smith (then Leader of the Opposition) said:

'the people of this country do not understand why they have a Government who wants to deny them the social rights, the social opportunities and the social advantages which the whole Community wants for its citizens'.

Later, in 1997, the then Labour Government finally agreed to be bound by the provisions of the Social Chapter.

It will be seen, as we go through the various areas of employment law which have been affected by the EU, that many new minimum employment rights and obligations imposed by the EU were resisted by the UK government during EU negotiations and in some cases only the very minimum requirements have been implemented into UK law, whereas in other cases the UK have 'gold plated' rights by extending and expanding upon what the EU has set down as minimum requirements.

12.1.2 Employment legislation which derives from the EU

Working time

Prior to the implementation of the Working Time Regulations 1998[1] employees in the UK did not have any minimum statutory right to paid holidays. These regulations were implemented by the UK following the EU Working Time Directive in 1993. This EU Directive was enacted as a health and safety measure to ensure that all workers in the EU are provided with sufficient breaks during the working week and a minimum number of days holiday each year.

The UK government was heavily opposed to the Working Time Directive. The UK negotiated concessions to the original proposals including the ability to include an opt-out from the maximum 48-hour working week, and they even abstained from the final vote. In 1996 the UK government went so far as to challenge the EU Council as to the legal basis of the Working Time Directive in the case of *United Kingdom of Great Britain v Council of the European Union*[2] but they failed in this challenge. The UK government only enacted the legislation complying with the Directive – the Working Time Regulations 1998 – two years after the deadline to comply and were therefore clearly reluctant to do so.

It would therefore be an understatement to say that this Directive is not very popular with the UK government. However, in one respect the UK Regulations go further, and 'gold plate' the Directive which is in relation to holidays. Under the European Directive the minimum number of paid holidays which must be provided to workers is 4 weeks per year (or 20 days for a full time worker) but under the UK Regulations the minimum is 5.6 weeks per year (or 28 days for full time worker).

---

1   SI 1998/1833.
2   Case C-84/94, [1996] ECR I-5755.

Discrimination

The majority of our anti-discrimination laws in the UK are currently set out in the UK Equality Act 2010, which consolidated previous pieces of anti-discrimination law into one act. The Equality Act provides protection for workers against discrimination on the grounds of a defined list of protected characteristics: gender; race or nationality; disability; marriage or civil partnership; pregnancy or maternity; sexual orientation; gender reassignment; religion or belief and age.

As an EU member state, the UK must comply with the EU Equal Treatment Directive 2006 (which was updated from the original Directive in 1975) which sets down minimum protections against discrimination on the grounds of sex; marriage and civil partnership; pregnancy and maternity and gender reassignment. At the point that all member states had to ensure compliance with the updated Directive, in 2008, the UK's existing anti-discrimination laws already complied.

The UK is also required to comply with the EU Equal Treatment Directive 2000 which covers age; disability; religion and belief and sexual orientation discrimination protection.

Although in recent years the UK's anti-discrimination legislation had been led by the EU, historically and before joining the EU our workers were protected from some forms of discrimination and within Europe the UK was at the forefront of implementing anti-discrimination legislation. The first anti-discrimination law affecting workers in the UK was the Race Relations Act 1965. The Sex Discrimination Act and Equal Pay Act followed in 1975 and in 1995 the Disability Discrimination Act was enacted. These were entirely domestic pieces of legislation.

The UK's domestic anti-discrimination legislation must be interpreted to comply with the various EU directives. This has therefore shaped UK law and for example meant that in 2004 the UK had to remove the exemption for small businesses (with less than 20 employees) not to discriminate on the grounds of disability, in order to comply with EU law. Also in relation to the burden of proof in discrimination cases, in order to comply with the EU Directives, it is a requirement that the respondent employer must bear the burden of disproving discrimination, once the claimant employee has established 'facts from which it may be presumed that there has been discrimination'.

Several areas of anti-discrimination law have been introduced entirely as a consequence of the UK's membership of the EU. Religion or belief, sexual orientation and age discrimination legislation were all enacted because the UK was obliged to comply with the EU Equal Treatment Framework Directive. These were originally enacted by way of the Employment Equality (Religion or Belief) Regulations 2003,[1] the Employment Equality (Sexual Orientation) Regulations

---

1   SI 2003/1660.

2003[1] and finally the Employment Equality (Age) Regulations 2006.[2] Age discrimination protection has not been popular with the UK Government and the necessary legislation was introduced at the latest possible time.

Business transfers

What happens to employees when a business is transferred from one party to another is currently governed in the UK by the Transfer of Undertakings (Protection of Employment) Regulations 2006[3] ('TUPE'). These UK regulations were implemented in order to comply with the EU Acquired Rights Directive 2001.

Prior to the original TUPE regulations of 1981, the position in the UK was that on a business transfer, the employment of the employees in the business ended immediately, as the employment was considered to be personal to the employer and employee. Provided that the employees were given the correct period of notice and provided with redundancy pay if they had been employed for long enough, they would have had no claim against their employer or the new company upon the transfer for the loss of their jobs. This position therefore radically changed when the TUPE regulations came into force in the UK.

Currently, the employment of employees who were 'assigned to the organised grouping of resources or employees that is the subject of the relevant transfer' automatically transfers to the new employer, by law. Relevant transfers include not only standard business transfers but also outsourcing, where a client engages a contractor to do work on its behalf, changes that contractor or brings the work back in-house. The employment contracts of those employees transferring continues on their existing terms and conditions (save for certain pension benefits) and the employees are also protected against dismissal, unless the dismissal is for an 'economic, technical or organisational reason entailing changes in the workforce.'

Atypical workers

Part time workers and fixed term workers are afforded protection against being treated less favourably than full time workers or permanent workers by two EU directives – the Part-time Work Directive 97/81/EC and the Fixed-Term Work Directive 1999/70. In relation to fixed term workers the directive requires that measures are put in place to ensure that employers do not use a succession of fixed term contracts to avoid the worker accruing employment protection. These have been implemented into UK law via the Part-time Workers (Prevention of Less Favourable Treatment) Regulations 2000[4] and the Fixed-term Employees (Prevention of Less Favourable Treatment) Regulations 2002.[5]

---

1   SI 2003/1661.
2   Si 2006/1031.
3   SI 2006/246.
4   SI 2000/1551.
5   SI 2002/2034.

The Agency Workers Regulations 2010[1] were enacted to implement the EU Temporary Agency Work Directive 2008. Under the Regulations, once an agency worker has been engaged by a company for 12 weeks they are entitled to receive the same pay and main conditions as the permanent staff of the company. This includes the same holidays, working hours, maternity benefits and access to facilities in the workplace such as canteens or workplace gyms.

Collective consultation

The current regulations in the UK which require employers to inform and consult with employees, employee representatives or unions before making certain changes which affect employees are generally derived from EU law.

Under the Trade Union Labour Relations Consolidation Act 1992, which implements EU European Collective Redundancies Directive 98/59, where an employer proposes to make 20 or more employees redundant within a 90-day period a process of collective consultation must take place for at least 30 days and where the proposal is to make 100 or more employees redundant the consultation period must last a minimum of 45 days. These Regulations also apply where changes to terms of employment are imposed by an employer who proposes to dismiss their employees and re-engage them on new terms.

In relation to business transfers, under TUPE, which implemented the EU Acquired Rights Directive 2001/23/EC, the buyer and seller of a business must inform employee representatives about the timing and reason for the transfer of the business and what the legal, economic and social consequences of the transfer will be; they must also consult with the employee representatives about any measures which may need to be taken regarding the employees.

Health and safety

A significant amount of health and safety legislation in the UK comes from EU Directives, for example the Work Equipment Directive 2009/104/EC, the Personal Protective Equipment Directive 89/656/EC, the Display Screen Equipment Directive 90/270/EEC and the Manual Handling Directive 90/269, to name just a few.

12.1.3 The influence of the European Court of Justice

In addition to EU Directives, which require the UK to implement legislation complying with minimum rights or protections, changes to UK law can also currently be effected through the case law of the European Court of Justice ('ECJ'). When a question of EU law arises, courts of each Member State must refer the particular point to the ECJ. The domestic court must then apply the opinion of the ECJ to the case, to ensure the interpretation is consistent between Member States. This has had a big influence over the shaping of UK employment law as can be seen in the following significant examples.

---

1   SI 2010/93.

Cap on discrimination awards

Historically, in the UK discrimination awards were subject to a maximum cap in the same way that unfair dismissal awards are today. However, this changed as a result of a decision of the ECJ. In the sex discrimination case of *Marshall (No 2)*[1] Ms Marshall challenged the fact that her compensation was capped at the then maximum award of £8,500 as being contrary to EU law. In considering this question, the ECJ reviewed the wording of the Equal Treatment Directive which states that 'compensation had to be adequate....to enable the loss and damage actually sustained...to be made good in full'. The ECJ interpreted this to mean that in order for compensation to be adequate, it cannot be subject to an upper limit. Following this case, and additional cases relating to other forms of discrimination, the UK now has no upper limit on awards for discrimination.

Accrual of holidays during sick leave

The Working Time Regulations 1998 specifically state that the four weeks holiday per year which are guaranteed by the EU must be used in the year that they accrue and cannot be carried forward to a subsequent leave year. It was therefore previously thought that if an employee was on long term sick leave at the end of the year and was therefore unable to take all of their holiday entitlement, that they would lose the remainder of their entitlement.

However, in the cases of *Stringer and others v HM Revenue & Customs and Schultz-Hoff v Deutsche Rentenversicherung Bund*[2] and *Pereda v Madrid Movilidad SA*[3] the EJC held that holidays continue to accrue during sickness absence and that a worker who has been on long term sick leave must be allowed to carry forward their holiday to the next holiday year to ensure that they are able to take it.

Calculation of holiday pay

In the UK it was previously the position that the amount of pay due to an employee during annual leave was equivalent to their basic pay only. However, this position has recently changed following a number of decisions of the ECJ.

The first in this string of important cases was Williams and others v British Airways plc.[4] In this case, British Airways pilots argued that during periods of annual leave they should not only receive their basic pay but should continue to receive the supplementary payments for flying time and time spent away from base that they would receive if they were working during that time. The ECJ agreed with the pilots and held that in addition to basic pay, workers should receive any remuneration which is:

---

1   *Marshall v Southampton and South West Hampshire AHA* (C-271/91) [1993] ICR 893.
2   [2009] IRLR 214.
3   [2009] IRLR 959.
4   [2011] IRLR 948.

'intrinsically linked to the performance of the tasks which the worker is required to carry out under his contract of employment and in respect of which a monetary amount, included in the calculation of his total remuneration, is provided'

and also remuneration which relates to the 'personal and professional status' of the worker, such as payments which relate to a worker's seniority, length of service or professional qualifications.

This decision of the ECJ was followed in the cases of *Lock v British Gas Trading Ltd and others*[1] and *Bear Scotland Ltd and others v Fulton and others*[2] which clarified that holiday pay must be based on normal remuneration and should include the following normal payments:

- Commission payments;
- Incentive bonuses and productivity or performance bonuses;
- Overtime payments, regardless as to whether overtime is guaranteed;
- Payments that relate to the 'personal and professional status' of workers, such as those based on seniority, length of service or professional qualifications;
- Shift allowances and premiums;
- Standby payments and payments for emergency call-out duties; and
- Travel allowances (but not travel expenses).

Collective redundancy consultation

The duty to collectively consult with employee representatives where redundancies are proposed applies where an employer proposes to make 20 or more employees redundant in any 'establishment'. The ECJ was called upon to decide what an 'establishment' meant in the case of *USDAW and another v WW Realisation 1 Ltd (in liquidation), Ethel Austin Ltd and another*[3] – more commonly known as the *Woolworths* case as it related to claims made by employees of Woolworths branches when the company went into liquidation. The employees argued that as the branches were centrally managed, the number of employees in all of the branches who were at risk of redundancy should have been aggregated to decide whether collective consultation should have taken place. However the ECJ disagreed and held that an 'establishment' meant the 'local unit or entity to which the redundant workers are assigned to carry out their duties' – in this case, each individual shop. Therefore if less than 20 people worked in any shop, Woolworths were not required to follow a process of collective consultation.

Pregnancy discrimination

A number of decisions of the ECJ have significantly affected the extent of sex discrimination law in the UK in relation to pregnancy discrimination. Previously,

---

1   [2014] IRLR 648.
2   [2015] IRLR 15.
3   Case C-80/14 [2015] ICR 675.

for a woman to claim that she had been discriminated against on the grounds of her pregnancy, she had to show that she had been treated less favourably than a non-pregnant employee in similar circumstances. Therefore if an employer could show that a male on long term sickness absence would have been treated in the same way as a pregnant woman, the woman's claim would fail. However, the ECJ in the cases of *Dekker v Stichting Vormingscentrum voor Jonge Volwassen (VJV-Centrum) Plus* (1990) *and* of *Webb v EMO*[1] held that treating a woman less favourably because she is pregnant is direct sex discrimination and it is not necessary to identify a non-pregnant comparator to prove discrimination. Today this principle is set out in the Equality Act 2010 which includes pregnancy and maternity as a protected characteristic.

Equal pay

In relation to the right for men and women to receive equal pay, the ECJ extended equal pay laws to include all types of pay from employment, including pensions, in the case of *Barber.*[2] The case was brought by Mr Barber who was made redundant at age 52. Due to his age, he was not entitled to be granted an immediate pension, whereas, if he was a woman he would have qualified. He argued that this breached the right to equal pay and the ECJ agreed.

It was also the ECJ, in the cases of *Enderby*[3] and *Danfoss*[4] which clarified that the right to equal pay includes work of equal value. This means that a person of one gender does not need to compare themselves with someone of a different gender doing exactly the same job, they can instead show that they are doing a job which is of equal value to the other person's job and that they should therefore be paid equally. In the *Danfoss* case, female speech therapists successfully argued that they were doing work of equal value to male pharmacists and psychologists and should therefore be paid an equal amount. These decisions led to the public sector bonus claims which resulted in back payments to thousands of women.

Associative discrimination

Before the intervention of the ECJ it was only possible for an employee to claim discrimination on the grounds of their own protected characteristic. However, the concept of associative discrimination was formed by the ECJ in the case of *EBR Attridge LLP v Coleman*.[5] The case was brought under the Disability Discrimination Act 1995, by a mother who was treated less favourably by her employer because she was the main carer for her disabled son. Although Ms Coleman was not disabled herself, the ECJ held that she should be able to bring a claim for disability discrimination by association in relation to her child's disability. As a consequence of this ECJ decision, protection against associative

---

1   [1995] ICR 1021.
2   *Barber v Guardian Royal Exchange Assurance Group* (C-262/88) [1990] ECR I-1889
3   *Enderby v Frenchay HA* (C-127/92) [1994] ICR 112.
4   *Handels- og Kontorfunktionaerernes Forbund i Danmark v Dansk Arbejdsgiverforening ex p Danfoss A/S* (109/88) [1991] ICR 74.
5   [2010] ICR 242.

discrimination is now included in the Equality Act in relation to all of the various protected characteristics.

12.2 WHAT WILL HAPPEN TO EMPLOYMENT LAW AFTER BREXIT?

As can be seen in Part 2, the EU has had an enormous impact on employment law in the UK and the vast majority of the various areas of UK employment law have either originated from the EU or have in some way been influenced and shaped by the EU. Can we therefore expect the laws governing employer and employee relations to change overnight after Brexit and if so, what will be the position going forward?

On 2 February 2017 the government published a White Paper entitled 'The United Kingdom's exit from and new partnership with the European Union' setting out its plan for Brexit. The White Paper confirms that upon leaving the EU the government will introduce the Great Repeal Bill to remove the European Communities Act 1972 from the UK statute book and convert existing EU law into domestic law. The White Paper states that this means that 'wherever practical and appropriate' the same rules and laws will apply on the day after we leave the EU as they did before. However, it goes on to state that:

> 'Once we have left the EU, Parliament (and, where appropriate, the devolved legislatures) will then be able to decide which elements of that law to keep, amend or repeal.'

At the time of writing, a White Paper on the Great Repeal Bill is awaited, which should further explain how the government plans to transfer current EU employment law into UK law.

In the recent White Paper, the section entitled 'Protecting workers' rights' is surprisingly short and unfortunately reveals little as to the government's future plans. It states that the government has 'committed not only to safeguard the rights of workers set out in European legislation, but to enhance them'.

It therefore appears, at the time of writing, that the day the UK exits the EU, the rights and obligations of employees and employers will not immediately change. However, in future the minimum employment rights currently guaranteed by the EU will no longer be guaranteed by our membership of the EU and so the government could in future seek to remove or alter some of them. Whether the UK will in future be required to transpose EU employment law into domestic law or not will depend upon what is agreed in the negotiations in relation to the UK's place within Europe.

After Brexit, whether changes will be made to UK employment law will largely depend upon the intentions of the government of the day. It is often said that the best predictor of future behaviour is past behaviour and given that there are a number of areas of EU employment law which the UK government has been opposed to, challenged or brought in at the last possible moment, it is likely that we will see some changes in the course of time.

12.2.1 UK employment law unaffected by Brexit

There are a number of areas of employment law in the UK which are purely domestic rights and have not been affected by the UK's membership of the EU. The following rights and obligations will not therefore change as a consequence of Brexit:

Unfair dismissal

Employees will continue to be protected from unfair dismissal under the Employment Rights Act 1996 once they have achieved two years' continuous service. As at 6 April 2017 compensatory awards for unfair dismissal are capped at £80,541 or a year's gross salary, whichever is lower.

National minimum wage

Since the introduction of the National Minimum Wage Act 1998 the UK government has set minimum hourly rates of pay which apply to all workers.

As at 1 April 2017, the rates are as follows:

National Living Wage (Workers aged 25+)	Standard Rate (Workers aged 21+)	Development Rate (Workers aged 18-20)	Young Workers Rate (Workers aged under 18 but above compulsory school age and not apprentices)	Apprenticeship Rate (Apprentices aged under 19 or within their first year of apprenticeship)
£7.50	£7.05	£5.60	£4.05	£3.50

Protection for whistle blowers

In the UK, the Public Interest Disclosure Act 1998 protects workers who 'blow the whistle'. Where a worker makes a disclosure about malpractice by their employer, such as a breach of a legal obligation or criminal offence, they are protected against being dismissed or suffering a detriment because of their disclosure.

Unauthorised deductions from wages

Under the Employment Rights Act 1996 it is unlawful to make a deduction from a worker's wages, unless the deduction must be made by law (such as income tax and National Insurance Contributions) or the worker has given their prior written agreement to the deduction. There are also some exceptions in relation to retail workers.

Unlawful deduction from wages claims can be brought in relation to unpaid holiday pay, bonuses and commission, in addition to wages. This right will not be affected by Brexit.

Redundancy pay

In the UK, under the Employment Rights Act 1996, where an employee's employment is terminated by reason of redundancy, provided that they have achieved two year's continuous service they are entitled to receive a statutory redundancy payment.

Family friendly rights

The right for the partner of a child's mother or adopter to take two weeks' paternity leave and to receive paternity pay was enacted under the Employment Act 2002. More recently, Shared Parental Leave and Pay was introduced in the UK for parents and adopters under the Families Act 2014 allowing parents to share caring responsibilities for a baby or newly adopted child.

Since 30 June 2014 all employees in the UK with at least 26 weeks' service are entitled to make a request for flexible working under the Employment Rights Act 1996 (as amended) and the Flexible Working Regulations 2014.[1] An employer who receives such a request must consider it within a three-month period and can only refuse the request on the grounds of one or more specific business reasons.

These family friendly rights come entirely from domestic legislation and will not therefore be affected by Brexit.

Other family friendly rights, such as the right to take maternity leave and adoption leave are protected by EU law but have been significantly extended by UK law. For example, under EU law mothers are entitled to 14 weeks' paid maternity leave whereas in the UK we have a far more generous provision of up to 52 weeks leave, of which 39 weeks are paid (at the rate of statutory maternity pay, which as of 2 April 2017 is £140.98 per week).

In January 2017 the government published a response to a report by the Women and Equalities Committee of MPs, into pregnancy and maternity discrimination. In its response, the Government acknowledged that some women in the workplace face discrimination due to their pregnancy or taking maternity leave and confirmed that they are committed to taking action to tackle this problem. This issue is currently being reviewed by the government as part of the 'Employment practices in the modern economy' review by Matthew Taylor.

---

1   SI 2014/1398.

The recent tendency of the government has been to extend family friendly rights and it does not therefore appear that leaving the EU will affect these rights in the UK.

12.2.2 Employment law changes post-Brexit

At the time of writing the government have not stated any intention to make any changes to employment law in the UK following Brexit. However, given the current political climate and general mood of the UK it is unlikely that now would be the time to make such announcements. What changes will be made to employment law in the UK's post EU future is therefore conjecture. We believe that the following areas are the most susceptible to change post Brexit:

Cap on discrimination awards

Currently, compensation in the Employment Tribunal for cases of discrimination do not have an upper limit. In the previous coalition government's Employment Law Review, which was carried out before the implementation of fees in the Employment Tribunal, the government stated its commitment to review discrimination awards, but acknowledged that it is currently prohibited by EU law from setting a fixed cap on discrimination compensation.

This therefore gives a strong indication that post Brexit the government may seek to set a statutory cap on compensation for discrimination awards. This would also fit with compensation for unfair dismissal awards which are subject to a maximum cap, and which cap was recently reduced by the Conservative government.

Working time and holidays

The Working Time Regulations, which set out the maximum hours that a worker can work each week, the daily and weekly breaks that they must be given and the holidays that they are entitled to, have always been unpopular with the UK government and this is an area which is likely to be subject to some changes.

It is highly likely that the government will abolish the maximum 48-hour working week which currently applies as it is seen as being unnecessarily inflexible for British business. The ability for workers to opt out of this provision will therefore become obsolete. Although this would leave the UK in a position where there is no specific statutory protection against working long hours, this is always subject to an employer's general duty of care for its employees' health and safety. Therefore employers would continue to be under a duty to ensure that an employee's hours are not so long as to cause any problems with their physical health or mental wellbeing.

As can be seen above, a number of recent European Court of Justice decisions have brought about significant changes in relation to the calculation of holiday pay and the entitlement of employees to accrue holidays during sick leave. The obligations on employers are currently not entirely clear and it is notable that the government have not chosen to amend the relevant legislation in order to clarify the position. They did, however, quickly introduce the Deduction from Wages (Limitation) Regulations 2014[1] which limit many unlawful deduction from wages claims, including in respect of holiday pay, bonuses and commission to the past two years of arrears only, which shows that the government are keen to limit employers' liability.

Following Brexit, the government may bring in legislation which reverses the changes made by the European Court of Justice in this area as they are seen as imposing too heavy a burden on employers. It is likely that the UK will therefore return to a position where holidays are not accrued during long term periods of absence and where sick pay only needs to be equivalent to basic pay.

Given that the number of days' holiday that workers are entitled to in the UK of 5.6 weeks per year (equivalent to 28 days for a full time worker) exceeds the minimum entitlement guaranteed by the EU of 4 weeks per year, it is unlikely that the UK government would seek to reduce this post Brexit.

Equal pay

Workers who bring a claim that they should be paid equally to a worker of a different gender who is fulfilling the same role, or a role of equivalent value or rated as equivalent, can currently be awarded arrears of pay of up to six years. In the same way that the government has limited claims for unlawful deductions of wages to a maximum of two years' arrears and is likely to seek to impose a maximum cap on compensation for discrimination post Brexit, the government may also seek to impose a cap on equal pay claims, in terms of the maximum period that compensation can be claimed for. This was previously the position in the UK prior to the European Court of Justice decision in *Marshall (No 2)*.

Atypical workers

Under the Agency Workers Regulations 2010, once an agency worker has been engaged by a company for 12 weeks, they are entitled to receive the same pay and main conditions as the permanent staff of the company. The EU directive which led to the implementation of the Agency Workers Regulations 2010 was strongly opposed by the UK government and the regulations only provide the lowest level of protection which is required by the EU Directive. In the Beecroft report on employment law, which was a review prepared for the last coalition government in 2011, the report went so far as to suggest that the government should break EU law by refusing to implement the EU Directive. The regulations have clearly been very unpopular with the government and with businesses, and it is therefore highly likely that they will be amended or repealed. If they are repealed, without additional legislation being put in place, agency workers would not have a right to bring a claim if they are treated less favourably than permanent staff in relation to their terms and conditions.

---

1   SI 2014/3322.

The current regulations which provide protection to fixed term workers and part time workers against less favourable treatment than permanent and full time staff are rights which derive from the EU. These EU Directives were unpopular with the UK government and previous Conservative governments vetoed earlier attempts to adopt Directives which allowed for equal treatment of atypical workers. Prior to the EU Fixed-Term Work Directive, in the UK fixed term workers were in fact specifically excluded from the right to claim unfair dismissal and redundancy pay. This exclusion was only repealed in order to comply with the EU directive.

Given their unpopularity, the rights of fixed term workers may be eroded after Brexit. However, we believe that is it unlikely that the rights of part time workers will be reduced, because the majority of part time workers are female and reducing these rights would therefore disproportionately affect women.

At the time of writing, the government is currently undertaking an independent review entitled 'Employment practices in the modern economy'. The Government's White Paper on Brexit states that the review:

> 'will consider how employment rules need to change in order to keep pace with modern business models, such as: the rapid recent growth in self-employment; the shift in business practice from hiring to contracting; the rising use of non-standard contract forms and the emergence of new business models such as on-demand platforms'.

Following the outcome of this review, it is likely that the Government may seek to amend or introduce legislation in relation to atypical workers in order to better suit modern ways of working.

Business transfers

The rights and obligations which apply in relation to employees where there is a transfer of a business from one party to another, or where there is a service provision change, derive from EU law. The TUPE regulations are extremely complex and often seen as a major burden on businesses. This is an area which the government are likely to take the opportunity to amend once the UK are no longer obliged to comply with the EU's minimum requirements. However, as these rules have been a part of UK law for over 30 years it is unlikely that they would be revoked in their entirety and we believe that instead the government will seek to tweak the regulations in order to reduce the burden on businesses.

The rules in relation to service provision changes which can currently be found in TUPE give employees the right to retain their employment with the transferring employer, on the same terms and conditions where a service is outsourced, where a contract is transferred from one contractor to another, or where a service is brought back in house. This part of the regulations go further than is required by the EU, however the reason this was brought in by the UK government was to provide clarity as the previous position in relation to service provision changes was unclear. Following Brexit the UK government may seek to tone down these regulations or to remove them entirely. If that were the case, employees would not be automatically transferred to the employment of the contractor and if the need for work of the type that they were carrying out for their employer has reduced, their roles may instead be redundant.

A further area of TUPE which the government is likely to amend post Brexit, is in relation to the harmonisation of employees' terms and conditions following a transfer. Currently under the TUPE regulations, the employees who are automatically transferred to the transferee business automatically transfer on their existing terms and conditions (save for certain pension benefits). If an employer attempts to change the terms and conditions for a reason connected with the transfer, any such changes will be void (unless made for an economic, technical or organisation reason entailing changes in the workforce and in other limited circumstances). Therefore in practice what often happens is that the transferee employer is left with a 'two-tier' workforce where their existing employees may be on completely different terms to the newly transferred employees, such as in relation to their holidays, working hours and sickness pay entitlement etc. This can cause administrative difficulties for business.

It may therefore be the case that the TUPE regulations will be amended, to enable certain contractual terms to be harmonised with the terms of existing employees after a transfer. The obligations to inform and consult with employee representatives are also an area which may also be softened in a post-Brexit future.

Data protection

Currently in the UK the legislation which sets out how personal data can be collected and used is primarily set out in the Data Protection Act 1998. This legislation was brought into effect to implement EU Data Protection Directive 95/46/EEC; however it replaced previous domestic legislation under the Data Protection Act 1984 and data protection regulations were not therefore new to the UK when the EU directive came into force.

On 25 May 2018 the EU data protection law Regulation 2016/679 on the protection of natural persons with regard to the processing of personal data and on the free movement of such data – commonly known as the General Data Protection Regulations ('GDPR'), come into effect. These regulations will apply to all member states of the EU and are an updated and overhauled version of the previous data protection regulations, which are being put in place in order to take into account the fact that information technology has moved on significantly since the original directive in 1995. In November 2016 the government confirmed that the UK will adopt the GDPR, as the UK will still be an EU member state on 25 May 2018. Shortly after the result of the UK referendum on 23 June 2016 the UK's Data Protection Minister published a statement explaining that if we have a soft Brexit and the UK stays within the single market, the EU rules on data protection may continue to apply. However, if we have a hard Brexit and leave the single market, whether we will replace the EU rules with national rules will depend upon what happens in the negotiations regarding the UK's place within Europe. In any event, for companies who wish to share data with other EU member states or to handle EU citizens' data they would need to be able to show that they are providing an adequate level of protection in accordance with GDPR.

A particular area of the data protection regime which is often an issue for employers is in relation to data subject access requests. Any person for whom a company holds personal data, including an employee, can make a data subject access request to obtain details of the personal data about them and information as to why and how it is stored and used. Currently a data controller has 40 days within which to comply with a data subject access request but under the GDPR this period will decrease to one month. The information required under GDPR is more detailed than currently required under the Data Protection Act and a further change is that the data controller may not charge a fee for the information, unless the request is 'manifestly unfounded or excessive'.

Health and safety

The UK has a long history of strong health and safety legislation and it is unlikely that the government would seek to decrease the protection for employees in this area. However, the government has been keen to reduce what companies see as unnecessary 'red tape'. This agenda can be seen in a decision by the Coalition Government in 2013 to repeal the right to bring an individual civil action for breach of health and safety regulations. Since April 2013, breaches of health and safety regulations can therefore only be enforced by way of criminal prosecutions via the Health and Safety Executive or the Director of Public Prosecutions. It has not yet been established whether this is legal and compatible with EU law.

Following Brexit it may therefore be that some of the specific health and safety regulations would be repealed, to reduce the burden on businesses. Should this happen, employers would still be under a general duty of care to protect the health and safety of their employees at work.

Collective consultation

The current regulations requiring employers to inform and consult with employees, employee representatives or unions, which derive from EU law, have not been popular with the UK government as they are seen as imposing an unnecessary additional burden on businesses.

The regulations relating to collective redundancy consultation under the Trade Union Labour Relations Consolidation Act 1992 were amended in 2013. Previously, where an employer proposed to make 100 or more employees redundant within a 90-day period, they were required to consult with employee representatives for at least 90 days. However this period was reduced to 45 days.

This is an area which the UK government may seek to modify in order to make it easier for businesses to implement change more quickly. This could include increasing the point at which the collective redundancy consultation rules apply, in terms of the number of employees which must be affected, from the current figure of 20 or more employees. However, should the government try to implement such changes, it would be likely to meet strong opposition from trade unions.

12.2.3 Freedom of movement and immigration

The biggest immediate change that is likely to affect employers when the UK exits the EU will be the changes to freedom of movement. Currently, as citizens of a member state we all have the right under Article 45 of the Treaty on the Functioning of the European Union to live and work anywhere within the EU and this is unlikely to change until at least 2019 when the UK is due to leave the EU. As at November 2016 there were 2.35 million EU nationals working in the UK and around 1.2 million British people living in other parts of the EU. What will happen to these people post Brexit is currently unknown and will be a contentious issue in the negotiations with the EU over the next two years. However until such point as the negotiations are concluded, it is likely that the status quo will remain and that EU citizens currently in the UK will continue to have the right to live and work here.

Immigration skills charge

Since April 2017 the new immigration skills charge has applied to all employers sponsoring skilled migrants from outside of the EEA under a Tier 2 visa. The charge is £1,000 per sponsored employee per year, with a reduced rate of £364 per sponsored employee per year for small employers and charities.

The government have stated that the purpose of the immigration skills charge is to 'reduce demand for migrant labour' and to 'incentivise employers in training British staff'. This additional charge on employers is clearly designed to discourage UK employers from employing overseas workers.

It remains to be seen whether the government will consider expanding the charge to employers employing skilled migrants from the EU after Brexit.

Immigration points based system

The UK currently has a points-based system, under which employers can sponsor non EU overseas workers to work in the UK, subject to specific requirements. Under Tier 2, which applies to skilled workers, a worker must be sponsored by an employer for a particular role, which role must be of a sufficient skill level and attract a minimum level of salary. The employer must first obtain a sponsorship licence and in relation to each role that they wish to fill, they must pass the resident labour market test in order to show that they could not find a suitable worker from the UK. The process to obtain a sponsorship licence, a certificate for each worker that they wish to sponsor and for the worker to then obtain a visa is complex and lengthy and the assistance of a specialist immigration solicitor should be sought to handle this.

Following the UK's exit from the EU, if in its negotiations the UK government agrees that the freedom of movement will no longer apply to EU citizens, it is likely that the points based system will be extended to apply to EU workers. This would add an additional administrative and financial burden to businesses in the UK who are unable to find the skilled labour that they require from the UK workforce. The current provisions under Tier 2 relate to skilled workers only and there is currently no provision in place in relation to low skilled jobs. Should the right to freedom of movement for EU citizens be removed post Brexit, the UK could therefore suffer from a shortage of low skilled labour.

12.3 PREPARING YOUR BUSINESS FOR BREXIT

How do you prepare for the unknown? Although nothing will be certain until Brexit takes effect, it does not mean that businesses should not be alert to likely change and continuing developments, taking time now to prepare for what is already known and whatever else may come.

With at least two years clear warning of when Brexit will be executed, organisations in the United Kingdom have no excuse to be caught out by it, although how it will take effect and what the true impact will be may not be known for some time. Will the UK be driven off a cliff-edge as it has been warned, or will the government have a strategy in place to see the UK land safely on its feet when the time comes? The answer is far from clear right now, but with little confidence shared by the business community, responsibility falls to each business to start thinking about its own future and what it needs to prioritise.

In the six months' following the referendum and before the trigger of Article 50 by the UK government, the concerns of UK businesses related primarily to the future of European trade and instilling confidence in the business community. According to a survey of its members, the Institute of Directors ('IoD') stressed the importance of a good trade deal with the EU. So important was security of trade to the UK economy that the IoD and the British Chamber of Commerce called upon the UK government to extend the two-year negotiation period, which would automatically follow the trigger of Article 50. Although the act of uncoupling from the EU is not generally anticipated to take two years, putting in place an economic framework for trade is expected – by both the UK and senior figures in the EU – to take much longer. The only way that any extension can happen is by unanimous agreement between the UK and each member state. Whether that can be agreed forms part of a much broader, politically charged discussion.

Without any guarantees from the UK government or any clear indicators from the EU, the timeline for when Brexit will take full effect remains unfixed, let alone what Brexit will actually mean when it does eventually arrive. Without any clear direction, responsibility and risk is placed firmly onto businesses to manage their own affairs and to plan ahead, albeit without the security or confidence offered by stable laws or certainty of trade.

Although there has been some reluctance for UK political parties to agree, even for the sake of economic stability, that they will not seek to question, query or criticise whatever deal is agreed at the end of the Brexit negotiation process, Brexit in one form or another, is assured. Until that time comes, political games will continue and business must be flexible and responsive to change.

12.3.1 Workers' rights

For the vast majority of companies operating in the UK, employees will be the greatest cost centre and most important resource. In spite of this, the concern for employees did not feature heavily in the UK government's hastily delivered White Paper, delivered prior to the trigger of Article 50. Despite the hope that the White Paper would reassure business leaders (as well as politicians) about the Government's plans for the post-Brexit UK and how it would approach negotiations with the EU, it offered little that could be relied on. With only two mentions of employees across the whole document, there is a real risk that workers in and out of the UK are not at the top of the UK government's list of negotiation points.

That said, there have been some lukewarm assurances from Prime Minister Theresa May that the legal status of EU workers in the UK will be dealt with as a 'priority in the early stages of negotiations'. What that means in reality has not yet been seen.

In the short term, workers' rights are unlikely to diminish. The White Paper states clearly that 'this government has committed not only to safeguard the rights of workers set out in European legislation, but to enhance them' and that '[t]he Great Repeal Bill will maintain the protections and standards that benefit workers.' Given there is otherwise very little about employment rights, we should read this as a clear, if brief, statement of future intent.

When it comes to future-proofing a business against an uncertain post-Brexit United Kingdom, there are many areas that involve employees and the wider workforce. Some of these areas may require immediate attention, others may be some way off, but having a plan in place will be essential. The next section looks more specifically at what organisations can do now and considers the issues that might arise from an uncertain immediate future.

When it comes to your business, it may be premature to think of Brexit as a crisis situation, but being prepared for the unknown should be part of any organisation's strategy over the coming few years as the UK pushes in an uncertain new direction. A business that is prepared for the worst will be in the best possible position to respond quickly and take advantage of whatever new opportunities present themselves. To maximise those opportunities, having a flexible and engaged workforce is just as important as knowing what future risks will have to be mitigated.

12.3.2 Employee audit

Having the right number of people, in the right places, in the right roles is a continual challenge for any organisation, but during a period of change and transition, such as now, it is an essential element of keeping an organisation operational.

With around three million EU citizens living in the UK, there is a good chance that your workforce will in some way be affected by restrictions on their ability to work, should such expectations come true. Although guarantees around the rights of these residents are high on the list of priorities during the negotiation process, this is an important bargaining point for the discussions. With 1.2 million British citizens living in other EU member states, the government will be keen to secure a similar deal in the process

Knowing who your employees are and how they may be affected by whatever changes Brexit brings about is an important part of being prepared. European labour mobility restrictions and immigration controls may affect not only EU workers in the UK, but also any UK nationals who work in or around Europe. Workers in or from Norway, Iceland, Lichtenstein and Switzerland may also be affected by any post-Brexit models.

Costs of relocation and/or redundancy are likely to be a significant cost factor in some circumstances for which employers are advised to be prepared and to have contingencies in place.

Atypical employee or worker relationships could also be affected by Brexit. Secondment agreements with associated or third party organisations, expatriate and Europe-wide education or apprentice type arrangements (such as the student Erasmus programme amongst sector specific opportunities), will undoubtedly come under scrutiny during the transitional period. Review the terms of any such agreements, noting any reciprocal rights or obligations between affected organisations. Notice provisions and financial consequences (such as contractual relocation or repatriation packages for UK workers) should be reviewed in anticipation of quick decisions becoming necessary.

There is a legal obligation on employers to verify and document the right of employees to work in the UK. If an organisation has not checked and retained relevant documentation for all workers, it will be liable to significant fines as well as criminal sanctions. If you are not confident of the status of each employee, it is imperative that checks are made, regardless of any wider employee audit. Making such checks will not only protect organisations from future prosecution, but provide valuable information in preparing for Brexit.

Recording and regularly reviewing details of the nationality of workers and their current and future rights to work in the UK will assist in preparing for what Brexit negotiations may deliver and in recognising potential skills or labour gaps. Tracking the status of workers, with a contractual obligation for them to inform you of any changes to their status, will be of increased importance in the coming years as Brexit approaches.

It is also important to check the status of any UK nationals working in Europe (and further afield). Rights of residency and the ability to work, as well as free movement through Europe, are top of the agenda in the UK and it is quite possible that not all countries will be as accommodating to UK nationals as they are currently obliged to be. Communication with employees working outside of the UK should not fall through the cracks. These workers may already be feeling increasingly isolated and uncertain of their future – personal and professional. From a practical point of view, an open line of communication means that any plans they may have – for example, to seek residency in the member state where they are working – are more likely to be shared in good time.

Employers are well advised not to single out employees for immigration status checks. To do so could give rise to feelings of discrimination and future claims. If checks are to be made, they should be applied equally and fairly across the whole workforce unless there are documented special circumstances.

12.3.3 Planning for EU workers leaving and UK citizens returning

Although looking to the future is important, it is essential that in doing so, organisations do not fall foul of their continuing statutory and contractual obligations to employees and prospective employees. Preparing for Brexit is encouraged and perfectly acceptable so far as prevailing law continues to be respected. For example, in recruitment it is not lawful to refuse to consider an EU migrant for work or discount them from a recruitment process based solely on what may – or may not – happen. For the immediate future, EU migrants have a right to work in the UK and any failure to honour this will be in breach of the Equality Act 2010.

It is anticipated that any transition period will allow sufficient time for employers and EU employees based in the UK to make arrangements for the termination of employment, if necessary, and facilitate relocation out of the UK. At the time of writing, there is a strong feeling that all EU citizens working in the UK should be granted permission to remain. An early agreement on this point will alleviate many concerns for UK businesses and those millions of workers whose futures hang in the balance.

Specialist advice and support can assist employers and employees in understanding what the consequences of Brexit may be on their workforce. Companies that employ EU citizens in the UK may consider extending support to workers who could establish a right to remain in the UK, either as citizens, dual-citizens or permanent residents. Any provision of support or advice to employees in this specialist area should be applied equally and fairly, but there may also be good business reasons for supporting key workers more fully if there are good reasons to do so. Employers should be cautious of directly or indirectly favouring certain classes of worker, however, in light of the Equality Act.

As already suggested above, the future is uncertain for many thousands of UK citizens working across Europe on behalf of UK companies and under UK contracts of employment. Employers should take time to open discussions with such workers and, as with EU citizens in the UK, try to understand what their current motivations and plans are. Some, for example, may have settled in places where they are resident and may already have leave to remain as citizens or residents of their adopted countries.

On the other hand, if free-movement throughout Europe is an important part of their role, any restrictions on free movement may put their future employment in jeopardy if they cannot fulfil their roles. At the appropriate time, companies should consider any exposure they may have if they are unable to accommodate workers whose roles may no longer be required, or if there is no potential to accommodate them in the UK, should continued remote working not be possible.

For those who are eligible to claim residency or citizenship, employers may consider supporting them locally with specialist advice, especially if their services will be of future use to the company in their adopted state.

12.3.4 Review employee contracts and incentives

As it currently stands, Brexit itself will not automatically trigger any legislative changes that will impact immediately on the rights of employees or statutory obligations on employers. Indeed, any change in the short term is not thought to be likely given the assurance in the White Paper that the UK government has 'committed not only to safeguard the rights of workers set out in European legislation, but to enhance them.'

Although no immediate legislative change is anticipated, prevailing statutory requirements as well as continuing contractual opportunities should not be neglected. Indeed, in anticipation of the economic instability that is predicted, reviewing and revising contracts of employment that are sufficiently flexible and adaptable to an uncertain future will be invaluable.

Having terms and conditions of employment that are suitable will be as essential as it is throughout the entire employment relationship. It is to be expected that over time, terms and conditions will change and employees are generally aware and accepting of this. Preparing for Brexit may not be an immediate reason in itself for a wholesale review of terms, but there may be opportunities to enhance and update terms for incoming employees and for existing employees who are changing roles, for whatever reason.

New contracts should not only set out terms of the current engagement, but also look to the future. Notice periods and restrictive covenants are especially important terms in the contracts of senior or key employees. Alongside enhanced salary and benefits, clear obligations should be included in their contracts of employment or service agreements.

Notice periods should reflect not only the seniority of an employee, but also how critical they are to operations. A notice period allows time for an employer to replace exiting employees. As it has already been noted, indications already suggest that there will be a depleted pool of talent across most, if not all, sectors in the coming years. The time spent to locate talent, domestic or otherwise, may be longer. With this in mind, the incentives offered by employers to encourage talent to move from a secure role to new employment, without statutory protection against normal unfair dismissal in the first two years, may have to increase to match urgency and demand.

Just as important as attracting new talent is retaining an existing workforce. An uncertain economic future for business and trade is likely to see organisations cut back on unnecessary or non-essential expenses. Any attempts to reduce or consult on the reduction of employees' contractual entitlements will almost always be met with resistance, particularly in unionised workplaces. However, there may be the option to reduce or realign certain benefits and financial policies.

Annual pay reviews, for example, will typically be discretionary and in times of austerity, an organisation might be forgiven for not raising salaries. Employers are advised that if they make any pay awards outside of any publicised organisation-wide freeze on pay increases, they may leave themselves open to criticism from aggrieved individuals (or unions). It is essential to exercise any contractual discretion fairly and evenly, but not to make wholesale policy points across the workforce if they cannot or will not be observed.

Similarly, bonus payments are a significant incentive for employees in some sectors. Bonus schemes are often non-contractual, labelled as being awarded at the discretion of the employer. Alternatively, bonus policies that are revised annually provide an opportunity for employers to properly consider what it is they want to incentivise and where savings may be made. By tailoring a bonus policy to maximise any investment or reward that may be due to employees, linked to the objectives and strategy of the organisation, it will be difficult for those failing to reach such expectations to later claim they have been treated unfairly.

When bonus policies are reviewed, consideration should also be given as to when payments can be made under such schemes. It is not unusual, or indeed unlawful, for bonus payments to be likened to incentives for employee retention. For example, bonus payments will be paid in instalments over the course of the following year, provided the employee continues in employment and is not serving out a period of notice (either given by the employer or the employee for whatever reason). However, there is a risk that any unsupported or unreasonable delay in rewarding employees by making a bonus payment that has already been awarded may constitute an unenforceable penalty clause and advice on this point is recommended.

Unexpected costs may come from the recruitment of new employees, which could easily rise as the net must be cast wider to target a broader range of candidates, or to engage more expensive temporary labour to meet short or medium term demand.

Restrictive covenants that are fair and enforceable are an important part of protecting a company from damage as employees move on to other opportunities.

Consideration to what protections are appropriate in light of Brexit is something to which thought should be given at the earliest opportunity. Senior and key employees who are not subject to reasonable restrictions or who have restrictions that are too broad or not detailed enough can be problematic, if there is ever a need for them to be enforced.

Always ensure that there is a genuine business interest to protect and a proportionate employee restriction in place at the time of agreement and/or when enforcement measures are contemplated. Although it is good practice to review restrictions regularly, in the period running up to and post-Brexit, it will be essential for any employees working in or across European markets.

If restrictions on an employee's future employment and/or ability to deal or engage with existing and prospective customers, clients or suppliers are appropriate, agreeing those in the continuation of employment will afford employers a preferable bargaining position and be more effective than negotiating on exit or as part of any settlement agreement.

12.3.5 Review company policies and procedures

As we know, the legal and regulatory impact of Brexit is unlikely to be settled for many years to come, but as with contracts of employment, there are some policies which allow employers to take a more flexible approach.

It is not unusual for companies to 'gold-plate' the minimum legal benefits and other financial and non-financial matters affecting employees. How easy it is to make changes to these policies will depend on many things: the presence of a union or work council; whether the policies are deemed contractual by fact of custom and practice or precedent and the bargaining strength of the employer (or relevant employee(s)).

Although organisations may have policies covering many quasi-contractual arrangements, there are two policies that seem most likely to be affected by Brexit: redundancy and relocation.

Enhanced redundancy terms are not unusual, whether in writing or rendered contractual by custom and practice over many years. Following a period of recession over the past decade, many organisations have already reduced or limited their obligations on redundancy. At one time, it would not have been unusual to see employers compensate redundant employees with generous financial packages. However, some organisations still recognise and reward employees at these levels. If there is a risk that redundancies may follow Brexit, or restructuring may be required before, efforts to reduce expectations and quasi-contractual entitlements should commence as soon as possible and before any such policies need to be relied upon. Often, this will be done at the same time as a more general review of benefits and policies, to allow employees to continue in work on no less beneficial terms.

When it comes to relocation and repatriation arrangements for employees working outside of the UK, agreements may be personal to the individual or contained in a corresponding policy. As with any personal contract, an individual arrangement can be varied with consent and this is preferable. Unilateral variation is less desirable, as is the familiar dismiss and re-engage procedure (which must, of course, be done on notice). Often, substantial benefits will be included, such as family flights, rental costs and cash incentives. If it is expected that large numbers of employees will be required to return to the UK, account should be taken in planning.

12.3.6 Communication and leadership

Throughout this period, employee engagement will be essential. Having a workforce that not only knows the pressures facing their employer but one that actively understands why decisions are being made and the longer term objectives, goals and aspirations of the business can add to corporate stability, even in uncertain times.

Words are all well and good, but in relation to Brexit, what does engagement mean in practical terms? In this situation, leadership and communication are fundamental.

The press have and will continue to report widely (and sometimes, hysterically) on developments between the UK and the EU as negotiations continue. Brexit will be part of the national conversation now and beyond the next few years. It will be impossible to ignore and employees will be well aware. By ignoring them or excluding them from important decisions that affect them, even if the intention is to protect them in the short term, can cause irreparable damage to the inherent trust and confidence that exists between an employer and employee. That is not to say that all employees should be offered a place at the board table and invited to comment on any decisions being made. Simply keeping employees informed of plans at an appropriate time, involved in issues affecting them (where appropriate) and engaged in the successes (and from time to time, failures) of a business can build long term loyalty, trust and mutual respect at each level of the organisation.

It will also be important to have clear corporate vision and confident leadership. From the boardroom and throughout the management structure, positivity and encouragement can filter down and throughout the workplace. There is a real risk that all employees may be unsettled by the events they have little control over, not only those EU workers who are in the UK and facing an uncertain future. Maintaining a positive workplace and 'business as usual' mind-set may mean that the workforce remains as stable as possible too.

Employers should be wise to the risk of bullying, victimisation or racist attacks in the workplace as they have become an unfortunate feature of public life since the Referendum in June 2016. Any malicious, offensive or prejudicial behaviour must be dealt with quickly and decisively, whilst in-keeping with any formal procedures. At this time, a positive, safe and productive working environment should be secured for the benefit and safety of all workers.

Far from being specific to the events around Brexit, having a workforce that is fully absorbed into a company and engaged in its strategy can make it easier when delivering bad news and all the more rewarding when delivering good. It can also encourage employees to be proactive in their ideas and their support of decisions being made by their employer in the best interests of the organisation, even at times when it may not directly advantage them personally.

12.3.7 UK labour market

It is fully expected that the greatest impact of Brexit will be on the UK labour market, but waiting for Brexit to happen before addressing future employment needs may be too late.

It has already been reported that there is a shortage of workers in certain sectors brought about as a consequence of EU workers leaving the UK in anticipation of Brexit. According to the Chartered Institute of Personnel and Development ('CIPD'), by February 2017, one in four employers had reported that EU Nationals already resident and working in the UK were planning to leave their organisations, or the UK entirely, by the end of 2017. This figure rises to almost one in two organisations in the education and healthcare sectors. Shortages in the food supply chain, manufacturing, hospitality and healthcare have already been identified. Although many of these high volume, labour intensive posts are filled by lower-paid, lesser-skilled workers, it is fully expected that high-skilled, professional and well-paid EU Nationals are considering their future in the UK, pre-empting any formal decisions or agreements being settled between the UK government and the EU.

Compounding this further, fewer EU workers are coming to the UK since the June 2016 Referendum. In part, this may be due to the insecurity offered by the UK, but there is evidence to suggest that businesses are delaying the hire of permanent employees and recruitment is slowing as the UK goes through a period of political and economic flux.

Although the UK government's Budget in March 2017 set aside significant financial resource to provide investment in training and education to a new generation of skilled, technical workers, the rewards of such investment may take years, if not decades, to reap.

Anticipating skills, knowledge and service gaps that may result from Brexit can allow time to train or re-train the existing workforce or to recruit trainees to learn before there is any real impact on productivity or inability to meet customer demand. This may be necessary not only in the UK, but within any European operations that the company intends to continue with and needs to resource.

Many EU workers are engaged in labour-intensive and often physical roles. There is a real risk that younger, physically able and predominantly male workers will be in short supply post-Brexit, especially in the manufacturing, farming and hospitality sectors as well as heavy industry. Employees in these areas specifically should be aware of the significant short and medium term impact on losing access to those workers. The UK is forecast to have an ageing population and increasingly ageing workforce, not only because of the anticipated disbursement of EU nationals, but also the effect of reducing pension provision and individual savings.

In the UK, short and medium term gaps in labour can be readily filled by fixed term, casual and agency workers, but as demand rises, employee shortages can be expected in most sectors. Employers will be wise to work closely with recruitment agencies as well as their own internal teams to secure access to the pools of workers that they have identified as being most urgently required. For organisations that rely on labour for turnover of goods or services, any reduction can have an immediate impact on productivity and risk falling short of demand.

Retaining EU workers, or bringing in labour from outside of the EU, may incur additional costs for business that have not previously been anticipated or accounted for. The Immigration Skills Charge may be applied to any EU workers who continue in employment in the UK post-Brexit, and see employers burdened by significant immediate sponsor fees (currently £1,000 per employee with some reductions for smaller employers and charities). Employers currently reliant on EU workers because of a national skills shortage may have little alternative but to prepare for the increased costs and administrative burdens of migrant worker sponsorship. Preparing to employ migrant workers can be done before Brexit occurs, and with many organisations expected to require sponsorship licences, delays in the process are increasingly likely the more immediate the demand.

The government's review of modern employment practices, being conducted by Matthew Taylor, is expected to be critical of the growing number of zero-hours contracts being utilised across every sector of UK industry. The combination of Brexit, an uncertain economic outlook and revisions to employee rights may produce a perfect storm, leaving many companies unprepared, underfunded and under-resourced.

As has already been identified, for organisations reliant on skilled workers, having a commitment from your key employees can be of huge significance to forward planning. Again, employers must be careful not to discriminate against existing workers by demanding to know what their future plans may be, especially when so little has been guaranteed by the UK government at the early stages of the Brexit negotiation process. What might seem like straightforward questions to support and inform business planning, may be construed as harassing or bullying behaviour, and based solely on nationality. This is to be avoided and may lead to a claim of direct discriminatory behaviour under the Equality Act 2010. By involving employees, inviting them to discuss any questions they have and to share their concerns throughout the pre-Brexit period and beyond, there is a likelihood that valuable and beneficial information will be forthcoming or able to be elicited.

12.3.8 Information and consultation

Should workplace restructuring, redundancies or wholesale changes to terms and conditions of employment result from Brexit, time and resource will need to be allocated and accounted for. Advance planning, as already discussed, will assist in managing any formal information and consultation processes, where timing is essential and often dictated by statutory requirement. If redundancies are contemplated, reporting obligations to government must not be overlooked.

If your company has a European Works Council (EWC) agreement in place, consider how Brexit may affect how it is structured and, in particular, employee representative thresholds. Any restructuring or organisational changes triggered by Brexit are likely to invoke the duty to inform an EWC and an early review is recommended.

12.3.9 Pensions

A substantial amount of EU pensions law is already incorporated into UK legislation, and this will remain unchanged for the foreseeable future. However, alterations in some areas are likely over time, but this will be dependent on the broader Brexit negotiations. Employers are advised to be aware of the potential for change and await further guidance in due course.

Pension scheme trustees should consider if any contingencies need to be put in place and when.

12.3.10   Data protection

The General Data Protection Regulations ('GDPR') will be incorporated into UK legislation on 25 May 2018, before the two-year Brexit deadline is reached. With little confidence that negotiations will be complete within that period, the UK will be obliged to follow the GDPR. Whether the GDPR will remain the basis of data protection regulation beyond Brexit is yet to be determined, but a sensible employer will be wise to follow it closely and abide by the obligations and procedures introduced into UK legislation in due course.

12.4 CONCLUSION

Having reviewed the impact that being part of the EU has had on UK employment law over the past half century, it is evident that there are a great many rights that employees have come to enjoy that might not otherwise have been available. However, the UK has frequently led the way and given more to its citizens than it has been obliged to provide. It should not be expected that this will change. The UK will not abandon the rights, protections or opportunities that workers and employees have grown to take for granted – at least not totally.

There is no doubt that a period of flux will follow. Businesses must be prepared for that. There will be opportunities though, whether that is with new trading partners, free-movement agreements or a skills boom across the UK workforce. Organisations that are successful will be prepared for change, ready to adapt and evolve as quickly as they can.

Recruitment may be strained for some time, but the value in maintaining a positive, confident and engaged workforce should not be discounted. Whilst policy and trade deals are negotiated at the highest level, it is for UK employers to pass on confidence to their employees and build a foundation for growth when the time comes.

CHAPTER 13

INSOLVENCY

Howard Morris and Jason Mbakwe, Morrison & Foerster (UK) LLP

INTRODUCTION

The UK is widely regarded as a global centre for restructurings, something evidenced by the number of non-UK companies that take measures to bring themselves within the jurisdiction of the courts so they might restructure, principally using the scheme of arrangement. In addition the UK is an important capital market with so many banks, investors and the specialist hedge funds that are active among distressed companies, based in the country. English law is commonly the governing law of a material part of debtor companies' obligations so the UK is the obvious and convenient venue for consensual restructurings hammered out between the debtor and its stakeholders. It is not simply UK insolvency laws (some would say 'in spite of') which are, again, the subject of reform proposals, that make the UK so attractive as a place to restructure but the respect felt internationally for the quality of professional advisers, the flexibility and predictability of English law and the sophistication and reliability of the UK courts. A number of these critical factors will be unaffected by Brexit and so, notwithstanding leaving the EU, the UK can remain a hub for international restructurings, even following Brexit.

However, it is clear that the loss of EU membership and the disapplication of EU laws will have some negative effect on the perceived attractiveness of conducting a cross-border restructuring in the UK. The UK recently slipped in the World Bank's annual Doing Business league table which suggests that perception of the UK's insolvency laws are not as favourable as they once were. By removing the added advantage of EU-wide automatic recognition of judgments and proceedings and cooperation between insolvency office-holders – that perception may fall even further.

Conversely, the US rose ten places in the same World Bank league table. American restructuring tools, and in particular, the Chapter 11 process are being increasingly viewed as best practices by organisations such as the World Bank and UNCITRAL. In the absence of measures modernising the insolvency processes in the UK (which remain at consultation stage[1]), there is a risk that following Brexit, companies may seek to find a nexus which allows them to conduct their restructurings in the US rather than in UK and credit institutions may seek to create establishments in other EU member states in order to retain access to the EU-wide tools available to them currently. A significant effort

---

1   https://www.gov.uk/government/uploads/system/uploads/attachment_data/file/525523/A_Review_of_the_Corporate_Insolvency_Framework.pdf

towards harmonisation of EU insolvency laws to establish a framework across the community that would, like the UK's reform proposals, bring the EU closer to the World Bank and UNCITRAL ideals, as well as competition from Singapore and other nations aspiring to be international restructuring centres, means that there is no guarantee the UK will remain such a powerful hub.

13.1 CORPORATE INSOLVENCY AND RESTRUCTURINGS

Currently, the main operative piece of EU legislation that affects UK restructuring/insolvency proceedings is the European Insolvency Regulation (Council Regulation (EC) 1346/2000 (the 'EIR'). The EIR is aimed at increasing cooperation and establishing common rules on cross-border insolvencies and has direct effect in the UK (as well as in every other EU member state except Denmark). For companies, it applies to compulsory winding up proceedings, creditors' voluntary winding up proceedings, administrations and company voluntary arrangements. It does not include schemes of arrangement or any type of receivership.

The EIR provides clarity over the effect of the location of insolvency proceedings:

- the courts of the member state in which the debtor has his centre of main interests (COMI) have jurisdiction to open insolvency proceedings, which are referred to as the 'main insolvency proceedings';
- once main proceedings have been opened, 'secondary insolvency proceedings' may also be opened, which run in parallel in one or more other member states in which the debtor has a place of operations where it carries out a non-transitory economic activity with human means and goods (an 'establishment');
- before main proceedings have been opened in an EU member state where the debtor has its COMI, local insolvency proceedings can be opened anywhere the debtor has an establishment. Such proceedings are referred to 'territorial proceedings' and are restricted to the assets located in that member state. This can apply to either winding up or reorganisation proceedings.

The EIR creates a duty for office holders in main proceedings and secondary proceedings to communicate information with each other and to cooperate with each other in general. The office holder in secondary proceedings has to give the office holder in the main proceedings an early chance to submit proposals on how the assets in the secondary proceedings should be used. This had been seen as a fairly radical development in cooperation in cross-border insolvency provisions but appears to have been hampered by the lack of a central database of court orders made in insolvency proceedings located in the EU.

13.2 BREXIT EFFECT

On leaving the EU the UK will cease to benefit from the EIR. The country will be going back in time to before the EIR but with a significant difference, the mismatch described below. The following will be the principal consequences:

- No automatic recognition (and mismatch):

  The automatic recognition in EU member states afforded to insolvency proceedings (such as administration) under the Insolvency Act 1986 (UK) and of the UK insolvency office holder (such as an administrator) will cease (except in those EU member states that have implemented the UNCITRAL Model Law on Cross Border Insolvency (the 'Model Law'). Only Greece, Poland, Romania and Slovenia (and the UK) have yet done so).

  This means, for an administrator in a UK administration with assets or operations in other EU member statess, she or he will need to make a separate application for recognition (and possibly open local proceedings) in each of those other EU Member States in order to:

  - benefit from the relief (such as a moratorium, discussed below) necessary to protect those assets and operations from litigation and attachment by creditors, and
  - deal with any assets or operations in that jurisdiction.

  The application will fall to be determined in accordance with the laws of private international law of that EU member state and/or judicial co-operation unless a bilateral treaty is put in place between the UK and that state. Alternatively the administrator might have to trigger an insolvency proceeding in that EU member state.

  Moreover, an insolvency proceeding in another EU member state will not be secondary proceedings (as it is under the EIR) and confined just to the assets and liabilities of the company in that member state. It will be, potentially, a separate independent proceeding, competing with the UK proceedings.

  It will therefore clearly be more expensive, time-consuming and cumbersome to run a UK administration if the company has assets and operations in the EU. Companies with assets and operations in the EU may consider moving their COMI from the UK to an EU member state so as to benefit from the reciprocal automatic recognition and relief and the detailed framework for resolving conflicts of law provided under the EIR, and the reformed insolvency regimes introduced in recent years by a number of EU member states may thus become more popular. However, such a decision would need to be weighed up against the very real benefits – which will not change – of the UK court system and administration process, which are known for their commerciality, transparency and predictability.

  Joining the European Free Trade Association ('EFTA') will not avoid these problems since the EIR does not apply to the members of the EFTA (and, in any event, the EFTA requires acceptance of the principle of freedom of movement of people, the rejection of which was a central pillar of the Leave Campaign). There is currently no option for non-EU member states to accede to the EIR.

- Mismatch: EU member state insolvency proceedings will continue to benefit from recognition in the UK.

Conversely, the UK's obligation (following a 'set-piece' application without regard to the merits) to grant automatic recognition in the UK of the insolvency proceedings of a company in an EU member state (and whose COMI is in that state) and to the officer appointed to supervise that company's insolvency, will continue (since the UK has implemented the Model Law).

- No automatic relief:

  The reliefs and protections (such as cessation of litigation and enforcement of security) that the UK's Insolvency Act 1986 confers on a company in administration will lose automatic recognition across the EU member states. An application for relief will need to be made and, again, will fall to be determined in accordance with the private international law of the relevant member state. The purpose of the relief is important – it provides breathing space for the administrator to assess and gather all of the property of the estate without creditors seeking remedies to protect their own interests. It therefore assists in maximising value for all creditors.

  - Mismatch: EU member state insolvency proceedings will continue to benefit from automatic relief in the UK.

  Conversely, EU member state insolvency proceedings in respect of any entity whose COMI is in that EU member state will continue to benefit from relief in the UK by virtue of the Model Law (as described above).

- Which laws apply?

  The EIR establishes that the 'State of opening of proceedings' determines the procedural law for the opening, conduct and closing of insolvency proceedings including the following matters:

  - the assets that form part of the estate;
  - the effect of insolvency proceedings on current contracts to which the debtor is party; and
  - who is to bear the costs and expenses incurred in the insolvency proceedings.

  The EIR also provides that other matters are to be determined otherwise than by reference to the 'State of opening of proceedings'. Examples are:

  - set-off rights;
  - rights in rem and reservation of title;
  - employment rights; and
  - detrimental acts.

Following Brexit, these and other complex procedural and substantive matters will again fall to be determined in accordance with the rules of private international law of the laws of the relevant EU member states and the UK. The determination of these issues will be time-consuming and difficult to predict.

13.3 SCHEMES OF ARRANGEMENT

As already mentioned the scheme of arrangement, not a creature of UK insolvency legislation but a venerable procedure from the Companies Acts that has enjoyed a surge of popularity in recent years as an effective tool to restructure companies notwithstanding up to 25% of the stakeholders with an economic interest in the company, vote against the proposal, is an important reason why non-UK debtor companies make their way to the UK to achieve a deal.

The main area of uncertainty in relation to application of schemes to EU member state companies relates to the role of the EU Recast Judgments Regulation. Specifically, the regulation's bearing on the question of whether there is a 'good prospect' that the Scheme will take effect in those EU member states where assets of the scheme company are located. And that is an issue for a non-UK company or a UK company if they have assets in other jurisdictions. An English court asked to sanction a scheme relies on expert evidence to answer the 'good prospect' question. As recent cases show the answer has not been found in the Recast Judgments Regulation, but rather in the rules of private international law as found in the relevant member state's law (eg *Re Van Gansweinkel Groep BV and others*[1]). Therefore on this basis, the falling away of the Recast Judgments Regulation should not affect the sanctioning of Schemes.

However, it is a possibility that it will prove in practice to be more difficult to obtain the same expert opinions on which the English court have relied if the UK has exited the EU on acrimonious terms and with no appropriate replacement arrangements in place. The popularity of schemes for restructurings over the limited solutions offered by the other EU member states has prompted reform of restructuring laws in some EU member states in an effort to bring restructurings back 'home'. These efforts to date have not had much tangible impact. However, as mentioned above, the loss of automatic cross-border recognition for the UK could also see an increase in the number of companies who seek out alternative restructuring solutions. Brexit may lead to a change in sentiment about the attractiveness of going to England to use a Scheme.

(If there were any doubt about the role of the Recast Judgments Regulation, the Lugano Convention may provide a substitute.)

13.4 CREDIT INSTITUTIONS

Formal reorganisation and winding up proceedings under the Credit Institutions (Winding Up) Directive (2001/12/EC) ('CIWUD')

CIWUD provides rules for mutual recognition and effectiveness of reorganisation and winding up measures in respect of a credit institution taken by EEA States. It assists in ensuring that the measures will be applied to branches of an institution located in another EEA State.

---

1   [2015] EWHC 2151 (Ch).

- No automatic recognition:

  Following Brexit, the UK authorities would lose automatic recognition across EU member states (as well as members of the EFTA) as CIWUD would cease to apply to the UK. The relevant UK authority may be required to apply for the opening of local proceedings for branches of the institution that are located in an EEA State. The benefits of the single proceeding facilitated by CIWUD would therefore be lost.

  For UK measures to be granted recognition in relation to branches in other EU member states the following options apply:

- the UK could negotiate bilateral arrangements with the relevant EEA States individually, or

- the UK could seek to become a member of the European Free Trade Association ('EFTA') (as CIWUD applies to the EFTA members).

  - potential mismatch of recognition.

  On the other hand, unless and until the UK amends or repeals its equivalent domestic legislation implementing CIWUD, measures taken in EEA States would continue to benefit from recognition in the UK.

13.5 RECOVERY AND RESOLUTION MEASURES UNDER THE BANK RECOVERY AND RESOLUTION DIRECTIVE (2014/59/EU) (THE 'BRRD')

The BRRD grants powers to 'resolution authorities' in EU member states in respect of banks and certain other investment firms in their jurisdiction. These powers allow them to intervene at an early stage of a failing institution (including to use the controversial 'bail-in powers' on creditors). The BRRD provides harmonisation of those powers and mutual recognition and enforcement across all EU member states of their exercise. For example, if a Portuguese Resolution Authority exercises a 'bail in power' in respect of English law bonds issued by a Portuguese bank, this will be recognised in the UK; absent 'supra-national' authority such as the BRRD, there would be limited ability for a foreign government to interfere with rights and obligations governed by an English law instrument.

- No automatic recognition: The UK authorities lose automatic recognition across the EEA

  The principle of automatic mutual recognition of resolution measures will cease to apply and the issues noted above in relation to CIWUD would apply equally here also.

  In order for UK measures to be granted recognition in other EU member states, in addition to taking the steps referred to in the CIWUD section above, it may be possible to negotiate a 'third country' agreement. The BRRD allows the EU Council to negotiate agreements with countries outside of the EEA to facilitate the establishment of principles of cooperation and recognition between the EEA countries and these third countries.

- potential mismatch of recognition.

As with CIWUD, domestic legislation implementing the BRRD would not cease to be in effect if the UK was to leave the EU. On that basis, automatic recognition of resolution measures imposed by EU resolution authorities should continue to apply in the UK unless and until such legislation is amended or repealed.

13.6 CONCLUSION

Depending on a deal the UK and the EU negotiate, and which the Prime Minister has asserted is not guaranteed to be agreed at all, UK insolvency and restructuring may find itself outside of the EU system completely. The Great Repeal Bill may tackle the domestic issue of which EU laws continue to apply in the UK, but it will not in itself be able to resolve the mismatch issues described above or coerce cooperation in insolvency proceedings from the remaining EU member states. There are a range of possible outcomes. It is possible that the UK and the EU negotiate and agree a multilateral treaty effectively recreating the effect of the EIR and similar measures are agreed in respect of the other Brexit consequences. However, certainly in the short term, this is widely considered as unlikely, not least because restructuring and insolvency are not seen by either the UK or EU negotiators as critical issues.

Conducting restructurings in the UK following Brexit is unlikely to substantially change or experience significant short-term decline. However, Brexit is set to intensify the need for modernisation of UK insolvency procedures to remain attractive in the spectre of the growing popularity of US methods and the attempts of other EU nations to revamp their procedures.

To summarise, the likely effect of Brexit on UK restructurings are as follows:

13.6.1 Companies

- UK administrations: the UK will cease to be bound by and benefit from, the European Insolvency Regulation. This means material disadvantages for companies in administration that have assets and/or operations in EU member states, including:

  - there will be prolonged uncertainty regarding almost every aspect of the administration (discussed in detail below). Unless separate bilateral treaties with individual EU Member States are negotiated these matters will fall to be determined by reference to the varying rules of private international law of the relevant EU member state and the UK.
  - the automatic recognition of the administrator as the authorised office-holder throughout the EU member states and the automatic stay on litigation or enforcement of security will cease. The

administrator will have to apply for recognition and a stay in each
EU member state and the application will be considered on its
merits in accordance with the rules of private international law of
the relevant EU member state.

- Schemes: as it stands, there should be no change in the ability of an
  English court to sanction a scheme of arrangement in respect of a
  (foreign) company whose COMI is in another EU member state (but this
  may depend on there being no material departure by courts in the EU
  member states in the application of rules of their own private international
  law insofar as they apply them to the UK (as further discussed. However,
  Brexit may further incentivise the EU Member States to develop
  alternative informal restructuring processes in competition with the ever-
  more popular scheme.

13.6.2 Credit institutions

- Formal winding up tools: a UK financial institution that undergoes a
  formal reorganisation or winding up proceeding will be disadvantaged
  if it has branches or assets in other EU member states or has issued
  securities under the laws of another EU member state.

  This is because the proceedings will cease to benefit from automatic
  recognition and relief across all EU member states provided by CIWUD.
  Joining the EFTA would, however, solve this.

- Recovery and resolution tools: similar disadvantages will be experienced
  by UK credit institutions and other relevant firms in relation to so-
  called recovery and resolution tools (such as bail-in and good bank/
  bad bank arrangements). However, the UK may be able to negotiate a
  'third country' agreement with the EU Council as regards some matters
  covered by the BRRD. Joining the EFTA would also solve this.

Part II

Thought Leadership by Inspirational Leaders

JOHN TIMPSON, CEO, TIMPSONS

Even before I reached our office, on the morning after the Brexit vote, there were enough e-mails to indicate many of our colleagues were seriously worried. The Remain supporters' forecast of immediate economic disaster had hit home and some of our shop colleagues were anticipating a dramatic fall in demand. At 9.30am that morning I sent everyone the following message.

'Many of you, like me, will have been surprised that the electorate voted to leave the EU and will be wondering what this means for our business.

Despite the many gloomy forecasts made during the campaign I never thought that EU membership makes any difference to the demand for shoe repairs, dry cleaning or photo services. There will be just as many people wanting to get a key cut today as there were yesterday.

My guess is that the referendum result shows that the majority of voters don't want to be told what to do by politicians in either Brussels or Westminster and, at Timpson, with our upside down management approach, this is a view that is easy to understand.

I want you to know that we will continue to invest in looking after our colleagues, because we know that success, as ever, depends on providing great customer service which is best done by picking people with the right personality and giving them the freedom to do their job in the way they know best.

Leaving the EU will make no difference to the way we run the business or to our future prospects.'

The unsuccessful Remain campaign was based on three misconceptions:

(1) The merits of in or out can purely be measured by money;
(2) We can rely on economic forecasts;
(3) The public believe that government knows best.

In retrospect the majority didn't buy the Remainer's argument that 'anyone who understands the facts will realise the country is much better off within the EU'. Both sides waged war using economic forecasts as their main weapon, with dramatic claims of lower incomes from one side and more money for the NHS on the other. Westminster has become so obsessed with making evidence based decisions, even when no clear evidence exists, they are happy to rely on an economic forecast. But economics is an art not a science and forecasts are far away from being facts; like every other guess, they are full of speculation.

This evidence-based mantra reduced the Brexit discussion to finance – but it is not all about money. I, for one, voted to leave because I didn't want my country to be governed by a European parliament. I want to be free to do it our way. I have discovered how well a culture of freedom works in my business and am convinced it is the best way to run our country.

One of the joys of being in business is the fact that you can never be sure what will happen next. From my experience the future is no more predictable today than it was when I started work in 1960. Despite an army of economists and market researchers the next 20 years are still gloriously uncertain and the business winners will still be those entrepreneurs with courage, flair and intuition.

The vote in June 2016 should have settled the argument but it doesn't seem to have ended the debate. Apart from a fall in the value of the pound, there has yet to be even a glimmer of the gloom predicted by the pessimistic forecasters, but they still stick to the script. It is time to change the subject, stop the boring Brexit debates and start talking about how we can make the most of the opportunities that will come from ceasing to be a full member of the EU.

There is no point in waiting for Article 50 to run its full course; don't be tempted to use the inevitably lengthy negotiations as an excuse for doing nothing. You will probably be none the wiser about Europe in three years' time. While the politics are being played out, get on with developing your business by creating a culture which recognises that success is achieved by ideas and great people rather than process and best practice.

Luckily I learnt this lesson about 20 years ago. I have now reached the age when I can look back over a career that covers 56 years, three major economic crises, inflation as high as 26.8%, two management buy outs, over 20 acquisitions and a boardroom row that temporarily took the company out of family ownership. Despite a roller coaster trip fewer than ten major decisions have made a major difference to my long term fortunes and the biggest game changer was in 1997 when I suddenly discovered the secret behind great customer service.

For 21 years as our chief executive I always recognised the importance of customer care but missed the simple secret which I now know is obvious. I spent a lot of my time running customer care courses, writing a code of practice and designing behind the scenes posters telling our colleagues to 'SMILE', but you don't produce excellent service by giving your sales team a rule book. Orders don't work; the only way to give amazing service is to trust the colleagues who serve your customers with total freedom to do it the way they know best.

During the Referendum debate we were bombarded with economic forecasts and they still keep coming, I prefer to ignore the experts and trust my own judgement. No one really knows what a difference Brexit will make, but you can be certain that plenty of other unexpected major events will happen. Brexit isn't the only thing to worry about. Most of the things we will be buying and selling, in thirty years' time, have yet to be invented. There will be more recessions, perhaps an energy crisis and changes in UK taxation which will make at least as much difference as Brexit.

The winners won't be the ones who worry about future forecasts the prizes will be won by those who take an optimistic approach and look to see how life after Brexit can make business better. We are all bound to be thinking hard about the future but I won't bother going to any Brexit breakfast seminars. Strategic planning is my job because I reckon that I know our business much better than any outsider.

I'm lucky, Brexit can't make a massive difference to prospects at Timpson, but others with a high proportion of their trade coming from Europe may face a pretty torrid time. To survive, they will have to change, but standing still is never an option, with or without Brexit. Look at what happened to Woolworths, Dewhurst the Butchers, Radio Rentals, BHS and many more retailers who didn't move with the times. Changes forced on companies by Brexit may well be a blessing in disguise.

My favourite management tool and something anyone could use as a Brexit buster is an A4 pad. The best way to sort out your strategy is to find pen, paper, peace and quiet and have a fundamental think. Every three years I write my Chairman's Report for 15 years from now. By picking a year so far ahead I free my imagination from today's issues and try to find the main game changers and stumbling blocks that lie ahead. Some of my past predictions have forecast the growth of our supermarket concessions and our diversification into dry cleaning.

I am shortly due to write my report for 2032 and, of course, it is impossible to predict with any confidence what Timpsons will be doing or indeed where or how we will be doing it. We probably won't be repairing mobile phones because they will have been replaced by some other new invention. I'm pretty sure but not certain that we will still be trading on the traditional high street but more of our business will be connected to the internet (or whatever takes over from the internet). Despite having to fumble futilely into the future this exercise is far from being a waste of time.

In anticipating developments you are bound to be better prepared when some of the forecasts turn into reality. Writing the report is a sharp reminder that every business exists in a changing world and managing change is central to any company strategy. But by thinking so far ahead you also start to realise that some things don't need to change. It makes you work out what your business is good at, the critical secrets of success, the vital bits of magic dust that combine to create your company culture. Whatever we finish up doing in 2032 I still want there to be a Timpson business that gives great service by picking colleagues with personality and giving them the freedom to do their job the way they know best. The wish to be a family business that feels like a family will be just as important in 2032 as it is today.

We should never forget the benefits of a united Europe, I have been lucky to have lived all but two years of my life without there being a world war. Free trade also made sense, but when we entered the Common Market we didn't expect to acquire a parliament with a new set of legislation. The EU is bound to suit some countries more than others. Germany enjoys having a strong influence on European affairs, France seems to like having the rules and Italy probably needs the rules to control their economy. Each member will have a different perspective.

When the referendum result was declared I was amazed that everyone so freely told the world how they had cast their individual vote and I was shocked by the vitriolic reaction from many people living and working in London, who claim to have been betrayed by ignorant voters in the rest of the country. I can understand why merchant bankers and city professionals, who have been sitting in the Centre of the European economy, would have preferred a Remain vote. I can also appreciate that civil servants in Whitehall, who have suddenly been asked to play a completely new game, were happy with the status quo. But, for business, Brexit brings a golden chance to put process in its proper place. This is the opportunity to halt the relentless advance of the administrators and professional fee creators who surround us with so much regulation, good governance, best practice and risk assessment there is little time left to attend to running the real business.

Brexit gives business a chance to get back some freedom, but I'm not sure it is a chance that will be taken. Maybe we have got so used to a world of compliance managers that we will miss living in a world dominated by process. Perhaps we don't possess enough mavericks to take the opportunity of running their business on the back of flair and initiative. It is possible that few executives have the courage to face up to the rule makers and institutional shareholders in a fight for common sense.

I also worry whether Whitehall will have got the message. Despite a clear sign that a lot of voters do not want to be told what to do by 'the establishment' I fear that the senior civil service will continue to dictate policy and legislate for a process designed to produce the perfect result. I dream of something very different which I call 'Upside Down Government'. In my dream, government would set the scene for success rather than relying on a proscribed process. The Department for Business Innovation and Skills has the right objectives, it talks of supporting British business and that's exactly the right role, but, as the recent ill thought through Apprenticeship Levy has shown they still want to dictate how business is run. In 2004 I spent a week at the Department for Trade and Industry (predecessor to the current business department) where I spent a morning with the head of training. I asked how much of their training was about business and after a short silence was told 'we are discussing the idea of developing a business module in the near future'. During that week I learnt quite a bit about the civil service, enough to realise that it will be a miracle if my dream of 'Upside Down Government' ever comes true.

Finally, before I finish I think it is only right for me to say how I think Brexit will affect us at Timpson. Frankly, I don't think Brexit will make much difference. Apart from a small concession trial in China and a few shops in the Republic of Ireland, all our trade is done in the UK. If I have any concerns they are in the short term. We could all experience a bit of an economic wobble due to uncertainty during the period of negotiation. Although the outcome may make little long term difference a drawn out debate could do some damage to the economy. The biggest danger is that price rises could wipe out the benefits of the national living wage, further increasing the wealth gap and putting the biggest burden on those least able to afford it. The soon Brexit is sorted out the better.

Despite some short term concerns I am optimistic. My confidence in the post-Brexit world is based on the fact that we will continue to break the rules and run our business the way we know best.

Our future, as for every business, will not be determined by Brexit but by the strength of our company culture and the talent of our colleagues. We are all in charge of our own destiny.

For more information on Timpson visit www.timpson.co.uk

STEPHEN ROSSER, CHIEF EXECUTIVE, CLARKE WILLMOTT

My role at Clarke Willmott is a full-time, elected position and covers all aspects of the business. I was originally elected to the position in May 2010 and I am responsible for the day to day management of the firm, chairing its executive board, and defining and implementing the firm's strategy.

Clarke Willmott as a firm has its roots in South West England in the 19th century. We are now a full service national law firm with seven offices in major UK cities. Over 130 years in business the firm has weathered many storms. Our survival and success owes much to an overriding belief in a prudent approach to growth. Whilst we value growth, we also value the long-term success of the firm as a profitable organisation capable of supporting a successful future for our clients and our workforce. Post Brexit referendum, this more than ever is my focus.

The result of the EU Referendum on 23 June 2016, the subsequent triggering of Article 50 and the ultimate withdrawal of Britain from the EU will clearly have a huge impact on UK residents and businesses. From a personal perspective, I believed – and still believe – that Britain should remain a part of the EU. However, I respect the outcome of the referendum and my role now is to ensure that the firm and out clients are best placed to deal with the challenges that result.

Whilst the referendum determined that Britain should leave the EU, we have not yet done so. Furthermore despite months of wrangling, the detailed process for doing so remains unclear. It is, however, clear that any legislative changes will not be immediate and in fact may take many years to come into force.

Many have speculated wildly on the potential implications of Brexit. However, whilst a great number of questions have been raised by the referendum decision, our position now is that, in practice, Brexit is the new 'business as usual'. In this new environment we can almost certainly expect short term economic flux followed by a period of legal and regulatory codification as the UK seeks to transpose the significant EU legislation into UK law.

As a firm we are successful as a result of the expert legal advice provided to individual clients and businesses across a range of market sectors by our specialist teams. This has not been changed by the result of the referendum.

In the face of inevitable huge legal change on the horizon, informed, commercial and up to date legal advice will be more important than ever.

I am well aware that our clients' experience may well be different and I have reflected on the impact to date on some of our key service areas:

Real estate

The property market has been more resilient than was perhaps predicted by some. Following the recession nearly ten years ago, the UK has been in a property market that has expected flexibility and this remains unchanged. As a result, adjustments have already been made to make the market well equipped to cope with some of the uncertainties ahead post-Brexit. Following the referendum there was a drop in commercial property prices, certainly in central London. This, coupled with the devaluation of the currency that has occurred, has made the UK attractive to overseas investors. The market is likely to get more competitive and enhanced relations with the US and China, in particular, are on the horizon.

For property developers, the immediate aftermath of the referendum vote caused much concern and the falling share prices of the large PLC developers reflected this. Developers were shocked into withdrawing from larger transactions where the exposure was considered to be too great given the uncertainty of Brexit and each transaction was scrutinised much more closely by management. Since the summer recess, however, much of the initial shock has dissipated and the trading conditions are significantly stronger.

Corporate, commercial and employment

It is impossible to make a broad, sweeping assessment of the impact of Brexit on corporate/commercial aspects of our business. For some clients the change will create great opportunity, for others it may be the threat that has the potential to bring their businesses to an end. Periods of economic flux typically provide an impetus for businesses to enforce their rights in circumstances where in a buoyant economy they may seek to reach agreements through commercial arrangements. This can often cause or exacerbate losses for firms and individuals which make disputes more commonplace and keep litigators busy.

From an employment law/HR perspective our corporate clients have, on the whole, taken Brexit in their stride. We typically look after corporates that operate in the SME sector and whilst some have been a little more cautious on hiring new staff since last June, the majority have continued on as usual and we certainly have not seen any Brexit-related job loss programmes. There is a clear expectation that Brexit will in time produce a reduction in so called 'red tape', something that our clients welcome. Many recognise, however, that such a reduction is likely to be some years off. The one area of concern that we have seen for some – generally large manufacturers and some in the agri business sector – is the possible abolition of the current freedom of movement. These clients rely heavily on European labour and have a real concern that without freedom of movement they simply will struggle to fill job roles in the future. Indeed clients have already mentioned to us that these concerns are becoming a reality in certain areas.

Banking and Finance

Linked to comments above, one of the major impacts post Brexit will be on the banking sector. If, as is expected, UK banks lose their so called 'passporting' rights, there is an expectation that firms will adapt by moving significant parts of their operations, and people, to Europe – as I write this there are news reports that Goldman Sachs will move 1,000 jobs from London to Paris and Frankfurt. UK based lending is likely to be impacted by a period of lower valuations. New models of banking and financial services that have in recent years been buoyant in the UK – from peer to peer lending to FinTech – may feel a squeeze as entrepreneurs and innovators consider basing themselves in European tech hotspots rather than in the UK. This said, the UK has a rich history in banking and financial services as well as of creativity, innovation and entrepreneurialism and it is hard to see this changing as a result of a vote.

Retail

The retail reaction overall has been less positive. But there is more than one story in this sector alone. For retailers who rely on importing goods, the fall in the value of the sterling has made imported goods more expensive. Sterling is expected to fall further and until negotiations to leave the EU are complete the sector will endure inflated cost pressures. Retailers who depend on imported goods (particularly in highly competitive markets such as food and fashion) will either have to pass the cost on to their customer to protect profit margins, or bear the cost themselves in order to attract sales and remain competitive – the second option is easier for large national chains and supermarkets, but near impossible for smaller independents.

Conversely, the devaluing of the pound has benefitted other retailers, in particular those that sell goods online. UK goods are cheaper for customers in the EU and United States, so sales have increased, but retailers can also charge higher prices and increase profit margins. London-based retailers have also benefitted. The capital has always been a shopping destination for overseas visitors, but the weak pound has brought more shoppers to the UK – particularly over the Christmas period. British exporters have likewise profited from the situation. Britain has an opportunity to maximise on its reputation for good quality manufacturing so sales of luxury and GB branded goods sell well in new growth markets such as the Middle East, Russia and China.

Agri-business

Perhaps one area we expect to see far reaching impact is the area of agri-business. For the first time since the 1970s the UK government will need to introduce legislation to develop policies relating to UK agriculture, fisheries and trade. It is hard to see how this will not create challenges and opportunities right across this sector.

Social housing

For the social housing sector, it is clear that the uncertainty caused by Brexit has the potential to have a negative impact. The risk of higher inflation, the limitations on migration for construction labour and skills and higher costs of imported constructions materials mean that the capacity of the housebuilding industry may be affected. However with clear government backing and with social housing providers in a good place with regards to their finances and planned mergers and growth activity, the impact might be mitigated in the medium term. As with most areas, a lot remains to be seen in terms of the negotiations and the form of trade agreement that will be reached for Britain.

Since the Brexit vote, as a firm we have reviewed our own strategy and have largely reconfirmed our commitment to the strategy that we have been following since the last economic downturn. The key tenets of that strategy include:

- Financial prudence with a focus on sustainable profitable growth rather than 'chasing' growth with disregard for the longer term.
- Focusing on our clients' needs and enhancing our sector delivery by developing a more focused approach based on client groups rather than organising our external client offerings along purely team or legal discipline lines.
- Taking full advantage of our current spread of office locations and opening satellite offices where there are particular markets, clients and disciplines which we wish to access and where we are confident of success
- Valuing our people by listening and investing in our staff and partners, continuing to focus on attracting, developing and retaining talented people by offering development opportunities and clarity about career progression

In general terms, the advice we are providing to our clients to help them deal with Brexit – either to minimise any negative impact or to take advantage of opportunities that may result – is to broadly follow a similar strategy. We see strategic value in deep client focus and where possible a diversity of markets/income – too narrow a focus, we fear, may result in Brexit having a disproportionate effect. In challenging markets there is no option but to get close to clients and to deliver the goods and services that they want in ways that exceed their normal expectations. Valuing staff and putting in place excellent people structures and policies means that they will always be able to attract the best candidates to secure the future success of their business.

The old adage of 'times change, and we change with them' ultimately applies here – by building in flexibility and resilience into their strategies, businesses will be able to adapt to the new situation post-Brexit and the potentially tumultuous time until then. This said, the hard won experience of the last 130 years guides us as we move forward. Perhaps our biggest challenge is to remain alert enough to spot and then take the emerging opportunities rather than fearing what might come to pass. As I said at the outset, rather than spend too much time contemplating what might happen post Brexit, my role as CEO is to ensure my team grasp this new business as usual.

For more information on Clarke Willmott visit www.clarkewillmott.com

NIGEL BARRATT, HURST CORPORATE FINANCE

In this article I will set out for you the impact of Brexit on your business.

If only!

While I hope that Theresa May and colleagues have a clear plan and strategy I suspect even they have little insight into the eventual outcome not only of Brexit directly but the future for our trading with the EU and the rest of the world.

Given that uncertainty, businesses must plan their futures while giving consideration to a range of potential outcomes and risks. In this article I will attempt to identify the key issues that are likely to impact on the future business landscape and in particular on a company's ability to access funding and the mergers and acquisitions market. My day job is providing advice to companies seeking growth; achieving their aspirations will frequently require access to additional funds and skills. Solutions to these requirements are many and varied, ranging from agreeing new debt facilities, raising development capital from individuals or private equity institutions to merging/acquiring or selling to another company.

Before examining the long term impact of Brexit it is worth exploring the immediate impact of the referendum result. Our own experience was that the shock of the result had an immediate impact as decisions were stalled – people were so busy speculating about the impact that inaction was almost inevitable! However, that was short lived and our more recent experience is that it has made little difference to decisions by financial institutions and that to a significant extent it is business as usual.

There are however pockets of real pain where the slide in the currency has inflicted major damage on UK businesses importing raw materials from territories such as the US and Japan. For the most part, however, business is in good shape as is the confidence of the UK consumer. In turn these factors are driving the financial markets. GDP growth in 2016 and the forecasts for 2017 have allowed pro-Brexiteers to point out that Remainers were scaremongering when they warned of an economic catastrophe.

Although no doubt Remainers were trying to make a political point in forecasting gloom, the economic risk of Brexit is clear; the UK exports £230 billion of goods and services to the EU. However, we do run a significant trade deficit (£89 billion) in goods giving some credence to the argument that the EU needs the UK as much as we need it. There is also truth to the Brexiteers' suggestion that other parts of the world are becoming increasingly important – out of the top 20 fastest growing export markets only 4 are in the EU.

So there is much to play for as the government plans its approach to the negotiations. In my research for this article I read the government's White Paper and the bewildering complexity of the task faced by the government is obvious. In addition to the obvious issues such as migration, free trade and the customs union many of our major industries such as transport, energy, communications and nuclear interact heavily with the EU. Add to that the many EU standards that govern many aspects of our lives.

It is therefore obvious that the Brexit process will take years to complete. For most businesses and their owners the Brexit timeframes are well beyond normal planning timeframes.

In terms of planning, one thing the White Paper is relatively clear on is existing funding commitments. The government has committed to continuing to fund projects under the European Structural and Investment Fund if they were in place prior to 2016. The government has also committed to continuing payments under the Common Agricultural Policy until 2020. The government is also continuing to encourage bidding for other awards in the expectation that funding will continue.

Freedom from EU regulation may also give our government the ability to tweak its tax policies in connection with making investments in UK businesses. At present tax incentives are available to UK investors making direct or indirect investments into UK SMEs. However, such tax incentives are classified as state aid under EU regulations and therefore subject to rules on what type of businesses can be invested in. Freedom from the EU may enable the UK government to widen the scope of qualifying investments providing greater access to capital for SMEs.

While a UK government freed from EU state aid rules may in theory have greater freedom to support business, under the current government I do not see any potential for significant changes in direct government funding support for businesses in the form of grants and subsidies. So funding for growth will have to come from our financial markets.

In terms of funding, the UK's financial markets remain strong. Sentiment is currently in a good place in the banking, private equity and capital markets. Banks are keen to lend to sensible propositions and are doing so with finer margins and higher tolerance to gearing than for some time. Private equity institutions are well funded and keen to support businesses with risk capital to fund growth and facilitate ownership change, importantly there is now more private equity funding available for smaller businesses. Meanwhile; the capital markets have performed strongly providing access to capital for those companies that require it.

In the short to medium term I do not see the fundamentals changing (while expressing no opinion on the performance of the stock market!). The sheer weight of liquidity will continue to direct events. Nevertheless, bankers and investors must be discerning and the crash of 2007-10 hasn't been entirely forgotten so I anticipate an extra layer of due diligence in relation to Brexit.

So what issues will funders consider when looking at a proposition? I have set out my thoughts below.

Is your business UK-centric?

If your business is largely dependent on the UK market Brexit is likely to have less impact on you, other than its overall influence on the state of the UK economy. Any business plan that can support growth without the need for international trade will inevitably carry lower risk albeit that some of the other factors set out below will need to be considered.

Can your business benefit from Brexit uncertainty?

Business that are skilled in dealing with complex global logistics, foreign exchange management and interpreting customs/excise taxes for clients are arguably in a good position to win business as the world becomes more complex as Brexit unfolds. Companies that have traditionally dealt with such issues in-house will, in my view, be more prepared to outsource these functions as the world becomes more complex.

Is your supply chain dependant on overseas supply?

Any funder will want to understand supply chain risk. If your supply chain is highly internationalised (and remember that your suppliers in the UK could be dependent on overseas suppliers) then there are two issues you need to deal with; foreign exchange rates (see below) and vulnerability of supply if duties and tariffs are imposed. Lack of alternative suppliers will undoubtedly be seen as a risk.

Managing currency risk

If nothing else Brexit has livened up the foreign exchange markets. This is at two levels; firstly daily volatility seems to have increased, with oscillations driven by the latest Brexit pronouncement and secondly a more fundamental resetting of our exchange rate. While market commentary focuses on the US dollar and the Euro, other major currencies such as the Japanese Yen have appreciated significantly and, for the moment, seemingly permanently.

For funders the currency question is therefore twofold. First can you demonstrate an ability to cost effectively manage the risk? Businesses should in my view be exploring how they can mitigate short term risk. One issue facing SMEs is that banks are nervous about providing complex products to manage risk. Secondly, if the exchange rate has fundamentally been reset to your disadvantage how can the impact on your profitability be managed? In part this will depend on your ability to pass on increases to your customers (good luck if your customers are major retailers) and also your ability to make efficiencies/savings.

On the other hand if you are benefitting from the drop in valuation of the pound sterling, funders are likely to want to understand the extent to which this has increased profitability and cash flow and undertake sensitivity analysis should the gain not be permanent.

Access to skills and labour

For many, Brexit was about migration. Amongst the interesting facts in the White Paper is that there are in excess of 900,000 Polish people in the UK and over 200,000 Romanians and u with significant numbers from many other EU states. For many businesses access to EU labour is critical and this is not purely a cost issue. Increasingly employers in the UK are dependent on the skills of non UK nationals. As Brexit unfolds and assuming a restriction on migration UK employers are going to have to be smarter about retaining their workforces and will need to invest more in training.

In part the prevalence of EU nationals in our workforce demonstrates the UK's poor productivity which has been much reported. At present it is easier and cheaper to recruit labour rather than invest in training and/or technology to improve productivity. As access to cheap labour is cut off UK business will need to invest to improve productivity.

Reliance on EU markets

Given the level of EU exports and the potential disruption to that trade any company accessing these markets will need to consider the risk. However, it seems highly unlikely that there will be a drastic alteration in trade and certainly not overnight. The commercial pressure to find a workable solution will be significant and not finding a solution is unthinkable.

In the government's white paper the stated objective is to achieve 'frictionless trading'. It is the extent to which frictionless trade continues that the risk exists. At present the EU effectively operates as one market without borders. Such a market facilitates the seamless movement of goods and to lesser extent services. It is therefore possible to, for example, operate a just in time stock system even though your goods are coming from Germany.

If there is to be an issue I believe it is that trade will no longer be frictionless and that this will potentially increase the transactional cost of doing business in the EU making it potentially less profitable. In this context one obvious issue is that currently exports from the UK into the EU are exempt from VAT.

Can I operate in non EU markets?

Our major trading partner is the US followed by (some distance) other major EU nations who make up seven of our top ten markets. China and Switzerland are in our top ten markets. However, other markets such as South America and South East Asia are growing strongly. Quite apart from Brexit these markets must be a target for UK exporters as they are experiencing significantly greater levels of growth than the EU. Any funder will want to know whether your business can successfully enter into these markets.

Will an overseas investor be interested in my business?

Our recent experience is that overseas businesses are prepared to either invest in or acquire UK businesses. At one level the desire to do so is driven by the access to the EU and therefore the continuation of such inward investment will have a question mark over it. However, the UK will continue to be an attractive place to do business from a language, cultural and market perspective and I think this will continue to be the case.

In my view if you have an attractive funding proposition provided you can successfully address these risk factors you should have no issues in accessing multiple sources of finance for as long as the UK economy remains in good shape.

While the above issues are specific to Brexit there are a number of ancillary factors that businesses should in my view factor into their long range thinking.

Will Brexit collide with a downturn?

At some point the economic cycle will turn and given the potential time frame for the Brexit negotiations there must be a strong possibility that the two events will be running in parallel.

Will Brexit lead to Scottish independence?

The current Scottish government is dead set against Brexit and if the political situation in Scotland remains as is it seems highly likely that a further independence referendum is inevitable

Is Brexit the first crack in the EU?

There are major electoral tests in 2017 in France, Germany and the Netherlands. In each there are risks to the political status quo which could herald further cracks in the EU and even the Euro.

I can offer no particular advice on dealing with these issues other than recommending these potential risks are worth factoring into your risk analysis.

One final area that I wish to discuss is the potential impact of Brexit on those owner managers wishing to consider a sale of their business in the near future.

A business sale can be the right answer to challenges such as access to funding and skills or offer a solution to a lack of management succession. Generally a business sale will be easiest in benign economic times. Given all the factors outlined above, owners should factor the potential risks into their strategic thinking and maybe consider adjusting their timeframes accordingly.

My own profession is faced with multiple uncertainties from Brexit, for example, will our professional qualifications be recognised in the EU and will our regulatory framework continue to be strongly influenced by EU standards and procedures. No doubt every industry and profession has its own uncertainties.

If we dwell on all the uncertainties the risk is that Brexit will freeze our willingness to make key investment decisions. I hope this article will help you to focus your thinking and planning so that the Brexit risk is simply one of the many things you need to consider as you plan your business's future. Good luck!

Nigel Barratt is the Corporate Finance Partner at Hurst Accountants LLP. Hurst is one of the North West's leading independent accounting firms and is focussed on the needs of owner managed businesses. Nigel started his corporate finance career in 1988 and has advised owner managers on transactions of every description many involving the raising of capital.

For more information on Hurst Corporate Finance visit www.hurst.co.uk/ services/corporate-finance

MARK BLACKHURST, COO, DIGITAL NEXT
What Brexit means for the savvy digital marketer

Economies are always changing, but there's no industry that has such a huge impact on the world as the online, digital marketplace. From the days I used to type on my Commodore 64 in the mid-1980s, to the near £200 billion value the internet now adds to the British economy every year, it's clear the Internet presents a huge opportunity for growth, both domestically and internationally. Consequently, companies must learn to adapt in order to survive.

As of 24 June 2016 – whether they liked it or not – British business entered a brave new world of business and trade with the Brexit vote. Until we formally leave, UK businesses still benefit from tariff free movement of goods, shared laws (such as trademarking), and the free movement of people; all of which have been of great benefit for companies within the 28 EU nations. We must make the best of whatever resource or opportunity that is available to us, but at the same time realise that there will now be a drastic change of which many of us have never before seen. However, those who react positively to this change and make the right moves are the ones who will ultimately benefit.

In the last week of 2009, my brother Justin Blackhurst and I left our jobs to set up Digital Next, a digital marketing agency in Manchester. In just seven years, we have transformed our business from a two-man operation in our parents' back bedroom into a multinational success story. Our aim has always been to put together the best talent and skills in the digital agency sphere; investing heavily in our staff and resources to ensure our clients get the best advice in delivery and thought leadership with their projects. As a digital marketing agency, our job is to help businesses tap into the huge audience of regular Internet users.

As one of Europe's largest full-service digital marketing agencies, we have also expanded our operations into various worldwide offices including cities like Melbourne, Australia. With a projected turnover of over £4 million we've certainly followed through on my brother's mantra of 'Let's crack on and smash it!'. As founding members of the Sharp Project (a Northern powerhouse for digital companies), where our headquarters are situated, we have been able to bring up the profile of Digital Agencies in the North of England by moving high value business and marketing budgets out of London and into Manchester. We have evidence first hand that waves of London-based ecommerce businesses and websites are now opening their eyes to the reality that Manchester is home to some of the best high level and result-driven agencies in the world. Manchester is famous for its contributions to modern day computing and we take great pride in our heritage within such a historically significant city. From the famous Alan Turing to the creation of the Manchester computers led by Tom Kilburn, Manchester has always emerged as one of the most technologically-progressive cities in the UK. Beyond Brexit, we believe that Manchester will continue to flourish in the Northern Powerhouse.

Looking beyond our four walls, we constantly look to expand and develop the business. Acquiring businesses, attracting global investment from Sweden's Online Group, before adding the founder of ANS Group, Scott Fletcher, to our board. Scott Fletcher in particular a shining example of an ultra-successful, Northern-based entrepreneur who is passing his knowledge and investing his time to help the business community grow in the North of England.

Both Justin and I are extremely proud of what we have accomplished in such a short space of time, but we are by no means complacent. Brexit or not at Digital Next we have no intention of letting our progress falter, our plans are to actually accelerate our growth both for ourselves and our clients. With the business industry currently under a little caution and even stress due to Brexit, we adopt an approach that Brexit is actually an opportunity to lead the way and show the modern, savvy business owner that it's time to take control, and use the power of the internet to do so. Our extensive knowledge and experience within the digital industry is always on the rise this is particular advantage for our clients; in fact, the internet and its link with business is a passion and a hobby of the majority of our staff, not only does this benefit us as a digital agency, but also the companies we work with.

For companies working solely in the digital sphere, the same trading opportunities exist within Europe as they always have done. Without the necessity to import or export physical goods, Britain's withdrawal from the single market and the customs union should not impact us detrimentally. In fact, there is probably no better time than now to set up as an independent digital-only business. We believe that Companies that are allied with good owners and the right digital strategy are the ones who will prosper both here in the UK and internationally. Unfortunately, traditional businesses that fail to make a switch to digital are more likely to be affected, while online businesses will continue to thrive.

It is important to remember that the digital marketplace is very much a global marketplace, and always has been. Of course, the focus of many businesses has been EU-centric over the years because trade has been so simple but, as with many other sectors, British digital agencies are some of the best in the world. Theresa May has already discussed creating a 'truly global' post-Brexit Britain, and this could offer huge opportunities for those willing to explore new markets. As such, this is a very encouraging sign for us that we have a leader who really believes that we can be successful in this new world. Quite simply, trading agreements are aplenty and available all around the world now – unfettered by EU constraints – so there seems to be little actual cause for great concern.

According to PricewaterhouseCoopers LLP (PwC), Britain will grow faster than any other advanced economy over the next three decades. We already know that the UK's decision to leave the EU will exert some tension on our economy, but it may be argued that Britain is now in prime position to forge new ties with emerging economies. While Britain still has the largest Internet-based economy of any G20 country – with more than 10% of GDP contributed online – China, the US and other developed countries offer vast digital marketplaces for British business that can be explored. It is predicted that the global economy will actually double in size over the next 25 years, thanks to emerging markets such as India, Mexico and Russia. When it comes to projected growth rates, though, the UK comes out of top of the G7 economies.

In the uncertain environment created by Brexit, which has been further aggravated by mainstream media; markets are fluctuating after every speech and Parliamentary vote, but there is an opportunity for brands to become a calming, reassuring voice. We have always made a point of circulating our positive stories about growth and international aspiration, as we are proof that a British brand and its clients can grow exponentially abroad. Put simply, we purely want to encourage others to adopt a positive mindset.

At a time of such economic unrest, it is imperative that the relationship between consumer and brand remains stable. However, with little or no immediately disastrous impact, this is also a real chance for brands to utilise their digital marketing strategies in new, creative ways. It is time for businesses like ours and the wider creative industry to now demonstrate their value to the wider marketplace, which should be viewed as an extremely exciting challenge – not a daunting one.

At Digital Next, we truly believe Britain can become a true breeding ground for start-up and aspirational business businessmen and ladies who want to become the next Unicorn or large scale operation; we are proof of that ourselves.

Admittedly, many of the companies we work with – both SMEs and large scale brands – are now realising that Brexit could mean it's time to prove their true value. This notion is especially true for growing businesses that lack the security of huge contracts and well-funded campaigns, so Brexit should be an opportunity to show that even smaller businesses with naturally lower marketing budgets can develop successful digital strategies. This effect of 'punching above their weight' is one we have seen countless times in recent history, as it's fair to say the Internet has levelled the playing field between small and large organisations.

One imminent worry that has emerged thanks to Brexit, however, is the concept of the EU's free movement. When the curtain finally closes on this, it's could be become increasingly difficult to plug the skill gaps across many of our industries. It's important to remember, though, that while it may become more difficult, the global workforce is still on-hand to some extent. This shouldn't be a scary thought though, as the British workforce might have shortages in skills, but this presents a training opportunity. In this respect, companies like Digital Next are leading the way already.

With active partnerships with universities and schools, we are looking to ease the passage for students from study to work, equipping the future of tomorrow with the right set of skills to succeed. With an extremely positive partnership with Staffordshire University, on the MSc Digital Marketing course, we are doing our part to educate the next generation. We have proven also that hiring locally and training up staff members can create brilliant results, both in the industry of digital marketing and general business skills. We have invested great time and resource in putting many of our staff not only through credible Google, Facebook accreditations; including our recent Premier Google Partner status award, but also Accounting, Business and Marketing qualifications. This is further proof of this; skilling up the nation involves this important step of educating internally.

The digital marketing industry and the Internet as a whole presents a huge opportunity to our country and, by embracing this, anyone can become an entrepreneur and develop and idea in front of the biggest possible audience. The millennial generation, and those coming after, are already experts in being internet savvy. For many of them, working in an agency environment is an exciting prospect; something that is positive for any savvy business owner post-Brexit. Britain is still held in high esteem across the globe, and there's never been a better time to capitalise on just how advanced our industries are. While Brexit negotiations continue, and countless debates ensue within the EU and Parliament, the UK is already in early discussions with the likes of the US and Commonwealth partners; presenting further reasons to feel positive.

As it's predicted, the so-called 'globalisation' of this post-war world is beginning to retract, and the online revolutions continue to grow apace. With every new technology, comes new potential for revenue; and the online economy shows no sign of slowing down. We are here to help business owners harness the power of the Internet and distribute their products or services on a greater scale. At a digital marketing agency such as Digital Next, we are in a unique position and have particular insight to understand just what industries will require when it comes to online business. Through our own marketing skills, we have aimed to educate and help savvy business owners realise that Brexit does not have to mean the end of all things good. Instead, it's time to be proactive and look into the idea of digital strategies. It is, therefore, the responsibilities of Digital Next and other such companies have to be the catalyst in ensuring business owners understand how this can result in growth and success.

The vote in June may have felt like the beginning of a long and arduous break-up, but it should hopefully be a wakeup call to those in digital marketing and the wider business industry to ensure they truly know their consumers and what matters to them. Brexit is the hand all British business have been dealt and there is no avoiding the ramifications, whatever they may be, but nor is there any point delaying key decisions or stalling on plans for expansion. This is a time of disruption no doubt, however, it will be those who react to the disruption with the right strategy that are the ones who will prosper in the future. Subsequently, the country and its citizens must unite in order to move forward; for those who voted 'Leave', now is their time to seize their opportunity for a prosperous future; for those who voted for 'Remain', it doesn't have to be all doom and gloom because the best days are ahead of us. For too long have we been under the constraints of the EU, but the vote to 'Leave' demonstrated that the ideals of a Great Britain still remain; spirit, courage, determination and grit. As Britain has to now adapt, we will see our economy evolve and see us affirming the old status of leaders of the modern world. To summarise in the words of our most beloved Prime Minister, Winston Churchill, 'A pessimist sees the difficulty in every opportunity; an optimist sees the opportunity in every difficulty'. Now, it's time for us *all* to be optimists.

Playing a proactive role in the success of your company is something we know very well. By investing in your business and the skills of your staff, you give yourself the opportunity to grow despite the uncertainty of Brexit at every turn.

The Internet has levelled the playing field; offering the same opportunities to both small brands and large corporations, changing the landscape forever. If you're not already savvy in digital marketing, you'll find yourself slipping behind. It's more important than ever to stand out against your competition and prove your worth in the midst of leaving the EU. We are here to ensure business leaders realise that digital marketing campaigns are a fundamental way to stay ahead of the curve; Digital Next's job is to ensure that British business owners get the guidance they need.

As many more people continue to use the Internet for business, the door opens for more opportunities and challenges. Putting into action the art of being savvy starts now, through building strategies that future-proof your business.

What we do know is that we're at least two years away from our formal breakaway from the EU. Since the referendum, consumers are still spending, investments are still being made, and the media and digital world seems mostly unaffected.

The online economy is in a unique position to continue forging new relationships beyond borders, and the time to act is now.

For more information on Digital Next visit http://digitalnext.co.uk/

JOHN TREHANE, CEO, THE GYM GROUP

I set up The Gym Group in 2007 and when the company was listed on 9 November 2015, I knew this was a significant milestone for The Gym and I had proved that my initial vision to provide affordable access to exercise facilities was a reality and finally mainstream. When I first started this business, Easyjet and Travelodge provided 'no frills' low cost products yet there were no equivalent options in the health industry. Prior to The Gym Group, gyms had expensive monthly fees and long, inflexible terms with huge penalties to leave. I wanted to be the Easyjet of gyms – to be the low-cost gym with excellent work out equipment. I wanted to give the customer what they wanted.

The customer wanted an affordable, 'no-contract' flexible membership and gyms that are open 24 hours a day, seven days a week to be able to work out when they wanted. The Gym gives members the freedom and flexibility to improve their health and fitness on their own terms, removing the old barriers of fixed, high-cost contracts which have served to reduce accessibility in the past. Having lived and breathed gym businesses, man and boy, the IPO was a way to extend my vision to every town in the UK. Raising £125 million helped to open 15 to 20 new gyms every year. This year, I am delighted say that we have opened 89 gyms and have over 500,000 members. I have been following Brexit carefully to see whether it would impact The Gym Group.

The customers

If a hard Brexit hit, we would undoubtedly lose some of our customer base who originate from the EU, but gain as others trade in their old, more expensive memberships to low cost. With our gyms being open 24-7 our customer base reflects all types of people and we get many shift workers (about a quarter of our membership) joining to train outside normal business hours, many of whom are from the EU. However, we also get a lot of students joining, so I believe any loss in the customer base from the EU will be filled by the uplift in student memberships – as many of our gyms are, or are being opened, near to university and college campuses.

If Brexit and its uncertainty leads people to stop spending as much, this may actually help our company. Given the low-cost of membership and joining fee, we actually predict an increase in members – as people may switch from their current gym which may charge double or treble our fees to ours.

The equipment

Unlike other businesses who buy goods from Europe and are affected by the decline in the sterling, we've been fortunate that our equipment was bought from

China. We initially bought the equipment on a hire-purchase agreement but the Initial Public Offering funds have helped pay down our debt and resulted in The Gym Group owning their own equipment – an envious business position indeed.

The staff

The Gym and their business model essentially operates in an innovative, technology-led, disruptive business model and online-only registration process so there hasn't been a huge emphasis on staffing. In actual fact, the personal trainers in the gym are on an arrangement where each personal trainer would give 10 hours free to The Gym to man the gym, run the classes, give inductions, in return for keeping 100 per cent of their income from personal training. Therefore even the proposed changes in employment and immigration laws wouldn't affect The Gym Group significantly.

The company's revenue has increased from £22.3 million in 2012 to £45.5 million in 2014, representing a compound annual growth rate of 43% and continuing in 2016. Brexit has created uncertainty but we are in a strong position to weather these changes. I believe that the model where the managers manage is key. With a multi-site business I can't micro-manage. The company hires high quality managers and empowers them to work within budgets and targets. It clearly is a system that works as we've won employment awards and 90% of our original staff still work for us – which speaks volumes in an industry which has a high attrition rate.

My advice to you is to be in love with the business and not the game. For example, I see other operators struggle with their company because they only love the health game but forget it's a business. Most businesses go bust in 18 months because they run out of cash. Cash is still king and with our business there are no arrears to deal with – people pay online upfront and it is direct debited monthly.

Brexit was a sobering time for the UK but it's a time for the UK to also pause and really think what model we want to adopt. Just like the young people whom I mentor and speak to – when they have finished the whirlwind of A levels and degrees, they start wondering what to do for the next 50 years and it's daunting. My advice is to not rush things but get a good grounding from an established business before striking out on your own. Britain should be analysing the models out there and seeing what works best for us. Businesses out there need to be resilient and adapt to change irrespective of Brexit. We've embraced technology – which gives us a key advantage – a living, breathing database of gym goers who know, like and trust us. Like Easyjet, whose key premise was to open new routes, my focus is to open new gyms every year and get everyone fighting fit. After all health is wealth, and joining The Gym Group is affordable and you can work out 24/7 even on Christmas Day! So there's no excuse, even with Brexit.

For more information on The Gym Group visit www.thegymgroup.com

ANDREW PRESTON, CEO, DE POEL GROUP
Brexit: Our Views

de Poel is a 15-year established independent recruitment outsourcing expert, focused on delivering cost-effective, compliant, quality-driven solutions to transform the engagement and management of an organisation's temporary workforce. We can call ourselves truly independent because we are what you call a 'neutral vendor'. This essentially means we are *not* a recruitment agency, nor are we owned by, or financially affiliated with any, but rather the conduit between an organisation, ie the 'hirer' and a panel of pioneering, compliant recruitment agencies that supply high-calibre, around the clock talent.

With recruitment in our DNA and innovative technology at our heart, our 120 clients span both the public and private sector – with spend under management standing at £750 million. Our relationships with over 3,500 like-minded recruitment agency stakeholders have been, and will continue to be, instrumental in our continued success. Likewise, we are focused on using our influence and expertise within the market to not only generate significant efficiencies and improvements for our clients, but to support our recruitment agency stakeholders in supplying volumes for high-profile organisations they ordinarily would not have been able to tap into.

With the support of my senior management team, my role as CEO of de Poel group largely comprises driving forward our company ethos and vision, overseeing the overall operations and resources and maintaining constant awareness of both the external and internal competitive landscape, opportunities for expansion, customers, markets, new industry developments and standards, and so forth.

My global healthcare background spans over two decades and, after selling my clinical service business to Serco Group Plc, I joined the de Poel group in 2013 to head up the core business model specifically for NHS and health care sectors – de Poel health+care. After managing a period of significant growth, I subsequently assumed MD responsibility for our newly formed education business and business development across the entire group. Following on from this, I was appointed CEO after leading a management buyout in September 2016.

A strategic recruitment partner

An item high on my agenda, since taking the reins of de Poel group, is helping our clients to navigate the raft of new legislation and ever-changing political landscape that continues to present a series of complex, delicate and daunting challenges.

Over the last decade and a half since we've been in operation, we have seen huge evolution within a number of sectors including transport and logistics, retail, health and care and waste management to name but a few – and are proud to have played a part in delivering simple, innovative solutions to age-old problems. In present day, de Poel connects 60,000 temporary workers with hiring organisations each week, working collaboratively with our national panel of recruitment agencies. Together, we are raising industry standards and bringing significant cost savings, efficiencies and improvements, visibility and control and total compliance to the fore.

Examining real-time management Information from our clients, large and small, alongside the latest government reports and industry findings, we are constantly taking a temperature check of the recruitment market, providing solutions, suggestions and initiatives to future proof organisations from the challenges ahead.

Times of uncertainty

In early 2017, there appears to be a shared feeling that we're on the cusp of the most seismic period of change yet – set to impact us all in different ways and at varying degrees. 2016 will be forever etched in the history books as the year that brought us Brexit (and Donald Trump for that matter), defying polling experts and causing a period of public unrest as a result. However, exactly what this departure from the EU will mean in a tangible sense is still very much up for debate. Despite Prime Minister Theresa May's insistences that her agenda is unequivocally pro-business, there remains an air of great uncertainty, as we're set to take a first furtive step into the unknown at the end of March, as Article 50 is triggered. May's statement at the CBI Annual Conference in November last year – 'people don't want a cliff-edge; they want to know with some certainty how things are going to go' – is also yet to be backed up with any clarity or detail, further sowing the seeds of doubt.

What have we noticed since Britain voted to leave the EU?

From a de Poel perspective, we have already witnessed a slight shift in the UK labour market in general, and the thought processes and behaviours of our client base, although we have counselled how incredibly important it is to avoid a knee-jerk reaction. For the vast majority of businesses, when uncertainty creeps into the market the natural instinct is to 'wait and see what happens' – the appetite for risk, growth, and thus hiring drops as companies step back and assess their position.

The important word here is 'growth' – the UK recruitment outsourcing industry has been in a near constant state of growth since mid-2009. According to The Recruitment & Employment Confederation (REC)[1], the total value of the UK recruitment industry in 2014 stood at £26.5billion and increased by 9.7% to reach £31.5 billion in 2015. Recruitment agencies play a crucial part in helping our clients to access a workforce that is able to expand and contract with the ebb and flow of the market and their own individual requirements – to date, over 2 billion hours have been transacted via e-tips®, our proprietary software solution.

---

1   The Recruitment & Employment Confederation (REC): Recruitment Industry Trends 2015/16 Report

Whilst we expect the rate of *permanent* hiring to decrease slightly as employers become a little more risk-averse, people will always remain the most important asset for any business. With this, it is a possibility that employers may look to hire talent on a temporary basis in order to plug the gaps. Aligning with an independent, strategic recruitment partner like de Poel can be one of the most cost-efficient, compliant and effective methods of sourcing talent on a temporary basis – and certainly, our role in these turbulent times is proving more important than ever.

As the saying goes, 'Keep calm and carry on'

It is critical to ensure that our client base continues to be able to access agile, diverse and skilled talent required to fill the jobs available. Procuring this talent is absolutely vital to sustainable economic growth and prosperity, especially in sectors such as health and care, education, hospitality, construction and manufacturing – workers from the EU are vital and any change to our immigration system needs to recognise that.

With the Trump wildcard now thrown into the mix, there is an extra variable to add to the uncertainty, which in theory will compound the above slow-down theory. That being said, Trump's policies – if taken at face value – are on the whole, potentially quite beneficial for the UK. Firstly, our exports to the US total just over £30 billion according to Office for National Statistics (ONS);[1] so a President focused on growing their economy can, in turn, be good for British exports to the US. Furthermore, Trump is very pro-Britain – and Brexit for that matter. Speaking about a trade deal with Britain, Trump was quoted as saying: 'With me, they'll always be treated fantastically. You would certainly not be back of the queue', which of course bodes well for UK business – assuming of course, that Trump honours his promise.

What *is* certain at this stage, is that Brexit will undoubtedly influence the UK on various levels, with a high possibly that its economy will be detrimentally affected – certainly in the short-term. In addition, there are many changes on the horizon that will likely affect Britain's' workplaces, and impact key areas such as current laws and worker demographics. This is my take on what is most likely to be impacted:

EU Legislation

Whilst EU legislation has by no means been the only driver behind the development of employment laws over recent times, it has arguably become a leading source of UK employee protection legislation over the last 15 to 20 years. Discrimination, family leave rights, working time regulation, protection for atypical workers, health and safety in the workplace and the rights of employees on the transfer of a business are just a handful of employment laws, which are shaped in some way by the laws of the EU.

---

1   Office for National Statistics (ONS): UK Perspectives 2016: Trade with the EU and beyond

Much of the 'Leave' campaign centred on reclaiming sovereignty, and it is true that EU-related laws have a significant presence and effect in UK law. According to a House of Commons report EU-related laws account for over 13%.[1] Although, when it comes to the impact Brexit – and the potential abolition of some EU legislation – will have on *industry*, Sir Paul Jenkins, a former Treasury solicitor who headed up the Government Legal Department, says:

> 'The impact of EU law varies from sector to sector. In many areas – public order, crime, defence, and health – EU laws have minimal impact. But in others – workers' rights, trade – the impact is much greater because the single market and the free movement of workers are at the heart of what the EU is about.'

Let's focus on the transport and logistics industry for a moment, and use the Driver Certificate of Professional Competence (Driver CPC) as an example. Driver CPC came into effect in the UK in 2009, following an EU Directive on drivers' hours and working time. The question is, 'Is this likely to substantially change post-Brexit?'

Renowned transport law firm, Pellys, believes not, stating:

> 'It is unlikely that Britain leaving the EU would provoke a mass overhaul of our transport laws, and it is very likely that the great majority of EU laws that are directly concerned with road safety will remain as they are. Brexit may trigger some legislative changes, but the fundamentals of safe and compliant operation are not going to change.'

This is a view echoed by most commentators, making it extremely unlikely that current rules and regulations governing driver hours and qualifications will change in any obvious way.

However, irrespective of some campaigners in the 'Leave' camp's opinion that EU-derived laws are intrusive to UK workplace relations and present unnecessary red tape for UK businesses, it is highly likely Brexit will have an impact on *some* employment law in the UK. But exactly how *much* change is probable in reality, once the UK withdraws from the EU? It is highly doubtful that any UK Government (of any political persuasion) would seek to fully repeal (or even, considerably repeal) existing employment laws which implement EU minimum requirements. This is down to some of the following reasons:

A substantial amount of employment protection which flows from Europe actually reflects accepted standards of good employee relations practices.

Some fundamental employment laws of the EU merely supplement rights which were already embodied in UK law before the EU chose to legislate in that particular area. For example, UK equal pay rights and disability discrimination. Given this, it is difficult to see why and how any UK Government would legislate to substantially change the current framework, upon our exit

---

1   House of Commons: EU obligations: UK implementing legislation since 1993

from the EU. In addition, modern UK employment law is technical and detailed, and is already presents itself as a compliance challenge for employers.

Perhaps most importantly, is the case that, following Brexit, the UK will still seek and need to maintain strong trading relations with Europe. As with other areas such as data protection, the UK will need to demonstrate that it has minimum employment protections in place in order to make it a viable trading partner for other European Member States.

This means that, as part of the current rules of the EEA, the UK would remain subject to most of the key aspects of EU employment law in any event. Key aspects including working time and the Temporary and Agency Workers Directive (2008/104/EC) – implemented in the UK by the Agency Worker Regulations 2010.[1]

So what does this mean?

As a result of the above, it is far more likely that the outcome of Brexit will be a desire on the UK government's part to remove or change some aspects of existing UK employment regulation which have proved unpopular with UK businesses. Moreover, where the removal of such protection is unlikely to be viewed by the rest of the EU, trade unions, interest and pressure groups as well as the British public, as an erosion of the fundamental rights and freedom of employees and workers. This, however, will be a very delicate balance to strike.

Free movement of labour and goods

Turning to immigration, this has also divided opinion in the referendum debate. It is unquestionable that free movement of workers is a central pillar of EU membership, ensuring that EU citizens and their families can live or work in any other member state without needing immigration permission. However, with the level of net migration to the UK recently reaching a record high, some of those who campaigned for Brexit want to end the automatic right of EU citizens to travel and work freely in the UK.

Theresa May has expressed her intent to do a deal with the EU guaranteeing, after Brexit, the rights of EU citizens already living in the UK – as long as they do the same for the British expats using the free movement rules to live in other European countries. This would guarantee the rights of just fewer than 1.2 million UK citizens living on the continent and over three million EU migrants living in the UK.[2] Following this, British businesses and the trade union movement have made an unprecedented joint demand to Theresa May to immediately guarantee the rights of migrants to remain in the UK. However, European leaders have said they will not discuss the issue until May triggers Article 50 of the Lisbon Treaty, which begins the formal Brexit negotiation process.

---

1   SI 2010/93.
2   ONS: Population of the United Kingdom by Country of Birth and Nationality, August 2016

Despite May's promise, there *is* a possibility that once the UK is no longer in the EU, the government could impose new controls for future EU travellers to the UK and other EU countries may do the same for UK citizens. For workers, the UK could require, for example, that EU citizens are subject to the same immigration system that already applies for non-EU citizens. This visa regime, which includes a Points-Based System, ensures, for instance, that Tier 2 work visas are only issued to workers performing a sufficiently skilled role in the UK at a particular minimum salary, to avoid employers undercutting the salaries of UK workers.

There will be challenges for the UK if this happens. The first will be to ensure that the UK still has access to the talented workers that it needs, to fill substantial skills gaps in the 'local' workforce (be it for highly skilled roles or perhaps for lower-paid work). Then there is the practical reality of the negotiations with other EU countries. Other countries that are not in the EU, but that have the benefit of free trade – Norway, for example – have been expected to agree to free movement of workers as a condition of the trade advantages.

With yet another area of uncertainty surrounding Brexit and what it will actually mean for workers, there are a number of points to note. Firstly, a number of migrants currently residing in the UK hold positions in the healthcare, construction, transport and logistics, IT and engineering sectors, amongst many others, without which resource the UK will see a chronic skills shortage. With the UK already struggling to find its own home-grown talent, it may be even hard to draw in talent overseas, as foreign workers will no longer find UK working conditions attractive.

Using the transport and logistics industry again as an example, according to the latest House of Commons Transport Committee,[1] some 60,000 foreign lorry drivers are thought to be working in the UK. If correct, this would account for 20% of the latest ONS Labour Force Survey[2] estimates, of the total number of UK LGV drivers. Other reports from trusted sources (including Recruiter Magazine) place this figure far higher at 30%.[3]

Any sudden decrease in the pool of available driver numbers caused by Brexit (both to existing workers already here in the UK and to future workers arriving) would further exacerbate the shortages that are already affecting the sector. Especially given that 64% of LGV drivers are 45 years plus,[4] and a mass exodus from the industry is already expected due to natural retirement.

---

1   House of Commons Transport Committee: Skills and workforce planning in the road haulage sector Report
2   Office for National Statistics (ONS): EMP04: All in employment by status, occupation and sex: people, Q2: 2016
3   Recruiter Magazine, London Summit, September 2016
4   ONS: Quarterly Labour Force Survey, Q2 2016

So does this potentially signify the end of free movement as we know it?

Like with employment law – and many other areas within the Brexit discussion – it is impossible to predict with any degree of certainty how the free movement of labour and goods may change, following our departure from the EU. However, nothing will change drastically overnight, and some of these changes will take years for the true magnitude to be fully felt.

Early predictions are possibly best summed up by Philip Hammond, the former Foreign Secretary and new Chancellor of the Exchequer, who said: 'The fundamental dilemma at the heart of the Brexit position is that we will now have to make a decision about how much access to that single market we want and need to protect our economy, and how much freedom of movement we are prepared to accept in order to buy it.'

Indeed, free movement of goods and free movement of labour are likely to prove themselves intrinsically linked in any negotiations with the potential to cause, in the worst case scenario, double trouble for firms. Any resultant rise in costs will squeeze already tight margins, particularly for the smallest operators, with the added knock on effect of reducing the pool of cash available to train and retain new and existing workers – further exacerbating the current skills shortage.

How de Poel is helping clients to ensure a smooth transition to Brexit

Whilst, even at this stage, no-one really knows how Brexit negotiations are going to pan out, de Poel is already taking steps to future-proof our clients from a variety of possible scenarios. This includes:

1. **Gaining a clear sense of the percentage make-up of EU Nationals** in the UK workforce.
2. **We are committed to taking a clear message to Westminster** through lobbying efforts (alongside our recruitment agency partners) around the impact any drastic changes Brexit could have, in order to, first, ensure that temporary workers in certain industries are considered critical for any exceptions to any potential forthcoming rule changes on immigration, and secondly, that clearer domestic policies and incentives are put in place to ensure a pipeline of UK talent. For example, through reduction in costs for training.
3. **Talking to our supplying panel agencies about ways in which they can begin to broaden and develop their candidate pools** away from a reliance on EU workers, so that alternative talent pipelines and recruitment partner agencies are already in place – should there be significant curbs on the free movement of people.
4. **Helping new organisations to implement a vendor neutral solution** and realise cost saving benefits across their temporary agency recruitment, in order to improve margins and the bottom line. Although, perhaps best known in the industry for our work with the largest of

brands, typically de Poel is saving smaller clients (those most vulnerable to margin change) 6% which, on agency workers bills of £1 million+, is a significant saving. This, in turn, is providing both a cushion and freeing up funds to reinvest in training and employee engagement, and developing their talent pipeline.

5. **Helping our existing client organisations to understand their potential exposure**, under possible Brexit scenarios and assisting them to look at additional services from de Poel. For example, supporting 'Warehouse-to-Wheel' continuous professional development programmes for their employees. Multi-site employers can also look to increase labour mobility in their current pool of temporary workers, where regionalised planning, assessments and inductions may allow for workers to be able to work at a multitude of locations, within an agreed geographical area. By introducing regional or cluster assessment and inductions, teamed with a short, site-specific familiarisation programme, staff may be able to work at multi-site locations without the disadvantage of spending a large amount of unpaid time to do multiple assessments.

Workforce modelling may also look to bring more long-term solutions for employers looking to retain quality, long-term agency workers through providing tiered guaranteed hour contracts dependent on the worker meeting eligibility criteria. If teamed with an opportunity to attain a permanent role at the final tier of contract, this may further motivate workers to be engaged, assist employers in keeping a valued skillset and encourage efficiencies to be driven through the business from a more motivated workforce. Of course, analysis of historical usage would need to be carefully conducted to ensure that the risk of guaranteeing more hours than will be needed is mitigated.

What is the next instalment in the Brexit story?

Theresa May announced in a key speech on Tuesday 17 January 2017, a 12-point plan on how Britain can achieve a 'confident, clean and hard Brexit' and maintain a strong partnership with the EU. Significantly, May confirmed for the first time that the UK will pull out of the single market and the European customs union, in order to end the jurisdiction of the European Court of Justice and regain control of immigration.

May made the promise that EU citizens will very much remain to be welcomed to the UK, a 'magnet for international talent' – as she hoped would be the case with UK nationals moving abroad – and that more trade will result in more jobs, thus ensuring the not just the UK will continue to prosper, but Europe as a whole.

May also confirmed her desire to have a tariff-free trade deal and the greatest of market access, and promised there will be a parliamentary vote on the UK's deal to leave the EU. Market news that broke following May's speech that sterling enjoyed its best day in more than eight years was very positive, and showed that concerns about an uncontrolled Brexit have been considerably diminished. Brexit *is* happening and we have to do all we can to collectively embrace the positive changes it may bring. It is my hope too that a 'Global Britain' can prosper on its own, and that at some point soon the two sides of the Brexit debate will reconcile to unite and work together.

Conclusively, although some of these changes will take a long time to take effect in what May has promised will be a 'phased approach to ensure a smooth and orderly Brexit'; they will nonetheless be game-changing. With a departure from the single market and vicissitudes to immigration and UK employment law on the horizon, now, more so than ever, companies should be looking to a strategic recruitment partner with a proven track record to manage these workforce changes and ultimately, always ensure they have the right workforce in play through this arrangement.

By partnering with an independent recruitment outsourcing specialist like de Poel, individuals tasked with people and budget responsibilities can rest assured knowing all suppliers will work toward a common goal. This is alongside standardised, transparent rates and terms and conditions and a robust approach to compliance – one thing less to worry about, when making the transition to operating a business in a post-Brexit climate.

For more on the de Poel Group visit www.depoel.co.uk

HANS CHRISTIAN IVERSEN

Implications of Brexit for small and medium sized businesses in the United Kingdom

There is still a lot of uncertainty prevailing with regards to the future framework under which UK business will be operating once the UK leaves the EU planned for second quarter 2019.

It is now clear that the UK government will try and negotiate some form of transition between the UK leaving the EU, and a full implementation of all the changes required before the UK is totally out of the EU single market.

This chapter is not about the political, financial and economic implications of the UK leaving the EU and the single market but it is more on how SMEs in the UK can prepare themselves in the best way both before, during and after we leave the EU including any it will take transitional period, which we believe will be longer than most people think. It is the case as it takes a long time to untangle 40 years of an integrated economic, financial, trade, working and regulatory regime. On which the commercial regime has been used to working.

Neither the EU nor the UK can be interested in a cliff hanging break as everybody will be working closely with one another in the future. The UK prosperity will still be dependent on our relationship with the EU for many years to come, combined with a strong integrated security arrangement through NATO and other organisations.

It is in this context and it is about how businesses can best prepare for Brexit by 2019 and this will also be shown through a case study by a manufacturer in the transport industry and the current known consequences of Brexit for Ferrabyrne Ltd.

How to prepare for Brexit

There is no simple formula to prepare for a longer period of uncertainty and ever changing circumstances. Even if the UK government produces a clear plan on how to leave the EU, we are still heading for a long period of uncertainty and change. There is something distinct about SME businesses but in this chapter an SME is a business with less than 250 employees and less the €50 million in turnover and a balance sheet of less than €43 million, which accounts for more than 95% of all businesses in the UK and even more in the EU. They are generally also the sector which is the future basis for growth, employment and prosperity in most economies, but they are generally also more financially less strong tan larger companies.

However, SME segment is much more vulnerable to changes in the economic environment as most of the businesses are smaller and often less financially consolidated than more mature businesses. The UK government wishes to create a digital economy on the back of growth in areas such as Fintech, so the importance of the SME sector should not be underestimated neither in terms of future profitability nor in terms of the importance of new employment and economic growth. The SME sector is therefore a key growth part of the future economy also according to the government.

The complexity and difficulties of Brexit will be outlined for the SME sector in much more detail through the Ferrabyrne case study later in this chapter. The biggest challenges are linked to enabling the businesses to plan better during very uncertain times, when future trading relationships with our biggest trading partner is no longer certain both in terms of exchange rates, mobility, trading tariffs, covering both custom tariffs and more technical tariffs and standards. The uncertainty is the single biggest challenge for the SME segment in the coming two to four years.

A failure to bring stability to this very important segment of the UK economy could make a mature difference to the future prosperity of this country and lead to a significant exit to a more stable environment in the EU. The success of the SME sector depends on the entrepreneurship in the UK.

This chapter will talk about lot of different sectors and will both cover domestic and export oriented businesses be they in manufacturing, services or in the leisure industry.

The dramatic fall in the value of the pound, should make UK exports more competitive in the short term, although in the longer term a weak pound will add to price inflation, which has already started and eventually corrective increases in interest rates.

Those in favour of Brexit argue that:

(1) EU markets are declining in attractiveness, so we would be better off negotiating our trade deals independently with other trading blocs – particularly in the Far East and other developing regions. As the world's 5th largest trading nation, the UK has a good negotiating position.
(2) As it runs a trade surplus with us, the EU needs trade with the UK more than the UK needs the EU, so we will be able to strike a good deal in terms of trade and other issues such as mobility.
(3) We will have more control over key economic variables if we are self-governing and independent
(4) The EU's trend towards ever closer political union will mean ever less control if we had stayed in.

However, commentaries from think tanks and organisations such as the CBI and other consider that on balance the decision to leave will have a negative effect on the UK economy, but an effect which is still to materialise. For those who believe we should stay in the single market, a variety of factors include:

(1) The likelihood that the UK will not eventually be able to negotiate better trade deals outside the EU as its bargaining power will be considerable less than as part of an EU acting together. The combined GDP of EU member states is now larger than any other single economy.
(2) Now, that we are leaving the EU it may lead to Scotland leaving the UK, causing further direct disruption to economic activity and general levels of confidence in the UK economy.
(3) UK based companies that are highly dependent on trade with the EU and/or on trade with countries with whom the EU is considered good trade deals may relocate. This might affect financial services firms in particular to have as a high proportion of trade in euros is done through the city of London.
(4) Irrespective of what trade deals the UK may eventually be able to strike, the intervening uncertainty is the principal source of concern in most commentaries. It is argued that Brexit has already undermined business confidence and investment in the UK, arising from fears of higher costs of trading, reduced access to labour and lower credit ratings. (This is already happening from nurses for the NHS from EU, where enquiries is already down by 90%) This uncertainty has already made financial sector companies plan for some operations to move to EU and the US.

The negotiation process and possible future scenarios for the UK outside the EU.

When the government invokes Article 50 at the end of March 2017, it will be a long and complex negotiation, which will most likely take longer than the two year deadline under Article 50 which then expires, the government has talked about maximum of another two years for a transitional period, but this will probably prove not to be long enough either. Any extension of the period will also require the agreement of all 27 remaining EU Members.

The UK government will negotiate as hard as possible to keep some sort of market access to the Single Market, but there is likely to be some hard bargaining, and potentially punitive action, by certain Member States and on top comes the potentially explosive issue of money relations between the EU and the UK.

Possible future trade scenarios

The terms on which the UK can trade with the rest of the EU and with countries outside the EU are critically important to the UK economy; at present the rest of EU takes over 45% of all UK exports and represents the single most important market for us. Over 35% of these exports are in services. Overall we have a trade deficit with the rest of the EU, although in services alone we consistently run a surplus. (mostly financial services).

It should also be noted that so trade with non-EU countries as a % of total UK trade has been growing in the last five years. Exports to the EU fell from 55% in 1999 to 48%, mainly due to trade with Brazil, Russia, India and China, the 'BRIC Countries'. However, it should be noted that the UK did more trade with Ireland in 2016 than with China.

WTO Regulations

It has been proposed that the UK could leave the EU and still trade under preferential rules with the rest of the EU. This is possible with an overall trade-tariff of 4.8% with some goods subject to less and some to be more. The overall bill for UK exports to the EU would be around £5 billion a year, but subject to significant more for EU imports were we continue trading with EU on WTO rules on imports.

The tariffs are not necessarily the major barrier under WTO rules as opposed to more technical barriers like new standard regulations, technical regulations or quantitative barriers which can cause significant disruption to trade. It is particularly this sort of barrier which will cause problems, were we to decide to trade with the EU under WTO rules alone.

For the majority of UK exports such as professional services, legal and accounting services and financial services, even more restrictions could be an issue were we to leave the single Market completely without some sort of arrangement for services as there are still restrictions on services across the EU. In the case of other markets, for example China, for a number of services including financial services and insurance there are still major restrictions for foreign owned entities and individuals.

It is therefore of great importance that that most important part of UK exports are left to continue operating in some sort of single Market with some sort of reciprocity as has been outlined by the government, for example in the form of deep and comprehensive free trade agreement covering these areas where standards and regulations are already implemented in the UK.

In the case of train and railway equipment which we will be looking at in a case study, the tariff restrictions under WTO rules are only 2% but all other technical standards, barriers and the state procurement policies makes some markets nearly closed for foreign supplier such as Germany and France for their state railways due to domestic suppliers and manufacturers.

Changes by sector

The EU accounts for 48% of all UK external trade and is therefore the single biggest trading block for the UK by a long way. We will be looking at some of the major implications by sector and in terms of tariffs, non-tariffs, regulations, migration, employment law and legal framework.

Taking a sector by sector approach, a longer transition beyond the two years is most likely going to have to be implemented to enable business to adapt to potential new rules and regulations. Below are some of the challenges that have been outlined by each sector in the UK.

A   Some sort of access to the single market (aviation and transportation).
B   Continued high skilled immigration (aviation, finance, professional services, health services, creative sector).
C   Stable regulatory environment (most sectors).
D   Tariff-free relationship (construction).
E   Collaboration with European partners enhances UK research excellence (aviation, teaching, research, and telecommunications).
F   The UK and EU would both benefit from temporary transitional arrangements in financial services and by adapting the 'equivalent' principle for the financial sector in the UK, so trade and transactions can continue.
G   Much of the regulation of the food and drink industry is from the EU and transforming existing legislation into UK legislation would give the sector the stability and certainty it is looking for.
H   Mutual recognition of regulation (food and drink).
I   Much of the regulation for the life sciences sector stems from the EU, so a continuation of this regime would give stability to this sector as well.
J   Barrier free access for good and services is very important (services and professional services).

A smooth exit from the EU is important for many sectors in the UK, in particular retail and transportation, as regulatory confusion will create uncertainty and will make doing business even more challenging.

To gain full advantage of the continued relationship with the EU the needs of SMEs need to be maintained, ie. tariff-free or with minimal non-tariff barriers across every sector.

How to prepare for Brexit for SMEs

In order for SMEs to prepare for the uncertainty of the next two years and beyond a number of initiatives need to be taken at each corporate level and the planning needs to be done, to enable the businesses to quickly adapt to new circumstances as they arise both in terms of new limitations but also in terms of new opportunities that could present themselves in the market-place.

This is all about creating as much certainty as possible in an ever changing world and environment.

The planning should be scenario planning, which is all about strategic planning under uncertainty. In this instance the use of scenario based approaches to modelling and planning is the best way forward.

By looking at multiple and contradictory plausible outcomes, requires SMEs to develop more options and to achieve better preparedness and higher resilience.

One part that needs to be accounted for in the future is the political/economic consequences which going forward appears to be more important than in the past in this phase of the negotiations as part of the scenario planning. What if?

The planning can be done through a three phased approach.

(1) The short term
(2) The longer term
(3) Continuing

Short term

Identify specific areas that may be affected by Brexit and require further investigation, areas in the business in terms of products, staff, geography, health and safety, forex and supply chain.

Having analysed the affected areas a short-list of issues should be articulated and communicated to all stakeholders, who will want to see a plan on how the business will cope with the areas/subjects which will be affected.

Shareholders will want to see a plan, customers will want guarantees and employees reassurances of the effect on their work and future career.

Be prepared to take action where key opportunities have been identified and arise and also where there is a danger of losing business due to new tariffs or technical barriers.

Plan and monitor for changes in the unfolding situation and execute need for changes appropriately.

In summary the near term plan should focus on:
(a) Accelerating your thinking on Brexit.
(b) Identifying risks and opportunities most pertinent to you and your business.
(c) Identifying initial opportunities and options to mitigate risks.

This is all about risk managing uncertainty.

Longer term – strategic options/choices

Once the parts of the business affected by Brexit have been identified, the strategy is about choice.

The strategy does not need to be a long planning document. It is more a set of identified interrelated and powerful decisions that positions the SME to win during even more uncertainty. To move with the changes in the market and in the political-economic world on the areas that affect your key business decisions will be critical (for example what happens if future technical barriers are set in the EU for the gadget that we produce, we have to be sure UK regulations follow EU articulated standards)

The strategy is about prioritising risks and opportunities, so appropriate actions can be taken quickly.

It is all about adapting to ever evolving changes as we head into the UK leaving the EU and beyond.

Continuing – Monitor and Act

Once the key issues have been identified and prioritised, you need as an organisation to be on top of the changes to ensure your organisation continues to adapt and change as legislation/regulation and circumstances change.

How will the potential changes affect SMEs

In truth the impact is currently unknowable – we cannot be sure which trade agreement scenario we will follow, as we know that we will be leaving the single market but we do not know how a weak pound will increase prices or how the alternatives will take to put in place, the proposed two year proposed transition period does not seem realistic at this stage. It is a fair guess though that the uncertainty created by the vote to leave will have additional short term effect on investor confidence and hence on investment and growth, although this has happened less than anticipated.

The dramatic fall in the pound in 2016, has made UK exports more competitive in the short-term, although in the longer term a weak pound can be expected to add to price inflation and eventually corrective increases in interest rates.

I will take you through a case-study for a company I have worked with for many years as a non-exec chairman and director, to show the factors that are under consideration, ie. what are the real implications for an SME in day to day and long term operations of Brexit:

Case-Study: Ferrabyrne Ltd.

Ferrabyrne is a leading manufacturer of railway suspension systems and components with a global customer base.

The core strength lies in providing a design concept, to final delivery service for all customers, large and small, with emphasis on improving product life-spans.

The major customers are most of the largest train-wagon manufacturers in the world.

The company is more than 45 years old and financially stable.

The questions asked by the management of Ferrabyrne after the Brexit referendum are:

(1) With the changing exchange rate, what will happen to the cost of imports and energy?
(2) What will happen if the reaction from Europe is negative to our trade?
(3) Are we in or out of Europe and how are we going to react to the changes?
(4) A US trade deal will not solve all our issues as their train standards are very different from both UK and Europe.
(5) For our size of company India and China are important development markets, but Europe is next door.
(6) What does this actually mean for Ferrabyrne?
(7) What is the time-frame for the implementation for a new deal with Europe?
(8) We are currently planning in a vacuum.

What are the effects of Brexit for Ferrabyrne?

Markets/customers

The market that is seen to have the strongest potential for the railway industry in Europe is the UK, with forecast growth in passenger numbers requiring massive investment for the next 30 years. With train manufacturers Bombardier and Hitachi already having established manufacturing plants in the UK and others, including Alstom and CAF announcing that they will also be manufacturing in the UK, whether the UK is in or out of EU will not affect this business.

Following the exit of the UK from the EU it can be assumed that UK suppliers would be in at least as good a position going forward, but perhaps even more prioritisation of UK content would be a possibility for UK rail developments as before, if the divorce is less than balanced. So with regards to UK business of European trains destined for Europe we are probably in a good position.

Manufacturers such as Siemens (Germany) or Alstom (France) who have strong ties to customers in their own markets, ie DB and SNCF already utilise local sourcing policies, so there would be no real effect following UK exit.

There are a number of other European train manufacturers, who are not strongly tied to their State owned rail companies, export outside the EU and particularly where we have provided specific technical solutions for them , are probably less likely to be influenced by EU sourcing guidelines. So unless specific trade barriers/duties were imposed, this business is unlikely to be significantly affected to our business in Europe.

For markets outside the EU – USA, China, Japan, India, Australia etc – Negotiations of separate trade agreements with a number of countries will take years. However, it is likely that a continuation of the status quo would be expected during those negotiation periods having little disruption on Ferrabyrne's business

The two largest revenue streams are the UK and the EU markets. Future revenue growth will be strongly influenced by rail opportunities in the Indian and Chinese markets, but these opportunities will inevitable be growing at a slower pace. The Indian Finance Minister has been quoted as saying that India is well prepared to deal with the fall-out from Brexit and aims to strengthen its position as the fifth largest job creator in the UK over the past four years ahead of China. But why would we wish to lose the existing 'next-door' market – the EU?

Exchange rates

Ferrabyrne's immediate position is unaffected as sales and purchase contracts are hedged to remove the effect of currency fluctuations on all long term contracts.

Short-term – Following the vote to exit. Sterling has reduced in value against most currencies. It is not certain how long the drop in valuation might last, however if this level were to be maintained then it would certainly increase our competitiveness in export markets such as USA and China.

Long-term – Many of our costs are based on import pricing and energy (dollars) and our sales pricing will have to reflect that. Hedging removes the short-term exchange risks, but there is certainly a potential benefit of an improved competitive edge for the added value content if exchange rates were to stay as they are.

Barriers

Until we have an understanding of how the exit will be negotiated, it is a difficult one to hypothesise about barriers.

There is a significant trade imbalance between the UK and the EU, so it could be assumed that the UK should be in a good position to achieve a fair balance, particularly supported by a range of German and Scandinavian industrial exporters. However, it is of course difficult to anticipate at this early stage, whether the EU will be dovish or not. However, if the EU impose tough barriers in the form of tariffs and the UK responded with similar tariffs on EU imports, then it is likely that the business would benefit from being based within the strongest growth market (UK). So perhaps it would seem barriers into the EU should not logically cause problems.

People

The business does not envisage any staffing problems arising from Brexit either in the short or long term.

Overview

Clearly the total effects on the UK economy as whole have yet to be determined from such a momentous decision. The biggest concern would have been if there was a reduction in the UK's future investment plans for the railways.

It is interesting to note that the early noises from the government suggest that, in the current circumstances growth/development are higher priorities than deficit reduction. Although many issues are debatable (to say the least) this factor, together with the present exchange rate and potentially reducing Corporation Tax Rates suggests that the business could be potentially better placed following an exit from EU.

CONCLUSIONS

In the short term there seems to be a number of advantages for Ferrabyrne in leaving the EU as the major market is the UK railway industry.

The big issue is the uncertainty linked to the divorce process which will last at least four to five years or longer. A number of issues were raised by the Managing Director Ken Horton at the beginning of the case-study on the implications for Ferrabyrne at leaving the EU:

(1) Exchange rate

The raw-materials such as rubber, metal and energy is all imported and usually denominated in US dollars and Euros, there will be growing cost pressure over the next few years for Ferrabyrne, if the Pound remains low and if inflation therefore starts to pick up in the UK. These are all factors that Ferrabyrne has to take into account in their planning going forward and this will also mean rising wages, which will affect competitiveness negatively and this is not expected to stabilise for the foreseeable future.

Ferrabyrne will continue to hedge currency exposure for all supplies and contracts going forward as they have done in the past, but with the continued uncertainty this becomes even more important as import prices will increase, but due to the fall in the Pound the Ferrabyrne products might become more competitive.

(2) Negative reaction to our trade with EU

This is a very difficult challenge to predict at this early stage as we do not know what our future trading relationship with the EU is going to look like. Currently the Single Market works as one big domestic market for UK manufacturers. (including Ferrabyrne) We have no tariffs or technical restrictions for the Ferrabyrne products and we are able to compete openly with our European competitors on price, quality, design and after sales service and credibility. This could change drastically if we in the future are subject to general WTO rules on low tariffs.

However, this might not be the biggest challenge going forward in the future, the barriers are usually linked with technical trade barriers such as specific standards and hidden requirements which form artificial trade barriers. These sort of barriers could be imposed by separate EU countries if the UK does not obtain access to the single market as we are able to do today.

This is where the difference between a 'hard' and a 'soft' exit from the EU could cause a major problem for Ferrabyrne going forward. It is these sort of barriers and uncertainties which will be part of the planning process for Ferrabyrne over the next four or five years or even longer.

Hidden trade barriers or artificial barriers are the ones that could cause problems for Ferrabyrne's export business to the EU, if a satisfactory access for the UK to the single market is not found as part of an overall settlement.

(3) Are we in or out of EU?

This is the key question after 2019 and in particular for SMEs who are used to operating in the EU market. The uncertainty makes planning very difficult and in the case of Ferrabyrne the board has decided to continue operating in the EU as it has done in the past with the larger European train manufacturers as no other information is available at this stage. So, over the next two years operations will continue as they have done in the past.

After 2019, it is expected there will be at least a two year transition period before new potential rules will apply. In the case of Ferrabyrne contracts often run for about three years, so no new plans have been implemented for exports and trade with EU customers at this stage.

The uncertainty of our status with the EU is the single biggest barrier for long-term planning at this stage, which is why any changes are currently not considered in trade with larger EU train manufacturers.

The provisions made are only in relation to currency hedging and the articulation of contractual clauses beyond 2019, should trading relations between the EU and UK change significantly, contracts should be up for re-negotiation.

(4) A US trade deal would not solve all our issues as their train standards are very different

The biggest barrier for a company the size of Ferrabyrne is the very different standards used in markets outside UK/Europe – our home market. We have developed business in both China and India over the past ten years and we are aware of how long it takes to develop a significant business outside the EU.

All train standards are different and we have until recently operated in China as part of the supply-chain through the European market, not as a direct supplier to the Chinese market. We believe it takes five to ten years to develop new markets and it is therefore important to have certainty that we can continue operating in EU beyond the exit and we need this market for the foreseeable future to remain accessible.

Building up new markets in India, China and the US will take many years and in the case of China and India this process was initiated many years ago, however, the size of our market shares will be insignificant compared to our market in EU and UK for many years.

The size of Ferrabyrne makes the entry in new markets both difficult as all our products are specifically designed. Consideration has to be given to the time it takes to develop business relationships as a serious supplier in these new markets, given that one is competing with long established existing domestic suppliers/manufacturers.

Therefore, entry-barriers for new suppliers and manufacturers are very high and with our size and reach we can only be successful by working with local partners in joint ventures in these new markets.

This makes it even more important that the transition from the single market and potential leaving it is done over a longer period of time. If we were to lose this market during this transition, before being able to fully develop the new markets of India and China (let alone the US market), it would be very damaging to the business, despite the growth in the UK market

(5) For our size of company Europe is virtually our home market as it is next door, whereas India and China are not.

Having operated in the UK and EU as a niche supplier in a highly specialised market for over 45 years, we are known to the customers of the train manufacturers in the EU. This specialist business has been built up over many years and is the bread and butter of our operation.

The nature of this business requires in depth knowledge and long term planning, compliance with standards, regulations and customer specifications and a very collaborative approach to work with customers to execute their future plans for railway equipment.

The long-term planning cycles makes it very difficult to have to work with uncertainty only as to what the future will hold in one to two years' time and makes it even more even more important for Ferrabyrne, what sort of trading relationship the UK will have with the EU after 2019?

(6) What does it actually mean for Ferrabyrne?

Ferrabyrne are part of an integrated supply chain for a number of train manufacturers in Europe and we will continue to develop in our home growth market the UK, as well as our relationships and customer relationships throughout Europe. However, with the understanding that we are planning in a vacuum after 2019 but we are hoping we will be able to continue operating profitably in this market, post-2019 as our UK customers are also operating throughout the EU.

The uncertainty will of course mean that we will simultaneously also develop the markets in India and China with our partners but there is no alternative for our current EU home market for the next five years and it is therefore key to our future success and our relationship with our key clients, that we can continue operating in Europe after a new deal is implemented in the UKs relationship with the EU.

The longer this goes on the more difficult it will be for a SME business and with the EU it's our home market built up over many years as geographical diversification takes time, and is a very costly exercise.

Conclusions on leaving the EU for SMEs in the UK

For Ferrabyrne Ltd we have covered both the pros and cons of leaving the EU as an example of the far reaching implications it has for one particular business but also to underline the complexity and challenges facing for example the manufacturing industry in this country having operated with Europe as a home market for many years. In the case of Ferrabyrne, which is well placed due to the growth in the UK domestic train market, the short term challenges are smaller, but for the medium to long-term the situation is very uncertain and therefore the sooner we all know how we will move forward with the EU the better.

In the case of the EU the principles of unrestricted competition are a series of directives which member states have some discretion to interpret, but which must be complied with. Directives bearing on public procurement and state aid and on regulations affecting the operation and commercial freedoms of regulated utilities (such as requirement to separate the ownership of national rail assets and operation of services) have important implications for Ferrabyrne and their customers.

If the UK remains part of the EEA in some form, then it will have to comply with the relevant directives (as do Norway and Iceland) although being unable to influence them. Conversely, being outside these trading arrangements will remove the need to comply further with the directives and could provide the public sector and regulated utilities with more flexibility in the way projects are procured – no longer following OJEU procurement procedures, but excluded from EU procurement markets – and more flexibility in the way access to infrastructure assets are charged for and owned, eg vertical integration of rail and train operating services could in principle become a realistic option, or there could be greater flexibility in the way access charges are set. The scope for providing government subsidies may also be increased, although subsidies are also subject to WTO rules. This should all provide more growth to the UK railway industry.

It is important to understand that there is no such thing as free trade these days. Free trade agreements are deep and comprehensive and full of standards, mutual recognition, mutual acceptance of laws and regulations, so even if the UK is out of the single market, EEA, customs union but wants a free trade agreement with EU it will probably have to keep a lot of laws and regulations that are already transposed into UK law. On procurement, don't forget that much regulation is WTO, and not only EU, and if UK companies want access to the EU procurement markets, the same rules will have to be followed.

The case study of Ferrabyrne has shown us some of the challenges facing small and medium sized companies in the UK over the next five years and the challenges and uncertainty are not insignificant. We have also covered some of the subject matters such as mobility, which will have significant effects on certain sectors such as the construction industry, food and leisure and the tourist industry.

On the exchange rate we have discussed the pros and cons of a permanently weaker pound, both in terms of imports and exports, but also in terms of growing cost pressures and impending higher inflation.

We have not been able with the current information to know whether this will have further implications for investments and investment returns, although investment decisions have been postponed or given up on the back of the Brexit vote. But it does seem that investor confidence has returned, at least in the short term, after the initial vote.

The importance for SMEs is to be able to plan for the future with as little uncertainty as possible and as long as the negotiations are ongoing with the EU over the next two years and beyond there is only so much which can be predicted.

It is therefore important that planning at the corporate level is done in as flexible fashion as possible, using the scenario planning as a core model 'what if' by identifying the most important priorities for the business and for its future profitability. To concentrate all resources on the core business and identified priorities and continue with as little disruption as possible to enable the business to adapt gradually to the new reality outside the EU and the new trade agreements.

Hans Christian Iversen is a senior advisor for middle sized companies on Brexit, a professional leadership mentor and a professional non-executive director who has specialised in helping business internationalise their business development. He was previously a VP with Disney and a senior partner with Deloitte Consulting in Europe and with Roland Berger Strategy Consulting and is a mentor with the Princes Trust

ADAM SHUTKEVER, CO-FOUNDER AND NON-EXECUTIVE DIRECTOR, RIVERVIEW LAW

'There's no such thing as bad weather, only unsuitable clothing.'

Alfred Wainwright, A Coast to Coast Walk

Introduction

I will start with a confession. I am a recovering lawyer. Happily, immediately after qualifying I moved to a career in investment banking where I spent 15 years travelling the world, advising on mergers and acquisitions and equity offerings.

Around the turn of the century, one of my last clients as an investment banker, Karl Chapman, was kind enough to invite me to join the board of a business which he was starting and which was targeting outsourced HR advice for the large corporate market. That business, AdviserPlus, proved to be very successful, securing long-term contracts from a wide range of blue-chip corporate customers, and became a catalyst for the creation of Riverview Law.

The core strategy of Riverview Law is pretty straightforward – to deliver a full range of legal services designed around the needs of its customers. Not rocket science, perhaps, but in the context of a sector little changed over hundreds of years, it has turned out to be quite revolutionary.

In practice, this means that we operate with teams dedicated to individual customers, operating on a fixed-price basis, typically under multi-year contracts with a defined service scope depending upon the requirements of each customer. Our activities are focused upon the core day to day requirements of our customers. We do not set out to lead on mergers and acquisitions work, neither are we a legal processor. Both of these areas are very well served – by 'Magic Circle' law firms in the former case and offshore Legal Process Outsourcers in the latter. Happily, our sweet spot comprises perhaps 60–70% of most in-house departments' workloads and, crucially, it is an area where considerable business intelligence can be gained from the data generated by our activities.

Six years from launch we are now a well-established business, regulated by the Solicitors Regulation Authority, with over 100 employees based in four locations in the UK and the USA. Our customers are all global corporations, many of whom are operating in regulated markets such as financial services and telecommunications.

We are also now a technology business. Our proprietary technology platform, Kim (standing for Knowledge, Intelligence, Meaning), which we initially developed to facilitate the efficient execution of our work and, through comprehensive data capture and manipulation, to provide the foundation for artificial intelligence solutions, forms the core of our US-based subsidiary, Kim Technologies. This is a particularly exciting development for us, taking us into a high-growth global market beyond legal services. Arguably, having started out as a technology-enabled legal business, we are now a technology business with considerable expertise in the legal services market.

Brexit and Riverview Law

In the early stages following the UK referendum vote, once the more vitriolic recriminations had died down, the main theme became, and to a significant degree, remains, one of uncertainty.

As a general rule, an uncertain business environment is a bad thing for confidence and makes long-term planning more difficult. It would normally be expected to have a negative effect on major corporate investment decisions with a consequent drop in transaction volumes.

Whilst the post-referendum data has been inconclusive, skewed in part by the effects of a weaker pound and the dominance of global corporations in the FTSE 100 index, these are early days and as inflationary pressures threaten the end of an unprecedented period of low interest rates there remains a significant risk of a slow-down in investment as Brexit approaches.

All things being equal, this potentially spells bad news for 'traditional' law firms, whose business models tend to be geared towards transactional activity, whether in mergers and acquisitions or sectors such as commercial or residential property.

In contrast, Riverview's managed services business, which is very much focussed on its customers' 'business as usual' activity, is far less exposed to short-term economic shocks or shifts in investment sentiment whilst Kim facilitates the efficient management of operations and arguably should be expected to benefit from the greater cost pressures being felt by our customers.

Geographically, Riverview is not reliant on access to the Single European Market. It only practices English Law. This does not represent a handicap, given the dominance of English Law in corporate contracts and our ability to work alongside our customers' in-house teams on the occasions that non-English law points arise, but does mean that our business does not require passporting rights in order to service our customers' requirements. Kim, meanwhile, is universal in application and language agnostic, giving us a global reach not confined to the legal market.

So, all in all, I feel it is unlikely that Riverview will be adversely impacted by Brexit. Indeed, setting aside the potential long-term macroeconomic benefits which I will consider later, we are well positioned to gain both from additional work driven by corporate preparations for Brexit (discussed below) and from the ability of Kim to drive down costs and increase the effectiveness of information-heavy processes across sectors and geographies.

Advice for other businesses

Notwithstanding the initial and, judging from most economic indicators, misplaced hysteria in the run-up to, and immediately following, the referendum vote, I would start by noting that change is not of itself bad. What is bad is failing to prepare for change.

Even after Theresa May's Lancaster House speech, plenty of uncertainty remains as to what will come next, not least how rational the EU response to our negotiating position will be. The general shape of the UK's strategy is, however, becoming clearer and it seems highly likely that, subject to any transitional arrangements, we will not be a full member of the single market or the customs union post-Brexit.

What does that mean in practice?

There are two obvious areas where change can be treated as a given:-

    (i)   Cross-border movements of goods and services. We should expect at the very least additional documentation/red tape requirements for the movement of goods, with consequent delays in the process and the possible imposition of tariffs affecting post-Brexit sourcing decisions. It is also highly unlikely that UK businesses delivering services across EU borders will enjoy the same passporting rights which currently apply;

(ii) Recruitment of staff from EU countries and, probably, elsewhere is likely to be governed by a different, permit-based regime.

It is impossible to say where things will eventually land, but as a starting point it is absolutely essential that businesses understand what they are 'in for' with their existing arrangements and requirements. This can and should be done now.

Achieving this might be relatively straightforward for SMEs with a limited range of customers and suppliers but it is a mammoth exercise for large corporates working with integrated global supply chains and numerous counterparties. These will involve thousands or tens of thousands of contracts, the terms or application of which might be affected by the UK's status in relation to the single market and customs union. Riverview's experience in conducting large-scale reviews of corporate contracts suggests that many businesses will have significant work to do in finding, identifying and analysing their current contracts. There is no time to be lost – come what may, a comprehensive catalogue and review of existing contractual arrangements would seem to be an absolute requirement in preparing for Brexit.

The good news is that, given the rapid development of automated review and artificial intelligence capabilities in systems such as Kim (hence, combined with Riverview's expertise in review projects, my optimism in relation to the opportunities presented to Riverview by Brexit), this is not as labour intensive or time-consuming an exercise as it used to be. Indeed, it is arguable that it shouldn't take a 'shock' such as Brexit to act as a catalyst. Now the technology is here there is no excuse for major corporates to be in the dark as to their contractual environments.

For businesses taking advantage of passporting rights, obvious examples being professional and financial services providers such as lawyers, insurers, banks and investment managers, now is the time to consider establishing or developing regulated operations in countries which will remain members of the EU post-Brexit. We are already seeing significant activity in this area and much manoeuvring on the part of financial centres who see themselves as natural alternatives to the City of London. It remains to be seen how substantial these operations will have to be in practice in order to achieve the desired result from the perspective of the regulated businesses. Instinctively, it feels unlikely that a glorified 'brass plaque' plus local compliance infrastructure will be sufficient, but by the same token many of the principals of these businesses are firmly established in London and the businesses benefit from the long-established integrated professional infrastructure which London offers. What happens next in this area is a key area of uncertainty, but it is certainly prudent for UK-based regulated service businesses operating across EU borders to plan on the basis of a loss of passporting rights post Brexit.

Moving on to staff recruitment, this is a very tricky area given the significance of the control of immigration as a factor in the referendum vote and the Prime Minister's continuing emphasis on regaining control over immigration from the EU. There can be no easy answers to a problem which arises from arguably emotional rather than rational or economic issues. Many sectors of the economy at all skill ranges, from hospitality and agriculture to technology and financial services, are likely to be adversely affected by additional restrictions on immigration. The government's answer would appear to be that it is up to businesses to ensure that their workforces are trained to do highly-skilled jobs, but this takes time and is dependent upon an effective education system producing recruits with an appropriate grounding for such training. It also fails to take account of the difficulty of recruiting British staff for many types of unskilled and anti-social hours work.

Ultimately, we are left to hope that an enlightened government will understand the needs of British businesses and will implement an immigration policy which will ensure that businesses are able to recruit and retain the workforces which they require. It is incumbent on all business leaders and representative bodies such as the CBI to lobby government on this – it is a fundamental element in ensuring that Brexit is a long-term success for the British economy.

Brexit – a longer-term view

So, having considered Riverview's position and that of other businesses preparing for Brexit, what will be the longer-term effects of the change?

On the one hand, the UK is walking away from full membership of an economic bloc which is its largest single export market. On the other hand, the EU's share of global GDP is falling as developing market economies grow rapidly. Leaving the constraints of a frustratingly unwieldy collective trade negotiating structure will give the UK flexibility to negotiate trade agreements with high-growth economies freely. We will also be leaving behind a faltering social and political project, significantly weakened by a single currency experiment which appears increasingly structurally unsound.

We read daily reports of potentially serious downturns in trading activity with the EU and projections of the low likelihood of these being offset by the potential upside of deals such as the hoped-for early agreement with the Trump administration in the US. But by the same token, we see the troubles of the Italian banking system, the continued travails of Greece, the threat of far-right populist candidates in European national elections and the continuation of a ruinous European agricultural policy. Nothing is clear.

It is probably appropriate at this stage for me to disclose that I was a 'Remainer', albeit (like many of my peers) not an enthusiastic one. I have little time for the unelected and disconnected Brussels functionaries and much of the legislation for which they are responsible. However, we are where we are.

To return to Wainwright's observation, the weather has changed. It is up to us to don suitable clothing. The UK enjoys an attractive corporate tax regime, a well-educated workforce and the best financial and legal market infrastructure in the world. We must head out to face this brave new world with confidence.

For more information on Riverview Law visit www.riverviewlaw.com

REEN MAGNUS, CEO, THE HANZEL GROUP

The Hanzel Group

The Hanzel Group, comprising of Hanzel Investment Management Limited, Hanzel Ventures and Hanzel Hedge Funds, is a group of innovative growth companies with interest in property development, hedge funds, banking, and disruptive innovations and it is run by highly qualified and experienced professionals who make up the Board. The primary business focus of the group is centred on improving lives through disruptive innovations. These disruptive innovations are designed to support sustainable livelihoods for younger hard working professionals and families in the UK and internationally. The key products include FueDeal, a retail fuel, utilities, and energy price hedging product; Home*Advance, an innovation in homeownership and Flex* the tandem financial vehicle for Home*Advance.

Impact on listed UK company shares and the British pound sterling

The Brexit vote result had a significant impact on the stock price of UK listed companies. This would have had a negative valuation on long positions held in these equities. The Hanzel Group had taken a defensive measure by moving its long positions in equities to cash prior to Brexit votes. Once in cash, prior to a fall in stock price, that price fall represents value from the initial position. This discounted price impacts Price/Earnings [PE] ratio by reducing it. A reduction in PE ratio, all other factors being favourable, represents value. However, at that time, the question remained as to whether the UK was headed into a bear market and when it would reach the trough. In addition to devaluation of UK company stocks being an opportunity, immediate opportunity for shorting the FTSE indices was significant and positive. It was a volatile time but it stalled within the premise of market correction rather than a bear market. On Friday, 30 December 2016, the FTSE100 had rallied to an all-time high of 7,142.83 point bouncing back from Brexit lowest point of 5,982.20 on 27 June 2016 adding £232 billion to the value of Britain's top companies. Some mining stocks like Anglo American and Glencore rallied to over 100% return. The FTSE 100 rally must be taken with caution because of the implications of the weak pound. Since the Brexit votes result and the period ending Friday 30 December, 2016 the British pound sterling lost 17.4% against the US dollar. The implication of this is that the rally of FTSE 100 company stocks comes from three sources none of which is a direct positive effect of Brexit and these being mining stock rally which is attributable to stronger commodity prices worldwide, the 'Trump Bump', which is the US President's commitment to boosting infrastructure spending, and lastly but not the least simple currency correction from multi-national companies that make up the FTSE 100 the majority of which generate the greater proportion of their gross revenue from outside of the United Kingdom and who often do little or no business at all in the United Kingdom. Thus, these blue chip companies benefit hugely when the pound is weak. To put this into perspective, in the same period, the companies which generate their gross revenue from and within the United Kingdom fell by 7%. This is significant. When evaluated in terms of adjusted return, which take into consideration surge in stock price versus currency fluctuation of the pound, it becomes clear that the FTSE 100 was actually down by 5% over the year of the referendum. That is not a positive outlook.

Whatever positive points this rally may imply, the Achilles heel remains the stark reality of the implication of the sharp decline in value suffered by the pound since the Brexit vote. This, clearly, will increase inflationary pressure on the British economy thereby squeezing disposable incomes which will in turn mean that Britons will have less to spend. Reduced consumer spending will negatively impact British SMEs. Conversely, the ironic conundrum this poses is that the hardest hit will be the working class people.

In both difficult and expanding economic climates, consumers will find FueDeal, indispensable in hedging inflation and price movement of retail fuel, energy, and utility products. If Brexit causes a backlash of difficult economic climate which creates retail fuel and energy product inflation, this inflation will produce a positive opportunity for the usefulness of FueDeal. However, reduction in disposable income will cripple the retail consumer's ability to take advantage of this product, so whilst the former creates a positive effect, the latter is negative. Furthermore, if Brexit creates a difficult economic climate for the short to medium term, this will make it extremely difficult for working people to get on the property ladder of homeownership. Home*Advance, which is designed to make homeownership more accessible would be very useful but only in so far as lenders have an appetite to lend to homebuyers within this space. From an objective point of view, Brexit is in its infancy. It is therefore extremely difficult and premature to definitively determine its full impact on the British economy, SMEs, and consumers without the specific terms of the agreement with the EU having been decided.

The below chart which is courtesy of Bloomberg clearly shows the immediate negative impact of Brexit on the UK's stocks leading index and the British pound sterling [GBP].

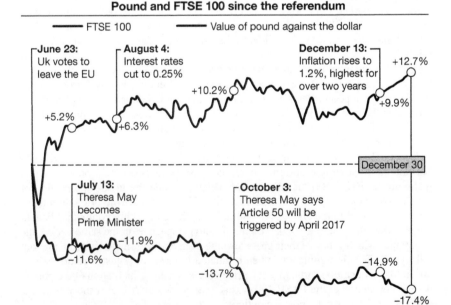

Pound and FTSE 100 since the referendum

264

Impact on property development lending and valuation

Another area where the Hanzel Group has noticed an immediate impact was the change in lending attitudes by many property development lenders. Development finance applications received prior to Brexit but which were not yet approved were generally suspended or completely terminated by some lenders. The attitude was very much that of 'Let's wait and see'. Whilst the requirement for new homes and the housing shortage crisis has not gone away due to Brexit vote, financiers were more concerned with devaluation of the property market as a result of Brexit and the implication of this on loan to value and the lender's exit strategy both of which ultimately underpins responsible lending criteria. Highest Loan to Value [LTV] in the property development finance space tends to be in the region of 70% of Gross Development Value [GDV] and highest Loan to Costs [LTC] is usually in the region of 80% of costs. Therefore, Brexit would only have a negative impact on lenders and their exit strategy if property prices slumped by more than 65% of 30% of the Gross Development Value and 65% of 20% of the development costs. As developers can only release 65% of the equity headroom, such reduction in the property valuation will have the impact of equity erasure which would leave lenders and developers in serious difficulties. This was however not the case, so it would be accurate to state that the lenders' reaction to withhold lending was more of a knee-jerk reaction.

Impact on UK government credit rating

Following the result of the Brexit vote, the United Kingdom lost its enviable AAA credit rating. It was downgraded from AAA to AA by S&P; this is a worrying two-notch downgrade. Following the British Chancellor of the Exchequer, Chancellor George Osborne's statement that the United Kingdom will face the future 'from a position of strength' Fitch downgraded the credit rating from AA+ to AA. Moody followed likewise and cut the UK's credit rating outlook to negative. The implication of this is glaring in economic and social terms. One such negative implication is that the cost of borrowing by the government in international financial markets will increase. This will invariably increase any applicable deficit. Higher credit rating allows a government to borrow at lower rate which in turns lowers its cost of funds or borrowing; hence it is crucial for any government to ensure that it protects its high credit rating. The rating agencies forecast a slowing down of the UK's economy, and further project that policymaking efficiency and stability will be negatively impacted by the deep divide between the Conservative ruling party, and the general public and the further complication of the prospect of a Scottish Referendum. The implication of this for UK businesses comes in many folds, one of which is the fact that there is the likelihood that the government may resort to finding alternative ways to compensate for the increased cost of borrowing in order to check or reduce any arising deficits. The government may seek to generate revenue from the private sector in taxes or other forms of revenue which will further squeeze and pressurize the private sector and SMEs leading to a potential vicious cycle of further slumps in Gross Domestic Product [GDP] and economic growth.

The Hanzel Group's focus on provision of housing

Our primary strategy is to focus on our business plan and deliver the products and services which the British people need. It is our professional opinion that the UK housing shortage will not be affected by Brexit. Therefore, the Hanzel Group is positioned to meet this need. We utilised a SWOT analysis that effectively addresses all four elements of strength, weaknesses, opportunities, and threats. Brexit falls under the 'Threats' category so we were fully prepared for either outcomes and determined to convert the threat to opportunities. The Hanzel Group went beyond positioning itself to provide housing needs, but also to consolidate this positioning by developing disruptive innovation products Home*Advance and Flex* that will facilitate, enhance, and empower more people to own their own homes and to remain on the property ladder of homeownership for the long term. These products have now reached capability for launch. Britons needed homes before Brexit and they will continue to need homes after Brexit. It is that simple. At the Hanzel Group, we have chosen to be adaptable and to create opportunities from Brexit for our company and for the betterment of the British people.

Focus on completion and roll out of innovation products

The Hanzel Group has two products outside of the property space. The first is FueDeal, a retail fuel, utlity, and energy price hedging product which harnesses returns from the stock market to hedge against inflationary influences on retail commodities and energy products. If in the worst case scenario, if Brexit's negative impact on the pound persists and this leads to decreased disposable income, purchasing power will become a real problem which will in turn mean people will be seeking value wherever possible. A retail price hedging product fits this need perfectly as it give a higher level of control over to the consumer to hedge rising prices. However as previously mentioned, lack of or reduced disposable income would negatively impact how much control a consumer could possibly exert on commodity inflation even within the FueDeal system.

Capital introduction from outside the UK – acquisition

With the negative change in lenders' attitude following Brexit, the Hanzel Group began to look for opportunities for capital introduction from outside Britain. Thus, we have been presented with an exclusive opportunity for the acquisition of a stable financial institution with a healthy, stable outlook for the purpose of funding our UK property development projects. Invariably, Brexit has created the necessity to source funding from outside the United Kingdom to provide housing for British people in the United Kingdom. This is not necessarily a bad thing as it creates further opportunities to broaden and diversify our portfolio internationally. Ultimately, this will also potentially enhance relationships between Britain and other countries that British companies like ours have to do business with or seek funding from.

Assets and regional diversification

At the Hanzel Group, we have always included in our business plan, diversification of our portfolio holdings. As a result, we have various complementary yet distinctly different products which we have discussed at length previously and therefore do not need to re-hatch. In the same vein, we made a conscious decision to diversify our holdings internationally. Diversification of holdings and by region is an indispensable tool to build for balance and resilience, and to curtail losses during difficult economic climate. This strategy forms an integral part of our long term risk management policy.

Currency hedging

Currency hedging provides opportunity to fix the rate of base currency against other currencies that the company relies on for frequent transactions, or occasional transactions. Hedging protects the business from fluctuations which would otherwise impact it negatively enabling the business to continue to transact its international trades and operations undisturbed.

Options contracts

With respect to FueDeal, the Hanzel Group would enter into and maintain options contracts with bulk hydrocarbons producers and suppliers in order to hedge the bulk price of these commodities. This enhances stability within the system. This is particularly important in stemming any negative impact that could arise from opportunity-driven events such as Brexit. When used appropriately, options agreements or contracts can be extremely valuable to a business.

Regional and asset diversification

The Hanzel Group would advise other companies to consider asset class and regional diversifications. The case in hand regarding the surge in FTSE100 at the close of the year 2016, clearly defines the advantage of diversification over non-diversification. Companies that did not sufficiently diversify their businesses geographically and generated their revenue principally from the UK lost 7% in value whilst those that diversified internationally and generated their revenue from sources outside of the United Kingdom, gained significantly over the same period and under the same negative impact of Brexit. Diversification can potentially reduce risk and its importance can therefore not be over-emphasised. Failure to diversify is akin to placing one's eggs in one basket.

Currency hedging

Another helpful strategy is currency hedging for companies that transact business in multiple currencies. The slump in the British pound sterling at 17% is significant and can cripple a smaller British business that relies on the US dollar in its operation. This would wipe out 17% of any potential income. Currency hedging takes the guess work out of foreign exchange costs.

Uncertainty and outcome of negotiations with Brussels

Besides the Scottish Referendum, there is a level of uncertainty as to what post-Brexit Britain will look like in terms of policies, trade agreements, and human capital mobility. Until these negotiations are complete and a clear agreement has been reached with the EU, it will be difficult to accurately predict if Brexit will be good for business on the long run. Also how long the long run will be depends on a lot of factors which will mostly be outside the control of both the UK Parliament and UK businesses. These factors include what relationships Britain will have with the EU and vice versa and importantly how the EU may want to conduct business, immigration, law, and politics with Britain. These factors will undoubtedly shape the outcome of the negotiations with Brussels and will have long lasting ramifications for Britain and the EU. If Prime Minister Theresa May is able to negotiate a structure that resembles that which Switzerland, Norway, and Sweden have with the EU, it may reduce the feeling of resentment from Brussels and the rest of Europe against Britain. It will be impractical and foolhardy to believe that there are or there will be no resentment from Europe against Britain because of Brexit. Europe knows how pivotal and important Britain is to Europe and was in as much shock at the outcome of the Referendum and Britain and rest of the world. It is also noteworthy that it would clearly be a more difficult task for PM Theresa May to succeed in these negotiations as easily as did the leaders of the aforementioned countries due to the fact that those countries took those decisions at a much earlier stage in the process of the formation of EU than Britain has chosen to do. It may be considered to be a little too late in the day to negotiate such status; however it is important to keep an open mind. It is also important to consider the effect of Brexit on Britons living abroad in Europe as there are already backlashes from Europe. Whilst it is not expected that European countries will seek the emigration of Britons from their respective countries, it is certainly a point to consider particularly in countries such as Spain that have a high population of British permanent residents. Finally, it is our opinion that a balanced and mutually beneficial agreement can be reached between Britain and the EU; it is a question of quid pro quo.

Positive outlook

At the Hanzel Group, we keep a positive outlook and rely on our SWOT analysis to harness opportunities from seeming threats. Brexit is such opportunity. We have therefore chosen to position our firm for profitability through Brexit.

Property development funding

The negative change in aptitude for lending was undesirable and quite counterproductive to profitability and business growth. This has gradually reduced, but the fear of possible future slump in property prices remains a concern for some lenders.

Regulatory changes – pan-European business and investment laws

Whilst that Hanzel Group has not been adversely affected by this at present, it is an issue for consideration in the near future if we decide to offer our hedge funds to UK and European investors. Some investment managers, hedge funds managers, and banks are considering moving from Britain to alternative jurisdictions, a move which the Bank of England has tried to discourage on the argument that the UK's effective regulatory framework which may not be matched in other jurisdiction is important for the effective regulation and monitoring of sophisticated products such as derivatives. Ultimately, the decision to move or stay in London cannot be controlled by the Bank of England or the Financial Conduct Authority; it will be down to the individual firms and asset managers.

Human rights law and social justice

There has been much said about European Courts 'meddling' with British domestic laws. The European Court of Human Rights (ECHR) in particular had endured endless criticisms. The crux of the matter is that this is rather misleading and factually inaccurate as the ECHR remained the last vestige of protection across Europe if domestic process has failed. There is no evidence to support the fact that the ECHR tampered with British law. Britain has enshrined the International Convention on Human Rights into its domestic laws, and enacted into law the Human Rights Acts 1998 which is consistent with the ECHR's stand on human rights. The criticism of the ECHR regarding the allegations of meddling with British law is therefore baffling, if British domestic laws recognise and protect human rights. The truth is that the interpretation of the Human Rights Act 1998 and the breaches of its articles by constituted authorities is where the problems remain. This will not change as a result of Brexit. The judges of the ECHR are drawn from member countries including Britain, and they do not seek to change domestic laws but to ensure that human rights laws as enshrined in domestic laws are being adhered to. Therefore, the glaring fact and question is if the United Kingdom abides by the articles of its own domestic Human Rights Acts 1998, there will hardly be any need for cases to be escalated from local county courts or the High Court to the Court of Appeal, and to the Supreme Court and finally to the ECHR. The fact is, whether Britain exits Europe or not, it will be a necessity that it protects human rights by adherence to its own domestic Human Rights Act 1998. Without effective human rights legislation, there could be breakdown in society and in law and order which no civilised society can afford. Placing the blame on the ECHR and using that as a reason to exit the EU is lame at best and misleading at worst. This will certainly become evident once the process of Article 50 has completed and Britain is no longer subject to the ECHR. The expected outcome is highly likely to be that access to effective administration of justice for the working class may be diminished as there will no longer be recourse to a neutral, external, independent court to take the matters of human rights to when all avenues within the country has been exhausted and justice remains miscarried. The issue of ECHR post-Brexit does affect our business directly because we are passionate about the protection of human rights and social justice, and are committed to promoting a healthy and lawful Britain.

Reen Magnus FRSA BSc, ACSI is the Group CEO of the Hanzel Group. She trained at Harvard Business School, and is a qualified stockbroker. She was a stockbroker with the Fortune 500 company, Edward Jones Investments; and previous to that, she was a banker with regulatory and operations oversight at Standard Trust Bank. At the Hanzel Group, she is responsible for overall growth and profitability, and heads the group's innovation drive which boasts disruptive innovations such as FueDeal, Home*Advance, Flex*, and B*Rent. She has a passion for providing high quality affordable homeownership for hard working younger professionals and families, whilst assisting the older generation to retire with dignity. Her passion for property development stems from her childhood exposure by her developer grandparent, and her passion for banking and investments comes from her father, a highly regarded central banker and Wall Street economist. She has over 25 years' experience, working in reputable multinationals such as Edward Jones Investments, UACN-Unilever, Royal Dutch Shell, and Standard Trust Bank. She is a member of the Chartered Institute of Securities & Investments [CISI].

For more information on The Hanzel Group visit www.hanzel.co.uk

PAUL WAN, TRUPROP PROPERTY

Definitive guide on doing business post Brexit

'It' is an important word in the English vocabulary and especially when it is preceded by 'Ex' creating Exit. Now the context to which this article refers actually relates directly to the extreme winters sending a chill down the spine 'Brr'.

Yes you have guessed it right! It's Brexit that got not only the UK and Europe talking for most of 2016 but the entire world as global dependence (however little or large) on this massive region changed perceptions on doing business here in the UK.

Outlook on economy:

While UK has always maintained a big brother approach within the European conglomerate so the global message of 'Business is Great Britain' should not see any change going forward.

At TruProp, we have always worked at creating value for our clients and all the stakeholders. Though a small business, we strive to deliver quality service in the Property & Estate Management industry. We strongly feel that UK businesses now will work at comparable terms as the businesses that worked here pre 1975 era before Britain joined the European Union. In our opinion, the real estate market in the UK will continue to grow albeit at a slower pace in the post-Brexit scenario. As mentioned previously that ease of doing business in the UK is quite high (amongst competitor countries) and this will still attract a lot of global citizens to be a part of UK economy. It is therefore very important that we study the UK population demographics to understand the impact it may have on the economy. Although the free movement of people from Europe to UK might stop and it may give a temporary slowdown however if we see the empirical numbers this impact might not be as huge as UK net migration from European Union for year ending June 2016 was only 189,000 out of a total net migration to the UK for 335,000 people. So if we were to see this in the context of overall UK population it is only 32%.

If you assume that the net migrants coming from the EU were to take up rented accommodations and go through UK lettings agents then just the admin fee for tenancy setup will be close to £50 million. This is the real money which would not be flowing into the small businesses and thereby could be taken as a potential loss to the UK economy. Another very important aspect is the impact on employment generation. It's a widespread fact that immigrants generally give a push to economy because they earn and spend in the local economy. So considering that net migration of EU is nil then it's a potential loss of £10 million per day or £300 million per month to the UK economy.

Understandably all this can be mitigated if the non EU net migration numbers go up considerably. However, if we recall correctly migration was the most important point on which Brexit was fought! While there are arguments and counter arguments on how the Brexit dust settles for UK businesses there's no denying the fact that it's going to be a steep climb ahead if UK is to maintain its lead amongst the other developed countries of the world in a post Brexit scenario.

Various media have published a lot of contradicting views from various individual and consultants on Britain's position as a gateway to Europe and we feel a lot will depend on how the present government lays down the rules of the game and negotiates a better deal for Britain. It's no secret that Britain took almost 15 years to convince the other European countries to be included in the Bloc and what we saw was a stronger Europe and a stronger Britain. Fast forward another 40 years and this strength has definitely been tested. There have been reports that a lot of multinational businesses have already put at least 30–40% of UK staff on a possible shift over to another EU country post the implementation of this divorce. The possible effects of this outcome may have a longstanding implication on UK businesses and it might not be easy to quantify this drainage from the UK economy.

When all's said and done, Brexit or no Brexit – people will still go out to work, they will still buy food to eat, buy clothes to wear, houses to live in and will still seek assets to invest in. Meaning thereby it will be internal demand and consumption that will keep the economy ticking on. While post Brexit will be an unknown territory for most of us but given the resilience in the economy Britain will see through this eventuality in a much matured way.

Outlook on property:

Our view on UK property & real estate is not quite hazy as we believe the demand and supply curve will determine the house price and the cyclical movements will continue. With almost 65% of UK population as homeowners there's a fair population who has to get on the property ladder some point in time and to top it with the vast global population wanting to own a UK property, we believe that UK property will be resilient in the post Brexit scenario. So anyone who has a long term perspective on real estate investing will continue to benefit from this growth.

The author, Paul Wan is a Landlord Property Specialist at TRUPROP Manchester. Paul has actively worked in the Manchester property market helping many of his landlords to participate in this vastly growing UK's second city. He is also a founding member of TRUPROP which was primarily setup to bridge the gap landlords have in the property management industry. TRUPROP sits between the online estate agents and high street agents delivering a High street service at online prices. Paul can be contacted on paul.wan@truprop.co.uk/0161 425 5930.

For more information on Truprop visit www.truprop.co.uk

RICHARD KOVAC, CHIEF OPERATIONS OFFICER

Food for Thought

My current business is a UK based Food Tech start-up. We deliver food platters to businesses for meetings through a technology based platform. In an effort to fast track the business and vertically integrate we have acquired a food production facility and a food distribution operation.

As with any investment funded business we have established short, medium and long term growth objectives.

Short term – integrate the business acquisitions to maximise sales and profitability and scale up the model in the UK

Medium term – build a successful UK business model and list on AIM to create capital for expansion into the EU

Long term – list on one of the US exchanges to generate funds to scale up in the US

Our executive team consist of nationals from the UK, EU and the US.

So we have the vision, we have the plan, we have funding, we have the product and most importantly we have the team to build a successful business model.

Then came the surprise Brexit vote. As our business is poised for initial growth in the UK followed by the EU, we find ourselves wondering if we need to reposition our strategy. As our strategy is to take the business internationally we are uncertain of the business environment in the EU and the US after Brexit.

I have worked in the in the global food industry for over 25 years for many multinationals. As our business and my experience is in food I will focus on the food industry for this chapter.

The UK relies heavily on the EU for food imports. This dependence will remain and the UK will feel the impact across the food supply chain. There is a myriad of topics that could be discussed regarding food and Brexit. I will concentrate on three key topics for this chapter:

- Food Safety Regulations
- Raw material import regulations
- Access to current and future EU labour

Food Safety Regulations

Currently the UK follows EU Food Safety Regulations, which are some of the best in the world. This creates an environment of consistency for import of products and for the development of products outside of the EU. As this is vast topic I will only focus on three key areas of food regulation; Protected Designation of Origin (PDO), standardisation of food regulations and food safety.

Protected Designation of Origin

Stilton cheese is a Protected Designation of Origin (PDO) product. This has been accomplished through EU Food Regulations and EU Law. With the UK leaving the EU Stilton Cheese will lose its PDO status in the EU. The UK will have to develop food regulations and laws that enable PDO status. If the UK develops PDO status it will then need to be accepted by the EU and other countries. This will be a long and costly process for what is a small niche product.

Will UK PDO be a thing of the past? Will PDO be replaced by provenance for the UK market only? At this point there are no clear answers. However, to protect regional interests such as Stilton cheese the UK will develop PDO regulations and laws but at what cost to the tax payers.

Standardisation of food safety regulations

A whole book could be written in relation to food safety regulations. The current food regulations are some of the best in the world and have been developed to protect consumers from food safety issues. The standardisation across 28 countries makes the regulations easy to adhere to, easy to regulate and easy to develop products against. In most EU countries the regulations are self-policing, which reduces the cost of the products.

Will the UK continue to follow EU regulations or let some of their own interests drive a change in the regulations? If the UK has different regulations this will drive the cost of products up, as different labels and production runs will be required to suit the UK requirements. Countries that established import standards against EU Food Safety Standards may need a different set of regulations for the UK only, driving up the cost for UK suppliers to export.

Today a food manufacturer can make a product that is applicable for 28 countries, which allows them to maximize their efficiencies. After Brexit they may have to produce for 27 countries plus 1 (UK). Anyone in manufacturing can imagine the inefficiency that would come from producing for one country.

There are many products the UK can't produce in sufficient quantity to satisfy consumer demands. There are also seasonal products that the UK can't supply to meet the demand. Most vegetables are imported during the winter from warmer EU climates. Will these have different import regulations? This will only add cost to the end consumer?

It would be beneficial for the UK to work with EU food safety regulations for the future.

Food safety

This is important to all of us and for the most part we take this for granted. However, many of us do not realise that due to the strict EU food regulations that much of the imported product is self-regulated. What is self-regulated? The manufacturer and importer are accountable for ensuring adherence to the food regulations. The risk to a manufacturer of getting it wrong is losing business in 28 countries. With Brexit the risk could be with only one country – the UK.

Will the UK continue with self-regulation or implement their own food safety inspection teams? If they do implement food inspection this will be an additional cost to the product. If the regulations have loop-holes will manufacturers or importers try to capitalise on these even if they risk food safety issues? Will special interest groups reduce food quality in an effort to increase margins?

You may remember 'Horsegate'. Will this be a common issue if the UK regulations are not aligned with the EU regulations?

We should hope the UK works with the EU to create common standards to ensure we are food safe.

Raw material import regulations

Imports from the EU

According to the UK Department of Environment, Food and Rural Affairs about one quarter of the UK's food imports come from the EU (source DEFRA Overseas Trade Data System (MOTS)). At present these products move freely across borders with no duties or tariffs. There is a risk that the UK will need to negotiate trade arrangements with each individual EU country and not as a bloc of trading partners. This will complicate the import process as there may be varied regulations, duties and tariffs by country.

Will the duty or tariff on a product be the same for each EU country or will it be different by individual country?

Will we need to establish new supply lines to source from a low cost country due to duties and tariffs?

With agricultural prices dictated by commodity factors, supply factors, freight costs and in the future duties and tariffs this will make it a challenge for SME's to source products cost effectively.

We can't forget EU subsidies to UK farmers. UK farmers received £2.4 billion in farm subsidies in 2015. (Source: UK Farm subsidies). These subsidies will cease with Brexit: currently farmers are unsure of the future subsidies.

Will the UK government continue to pay these subsidies?

Will they be in the same format?

If the subsidies cease after Brexit farm prices will surely go up or farmers will cease growing their crops. This will drive up prices and may drive down supply, requiring more imports. At this time, we can only speculate that the UK government will continue subsidies in some format.

There will be raw material price implications due to import regulations and subsidies; how much only time will tell. There will also be supply line implications that will be a challenge for SMEs to wade through to maintain their cost base.

We should anticipate subsidies to farmers to be funded by the UK government through taxes. We should hope that the UK government negotiates no duties or tariffs with the EU bloc of countries.

Access to current and future EU labour

Immigration was a key topic for the Pro Brexit team. It will be a key topic for the business community.

In 2014 about 16% of the UK's labour force was from the EU. This does not account for transient labour such as truck drivers who transport products to and from the EU. If we had to replace this labour force overnight it would be an impossible task.

Employers are already feeling the pinch on EU employees. For example, our business struggles to find full time truck drivers; this will be a harder task going forward.

Many of our EU staff are commenting on the value of the pound to the euro. They have had a 20% pay decrease due to the exchange rate. This starts to make jobs back in the EU more attractive.

The government will be faced with a dilemma on EU labour. Much of Brexit was predicated on restricting immigration; however immigration is a healthy part of the UK workforce. To date the government has not had much to say on this topic. This has created uncertainty within the EU and international labour working in the UK.

Things we are actively doing to prevent losses from Brexit

From the previous sections we can see there is a risk pf food costs increasing, labour shortages, labour cost increases, food regulations changing and the exchange rate. We recognised these early on and have put some actions in place to try and minimise the impact.

Food cost increases

We have worked with suppliers to try and extend contractual terms at existing costs. This was achievable with some of our SME suppliers, however our larger suppliers were not willing to extend terms. Overall we have been able to protect about 40% of our raw material costs from price increases for an additional six months.

Food Regulation changes

We have started to review our ingredients in an effort to try and source more from the UK. This will add cost in most cases but will protect us from food regulations changing. We are also looking at how we re-engineer our products to try and minimise the cost impact of changing to UK supply. We understand our customers do not want to see price increases, but do want to assured supply.

Labour shortages

As mentioned previously we have struggled to attract truck drivers. Many of these drivers come from the EU and have seen the value of the pound drop by almost 20%. We have had to implement more hours on overtime and pay increases to try and retain and attract drivers. Currently this has impacted our bottom line directly, but we need the drivers to make our deliveries.

Exchange rate

Unfortunately, we do not buy many items directly from the EU – we predominately purchase through agents in the UK. This restricts our ability to hedge on currency. We have discussed hedging with our suppliers. Many of our suppliers lack the sophistication or funds to hedge, so we will have to wear these increases as they come. To date the increases have been in the range of 8-20%.

With our employees in management we are not in a position to offer pay raises to those with EU roots. We will have a risk of them leaving to the EU or for another higher paying job in the UK. We have seen some of our IT developers leave for higher pay within the UK.

Advice you would give to other companies or SME's

We have another month before Article 50 could be triggered. The UK government are testing the ground around Brexit both for the EU and other countries. They are trying to develop a strategy to negotiate EU and global trade. We will live in uncertainty for the next month. Then a new realm of uncertainty will start with negotiations. We will definitely see costs increase, we will see the exchange rate shift as negotiations on both side commence and more importantly posturing and positioning will start, this will make markets jittery.

Raw material and input costs

This will be a large cost for any manufacturer, trader, retailer etc. Try to lock in fixed pricing for as long as you can. Cover as many input costs as you can. Remember the indirect costs to your business will add up, so try and cover these as well. I have a friend with a hair salon business, she received a 25% increase in rent. The landlord told her it was the impact of Brexit.

Locking in costs will minimize price fluctuations for your business, more importantly it will allow management to forecast costs further into the future.

Cash reserves

Start to build some cash reserves. There may be some wild price changes due to exchange rate volatility or overseas suppliers taking advantage of the UK position. Additional cash reserves will help you through challenging months.

Price increases to customers

If your business needs to increase prices with customers cover these soon. The first suppliers to discuss price increases tend to get them. The last ones are usually too late. You know your customers build a sensible proposal for the price increase but don't wait too long.

EU staff retention

If EU staff are an important part of your business let them know. Communicate with them on how you intend to retain them. They are uncertain as to what the impact of Brexit will be on them so let them know you are supportive of retaining them.

Unfortunately, at this time we are all uncertain as to the result of Brexit, we can be sure there is more turmoil to come as the negotiations start between the EU and the UK. We should prepare our business for the uncertainties so that we can get through them with as little impact as possible.

Economic/legal impacts of Brexit

We are definitely feeling the economic impact already. The legal impact has not hit us yet, but we anticipate feeling this when there are more details around the Brexit strategy.

The exchange rate dropped making exports cheaper and imports costlier. Below is a chart showing the change in the exchange rate against the Euro.

GBP/EUR chart

Performance in the last nine months

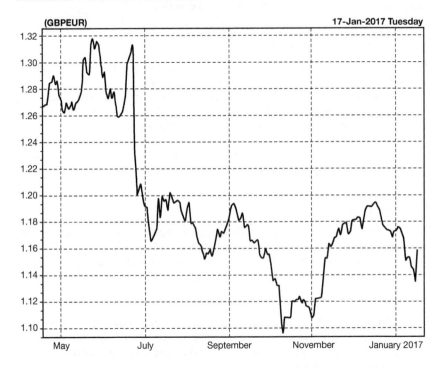

The exchange rate decline as had two distinct impacts on our business; the cost of raw materials and EU labour pay rates.

The cost of goods is starting to rise as most businesses were not prepared for the exchange rate to shift as much as it has. They had some short term cover such as goods in transit but nothing greater than this. We are having suppliers talk to us about price increases that are in the range of 10% to 15% due to the exchange rate. They are also proactively flagging the fact that import duties may change due to Brexit which could have a further impact on cost.

We are also seeing our employees from the EU realise that their pound has lost value. They are looking for pay increases to compensate for this. Many of our staff have families in the EU they support from their UK earnings. Many are also nervous about their ability to continue to stay and work in the UK.

In relation to contracts there is an uncertainty around supply, purchasing and employment contracts. Will they continue to be enforceable? Will they be valid? Will they need to be changed to accommodate Brexit? On top of this as a small business what will be the cost implications of making changes?

Long term implications

In order to understand the impact of Brexit into the future it is important to have view on what the future may look like.

Brexit

No one anticipated a 'YES' vote, so no one planned for the exit. This includes the EU. The process to exit will be long and drawn out. Both governments are still working through the full impact of what will need to be negotiated, changed and implemented. The cost will not only be monetary, but also time. It may take more than two years to complete the transition.

The world

Travel and trade will become easier to conduct as the global economy becomes more transparent and easier for businesses to work within. Operational efficiency through robotics and analytics will increase. The ability for individuals and business to complete transactions across platforms such as Amazon and Alibaba will become a standard. This will lead to country borders being less relevant.

If this is the future, then being part of a trading bloc will make business transactions easier.

The Prime Minister has flagged the UK is prepared for a hard exit. This could make the UK an independent trader surrounded by a trading bloc. This will increase operating costs for businesses. Multinationals may need to run two business entities EU and UK. Small businesses will need to have two sets of operating processes EU and UK. Trade around the region may be harder to conduct.

It is difficult to predict the long term impact of Brexit as the rules for the game have not been agreed yet. It is easy to speculate that the cost of separating will be felt across the UK for several years. The uncertainty of how to position your business will lead to executives making conservative and safe decisions. The safe decisions will have implications on business growth in the medium term. While Brexit will not damage the UK economy it will inhibit it for the next three plus years while the UK and the EU goes through the turmoil of negotiations and the process of change.

ANDY BEADEN, CFO, LUXFER PLC

It is Brexit!

It is 23 June 2016, I am sitting on a plane from Newark to Manchester, after a team conference for my Luxfer US finance staff in New Jersey. That day I had taken a call from one of our longest and biggest investors. He had been investing in Luxfer for many years and noted the share price had ticked up. We felt it must be the fact the UK would vote to stay in the EU. After some banter over the bad way the 'Remain' politicians had handled the campaign we had agreed, 'no major political change', was usually best in business and the investment world. Though I didn't believe Luxfer would be greatly impacted by the UK leaving the EU, we didn't need the stress of many years of uncertainty, plus we were fully hedged on the FX either way, so no need to worry.

My aircraft gets delayed on the runway, so now it is 19.00 US-EST, 12.00 BST. I start watching the BBC from my phone. All the people around me have suggested they voted Remain or would have if they were UK citizens. The British pound had already hit an annual high against the US dollar of over $1.50. Nigel Farage had admitted defeat hours before, Boris Johnston had told a stranger on the tube he accepted he had lost. Then – 12.01 BST – Newcastle votes Remain, but there is a sting in the tail, the commentator quickly realises the vote was too close for an obvious Remain win. This should have been a safe result. The minutes tick by and Sunderland announce at 12.20 BST, 19.20 US-EST, it had voted to 'Leave'. The British pound starts to collapse against other currencies. My phone is switched off and we take-off. Though nothing was certain for some time, it was on a knife edge, but I slept on my aircraft. I landed at 07.00 BST in Manchester, switched on the phone to see the text from my wife, with one word, 'BREXIT!'

Key communications

We communicated first thing next day to all employees, a letter from our CEO. He explained we did not believe Brexit would have a major impact on Luxfer and therefore staff should not be concerned. The Stock Exchanges were going south and the pound had weakened further. People were in panic mode. The communication was a good one and showed great leadership from our CEO, he had drafted it himself and had it ready and signed before 09.00 BST. Communications to major stakeholders followed and in the following days financial markets started to stabilise, unlike politics, which started to go through a series of shocks and further panic. In some ways it was a case of adults and children, business and politics, until the Conservatives decided Mrs May was their best adult. Though it always good to know who is the Prime Minister of the UK, it was a sign of things to come and a lesson to be learnt for business in this post-truth Brexit world.

What is Luxfer

Luxfer is an international material technology business. We sell to our customers the development and beneficial utilisation of advanced materials. For us a key strength remains having our research and development functions located next to the manufacturing, providing an integrated solution to customers. Management and sales staff are often technical experts or working closely with R&D. This is not an easy business to get right, it takes time to develop a new material or new application for an existing material, often longer to fully commercialise, but the returns can be high when measured as a return on capital invested. Products go through life cycles and new products are always required as we transition from one generation of technology to another. On average, UK sales range at 8% to 10% of our global sales, the North America over 50% and the EU in total 35%. Approximately 35% of our production is in the UK, but 50% in the US. Though we are headquartered in Salford Quays, UK, close to Media City, we are truly international, listed on the New York Stock Exchange and therefore the vast majority of our equity investors are US investment fund managers, as are many of our own employees and customers.

Immediate impact

The immediate impact from the Brexit vote was on exchange rates. At the end of June 2015 the ISE British Pound Index was 63.67, before the vote it closed in May 2016 at 69.04, but by the end of June 2016 it was 75.12. The higher the index number the weaker the currency, so you need more of a British pound to buy a basket of other major international currencies. After a 'hard Brexit' became a potential reality the index closed at 81, helped also by a strengthening US dollar. Using this index we can see the value of British pound fell by 8% in the year before the vote, then nearly 9% in June 2016, as the vote happened and again another 6% over the coming months. In total, a devaluation of approximately 25% with other major trading currencies.

What is harder to analyse is what might have happened if we had voted to Remain? There was a view that the pound would have strengthened to a higher position. What we do know is the result contributed a major devaluation in the pound. My personal estimate is there is probably a 30% plus difference between a Remain and Leave vote in the currency valuation.

For Luxfer this was initially a negative. We had hedged short-term the prices for our imports and exports and therefore the net FX transaction benefit from exports being priced higher was not yet tangible. We also reported our financial results to investors in US dollars, so our non-US revenue and earnings, which are mainly from the UK, were now worth less when reported in US dollars, a FX translation loss. This however is all short-term thinking, most of what we make in the UK we export, so over time, the devaluation of the pound will have a much larger benefit to our results and so will offset the translation loss. Any new business would also be priced at favourable rates. For Luxfer's UK operations, as for many UK manufactures, mainland Europe is its largest export market, and most of that is priced in the euro. Brexit weakened the British pound, but the exiting of such a large economy from the EU was bound to put further pressure on the euro too.

The pound to euro exchange rate is an important variable in the economic debate and one lost on the Remain camp during the referendum campaign. When the euro was set up, one key impact was it locked in Germany to a rate with many of its trading partners, the euro also started as a fairly weak new global currency, and so Germany's own export driven economy had an excellent opportunity to exploit this. This is exactly what German companies did and did very well, not just within the EU, but globally. This also put significant pressure on many UK exporters at the time, direct competitors of German and other EU companies. The result is since 1999, UK manufacturing has had a number of periods when competing with industry based in that wider Germany economic region has faced unfavourable exchange rates, when compared to what would have been in place if Germany had just its own currency. You might argue this is unreasonable in a free trade zone. Brexit has helped reverse that position and the weaker British pound is beneficial globally to UK exporters. With the British pound weaker to so many other currencies, particularly the US dollar, the largest international trading currency and also the Chinese Renminbi another major exporter like Germany.

In the analysis of traded goods, the trade with the EU dominants statistics (as shown in Table 3 below). The euro to pound exchange rate has traded post Brexit vote mainly in a range of €1.10 to €1.20, during the voting campaign it was more in the range of €1.20 to €1.30 and before that had been €1.30 to €1.45. There had been an expectation of a Remain vote leading to a rise back to a €1.35 to €1.45 trading range, so the delta that I felt Luxfer faced was around a 20% swing in rates from Remain versus Leave. That is a 20% price differential on our goods made in the UK and sold to key mainland European customers, just through a political vote. Therefore I had hedged my bets and fixed the rates for the next year in the middle of this range to protect the business and provide a platform for stability with our customer base.

For Luxfer, we will start to see benefit of beneficial export pricing in 2017 and through the use of FX contracts we can lock into these benefits for future years too. Of course rates can change, in fact that is certain, but the alternative of a Remain win was much worse. This is a big variant in margins and as we will see with World Trade Organisation ('WTO') standard duty tariffs, exchange rate movements like this are a bigger factor than the percentage rate of a tariff on imports and exports.

So what happens if there is no 'free' movement of goods? The main impact that most people consider is the use of tariffs or duties charged by countries on imports from other countries. If no special trade deal has been established then the WTO rules would be applied, which means the tariffs and rules the EU puts on other countries importing into EU would now apply to the UK. This means we already know the worse-case scenario for tariffs. The EU cannot impose punitive tariffs on the UK, without the same on every other country, because it would be in breach of international rules on trade. For a lot of manufactured goods these tariffs are only 3% to 6%, therefore, though not insignificant, they are dwarfed by the movement in exchange rates of 25% to 30%. Maybe the bigger issue for the EU, is this is a two way process. If automotive vehicles made in the UK are impacted then so are German, French, Spanish and Italian manufactured vehicles destined for the UK market. It maybe such tariffs are imposed, though why do that to your closest G7 export market?

What about other rules around trading goods? Well the EU is famous for setting standards for various products and getting into a laughable public relations mess, such as trying to ban curved bananas However you do need product standards, particularly safety ones. In any country or region you export into you have to meet their local standards, it is a pretty reasonable requirement. Again, the UK manufacturers like Luxfer remain in the same position post-Brexit, we will still be exporting into one common market, with one set of rules, which we will have to meet. If the UK rules vary, then we have to deal with this, as would any importers into the UK, so no real competitive change? Currently you can register new products anywhere in the European Economic Area (EEA) and gain a CE marking for a regulated product throughout the EEA including all of the EU. What we do not know is if the UK will be leaving the EEA too or remain an associate member? This is a bigger issue than just leaving the EU and is purely about trade and hopefully common sense would see the UK remaining part of the EEA, if not, then there will be the risk of two sets of standards to follow and two registrations to make. This is easily fixed by the UK accepting CE marking standards and again common sense is required and in theory it will be in the UK government's own powers to implement.

If we did end up with different product standards, smaller businesses would find this the hardest, with their ability to scale up a winning product into export markets in Europe hindered. One of the major legal issues could be around intellectual property rights and registering patents or re-registering them (see Chapter 10).

What about those legal issues? For Luxfer, like all international businesses, legal and regulatory issues are something we need to invest time and effort into. Luxfer is already a highly regulated business. One major issue on Brexit is understanding if we remain in the EU's free trade zone or EEA, as well as transaction taxes to administer with import/export documentation, there is also a wide range of registrations to consider too, these include the product registration points I have made, along with employee documentation for EU citizens working into the UK. We do not know what the fine details of the Brexit deal will be and the knock-on impacts to these legal and regulatory positions. For larger businesses like Luxfer, an audit of these points can be carried out, which will help flush out the potential issues, though never welcome, it is all part of doing international business. My concern will be for smaller businesses and their advisers.

It is also the removal of the 'easy route to market' to the main European economy within the EU which would be of concern when overseas investors consider where to setup in Europe. It may well be that FX and potentially lower UK corporate taxes still attract investment into the UK, but the government would need to help ensure any additional compliance issues are clear and easy for all businesses to adopt. The UK is also business friendly in a number of other employment and legal areas, which will remain an advantage over other European countries.

Investment considerations in Europe

Businesses thrive on the economies of scale and international trade helps boost that scale and provide new avenues for growth. Throughout Europe, it would be common practice to achieve scale through focussed manufacturing facilities to meet demand across the entire common market. You may have sale resources more spread out over various countries, but manufacturing facilities are likely to be concentrated with larger or single facilities in European. If someone is making an investment in Europe, they will think twice about that investment in the UK, until it is clearer what the post-Brexit regulations are going to be. Lower inward investment in the UK would have several impacts including weakening the balance of payments position and reducing economic growth. The British pound is also likely to devalue more, due to negative currency flows – though this could have benefits as I have identified earlier. The government has indicated changing tax rates to help incentivise inward investment, though rates can be cut in EU countries or some incentives provided there to counter this.

The main damage to investment is the uncertainty and fear of the unknown and I believe this is likely to put at risk some large potential investments into the UK by multinational businesses. Luxfer has focussed much of its European production requirements into the UK, with some manufacturing in France and Czech Republic. As an established business in Europe it would be hard to envisage opening up new facilities in the reaming EU just because of Brexit and unlikely the economics would work. My concern would be for businesses running on lower margins such as the automotive industry or relying more on new overseas investment, where I believe Brexit considerations and the current uncertainty could play a larger role in the decisions making process. The main issue is avoiding unnecessary risks.

For Luxfer, I am sure the UK will remain a good place for business. I am struggling to believe exiting the free trade zone and EEA would be a positive for business, but the negatives can be overcome.

Europe is a good place to do business

One area of international trade that is not always taken correctly into account is the economic status of the country you import into. In general, Europe, like the USA, is a good place to do business. It contains many of the wealthiest countries per capita in the world and so provides rich picking for advanced and innovative businesses.

Table 1: Gross Domestic Product per Capita (per person)

$ US dollars	2000	2010	2015
UK	26,034	35,745	41,779
China	2,919	9,310	14,388
EU	22,594	33,325	38,621
Germany	27,530	39,993	47,999
USA	36,419	48,302	56,066
Source: OECD data			

If you compared the GDP per capita for the EU with that of China, you soon realise that for many businesses that are manufacturing premium products, Europe is a key market. The UK is an advanced manufacturing economy and so the products it makes are going to be targeted to wealthier economies. There is a big risk of having a weakened trade deal with the mainland European economies for the sake of trade deals with countries that may be growing quicker, with a question mark over whether their economies are wealthy enough to support premium advanced manufacturing from the UK. What this points to is though businesses in the UK may want to take advantage of new trade deals with other countries, it will really depend on the market opportunities in that country and region. A trade deal with the USA is clearly attractive, but one with China may not be as helpful. What UK businesses will be doing or should be doing is ensuring they continue to secure business in fellow European countries. Of course, the UK itself, is part of Europe and is one of those key countries every business should be targeting. We will see later that the USA is the single largest country for UK trade and is highly beneficial for the UK economy.

We need clarity on the big default issues – What would help with business uncertainty? What would help is clarity of big themes around Brexit and what is the 'End Game'. The Prime Minister's statement in January 2017 of her objectives for Brexit negotiations was helpful in at least seeing what the UK government would try and achieve, which would include no tariffs with a new customs union and free trade agreement. What is much less clear is how, if these objectives are achieved, trade regulations would operate. You have to assume common standards around goods and services would have to prevail, which makes sense given the EU would remain our largest export market.

Political uncertainty and unrest is not helpful. Britain should continue to support the political existence of the EU, even outside it. For business, socio-economic stability is extremely helpful to stainable growth and investment. The EU provides a stable political and economic system to a wide range of countries and those surrounding it. I believe this is of significant economic benefit, though hard to measure.

Free movement of workers is unlikely, and again we would need to see what regulations emerge and competition for skilled labour will increase. For businesses in the UK this could be a major headache and manufacturing will be no different to other industries seeking a quality labour force. For Luxfer, our manufacturing operations require a skilled labour force. Given the potential constraints coming on labour movement from the EU and with labour maybe not wanting work in the UK, post-Brexit, a renewed effort to recruit the young and train up employees through apprenticeships will be essential. Manufacturing has struggled in its PR credentials when compared to other industries and again at Luxfer we are conscious of the need to promote the positive benefits of working in a modern manufacturing business. These include the international nature of our business, its links with real scientific innovation of real products you can physically see and the strong team work ethics. There are a lot of skills to be developed to compete internationally and the full range of business functionary skills, not just production based, but in sales, marketing, finance, research and development, logistics and human resources. In production the standards are high, with manufacturing businesses having a series of continuous improvement initiatives and use of higher technology machinery, including robotics. All this is essential if we are to compete globally and take advantage of international trading relationships and is also a very attractive reason for younger people to work in this industry.

Table 2: International comparisons on productivity
GDP per hour worked by country

UK = 100

	Canada	France	Germany	Italy	Japan	UK	US	G7	G7 exc. UK
1990	104	116		113	83	100	120	108	109
1991	103	115	119	112	84	100	119	106	107
1992	101	113	117	109	81	100	118	104	104
1993	99	110	114	109	80	100	114	103	104
1994	98	110	115	110	79	100	112	104	104
1995	98	112	116	113	80	100	112	102	104
1996	95	109	115	109	79	100	111	102	103
1997	94	109	113	108	78	100	110	102	102
1998	95	112	113	109	77	100	112	103	103
1999	96	113	116	108	78	100	114	105	105
2000	93	112	112	105	76	100	110	102	102
2001	92	114	113	106	76	100	111	102	102
2002	89	115	112	99	76	100	109	101	101
2003	91	112	115	99	76	100	112	102	102
2004	89	108	115	94	76	100	112	101	102
2005	92	109	115	94	76	100	113	102	102
2006	90	111	113	94	74	100	110	101	101
2007	91	114	116	98	77	100	113	103	103
2008	92	116	118	101	77	100	115	105	105
2009	94	119	119	104	78	100	119	107	108
2010	99	126	127	108	84	100	126	113	115
2011	100	127	132	110	83	100	127	114	116
2012	99	126	133	111	85	100	128	115	116
2013	102	130	134	112	84	100	127	115	117
2014	104	128	136	111	83	100	130	116	118
2015	100	127	135	109	84	100	130	116	118

Note: This table should be read horizontally

Sources: OECD, Office for National Statistics

In the UK, productivity improvements have lagged many other modern economies and I believe one reason has been the lack of constraints on labour availability. In the future this needs to be reversed and that in turn would help UK manufacturing be more competitive in the longer term.

The table above shows how in recent years the UK, measured as 100 in the index, has lagged other major economies on productivity. If a country has an indices measure of above 100 it is more productive and below 100 it is less productive than the UK. Therefore in 2015 German industry was on average 35% more productive and USA 30% more. Japan is less and Canada the same as the UK. France is 27% more productive or efficient per worker. What the table does not show is a UK worker will work more hours than a French worker, so per worker, the UK can still make more goods than other countries per worker, but that does not mean the products being made are cheaper or the businesses are more efficient. It is also a reason the UK needs more immigration than others countries, because in simple terms it needs a larger labour force to make the same amount of goods when compared to other major economies.

The UK trade deficit for physical goods has continued to widen in recent years and the main focus on reducing this deficit has been to increase exports, but we also need to think about making more for ourselves. Brexit provides an opportunity here, with imports increasing in price, for domestic manufacturers to be more competitive in the UK itself. The challenge here may well be a rising cost of labour, with restrictions on immigration and the potential for inflationary pressures increasing labour costs too. Again, investment will be the key and modernisation essential, but with imports rising this is part of the solution to a stronger UK economy.

Table 3: UK Trade in Goods only (excludes services)

£ Billions	1999	2000	2001	2002	2003	2004	2005	2006	2007	2008	2009	2010	2011	2012	2013	2014	2015
Exports	166.4	188.0	189.5	186.6	188.4	191.5	211.9	243.8	222.9	254.4	229.0	270.0	308.0	301.5	303.1	292.8	284.8
Imports	(195.9)	(221.5)	(231.4)	(235.6)	(239.4)	(253.4)	(282.1)	(322.8)	(313.4)	(349.5)	(315.8)	(367.4)	(402.9)	(412.3)	(423.6)	(415.2)	(411.0)
Net deficit	(29.5)	(33.5)	(41.9)	(49.0)	(51.0)	(61.9)	(70.2)	(79.0)	(90.5)	(95.1)	(86.6)	(87.4)	(94.9)	(110.8)	(120.5)	(122.4)	(126.2)
Exports to EU	101.9	113.1	115.1	115.7	112.4	112.9	123.1	151.8	128.5	142.8	125.5	145.2	165.1	150.7	151.3	145.5	133.5
Imports from EU	(110.1)	(118.5)	(128.3)	(138.8)	(140.7)	(146.3)	(161.9)	(185.1)	(172.5)	(184.8)	(166.1)	(189.1)	(204.6)	(209.0)	(220.7)	(224.7)	(223.0)
Net EU	(8.2)	(5.4)	(13.2)	(23.1)	(28.3)	(33.4)	(38.8)	(33.3)	(44.0)	(42.0)	(40.6)	(43.9)	(39.5)	(58.3)	(69.4)	(79.2)	(89.5)
% of total deficit	28%	16%	32%	47%	55%	54%	55%	42%	48%	44%	47%	45%	42%	53%	58%	65%	71%
Exports to Germany	20.7	23.0	24.0	22.4	21.1	22.0	23.5	27.1	25.0	28.3	24.6	28.8	34.9	32.5	29.8	30.7	30.5
Imports from Germany	(27.0)	(28.7)	(30.5)	(32.9)	(34.5)	(39.3)	(40.1)	(42.2)	(45.3)	(45.6)	(40.9)	(47.2)	(51.1)	(53.4)	(56.8)	(60.6)	(61.8)
Net Germany	(6.3)	(5.7)	(6.5)	(10.5)	(13.4)	(14.3)	(16.6)	(15.1)	(20.3)	(17.3)	(16.3)	(18.4)	(16.2)	(20.9)	(27.0)	(29.9)	(31.3)
Exports to USA	22.6	27.2	27.6	26.0	28.5	28.2	30.4	32.2	32.1	35.3	34.0	38.1	40.1	41.3	39.6	37.1	47.2
Imports from USA	(24.3)	(28.4)	(29.8)	(24.9)	(22.6)	(21.7)	(21.7)	(25.5)	(25.6)	(25.5)	(24.2)	(26.9)	(28.7)	(29.8)	(27.6)	(28.1)	(34.7)
Net USA	(1.7)	(1.2)	(2.3)	1.1	5.9	6.5	8.7	6.7	6.5	9.8	9.8	11.2	11.4	11.5	12.0	9.0	12.5
Exports to China	1.3	1.6	1.8	1.5	1.9	2.6	2.9	3.5	4.5	5.8	5.6	8.1	10.3	11.3	13.5	15.5	12.7
Imports from China	(3.6)	(5.0)	(6.0)	(7.2)	(8.8)	(10.5)	(13.2)	(16.1)	(19.0)	(23.7)	(25.3)	(30.9)	(31.8)	(31.7)	(35.9)	(36.9)	(38.0)
Net China	(2.3)	(3.4)	(4.2)	(5.7)	(6.9)	(7.9)	(10.3)	(12.6)	(14.5)	(17.9)	(19.7)	(22.8)	(21.5)	(20.4)	(22.4)	(21.4)	(25.3)

Source: UK ONS Annual trade data

288

The table above also shows the extent that the other EU countries have benefited from UK membership in the trade of physical goods. Since the existence of the euro imports from the EU have doubled but exports from the UK have only risen by a third. This has been the primary reason for the UK's physical goods widening trade deficit. China being the secondary cause and US net exports have partly offset this. Armed with these statistics it is hard to believe the EU would really want to have anything other than a soft Brexit for the physical trade of goods. For the UK, a deal on free trade with the USA and tariffs on EU goods would not be as damaging as we might have thought.

There are a lot of political and economic or business related points you can make to avoiding Brexit, but we cannot deny the nation voted to leave and I believe the primary reason was the population wanting some restrictions on immigration. This will require a change in our economy to rely less of use the use of labour and more on the use of modern technology, with investment being the key driver to this working.

What should business do next?

I believe every business does need to now think about their own next steps. This should be in the form of its own Brexit plan. This will have to be flexible as political events unfold. The key elements of the plan need to address the following:

- FX – what are the risks and rewards and how can a business take advantage? All businesses can now fix into the new FX rates and should work with their banks to do this. This will be through forward contracts which fix rates for future transactions. Contracted new business should be fixed as it is won to avoid unnecessary FX risks.
- Employment – Businesses should assume labour will be harder to find. Resource planning and development of staff will be more critical going forward.
- Legal issues – This could be a major headache to businesses. Key areas to review and prepared for change are around employment laws on immigrate workers and intellectual property rights across the EU and UK. Legal advice should be sought, particularly where there is a lack of in house knowledge.
- Maintain strong links with customers and suppliers – everyone is in the same boat of uncertainty, but a business can counter this by focusing on its relationships with customers and suppliers. Much of manufacturing is business to business and therefore commercial relationships are the key. Keeping close to your cross-border supply chain contacts in the EU and elsewhere is essential in this world of political uncertainty.
- Investment for efficiency – whatever the outcomes, investment to be more competitive will remain critical to long term success. Maybe more so with restrictions on labour movement. In the UK we have fallen behind in this area and used additional labour to support the need for higher production requirements, this will have to change as labour movement is restricted.

Maybe the final conclusion is that though Brexit was not welcomed by most of the business world, we now have to get on with building our own mini-EU and trade arrangements, with our own customers and suppliers and were possible plan around the disruptive nature of the Brexit process.

Good businesses will survive and should survive.

For more information on Luxfer PLC visit www.luxfer.com

NIEL BETHELL, CEO, HIGH ACCESS

High Access has grown into a £6 million turnover business employing 80 staff since being founded by Chief Executive Niel Bethell in 2005.

Hitting the pause button was never going to be an option for High Access once Brexit became reality.

I've spent the past decade nurturing this business to a size and scale of which I'm extremely proud and I determined from the start to treat any fallout from leaving the EU as a bump in the road on this company's inexorable path to success.

We're still pressing ahead with our ambitious expansion plans; the most junior members of our team will continue to receive the UK living wage; and we're actively investing in the company's state of the art plant and equipment to ensure our continued success and longevity.

Indeed, it's been business as usual for High Access since the EU referendum took place – and that's not going to change.

Writing as an entrepreneur at the helm of a company that's grown to have a £6 million turnover during one of the worst recessions on record, my team and I have become accustomed to getting the job done even when circumstances are difficult.

And I think that the tough trading conditions every business has faced head-on over the past decade should give us all the confidence to know that we can traverse those choppy waters Brexit's predicted to throw at us.

The main problem is this…

At the moment, we simply don't know how rough those waters will get. In my opinion, we're not going to know with any real clarity what the post-Brexit trading conditions will be like until some considerable time after Britain finally leaves the EU in April 2019. Nonetheless, I'd be the first to accept that High Access might be far better placed than many businesses to ride out the uncertain economic times which so many analysts are predicting. And this, I'm certain, is one of the reasons why I'm possibly more relaxed and upbeat about the potential impact of Brexit than many other entrepreneurs.

It's possibly most useful at this point for me to explain a little about how High Access came into existence, how we've grown and what we intend ultimately to achieve.

Prior to founding the company in 2005, I'd built up a successful career as an industrial property electrician when I spotted the opportunity to develop a more specialist service.

I'd been repeatedly asked to repair signage positioned high above the street for a Manchester-based commercial property landlord. But I quickly realised that this wasn't going to be straightforward due to the health and safety constraints of working at height combined with the ridiculously high cost of hiring scaffolding. It was only when I teamed up with a former army climbing instructor that High Access started to gain traction. To cut a long story short, we developed abseiling as a rapid and flexible way to deliver those services we were consistently being asked for and this remains at the heart of what we do, but we've grown well beyond our beginnings.

Today, High Access employs more than 80 staff and offers a complete high-level building maintenance and cleaning service to the commercial property sector. What differentiates us in the market is that we provide a one-stop-shop offering everything from survey to resolution. Our services include: building maintenance; roof and gutter maintenance; safety systems testing and installation; lighting maintenance; high-level specialist cleaning; coatings and glazing. As our reputation has burgeoned, we've been able to purchase a range of bespoke mobile mechanical platforms. These have been specially designed to enable colleagues to reach those difficult to reach aerial areas, enabling us to get the work done even more efficiently and cost-effectively. Down the years, we've build up excellent working relationships with some of the major property management companies earning their trust as the go-to property maintenance and service provider.

Among our many household name clients today are Savills, CBRE, GVA, Jones Lang LaSalle and Allied London. But far from resting on our laurels, we constantly look to the future at High Access. Shortly before the EU referendum, we opened a depot in the Berkshire town of Slough to ensure that we're even better positioned to care for our increasing portfolio of clients based in London and the South East. In the coming months, I've every intention of opening further depots in Birmingham, Scotland and Yorkshire.

But this question remains: how will Brexit affect a business like High Access?

For a start, we remain well funded as the full effect of leaving the EU begins to unravel.

Last year, we secured a £3.3 million investment from the Business Growth Fund (BGF) which allowed us to open our Slough depot in earnest and make ambitious plans to open elsewhere.

While our ongoing success is linked closely to the prosperity of the commercial property sector, our turnover isn't inextricably linked with the number of cranes to be seen across the skyline of Britain's major towns and cities.

So if a downturn in construction activity materialises, it's unlikely to have an immediate knock-on impact on a business like this that specialises in maintaining and servicing existing high level buildings. Maintaining old stock is also fruitful for us.

Additionally, it's been well documented that many construction companies – like businesses in myriad other sectors – are concerned that Brexit will ultimately impact on the availability of EU workers who often form the backbone of their teams.

High Access isn't exposed in this respect either.

Whenever we've advertised for new recruits in the past, those positions have always been applied for – and successfully filled – by UK residents. Long before the EU referendum took place, I decided to pay the most junior members of my team the UK living wage and I'm certain that this is a major reason why we get inundated with applications for each new job we post. To say that introducing the UK Living Wage has been a beneficial step for this company would be an understatement. It has generated massive goodwill across the entire organisation while simultaneously resulting in an improvement in productivity and employee morale. I fully recognise that one of the main reasons why High Access is doing well is only because of the people we employ and, from the start, I've wanted to ensure that they're rewarded appropriately for their hard work. This ethos underpins all that we do at High Access and we're currently in the process of being accredited by Investors in People.

Another major reason why I don't fear the potential impact of Brexit as greatly as some entrepreneurs is because we've minimised our exposure to any issues arising in our supply chain.

We've invested heavily in our own plant and equipment since the start. In my experience, the main benefit of owning your own plant and equipment is that you know exactly how your balance sheet stands at any point in time and can plan accordingly. By contrast, the cost of hiring in the equivalent plant and equipment from a third party – if it's actually available – can fluctuate wildly. While I remain fully committed to investing in whatever bespoke equipment and vehicles we require in the future, I also recognise that there's a chance we'll have to pay more than has previously been the case when sourcing those items from Europe. For example, shortly before the EU referendum took place we bought a bespoke cherry picker for our newly opened depot in Slough direct from the manufacturer in Italy. It has been well documented that the value of the pound plummeted immediately after the EU referendum – and I don't expect that we'll be able to buy the same vehicle from an Italian manufacturer for the same amount of money for the foreseeable future. Whether this ultimately results in us looking more closely at what British manufacturers can provide will depend on their ability to meet our precise specifications as well as the cost.

Finally, if Britain's legislation evolves as a result of leaving the EU, High Access is – once again – likely to be largely unaffected.

Ever since this company was established, I've placed an emphasis on enshrining the highest health and safety standards at the heart of everything we do and we consistently go far beyond what's expected of us.

In conclusion, it's my residing hope that the politicians and policymakers get it right for Britain, right from the start. My worry at the moment is that an ever-increasing number of businesses will hit the pause button in the coming months as the precise nature of Britain's post-Brexit trade deals unravel. That would be a massive mistake on so many different levels for those companies as well as the continued prosperity of UK plc. At this point in time, this country's entrepreneurs need to set an example by looking to the post-Brexit future as positively as possible. I've every intention of ensuring that this business attains even greater success regardless of what leaving the EU throws at us.

I owe it to my colleagues and my clients to ensure that High Access remains at the vanguard of what we do.

For more information on High Access visit http://highaccess.co.uk

SARAH E KEEGAN, CEO, THE CS PARTNERSHIP

My co-founder and I have worked together for over 11 years. We managed a residential conveyancing department at a large regional firm, and we took that department from a turnover of £1.8 million per annum, to a turnover of £3.96 million per annum in 18 months. We had a staff of 100, and we were one of the largest departments in the country at the time, submitting 4,000 applications a month to Land Registry to change the register. It was a fast-paced environment, and we needed to constantly innovate and adapt, to suit client requirements, and changes in practice and procedure. When the markets crashed in 2008/09, the firm had no appetite to indefinitely wait for the markets to pick up, and we were invited to work for a firm in the Midlands, to build a property department in one of the cities that the firm practised from, and to build case management systems across the firm. In 2009, therefore – through no fault of our own – we went from delivering 4,000 transactions a month (and all that entailed with dealing with staff, complaints, our regulators, training the teams, sitting on the board of the firm, budgets, clients, marketing and PR), to starting completely from scratch with a blank piece of paper and a pen. The recession gave us the opportunity to question everything about the systems and procedures and the way that they had always been done, and it frightened us into being less sure footed that a market existed for us, and forced us to become sharper, faster and better. Three years later, as our Midlands firm merged with a bigger firm, we decided that it was our opportunity to take our ideas and concepts (which were considered ground breaking) into the market place, and branch out alone.

Our ground-breaking concept is that the delivery of all legal services should be as comparably slick as Amazon is in delivering their products (as a consumer experience).

It is 2017, and an increasing percentage of the public deal with their lives by using the thumb of whichever hand is holding their phone. According to the

Media Consumption Forecast 2015 in the UK (written by ZenithOptimedia), the average minutes of internet consumption per individual has risen from 82.0 minutes per individual per day in 2010, to a forecast of 176.80 minutes per individual per day in 2017. There is a slight dip in people using desktops to access the internet in those years – but there is a massive hike in mobile usage in the same period from 13.2 minutes to 99 minutes (as an average across all people in the UK). Smartphone ownership in the UK is approaching two-thirds of the population – 63% of us owned a smartphone in 2014 up from about 40% in 2011 (according to IPSOS Tech Tracker). And the last statistic for the moment – about 90% of all 15–34 year olds have smartphones.

Those statistics are staggering – and that change has occurred in the last six years. We are living in an economic and social revolution, which is as disruptive as the agrarian and industrial revolutions were. We can learn any fact within seconds; access vital documents over smartphones, communicate with each other at any hour; track our children's whereabouts 24 hours a day; pay bills whilst sitting on the bus; turn up the heat in our homes from the office; and have almost any product delivered to our door within 24 hours. That is why I constantly refer our clients to 'The Amazon effect'. A law firm's clients are now so used to this revolution, and social media, that our key question is 'How long will those same clients put up with quaint and antiquated lawyers?'

Certainly, not much longer – and it is very likely that those firms will disappear as that bracket of 15–34 year olds referred to above (with their smartphones), become the managers, directors and CEOs of tomorrow.

As if that isn't a big enough change for lawyers to embrace, in addition to this technological revolution, on 23 June 2016, the UK voted to leave the EU – and so we must also consider what impact that decision will have on the economy, and how to prepare accordingly. The only certainty is that the future is uncertain. Negotiations with the EU will be a drawn-out process, perhaps even beyond the two-year guidelines. Negotiations with potential new markets cannot begin until the EU situation is resolved – there is no way to gauge the impact which delays will have on the Economy.

As it stands at the beginning of 2017, the reports are that the property market is fairly robust. According to HMRC data, the property market has had a healthy start to 2017, with seasonally adjusted transactions showing growth in January 2017 in both residential and non-residential transactions – 8.8% higher in non-residential, and 4.9% higher in residential transactions than 2016. But as a partnership, we are extremely reluctant to rely on the statistics being tweeted about the robust property market, and instead are looking at the stark reality of what Brexit may do to the market.

It is an uncertain time ahead. My thinking is that despite the robust looking property market, at the moment, by 2020 house prices could have fallen by 10–15%. Our house prices are an indication of the strength of the confidence in our economy. Britain has the biggest current account deficit in its history – put bluntly, we are living beyond our domestic needs. We are the second largest recipient of overseas money (America is first; China is numbered 56). We received that level of overseas investment because we were in the EU. If even a portion of that overseas investment falls away as we exit, then the only way we can balance our current account as a country is to either raise the interest rates or allow sterling to drop to the level of the Euro or the dollar, but if we allow that, then our interest rates will rise. There is an argument that new markets would be created post Brexit, but there WILL be a delay between exiting the single market and establishing new markets.

I am not an economist, but I do know the residential property market, and it relies on confidence in the market to be strong. It relies on confidence to enable buyers to take out mortgages, and as fewer buyers want to do that in uncertain times (with interest rates higher than some of them have experienced before), the balance favours the buyers as sellers become desperate to find a buyer, and drop their house prices accordingly. I also know that a weak property market means a recession. When our house prices are controlled, our economy is strong. As an example, when George Osborne announced the Help to Buy initiative, house prices increased, because of the perception that the government was driving a house boom. Whether Brexit is a good thing long term or not, in the medium term I suspect that the UK will hit another recession by 2020.

With a background of massive technological change, and Brexit indicating uncertain times ahead, our advice to our clients is very clear. In our experience, all law firms present a façade to the outside world that they are as streamlined and organised internally as they could be. If they have merged with each other, they refuse to publicly confess that they have multiple IT systems, procedures and staff that do not communicate with each other. They point to expensive software that they have purchased, or the fact that their IT is 'in the cloud', as evidence that they are moving with the times. Without fail, each lawyer will painstakingly tell us that they understand why our services are important for other lawyers/types of work/their colleagues, but will not do for them, because they have very 'bespoke' transactions, and their clients are high end/need a personal touch. We are always at pains to explain that we will never 'dumb down' their work – far from it. Our aim is to allow them to continue to carry on their work faster, sharper and better. Every transaction has a beginning, a middle and an end. Every transaction can be organised/systemised/streamlined – to look at that process across all work types with honesty is not dumbing down. It is intelligent. Why would anyone repeatedly perform tasks that they do not need to do?

Firstly, we sit with them and process map their transactions to remove the inefficiencies of the individual lawyers and their teams. Each lawyer/work type has their style and wishes taken into account. Fast track, low margin work is heavily computerised. High end corporate jobs are not. We write changes to their case management systems to reflect the more efficient ways of delivery, or we write bespoke case management workflows. We help them innovate their thinking behind the way that they deliver their services, and change their procedures as well as their case management systems. And finally – and probably most importantly – we help the partners and staff change their individual working habits, and their team and departmental habits and thinking. The market may be talking about innovative artificial intelligence, and the top firms here and abroad are certainly building it, but there is a lot of work to be done in changing the hearts and minds of the profession in order to embrace it.

We have lived through the worst recession since 1932, and we are embracing this technological revolution, and consequently our advice to all firms and companies is that survival is absolutely possible. In fact, thriving and growing in any market is absolutely possible. There is nothing to fear. None of us know any more than the next person what is going to happen following Brexit and whether the recession coming will be gentle or like falling off a cliff as it was in 2009. What we do know is that if you have removed your inefficiencies, and changed the mindset of your staff and Board, then you will be in a position to survive whilst remaining profitable.

For more information on The C.S. Partnership visit www.thecspartnership.com

PAUL FOREST, CHAIRMAN, MBN SOLUTIONS

Let me start with my interest in the subject matter.

As a portfolio non-executive director and board adviser to a number of businesses, Brexit as a concept and in practice is something of great interest to me and the organisations with whom I work. One of the key areas of concern for businesses planning their response to the impact of Brexit is their workforce. This for me extends to both the people themselves and more generally, resourcing issues. Since I am the Chairman of MBN Solutions, a full-service People Solutions business, I thought it would be an area worth exploring in more detail.

The impact of Brexit on HR, recruitment and business

Like many UK businesses, the decision to leave the EU in June has certainly led to a period of immediate uncertainty for MBN Solutions. Clearly, we all want to know the detail of how we will go about what is emerging as a relatively messy divorce. As a result of the uncertainty we have spent time building both research and thought leadership into the issues which for us create both opportunity and risk. What I discuss here are those that relate to issues around the people and the workforce.

The single question we are most frequently asked at MBN is how is Brexit going to affect recruitment and retention of employees in the future? Whatever the impact, once Article 50 is finally implemented in March, there's no doubt that Brexit is going to take time and a lot of energy to work out, and this is where the first key point needs to be highlighted and that has rapidly become our core mantra ... Don't let Brexit stand in the way of business as usual!

The role of HR and recruitment

If we go for a hard Brexit, as has been indicated, it will clearly impact on recruitment from current EU member states. Much of our work at MBN focuses on finding the very best talent in insight and analytics, data science and econometrics, and as such, we currently see many high-quality candidates coming to the UK from the EU where many countries have invested heavily in this important sector. These workers bring exceptional skills and competencies and can potentially add tremendous value to the UK economy. This, of course, will not be unique to workers coming from the data skills sectors. The role of client Hiring Manager and HR functions here is to find ways of securing such talented individuals without compromise and this requires planning. Our response? We consider ourselves the most appropriate business partner to facilitate this which represents an opportunity to deepen our client relationships by assisting the HR functions within client organisations.

We have spoken with such functions and there are many issues relating to Brexit that are particular to HR. There is already a high degree of uncertainty amongst members of staff about what the future holds and communicating with employees is therefore going to be vital. Anticipated changes may mean assessing the immigration status of employees and providing targeted support for EU nationals and perhaps even their families.

Calm and compassionate leadership is going to be needed and strong planning implemented to help ameliorate potential challenges not only in recruitment but for retaining key staff. There may be changes in regulations and the need to move some parts of the business to the EU for more direct access. There is certainly going to be a requirement to maximise efficiencies in line with cost pressures that could ultimately impact on recruitment. We have already found that the cathartic approach of talking to clients is helping them to understand these issues and helping them to remain calm regarding people issues whilst allowing MBN to be positioned as their 'go to source of intelligence' regarding how candidates are responding and where alternative domestic sources of resource may be available.

Business shouldn't panic

The process for Brexit is going to take some time and even when Article 50 is triggered there are two years of negotiation before we really have a clear idea of the actual trade and labour market landscape. There will be some economic turmoil as with any change and navigating this is key at MBN as we source candidates in the EU and provide recruitment services to many EU based businesses.

While we don't yet have a clear path, we have to prepare as best we can. That means creating a plan (there, that's the third time I have said it) and looking at current processes and procedures and examining alternative scenarios. Our plan in this narrow area of impact has involved us understanding more about different sources for key staff. That doesn't just mean looking for talent beyond EU borders! It also means implementing measures to retrain existing staff to fill possible skills gap or look at other parts of the UK labour market to explore the prospects of bridging gaps with domestic staff. Our feeling here is that planning now should see sufficient time to start to explore the detail behind these alternatives and identify future sources for the talent the business needs.

Will Brexit be bad for us?

For us, we have a global business, but our commercial activities in the EU are a sizeable proportion of our overall work. So, if like us, you have strong ties to Europe and rely on them disproportionately compared to other markets, there is going to be a lengthy period of anxiety as you try to navigate that path. We have accepted that there are certainly challenges ahead and trading agreements that need to be reached but there are also plenty of opportunities as with any major change. In the long term, there will be rules and agreements put in place which like us, you will need to comply with. The doom and gloom relating to missing out on the single market is very real but the good news is that most of the world's economies and businesses are not part of the EU and they manage to thrive and grow. Key for us will be to explore scenarios and understand what future trade direction the business has open to it to substitute any short-term losses as a result of exiting the EU – this is why we have made clear to our team that 'business as usual' is the order of the day!

The impact on recruitment businesses

Along with a hard Brexit, there are going to be recruitment issues that most agencies will need to face. We, like many agencies, have banks of contract staff, particularly in technical disciplines. Such contract staff from the EU may become vulnerable under a hard Brexit and in such circumstances, we need to understand and set out alternative scenarios for meeting client demands for contract staff by exploring future skills sources (a pattern should by now be emerging, we explore scenarios, we plan and we prepare).

One such scenario could mean ensuring staff recruited from EU countries comply with regulations and have the right immigration status and paperwork. That will probably add to the cost of employing key staff from this region. This is not new to us as we have non-UK contract staff and already deal with non-EU international recruitment. If this applies to you then you will find nothing different in this. However, there is a finessed approach here that can be adopted by recruitment businesses that will help with maintaining the quality of their candidate pool and much of this approach will also work for in-house recruiters – Focus on the talent!

So, what about the talent?

Given that much of the drive behind Brexit and the leave campaign revolved around immigration controls, we can almost certainly bank on changes to immigration law. As it stands, it is highly unlikely the UK will be a participant in the EU free movement principles and so thousands of employees, like EU nationals or even UK expatriates and their families, who work in various industries across Europe are likely to be affected. At present indications are that they are likely to be allowed to stay but who really knows? And that is the real issue for us, our clients and other agencies – the uncertainty. Perhaps the worst-case scenario is that these changes could actually be implemented in a way that may result in many of these staff having to leave the country in which they are currently based (UK nationals returning from Europe and EU nationals leaving the UK), thereby creating an employment nightmare. Surely here, common sense will prevail... Right?

Unlikely to be immediate in the sense that there is likely to be some lead time for this, the potential impact means that, we need contingency plans for the likelihood of some major changes to our workforce and our clients' recruitment strategies as soon as possible. I stress that if nothing else is done, this point alone will at least, like it has for us, help you to identify the key risks and their likely impact and to understand scenarios for dealing with it if it happens.

A key component in this plan is our ongoing need to determine where we will have to look to find people with the skills and competencies required (a recurring theme). We then need to determine the extent to which they will qualify to work in the UK and if not automatically, what conditions will need to be fulfilled in order to secure the appropriate visas and permits to work. We see our role here as a facilitator to help the in-house client teams with both strategy and making it happen.

What about pay and rations?

If EU workers are forced to leave the UK as a result of Brexit, this could bring about a shift in the balance of power in the labour market towards employees, with a new war for talent between businesses seeking out the best talent intensifying. The result will almost certainly be an increase in pay packages, particularly for those people with skills that are in high demand in the industries that have traditionally depended on migrant workers (technology, education, hospitality, healthcare, construction and manufacturing).

By way of example, if the influx of lower cost resource from Eastern Europe is stopped, the lower end of the job market could also see a pay boost. This is not such good news for British businesses that may have to pay more to fill positions and retain staff. Such an effect will likely harm the competitiveness of UK businesses. Further, if businesses struggle to find the people that they need, they may need to increase outsourced recruitment, particularly for more basic roles. This, of course, may result in a further increase in costs. This represents an opportunity for MBN since we are already exploring disruptive propositions whereby lower cost, semi-skilled recruitment is bundled or packaged by us in a quasi-self-service model. This will allow our clients to have access to a lower cost recruitment model whilst we focus on finding and securing the higher yielding, more strategically important candidates for our clients. Perhaps this is the start of the next generation of recruitment partners?

Providing information to candidates

Candidates' will also realise that Brexit leads to uncertainty. Concerns may arise as a result of fear of the uncertainty and perceived vulnerabilities in companies' abilities to deal with Brexit. Concerns with British businesses and changes to employment contracts as a result of withdrawal from the EU is only the start.

Others may find that the UK based business they join could decide to relocate some or, in extreme cases, all of their workforce to elsewhere within the EU. Other concerns relate to the potential for financial impact on their salaries or the prospects of failure to negotiate trade terms leading to reduced work and the prospects of layoffs and redundancies. We have focused on providing regular and clear communication within our own workforce and with potential recruitment candidates for clients. But here, it is also incumbent upon any decent recruiter to help facilitate this and identify what is important to the potential candidate or core of your workforce.

By keeping up to date with the impact that Brexit will have on employment and contract law, plus having a clear idea of our client's approach to the economic situation (even if that's simply, they are planning no immediate changes) we will be in a better position to reassure candidates of any concerns.

Brexit is a fast-moving situation. News is emerging on an almost daily basis. As it's revealed what 'vote leave' will really mean for us, other employers and their employees, we will need to be ready to digest legislative changes quickly and discuss them with our clients or internal stakeholders and candidates. Once again, the opportunity for us and other recruiters here is to cosy up to people who can rapidly interpret the legal changes and set these out in plain English to be distributed to our client base for action.

We have become the calming influence

It's inevitable now – there's no getting away from Brexit and the incumbent changes it will bring about. And for those who stand to be directly impacted, feeling concerned is an understandable and natural response. The reality is that we are already experts in helping people navigate a difficult and stressful time of their life – changing careers and finding talent. For business, it is time to engage those often kept at arm's length. If the new war for talent is a real prospect, it is only a matter of time before such recruiter/client alliances start to dilute sensible partnership opportunities and if you don't act sooner, you'll no doubt have reduced options later. For us, we can use our experience to play a very reassuring role in candidates' lives and work with them to allay fears and explain options. Further, we work with businesses in a truly collaborative way to help them understand the dynamic of the next generation labour market that will be born of Brexit.

At this stage, there is of course a limit to how much you can do to immediately answer candidates' concerns and debate options with client organisations. Until further government and EU legislation is announced, it will be a case of trying to stay on top of our plan – a sensible plan with a set of early warning indicators of the need for action. My advice? For businesses and HR teams, plan but continue with business as usual. For recruiters, take the opportunity to reinvent yourselves. Be ready to disrupt and collaborate rather than be a 'me-too' recruiter.

For businesses, building a relationship with a recruitment agency that has its finger on the pulse and can provide the advice and guidance needed is going to be even more vital.

Planning for Brexit

1. *Start now*: The conundrum that many organisations face is that they are having to plan for a future and they are not entirely clear what it is. You need, however, to assess the situation as best you can and try to make the most of all the opportunities. This is not a time to put your head in the sand and hope for the best. Your business needs to start planning now.

2. *Plan to grow not stagnate*: It might seem easy to put everything on hold, but what businesses actually need to do is build up resilience and protect themselves. Leadership is as vital now as it has ever been. Make sure you have the right people in the right places and figure out which strategies will pay off in this new world order. It's time to review growth plans and bring them into line with the new landscape.

3. *Attracting top talent*: If the rules are going to change for immigration, your business will need to review its policies and procedures in respect of attracting great employees. How is this going to impact your business if the immigration status of EU nationals is going to change? Can you develop existing staff to fill any possible skills gap? It's not just new employees that need to be planned for but how existing EU nationals working for your company are going to be treated and, hopefully, retained.

4. *Motivating employees*: With so much uncertainty, giving special attention to motivating your staff is going to be another key factor. That might include reviewing bonuses and incentives as well as providing the valuable support and strong communication that keeps everyone on board and engaged.

5. *The Brexit lull*: There's no doubt that the prospect of leaving the EU has already had an impact on doing business. A number of large scale projects have been put on hold, awaiting clarity from the government. Do you have the skilled employees available when things do start moving again and where can you source the best from? Once Article 50 is triggered, things will start to change quickly and businesses will have to make sure they are prepared to suddenly carry on with projects that were stalled.

6. *Processes and systems*: Remember to explore practical issues too; changes to paperwork, employment contracts and your HR systems and tools – they will most likely require change or reconfiguration to ensure you stay the right side of any new legislation that arrives as a result of Brexit.

7. *Implementing a plan of action*: Implementing your Brexit survival and growth plan may mean retaining key staff but also employing new ones who have the skill set to cope with the challenges ahead. You might need to explore new markets and look further afield for top quality employees who are going to make a real difference.

Stagnating is not an option. For all businesses in the current environment, planning as best they can for the future is important. It's not going to be easy but there are certainly reviews and changes that you could be putting in now to ensure that the future comes as less of a surprise.

Particularly for HR and staff hiring, it is the right time to build relationships with recruitment agencies that can help your business get the right procedures in place and plan effectively for the future.

For more information on MBN Solutions visit www.mbnsolutions.com

PAUL GRAINGER, CHIEF EXECUTIVE OFFICER, COMPLYPORT LIMITED
Brexit and the financial services sector

Brexit will have a direct impact upon the financial services sector both in the UK and in the European Union (EU). My firm, Complyport Limited, is a provider of regulatory advice and assistance to UK and EU financial services companies. This gives us an excellent perspective from which to assess what the impact of Brexit is likely to be. In this chapter, I shall explore the nature of that impact and the implications for financial services firms. I will also consider the implications of Brexit for Complyport.

What we do – Complyport Limited

Complyport Limited is a consulting firm that specialises in the financial services sector. Our expertise is in the fields of financial services regulation and in Governance, Risk Management and Compliance (GRC).

Primarily, Complyport advises firms on how to comply with the rules for the conduct of financial services business within the UK, the EU and further afield in Asia, the Gulf States and the USA. This involves helping firms to apply for authorisation to the Financial Conduct Authority (FCA) or the Prudential Regulatory Authority (PRA) in the UK or to regulators in overseas jurisdictions. It also involves providing guidance or hands-on assistance to clients relating to operating their business in compliance with the relevant regulatory requirements.

Complyport is a wholly owned subsidiary of the Al Imtiaz Investment Group, which is listed on the Kuwait stock exchange. Complyport has a sister company in Hong Kong and associate firms in Singapore, the United Arab Emirates, the USA and continental Europe. As a subsidiary of a publicly listed company, Complyport is subject to many of the same rules and constraints as our parent company and many of our client firms.

Complyport's clients

Complyport has clients who operate in wholesale financial services (financial markets, asset managers and financial product providers), who provide retail financial services to private individuals or smaller businesses (loans, insurance, financial products and advice) and some clients whose business activity spans both wholesale and retail markets.

Over the last 15 years, Complyport's clients have included investment banks, investment fund managers, stockbrokers, investment advisers, wealth managers, retail banks, payment services firms, mortgage lenders, mortgage brokers, insurance brokers and consumer credit firms. The types of clients we deal with pretty much covers the whole spectrum of financial services.

A key characteristic of many of Complyport's clients is that they are often based in the UK but do business in continental Europe by utilising the passport system within the EU Single Market for Financial Services. This is particularly true of companies owned by US or Asian corporations.

Some clients are the UK branches of businesses based in and authorised in other EU states, eg, France, Germany, Italy or Spain). They too operate in the UK under the passport system. A significant part of Complyport's business is advising firms on how to operate in the UK or in the wider EU under the passport system.

The impact of Brexit on Complyport

As Complyport is a service provider to financial services firms, any negative impact that Brexit has upon our clients will indirectly have an impact upon Complyport. This was clearly illustrated during the first six months of 2016.

During that time, uncertainty in the run up to the Brexit referendum of 23 June caused many clients to postpone or cancel work or projects that had been planned. Understandably, in the uncertainty arising from the Brexit debate, conflicting statements regarding the impact of Brexit, uncertainty about the referendum outcome and uncertainty about the impact of Brexit should the referendum result in a Brexit decision, many financial services businesses were reluctant to commit to or undertake any significant new expenditure or major commitments.

Additionally, Complyport would normally have expected to receive a significant number of enquiries from non-EU firms (particularly from the USA or Asia) wishing to enter the UK or European markets. However we found that the volume of such enquiries was much less than normal during the first half of 2016 and was somewhat less than normal for the balance of 2016. Again, it is clear that the uncertainty caused by the run up to the Brexit referendum and then the further uncertainty post referendum, caused many Non-EU overseas firms to postpone or cancel plans to proceed with business ventures in the UK and Europe.

Complyport was able to cope with such a downturn in normal expected business levels, as we had carried out appropriate risk assessment and had anticipated that it may occur. As a result, we had contingency plans in place. However, had we not anticipated the uncertainty, we could have faced a very difficult period.

The impact of Brexit on Complyport's clients

It is difficult to assess the impact of Brexit on clients without first understanding the start point. The UK first joined the European Economic Community (the predecessor to the EU) in 1973. Since then, there has been a process of integration and harmonisation in commerce and trade and in economic and social policies that has been slow, steady and almost imperceptible. This has particularly been the case in the financial services sector.

Although the UK has its own financial services regulatory law, rules and structures, this framework has taken account of the requirements of EU law as it has evolved. It has also taken account of regulations or rules imposed by other supranational institutions such as the 'Group of Twenty' (G20) Economic Forum comprised of the finance ministers and central bank governors from 20 countries with major economies. (The EU is represented at the G20 in its own right as the world's largest economic bloc/market.)

As a consequence, the impact of Brexit on Complyport's clients in the financial services market can only really be understood by understanding how that market has developed and how it works in practice. Specifically, it is vital to understand the influence of the EU on the financial services market.

How does it affect the financial services sector?

Although the Single Market applies to all areas of trade in goods and services within the EU, a major part of it is the Single Financial Services Market. Whilst not necessarily the single largest market sector, financial services is often cited as amongst the most important as financial services enable other areas of trade to function. Key examples are banking, payment services and insurance.

Single financial services market

Although there are no tariff (additional taxes or charges) barriers to trade within the EU Single Market, there can be other barriers to trade in the form of local laws and standards that sometime hinder or prevent the delivery of goods and services from one country to another within the EU. In many specific markets such as telecommunications, the motor industry, electrical goods or food production, the EU has overseen the harmonisation of standards to remove or significantly simplify such non-tariff barriers to trade.

The Single Market in Financial Services was broadly agreed and substantially completed by the Treaty of Lisbon.[1] When it came into force in 2009, the Single Market in Financial Services was substantially in place. However, the significant and growing sector of non-retail investment funds was not included. (These investment funds are sometimes referred to as alternative investment funds. They are not designed for retail investors but are intended for professional investors. Examples of such funds would be private equity funds or hedge funds.)

After significant development work by the EU, the European Parliament and national regulators, the last major component was completed as recently as 2013,

---

1   The Treaty of Lisbon was signed on 13 December 2007 and came into force on 1 December 2009.

when the Alternative Investment Funds Management Directive (AIFMD) of 2011 came fully into force. That significant development now means that there is a comprehensive Single Market in Financial Services within the EU and EEA.

The Single Market in Financial Services has provided harmonisation of rules and regulations and thus removed the vast majority of non-tariff barriers to cross-border trade in financial services within the EU.

Services covered

The Single Financial Services Market was created by more than 39 Tier 1 legislative documents (Directives and Regulations). They cover

- Banking services
- Payment services
- Mortgage lending
- Consumer Credit lending
- Mortgage Broking
- Consumer Credit Broking
- Non-Life Insurance
- Insurance broking
- Life assurance
- Occupational pension schemes
- Consumer Protection
- Retail Funds & Savings Products
- Alternative Funds
- Economic Stability
- Markets in securities (stock markets)

- Alternative securities trading facilities
- Trading in securities
- Trading in Derivatives & Commodities
- Trading in currencies (Forex)
- Credit Rating Agencies
- Clearing of banking and currency transactions
- Clearing of securities transactions
- Clearing of derivatives
- Investment advice
- Retail stock broking
- Wealth Management
- Asset & Fund Investment Management
- Prevention of Financial Crime

The list above is not exhaustive. It is possible to further sub-divide the categories above. Equally it is possible to recognise that many other areas of EU law, eg, the prevention of market monopolies or cartels and the prevention of unfair contracts, also have a significant influence on the Single Financial Services Market.

Common Regulation and Standards

The effect of the Tier 1 Directives and Regulations and the additional Tiers of Implementing Regulations and Technical Standards, is to create common standards and harmonisation within markets. They also set out the conditions for a company or firm (known in the EU as an undertaking) to be authorised to conduct financial services business, access markets, consumer protection, economic regulation, markets regulation and prevention of financial crime.

In certain areas of financial services, national law makers or regulators may on occasions add local requirements on top of the common minimum standard. This practice has generally declined and it is now less common to find additional requirements imposed. In certain areas that are closely related to financial services, there is also a lack of harmonisation, eg, taxation and social security contributions or benefits. This is seen by most Member States as an area of policy in which they do not wish to harmonise. However, this does not seriously impair the functioning of the Single Market in Financial Services.

Passporting

A key feature of the Single Market in Financial Services is what is known as 'Passporting'. This is a mechanism that permits a company that is authorised by a regulator in its 'Home' state to do business in one or more other EEA states without the need to apply for authorisation by the national regulators in those other 'Host' states.

Individual Directives dealing with specific areas of business, contain the passport provisions. As an example, the Directives dealing with banking, non-life insurance, life assurance, investment business, investment advice, insurance mediation and retail or non-retail investment funds, each contain provisions that permit a firm to apply for a passport to offer its services in another EEA member state. A firm may passport into one or more other EEA states.

There are generally two types of passport that a firm can apply for. The first is a 'Service' Passport. A Service Passport means that the company or firm concerned is permitted to do business in another member state, but will not have a permanent establishment (maintain an office or staff) in the Host State. Instead its relevant personnel will temporarily visit the Host State as and when needed to conduct business.

The second type of Passport is a 'Branch' Passport. Under this type of Passport, the company or firm concerned will have a permanent establishment (staff and an office) in the Host State.

According to figures provided by FCA Chief Executive Andrew Bailey to the House of Commons Treasury Select Committee, 5,476 UK firms authorised by FCA use passporting to do business elsewhere in the EU or EEA. As at August 2016, 8,008 financial services companies from either the EU or EEA depended on passports to access the UK market.

Options on leaving the EU

UK government options

The UK Government has ruled out adherence to the Single Market principle of the free movement of people across borders. This excludes the UK from membership of the EEA or EFTA. Similarly, the UK cannot join the Customs Union, as the UK government has stated it wishes to conclude trade agreements with non-EEA countries that are outside the scope of the EU common commercial policy.

There are only two options remaining to the UK government. The first is to negotiate a bilateral post-Brexit trade agreement (or series of agreements) with the EU. If this cannot be agreed or if the UK abandons negotiations, then UK trade with the EU/EEA will default to WTO rules.

Impact on financial services

Within the EU single market, non-tariff barriers to trade (sometimes referred to as 'Soft Barriers') have traditionally been more of a problem in the service sector compared with the manufacturing sector. Manufacturing standards can be harmonised and standardised relatively easily. Over time such barriers in the service sector have been reduced, (often very significantly) through harmonisation. However, the greatest progress has undoubtedly been made in the financial services sector with the creation of the single financial services market.

When the UK leaves the EU, the major issue for the UK financial services sector will be the terms of access to the single market. Whilst at present the UK financial services market is fully harmonised with EU standards (and indeed is often amongst the leading policy makers), upon leaving the EU there is no guarantee that harmonisation will be maintained at the same standards or at the same pace that EU rules and regulations change. Thus the terms of access will be a critical factor for all financial services firms that rely to any extent on supply of services from suppliers or business partners located within the EU/EEA. The same will apply to firms that supply services to clients or business partners located in another EU/EEA country.

UK financial services dominance

Financial services is very important for the UK economy. According to research published by City UK (Key Facts March 2016), the financial services sector directly employs nearly 1.1 million people in the UK plus a further 1.1 million people in related professional services jobs such as accountancy, legal and related support services. The sector is responsible for employing a total of nearly 2.2 million people which is over 7.4% of the UK total employed work force. Whilst the almost 50% (1.2 million) of those jobs are located in the Greater London and South East areas, financial services is a major employer in the North West, Yorkshire and Humberside, the South West, the West Midlands, the East of England and Scotland.

Financial services contributes £66bn (11%) of UK taxation to the UK Treasury and £58bn trade surplus to the economy in terms of net exports. The UK financial services sector is highly productive achieving an economic contribution to the UK economy of 11.8% compared to an employment level of 7.4% of the labour force. This means average productivity in financial services is well above UK average for the economy as a whole.

The picture is even more significant when the UK financial services sector is compared with competitors overseas. The UK financial services sector accounts for 7.51% of GDP as shown in the table below.

Finance and insurance international comparison

Contribution to GDP

COUNTRY	Finance & Insurance Value Added %
China (People's Republic of)	7.25
European Union	5.42
France	4.57
Germany	4.18
Ireland	8.76
Italy	5.79
Japan	4.37
Luxembourg	26.71
Spain	4.02
Switzerland	9.85
United Kingdom	7.51
United States	7.10

Source: OECD GDP Value Added by Sector 2014 – Finance & Insurance

Value Added is a measure of GDP contribution

However, the UK is a very significant participant in international financial services to an extent that far surpasses other financial centres. The UK is the world's largest net exporter of financial services. This means the UK sells more financial services outside of the UK (defined as financial services and insurance) than it consumes from outside of the UK. As the table below shows, the UK exports more than double that of its nearest competitor, the USA.

Major financial centres – net exports of financial services (finance and insurance) 2013

COUNTRY	NET EXPORT VALUE (USD)
UK	$71bn*
USA	$28bn
Luxembourg	$22bn
Switzerland	$21bn
Hong Kong	$13bn

Source: United Nations Conference on Trade and Development (UNCTAD) Stat Data

*Due to exchange rate fluctuations $71bn is approximately equivalent to £58.5 billion at the time of writing

According to the UK Government's Office of National Statistics (ONS) the UK exported £58.5 billion of financial services (finance and insurance) in 2013 of which £19.8 billion (approximately 34%) was exported to other EU/EEA member countries.

Given the dominance of the UK financial services sector in global markets and especially in the EU/EEA, it would be highly disruptive to the UK financial services sector and to the wider UK economy if access to EU/EEA markets was severely curtailed. Similarly, it would be highly disruptive to commerce and the wider economies of the remaining EU/EEA members if the supply of payment, clearing, banking, insurance and other financial services was severely curtailed. It is therefore to everybody's advantage for there to be an orderly and amicable agreement between the EU/EEA and the UK regarding continued cross-border trading in financial services post-Brexit.

Brexit options – clean break or transition

As indicated above, there are really only two options in terms of what Brexit will look like at the end of the two-year negotiation period. The UK will either have reached an agreement with the other 27 EU members (and thus by definition with the EEA countries too) or it will not. Failure to agree a bilateral trade deal will mean, de facto, a clean beak and 'Hard Brexit' and future trade with the EU conducted under WTO rules.

Negotiated exit and transition

The first option of a negotiated Brexit and negotiated access to the Single Market (presumably with reciprocal arrangements for the EU/EEA based companies to be able to trade into the UK) implies there will be a transition period for both the UK and the EU/EEA members to adjust to the terms of new trading relationship. The length of such a transitional period is uncertain and potentially, by mutual agreement, could extend beyond the two-year window that is specified in Article 50 for the negotiation of a new trading relationship upon a country leaving the EU.

It is clear from statements made by more reserved spokespeople on each side of the future Brexit negotiations that it is not in the best interests of EU members for there to be a Hard Brexit with major disruption caused in financial services markets by loss of access to important services provided by UK based financial services companies.

Equally, it is not in the best interests of UK based companies to lose ready access to a major export market, especially as the EU accounts for over one third of all financial services revenue generated outside the UK by UK financial services companies. There are calmer saner voices making precisely this argument to government ministers on behalf of the UK financial services industry.

However, it will be a condition of negotiated access to the single market (particularly the single market in financial services), that there are equivalent standards, laws and rules in place between the UK and the EU. The UK government has already indicated that upon triggering Brexit, it will pass an enabling Act through the UK Parliament to adopt all existing EU law as at the Brexit date, into UK law. That law must then be maintained in line with EU equivalence into the future. That will not be an easy task due to the volume and complexity of regulations.

Clean Break Hard Brexit

Brexit negotiations must be concluded between the UK and the EU within the two-year negotiation window. Teresa May (the UK Prime Minister) and several of her government ministers have indicated that the UK will walk away without a deal rather than accept what the UK government would consider an unacceptable Brexit agreement. Whilst this is clearly a negotiating tactic, it is one that does not add any clarity and only creates more uncertainty.

Additionally, at the time of writing, the UK government has not indicated what an acceptable negotiation outcome might look like. There is thus nothing to measure and monitor how close or far the UK and EU negotiators may be from reaching agreement. This again creates uncertainty.

The UK government has indicated that if no negotiated deal is possible or if it loses patience during the negotiations and abandons them, the UK will leave the EU and default to trading with the EU under WTO rules. There can be no transition period in this scenario.

As stated, the UK has indicated that upon triggering Brexit, it will pass an enabling Act through the UK Parliament to adopt all existing EU law as at the Brexit date, into UK law. Following Brexit, as EU law and its interpretation is often updated by Regulations, by new Directives, by guidance from EU regulatory bodies and by decisions made in the European Court of justice, it is possible that UK law may then deviate from EU law. Any significant deviation of UK law from EU law is likely to result in loss of access to the Single Market, as it requires equivalence and harmonisation for it to work efficiently.

Impact on financial services sectors

The major impact of the Brexit negotiations upon financial services companies in the UK is uncertain, which in turn is causing those companies to delay or even cancel investment or development projects in the short to medium term. Whilst confidence may return once the shape and terms of Brexit are known, that still leaves a window of up to two years of continuing uncertainty ahead

Many smaller and some medium sized firms that have little or no direct involvement in or exposure to cross-border financial services may be largely unaffected by Brexit negotiations in a direct sense. In some cases, they in turn, may provide services or products to clients who also have little or no Single Market trading exposure and thus are also largely unaffected by Brexit negotiations. For such companies and businesses it may well be a case of business largely as usual.

However, there is significant interdependency between financial markets. A significant number of financial services companies are owned by or carry out transactions with EU based parent companies that manage funds, provide products or accounts or that execute transactions within the EU. In this sense, many other companies may not be quite as separate from or unaffected by Brexit as perhaps first appears.

At first, it may seem that the adoption of WTO rules provides a degree of certainty. Similarly, the UK Government's proposal to pass an enabling Act through Parliament adopting all existing EU law at the date of Brexit into UK law would appear to provide a degree of continuity.

However, this is an illusion. With a Clean Break Hard Brexit, will come loss of access to the Single Market in general and specifically to the Single Financial Services Market. In the short term, there would be a dramatic loss of capacity to carry out cross-border trade and transactions with any legal certainty. Such a situation would be catastrophic for both the UK based financial services companies and for their clients and customers in EU member countries. It raises the probability of UK based firms having to apply for authorisation to multiple financial services regulators within different EU countries.

As referred to above, figures provided by FCA in August 2016, show that 5,476 UK firms authorised by FCA rely on passporting to access the Single Market in Financial Services to do business in EU or EEA countries. As at the same date, 8,008 financial services companies from either the EU or EEA depended on passports to do business in the UK financial services market.

There are a total of 13,484 companies in the EU/EEA that depend on the passport system in the Single Financial Services Market. However 40% of these firms are based in the UK, whilst the balance of 60% are spread over the 27 other countries. The impact on the UK financial services sector of a loss of passport access would be disproportionately harsh and severe compared to EU based competitors.

In the shorter to medium term, a Clean Break Hard Brexit is likely to have a very disruptive impact on the UK financial services sector. There is a very real possibility that it could result in the loss or suspension of the ability of UK authorised firms to access the Single Financial Services Market using passports.

Simultaneously, the lack of certainty arising is also highly likely to result in a drastic reduction of US and Asian firms entering the European markets via the UK. This is because US and Asian firms would be able to enter the same markets with more certainty via Ireland.

The Republic of Ireland is a full EU member country. It has a competent and responsive regulator (the Central Bank of Ireland), the same time zone and language as the UK, a legal and taxation system similar to the UK and ready access to major financial markets. Significantly, firms authorised by the Central Bank of Ireland can enjoy passport access into the Single Financial Services Market.

An area of business in which Complyport has always had an interest is that involving the delivery of financial services using new technological developments. This has become known as the 'Fin Tech' (often spelt 'Fintech') sector where transactional services are delivered to consumers or business users and 'Reg Tech' (often spelt 'Regtech') where it is used by financial services firms to monitor compliance and/or make reports to regulators. Complyport often advises both Fintech and Regtech firms on UK and European regulatory requirements and compliance issues, related to their product and service development.

A report in the Observer newspaper of 26 February 2017 indicate that Fintech firms established in the UK are beginning to establish offices in other EU countries and move some jobs there as a precaution against loss of access to the Single Financial Services Market post Brexit. Many of these firms have US, Asian or other non EU investors. There has also been a steady flow of firms seeking to establish a presence in Ireland, France and other EU countries as a contingency against Brexit.

A softer Brexit under a negotiated bilateral treaty or series of agreements providing equivalence to Single Market rules, will provide more certainty and much less disruption if that also includes a continuation of access to the Single Financial Services Market for UK firms within the passport system. Whilst there has been some talk from EU negotiators of a hard line approach to Single Market access, particularly the retention of free movement of people, at the time of writing there have been some statements behind the scenes that suggest a softening of the stance. Michel Barnier, the EU Chief Negotiator is quoted by The Guardian (a UK newspaper) on 14th January 2017 as having expressed the view in a meeting with Members of the European Parliament, that the EU should avoid financial instability as a result of Brexit and work instead for a managed transition.

Such a negotiated settlement, based on bilateral treaties or agreements, will allow for a period of transition and a much smoother future relationship. Above all it will avoid the potential of a Clean Break Hard Brexit scenario, which would be catastrophic in the short to medium term.

The longer term future for exports of financial services is potentially more optimistic. Forecasts estimate that in the longer term future, continued trade with the EU and USA, coupled with higher growth rates in the BRIC (Brazil, Russia, India and China) economies and others in the developing world, particularly in Asia, may compensate for relatively low projected future growth in the EU. This relatively optimistic view is based on the fact that whilst circa 34% (£19.8bn) of UK financial services exports go to the EU, the balance of circa 60% (£38.7bn) is exported to non-EU countries. The breakdown is shown in the table below.

312

UK Finance & Insurance Net Export Earnings Worldwide Comparison

CONTINENTAL UK MARKETS	UK Finance & Insurance Net Export Value %
European Union (EU) Total	33.8
Europe Non-EU Countries	14.3
USA	17.6
Rest of the World	34.3
TOTAL	100

Source: UK Office of National Statistics (ONS) Pink Book 2014

Additionally, it should be noted that there is a significant amount of financial services business exported to non-EU European countries. As the table below shows, this is approximately 14.3% which when aggregated with the volume of business conducted with EU member countries, means that just over 50% of all financial services net export business is done with companies based in Europe.

UK Finance & Insurance Net Export Earnings Europe Comparison

EUROPE MAJOR UK MARKETS	UK Finance & Insurance Net Export Value %
France	2.8
Germany	2.3
Ireland	1.6
Italy	1.1
Luxembourg	1.7
Netherlands	2.9
Spain	1.2
Other EU	2.4
Russia	0.9
Switzerland	1.4
Other non-EU	14.3
European Union (EU) Total	33.8
Europe Non-EU Total	16.6
EUROPE TOTAL	50.4

Source: UK Office of National Statistics (ONS) Pink Book 2014

The evidence above clearly demonstrates that whilst in the longer term, growth in financial services exports may come from exporting services to non-European developing economies and to the USA, there is also a significant prospect of some future growth in Europe, particularly from those countries seeking membership of the EU and from significant countries on the borders of the EU such as Turkey and Russia.

In the shorter-term, because over 50% of financial services exports are to companies based in continental Europe, it is imperative that the UK financial services industry remains as fully engaged as possible with both the EU Single Financial Services Market and non-EU continental European markets.

Financial services and Brexit: opportunity or threat?

Because Complyport is a service provider to financial services companies, our prosperity is very likely to mirror that of the wider financial services sector. In our view, there are likely to be some companies who will experience at least a temporary down turn in business as a result of Brexit. However, as companies will need to re-think how they continue to do business in the new environment, we also see an opportunity to advise UK companies on how to do business going forward, especially in relation to cross-border commerce. Similarly, there will still be non-UK companies who will seek advice and assistance to enter the UK markets.

Businesses such as Complyport will need to assess what may change and what is likely to remain unchanged in the financial services markets and how that may affect what clients require. This will also mean that companies need to assess the risks they face, identify which risks they can control, manage or insure against. Firms will also need to consider which risks they may need to avoid. Where necessary, this may mean withdrawing from those areas of the market that are considered to be beyond the firm's risk appetite.

Forward planning is essential. The boards and senior managers of companies in the financial services sector (and in sectors that supply services to it) must consider the impact of Brexit on revenues and costs over a reasonable period of time. This should, in our view, be at least 3 years and possibly longer, to reflect the length of time over which Brexit negotiations will take place and the time before the outcome can be assessed and the implications understood.

In the meantime, companies should consider how and where their business may need to change in response to new regulatory and market conditions. Depending on the outcome of such deliberations, companies should also consider what the impact will be on resources, both financial resources and people. There may also be significant implications arising in areas such as information management, data protection and software requirements.

A significant challenge that should not be overlooked is that the nature of work may need to rapidly evolve which may give rise to the need to rapidly develop new areas of competence.

The considerations raised above are by no means exhaustive. Indeed, it is most likely that for many companies they are only a starting point.

Conclusion

By the time this book is published, I expect that the UK will have triggered Article 50 and given notice to leave the EU. The UK being on the road to leaving the EU will be a fact. However the destination, in the form of the nature of the post-Brexit agreement with the EU for access to markets will not have been finalised and indeed may still be largely unknown.

I have set out above, that in my view, a negotiated agreement based on one or more bilateral treaties or agreements for access to the Single Financial Services Market, is the desired and least disruptive outcome. Hopefully, such an agreement will preserve access for UK firms to the Single Financial Services Market via the passport system. The alternative, a Clean Break Hard Brexit is likely to be catastrophic for all parties in the shorter to medium term.

Whilst never a pleasant experience, good companies can and will survive even catastrophic market conditions. Should these conditions arise, there will be opportunities in adversity for companies nimble enough to exploit them. Of course, it is much more preferable that such adversity is not allowed to occur in the first place.

Neither I nor my peers in the industry have a crystal ball. We cannot predict with any accuracy what may result from the Brexit negotiations especially when so much national interest is at stake and where so many volatile personalities are likely to be involved in the negotiating process.

Under such circumstances, the only thing we can do is to hope for the best outcome but plan for the worst.

Paul Grainger is CEO of Complyport, a specialist Governance, Risk and Compliance consultancy firm that provides regulatory and compliance advice, guidance and support to financial services firms. He brings with him over 34 years financial services experience including over 28 years as a financial services regulatory and compliance consultant dealing with wholesale and retail markets.

Paul is a Chartered Fellow of the Chartered Institute for Securities & Investment (FCISI), a Certified Financial Planner (CFP) an Associate of the Personal Finance Society (APFS) and is a Member of the Institute of Risk Management (IRM).

He sits on the Institutional Committee of the Association Professional Compliance Consultants (APCC), which is the trade body for Regulatory and Compliance consultancy firms. He is also a member of the Examinations Committee of the Chartered Institute for Securities & Investment. Paul is a former Director and Steering Council Member of the APCC and is the former Chairman of FPSB UK (Financial Planning Standards Board for the UK).

For more information on Complyport visit www.complyport.com

PETER HOLMES, WIREHOUSE EMPLOYER SERVICES LIMITED

Employment Law – an overview after Brexit

A significant proportion of UK employment law derives from European Directives, and has been incorporated into UK law. On face value, it is therefore surprising that there has been little discussion over the implications that Brexit will have on employment law in the UK.

When one considers the complexities of EU and UK employment legislation, both domestic and European case law, alongside the repeated promise of 'The Great Repeal Bill', and the White Paper on Brexit, it appears less to be a legal issue as to which laws may survive Brexit, and more to do with it being a political decision as to which laws will be repealed at the first given opportunity subsequent to Brexit taking effect.

To consider this in more detail, one needs to have some understanding as to the current status of employment law and case law within the UK, and whether or not they are primary or secondary legislation. By then considering Theresa May's Speech of 17 January, alongside comments of David Davis and other leading figures going into the Brexit negotiations, in addition to the albeit limited information provided in the White Paper;[1] there are some areas which could perhaps be vulnerable to an early repeal.

Clearly this does have an element of 'crystal ball gazing' and hypothesising, and it is appreciated that putting these opinions to print prior even to Article 50 being triggered and negotiations commencing, could lead to ridicule in years to come. As suggested above, it will be more of a political issue rather than a legal matter as to what is changed in employment law moving forward. This could result in logic and sense being rejected due to a sway in public opinion or persuasion, which makes the future of employment law even more difficult to predict.

Whilst considering recent opinion polls relating to the main political parties, it would appear unlikely that any General Election result in the near future is likely to result in a significant change in Government[2]. Although the next election is timetabled to be in May 2020, and a lot can happen in politics during this period, it is currently predicted that the status quo in politics is to remain for the near foreseeable future.

Employment law and case law

Prior to considering which areas of employment law are vulnerable to change after the UK leaves the European Union, there is a need to consider current

---

1   The United Kingdom's exit from and new partnership with the European Union, February 2017

2   https://yougov.co.uk/news/2017/02/24/voting-intention-conservatives-41-labour-25-21-22-/

employment legislation and case law, from where it law or judgment was made, and how this has been implemented and incorporated in to UK law.[1]

Some of the European legislation is incorporated into UK law with the use of primary legislation. An Act of Parliament is primarily legislation. In order for a Bill to become an Act it requires, in short, several readings in both the House of Commons and House of Lords, discussions in both committee and report stages in both Houses, and further consideration and amendments prior to Royal Assent. It is a significant and time consuming process which is completed normally over many months, and can be held up or delayed depending on amendments proposed by either the Commons or the Lords. Examples of primary legislation is the bulk of discrimination legislation which was then brought together under the one piece of legislation and renamed The Equality Act 2010.

The remainder of European legislation is incorporated into UK law by the use of secondary legislation. This could be by relying on section 2 of the European Communities Act 1972 which provides the power and obligation to implement the Directive via secondary legislation, or relying on a power contained elsewhere within an Act of Parliament already in place, or under a mix of the two methods. Because the power to introduce the European Directive may already exist in other legislation, it can simply require a Minister or Secretary of State to draft the legislation for the UK whilst remaining consistent with the European Directive, and then simply confirm the date at which it will be implemented and come into force within the UK. Obviously this is a much easier and far less confrontational way to introduce legislation. Examples of secondary legislation are The Working Time Regulations 1998, and the Transfer of Undertakings (Protection of Employment) Regulations 2006 ('TUPE') or indeed the bulk of Regulations and Orders implemented by relevant Secretaries of State or Ministers.

Although both primary and secondary legislation has the same power and force in real terms, the difference is more how the law is made, and also therefore perhaps more importantly, how the law could be repealed. An Act of Parliament as primary legislation would need Parliament to vote in favour of repealing the Act. This would come after debate and discussion, and therefore can be a prolonged and difficult process. Secondary legislation could in theory simply require the Secretary of State or Minister to repeal either part or whole of it without the need for Parliamentary consent, which is a much quicker and more straightforward process. It would therefore not have the same Parliamentary scrutiny, ability for MPs to vote on the matter, and would leave these parts of employment legislation vulnerable to amendment and repeal by using a remarkably simple process.

The 'Great Repeal Bill' is looking at transposing all current EU based employment law into UK law.[2] A key question is going to be whether employment rights will

---

1   Brexit: employment law by Doug Pyper, House of Commons Library, Briefing paper, number CBP 7732 10 November 2016
2   Legislating for Brexit: the Great Repeal Bill by Jack Simson Caird, House of Commons Library Briefing Paper, Number 7793, 21 November 2016

be preserved through the 'Great Repeal Bill' as primary or secondary legislation. For example, would the Working Time Regulations 1998 be 'transposed' into primary legislation of an Act of Parliament, or would they remain secondary legislation, and remain a mere Regulation thus vulnerable to repeal. It is perhaps this debate which is going to be one of the central battle grounds within drafting the so-called 'Great Repeal Bill'

The immediate difference in law between primary and secondary legislation is non-existent. For example, The Working Time Regulations 1998 would remain in place immediately after the Great Repeal Bill is made law, and business would still be required to comply with all it contains. The difference comes only in the ease and manner of how to repeal or amend the legislation should the government choose to do so. Currently, legislation cannot be amended due to the fact that the UK government is tied to remaining compliant with the multiple EU Directives on the issues. Once that requirement to remain compliant is removed, a piece of secondary legislation could be amended or repealed by the Secretary of State, or whoever has the delegated power, without the consent of Parliament.

It may well be the case that discussions surrounding the 'Great Repeal Bill' are required, and the matter to be closely studied in relation to which Regulations or Orders will remain as such, and which will be transferred into Acts of Parliament subsequent to the 'Great Repeal Bill' becoming an Act and it taking effect. The outcomes of this would certainly be a clear indication of which areas would potentially be the first to be amended and/or repealed, and which areas of employment law appear settled and unlikely to receive much scrutiny or change post Brexit.

Mark Durkan (SDLP, Foyle) succinctly raised this issue in debate in the House of Commons on exiting the EU and workers' rights;

> 'The right hon. Gentleman refers to the Greta Repeal Bill, which is in essence the Great Download and Save Bill for one day of Brexit. Who controls the delete key thereafter as far as these rights and key standards are concerned? Is it, as he implies, this House? Would any removal of rights have to be done by primary legislation, or could it be done by ministerial direction?'[1]

It would be naïve to assume that for the simple sake of ease, the UK Government will transfer all Regulations and secondary legislation into primary legislation, thus cementing them within UK law. It is more likely that many, if not all secondary legislation, could remain secondary legislation in order for it to be easily amended and repealed later or at a time convenient to the Government. It is unlikely for any government to make it more difficult than necessary to repeal or amend the law when transferring the laws across, and therefore only 'safe' areas of law created by EU Directives are likely to be transferred into primary legislation.

---

1   House of Commons debate, 7 November 2016 c1318

In regards to European case law, it is difficult to give a clear indication at this stage. The judgments of the European Court of Justice interpret the correct wording of the legislation. Taking the assumption that the legislation was originally compliant with the EU Directive on which it may have been based, then it stands to reason that EU case law relating to legislation which remains in place post Brexit would therefore continue to apply, but that any further case law on similar laws in Europe on such Directives would not hold anything more than a mere recommendation for UK law. As time elapses, and both domestic case law in the area increases, and potentially the legislation is amended, then this would reduce the significance of not only of future ECJ judgments, but also existing judgments too.

The other side of the argument is that the UK courts would no longer need to follow or be bound by existing or future judgments from the European Court of Justice, and could deviate away from it where it disagrees. This could result in cases returning to Tribunal to test certain elements of 'established' law, and whether UK judges wish to deviate from the ECJ. A clear example of this could be in regards to the calculation of holiday pay, which the UK had interpreted as merely representing basic contractual pay, rather than as the average of a worker's earnings as per recent case law discussed later in this chapter.

It would be difficult to unpick existing ECJ judgments away from domestic case law. Once a case law precedent is set, it is followed and developed over time. Likewise, it would seem illogical and legally impossible to simply pick and choose favourable judgments over decisions which the Government of the day deemed unpalatable, as this would be unprecedented interference in the judiciary by Parliament. Nor could the ECJ judgments merely be ignored in favour of the lower UK judgments due to the reliance and overlap between them and the reliance on existing case law.

In short, the most logical step once the 'Great Repeal Bill' takes effect, ie when the UK leaves the European Union, would be for all existing case law to remain the legal precedent. This would provide certainty and clarity in the immediate aftermath to employees, employers, and the judiciary, and then allow the Government at its own pace to commence concentrating on specific areas of concern to amend or repeal.

Theresa May's speech and the White Paper

'Brexit means Brexit' has been a mantra repeatedly chanted by Theresa May and the Conservative Government since the result of the referendum was announced on 24 June 2016. There have been other phrases, from all quarters; hard Brexit; soft Brexit; Red, white and blue Brexit to name some of the most notable phrases coined in the latter half of 2016 and early 2017, but all have been inane soundbites offering absolutely no indication as to what a 'Post Brexit Britain' would look like.

With the economy, immigration and the welfare of European citizens residing in the UK, and UK nationals living in the EU taking the significant proportion of the limelight when matters of Brexit have been discussed, it has left others areas, such as employment and employment rights, lingering nervously on the side lines waiting to be picked as a topic for discussion.

There has been, however, little discussion by either the Prime Minister or the government over how they anticipate the landscape of employment law subsequent to the UK leaving the UK. In Theresa May's speech of 17 January 2017, she highlighted protecting workers' rights as her seventh objective in her negotiations with the EU.

In her speech Theresa May stated;

> 'As we will translate the body of European Law into our domestic regulations, we will ensure that workers' rights are fully protected and maintained. Indeed, under my leadership, not only will the Government protect the rights of workers set out in European legislation, we will build on them. Because under this Conservative Government, we will make sure legal protection for workers keeps pace with the changing labour market'.[1]

It should be said that the government's intension to negotiate with the remaining EU member states in order to protect employment rights, or possibly improve them is not really a negotiation position to take with the EU at all. For one, the EU is unlikely to care that we are going either retain the status quo or indeed improve the UK's current employment rights. To be slightly flippant, the EU is not going to attempt to haggle the UK down on its maternity rights or holiday entitlement, for example. However, in the speech of 17 January 2017, the above quote is over half of what the Prime Minister had to say on issues surrounding employment law.

Also, protecting and building on workers' rights does not necessarily equate to a legal protection which keeps pace with a changing labour market. Arguably, the employment market is becoming more fluid and flexible, which includes the growth in the 'gig economy' which could result in the relaxing of legislation, as opposed to the strengthening of current legislation, which will be discussed later.[2]

Due to the lack of information from the government on the issue of how Brexit will impact on employment law and rights, it was therefore of some relief that the government agreed to publish a White Paper on the UK's exit from and new partnership with the European Union. This White Paper allowed employment lawyers, academics, the public, and UK businesses the opportunity to consider in more detail how employment law may be changed in the immediate aftermath of Brexit.

It was, and is, disappointing to see that chapter seven of the White Paper, which deals with protecting workers' rights has only been developed into seven

---

1   Theresa May Speech, 17 January 2017
2   http://www.bbc.co.uk/news/uk-england-london-38248949 In London alone, the 'gig economy' just in transport and storage grew by 72% between 2010 and 2016.

paragraphs within the White Paper, and thus gave very little detail in respect to the future of employment law in the UK.[1]

Chapter seven of the White Paper on Brexit is almost bullish in its desire to protect worker's rights. It is once more confirmed that there is the desire to convert the EU law into domestic legislation in order to both protect worker's rights, and providing certainty to employees and employers alike.

In a moment of pomp and circumstance the White Paper highlights some specific areas where UK employment rights exceed that of the minimum standard as laid out in their respective EU Directives to member states. It provides details of two of the most repeated examples of where the UK goes above and beyond the European Minimum, such as the UK providing for a minimum of 5.6 weeks annual leave for a full time worker, whilst the EU legislation provides that Member States need only provide 4 weeks.[2] Also, in regards to paid maternity leave, UK legislation provides for up to 39 weeks paid leave, which is significantly higher than the minimum required under the EU Directive, which is, perhaps surprisingly low on only 14 weeks.[3]

Chapter seven of the White Paper is perhaps a nice reminder that the UK does not simply provide workers with the European minimum, but can and does go above and beyond this minimum in many areas, the document does provide scant information as to how employment law will look in the UK in a few years' time.

What little to be gleaned from Theresa May's speech and the White Paper when considering the impact of Brexit on employment law is that in the immediate aftermath of Brexit taking effect, nothing will specifically change. Perhaps this will be a surprise to some who were hoping for or fearing widespread changes and repeal of the vast majority of European legislation. Whilst that is possible once the dust has settled, it is doubtful that any laws will change immediately upon leaving the European Union.

Taking the Great Repeal Bill at face value, current legislation which has been implemented due to European Directives will be transposed into UK law. In the grand scale of organising Brexit, this may be one of the easier tasks to complete, at least within the sphere of employment law.

If there is to be no change in the aftermath of the UK leaving the EU, this would explain the brevity in this chapter of the White Paper and even more limited content in the Prime Minister's speech.

This would therefore leave the UK government to consider the legislation as they then found it, and should they wish to amend or change any element of

---

1   The United Kingdom's exit from and new partnership with the European Union, February 2017, pages 31 – 33

2   Directive 2003/88/EC

3   The Statutory Maternity Pay (general) Regulations 1986 (as amended) http://www.legislation.gov.uk/uksi/1986/1960/pdfs/uksi_19861960_280215_en.pdf and the Council Directive 92/85/EEC

current employment law it would require an Act of Parliament or the Minister or Secretary of State to amend any specific law. Areas which became entrenched and transposed into an Act of Parliament would be more likely to remain due to the difficulty in repealing any such Act. That legislation which was left as secondary legislation subsequent to the UK leaving the EU would be vulnerable to change and no doubt the first to be considered for repeal.

Considering the timeframes involved for the Brexit negotiations, it is likely, even taking a 'best case scenario' to take 2–3 years to negotiate Brexit. In which case this will leave very little time for any amendments to employment law, or indeed any area prior to a future general election in May 2020. To a large extent, any changes to UK employment law would most likely become an issue in any manifesto for the 2020 general election and beyond. In many regards then, it is unlikely to significantly change prior to the end of the Parliament.

By considering the comments of main protagonists, and perhaps more usefully, on how the UK has responded to the introduction of certain pieces of legislation, one may be able to make an assertion over which pieces or areas of employment law are vulnerable to amendment or repeal, and which may remain safe. There are some areas EU Directives which have been universally unpopular with some political parties since they were first drafted. Whilst times, attitudes, and political will can change, some areas of employment law will remain vulnerable to repeal soon after Brexit takes effect.

The Secretary of State of Exiting the EU, David Davis wrote that although new regulation from the Europe would cease after Brexit;

> 'As long as the employment law environment stays reasonably stable it should not be a problem for business. There is also a political, or perhaps sentimental point. The Great British industrial working classes voted overwhelmingly for Brexit. I am not at all attracted by the idea of rewarding them by cutting their rights'.[1]

This would perhaps give some comfort to those who believe that there will be widespread amendment and repeal to current employment law. It is likely that there will be changes, but it is thought that these will be relatively limited in number. Some areas, it is acknowledged, are however, susceptible to early amendment or repeal.

The Working Time Regulations 1998

These Regulations are perhaps the most vulnerable to amendment or repeal after the UK leaves the European Union. Although these regulations are primarily designed as health and safety measures they have a significant impact and repercussion on millions of workers in the UK. Most people are aware of the paid annual leave entitlement contained within the Regulations, along with the

---

1   David Davis: Trade deals. Tax cuts. And taking time before triggering Article 50. A Brexit economic strategy for Britain. Conservative Home, 14 July 2016

UK opt out of the 48-hour working week provision. However, the bulk of the piece of legislation is primarily relating to rest breaks per day, week and averages over an extended time, along with rules surrounding night work.

Perhaps since they were introduced in 1998 people have forgotten, or indeed never been aware, of some of the practices which existed prior to the Regulations. Perhaps workers have taken them for granted, but although all the noises from the government, including Prime Minister May's speech and the White Paper, state that they will continue to protect worker's rights, it is not unforeseeable that the Working Time Regulations may be one of the first pieces of legislation amended by the UK post-Brexit.

There are several reasons for making this assertion.

1. Both main political parties have taken exception to parts of this legislation since it was first drafted as a Directive and then later introduced in 1998, which has continued to exist to date.
2. It could be argued that by removing the rules on rest breaks per day, week and quarter, it allows employees and employers to be more flexible and allow employees to work and earn more, and for business to be more productive. Rather than a reduction in worker's rights it could be argued that it could increase 'choice' and allow workers' rights to keep pace with the changing labour market. It would therefore be arguably quite easy for rhetoric to develop on relaxing these rules to assist British industry post leaving the EU.
3. Through recent case law it now appears that companies in the UK have incorrectly calculated holiday pay for probably millions of people since the Working Time Regulations 1998 were introduced, which has now had significant financial repercussions across many industries, and resulted in a uncertainty in the near to medium future over how to calculate holiday pay for workers.

John Major secured a complete British opt out of the Working Time Directive when it was being drafted in 1993 as part of the Treaty of Maastricht. This was seen by some quarters as a victory for him and the UK at the time. Tony Blair took the decision for the UK to then opt in to the Directive and implemented the Working Time Directive 1998, with the proviso for workers to voluntarily 'opt out' of the 48 hour maximum working week should they chose to do so. This was, perhaps, in order to appease British commerce and allow there to be flexibility in the workplace, and to also perhaps demonstrate that 'New Labour' also cared about the thoughts of commerce, and not just the unions. It is clear from this opt out, that both main political parties have taken issue with aspects of the Working Time Directive, even prior to its implementation.

As part of David Cameron's renegotiations with the EU he allegedly attempted to once more opt out of the Working Time Directives and therefore the Working Time Regulations 1998.[1] Whilst he was unable to include it as part of his

---

1   https://www.theguardian.com/politics/2015/jul/11/david-cameron-employment-law-opt-out-eu-membership-renegotiation

negotiations with the EU, it clearly demonstrated that MPs still have strong views on this legislation, some 20 years after it was first drafted.

It is therefore an area of law which has caused concern among both Conservatives and Labour politicians alike, to differing degrees. A clear example of the difficulty that the Working Time Regulations has brought to the fore is that of training of doctors and medical staff. Often medical unions have recommended to their members to remain limited to working a maximum of 48 hours per week on average. Others have alleged that this reduces the amount of training that they receive by up to 3,000 hours.[1] The quality of those hours training after regularly working over 70 hours plus per week is also arguably questionable. This is however, just one argument in one sector which has never been resolved since they were brought into force nearly 20 years ago. It is clear that there is a lot of political animosity to these Regulations, and an active political will to reconsider at least some elements of them.

The second point could be seen as a reduction of workers' rights, which would be contrary to both the comments made by Theresa May in her speech and the White Paper, but could easily be turned to suggest that nothing would immediately change for existing workers working under existing contacts. It could also be suggested that the removal of legislative working hour restrictions would simply allow employers and their workers to negotiate separate hours agreements based on their internal risk assessments or independent guidance. This could allow greater commercial flexibility for businesses, and allow workers to potentially earn more money and thus be 'better off' financially. Choice is already available to employees in regards to the 48-hour opt out, and therefore there exists a precedent for removing some of the regulation away from business in order to allow agreements in the workplace to be made.

The Regulations were introduced to protect workers from working excessive and dangerous hours. This is particularly important in areas such as manufacturing when tiredness could have significant health and safety implications. This is not to suggest that it could be possible for companies to complete risk assessments and put measures in place to make the workplace safe for workers working more hours than they have done in the past 20 years, but this could have no immediate risk to existing employees' 'rights' per se, it could just mean that the European catch all maximum levels of work would no longer be in place to protect workers from excessive hours. Currently, the UK is unable to turn the clock back on maximum hours for workers, due to the fact that the UK is bound by the EU Directives. Once that element is removed then it would simply come down to a decision of the ruling party, or even potentially, the specific Minister or Secretary of State to amend the rules surrounding rest breaks and working time.

It is unlikely that all such areas of work would be reconsidered or dramatically changed. The differences between UK and EU law on driver's hours are relatively nuanced, but once Brexit has taken effect, it is likely that drivers in the UK,

---

1   http://www.telegraph.co.uk/news/health/news/10980505/Junior-doctors-will-be-encouraged-to-opt-out-of-Working-Time-Directive-Department-of-Health.html

especially those with tachographs, will simply apply the UK rules and the EU rules will be ignored unless travelling within the EU.

But there is the potential for there to be an element of regression in regards to working hours, and allow for the potential for greater working hours, especially if there was no default maximum which currently exists. In Europe, action is being taken to reduce working outside of normal working hours and to fight against what appears to be the steady encroachment of work into the personal realm through technology. This has included the French 'right to disconnect' which requires companies to establish hours when staff should not receive or answer emails. The goal is to protect private time and avoid burnout, and reduce the encroachment of work into nonworking hours due to constant developments in technology.[1] In 2012 Volkswagon blocked all emails to employee's phones after hours, and Daimler deleted the emails received by employees whilst on vacation.[2]

The third point relates to the recent changes in the calculation of holiday pay, which has caused significant upheaval and uncertainty for businesses, specifically larger organisations with sales teams or those who complete significant overtime.

When the Working Time Regulations 1998 were introduced, it was the UK's understanding that this simply meant that annual leave should be paid at the worker's basic contractual pay. *Evans v Malley Organisation Ltd t/a First Business Support*[3] confirmed the position that commission was associated to the success in the role, rather than the amount of hours worked. Although this point was slightly softened by later case law, a standard rule applied that commission was not part of the calculation for holiday pay.[4]

Bear Scotland Ltd & Others v Fulton & Others[5] changed this, and subsequent legislation has confirmed that the annual leave should not merely be basic contractual pay, but must include an average of overtime that you would have been working prior to the period of annual leave. *British Gas Trading Limited v Lock*[6] developed this point and confirmed that commission should now be used in the calculation of holiday pay. In a nutshell, a week's holiday pay should mirror a normal working week, otherwise it could be seen as a deterrence to taking annual leave. This has had massive implications, not only on the sales industry where commission can make up the bulk of remuneration, but also in industries where overtime is regularly paid, industries such as engineering, care, and pubs and leisure. The case of *Bear Scotland Ltd* also required there to be no break of more than three months between periods of claimed unlawful deductions of wages, otherwise it would cease to be an 'ongoing deduction' up

---

1   https://www.theguardian.com/money/2016/dec/31/french-workers-win-legal-right-to-avoid-checking-work-email-out-of-hours
2   http://fortune.com/2017/01/01/french-right-to-disconnect-law/
3   [2003] ICR 432, CA.
4   May Gurney Ltd v Adshead & Others EAT 0150/06
5   UKEAT/0047//13/BI.
6   [2016] EWCA Civ 983.

to the point of the claim being lodged, which also reduced the potential liability against companies.

The UK government was able to combat a sudden burst of tens of thousands of claims for alleged unlawful deduction in holiday pay by limiting any claim to a maximum of two years from the date of the claim through The Deduction from Wages (Limitation) Regulations 2014, which came into force on 1 July 2015.

For a claim to proceed on this issue it now requires detailed consideration of when the period of annual leave was, the gap between that period of leave and the one most recent, what the individual was paid and what, following the new interpretation of the Working Time Regulations 1998, the individual ought to have been paid at that time. Needless to say this has resulted in significant time and cost being spent on these calculations, especially when being brought as mass litigation for several hundred employees at a time in any one workforce. From practical experience in this matter, litigation with larger workforces is often a drawn out affair, especially as the employees themselves often do not know the amounts of money they are claiming, and the forensic accountancy exercise which follows can be both costly and painfully slow for those involved.

Despite the *Bear Scotland Ltd* case, and others that have followed subsequently, no tribunal has clarified whether annual leave should be calculated at the average of the 12 weeks prior to the period of leave, or simply an average of their earnings over the course of 12 months.

This sudden spate of cases on what had been a previously well-established position does make it more likely that this is an area which is ripe for reconsideration after Brexit. Not only has Government already introduced legislation to mitigate against the onslaught of new claims against employers, but still questions remain unanswered over the manner in which it should be calculated, whether or not voluntary overtime should also be included in calculating annual leave, and whether or not it should only be sums of money which would actually deter an employee from taking annual leave, and if the difference was 'nominal' would a claim still succeed.

Politically, it could also be used as a sign of the European Court of Justice 'interfering' with UK law, and an easy way to demonstrate 'taking back control' of our laws. Whilst this rhetoric is likely to continue for several years, this is a current area of confusion within employment law, and by amending it soon after the UK leaves the EU it could be argued that certainty could be provided once again to both workers and business, and help move away from complex, prolonged mass litigation.

It is likely that there will be changes to the Working Time Regulations once the UK has left the EU. It is unlikely that the UK will reduce annual leave entitlement of 28 days per year (which, although higher than the Working Time Directive minimum, were brought in and implemented over time once the Working Time Regulations 1998 were introduced and have been enjoyed by workers for over

326

15 years), but it would be prudent for business to prepare for elements of the Working Time Regulations to be amended or repealed.

From a political point of view, there are fewer better ways to 'give back control' than to allow British business and employees to choose the hours they can work in a mature and sensible manner, and to revert back to the previous method of calculating holiday pay. Although the Trade Unions may take great exception to the removal of these regulations, it is easy to imagine hearing this rhetoric for repealing the bulk of these Regulations in order to provide business with greater flexibility in organising their workforce, and to allow business owners to decide on how many hours should be worked per week, or month and an employee's rest periods.

Transfer of Undertakings (Protections of Employment) Regulations 2006

Directive 77/187 was introduced in order to safeguard employee rights in the event of a transfer of the business, part of the business or an undertaking. These were introduced into UK legislation through the Transfer of Undertakings (Protections of Employment) 1981. Due to a series of judgments from the European Court of Justice these Regulations led to a great deal of confusion within this area of law. In April 2006 new TUPE Regulations came into force which significantly overhauled the Regulations, and was meant to make the area easier to understand, and bring the vast majority of service provision changes under the scope of TUPE, and also to promote a 'rescue culture' for employees to be transferred when a business is insolvent.[1]

In 2013 there was consultation over whether or not to remove the 'gold plating' that the 2006 Regulations had introduced. Despite threatening to overhaul the TUPE Regulations once more, the legislation was instead only slightly amended through the Collective Redundancies and Transfer of Undertakings (Protection of Employment) (Amendment) Regulations 2014 which confirmed some elements of case law into legislation, micro businesses of fewer than 10 employees could consult directly with their employees rather than representatives, and to provide employee liability information under reg 11 now 28 days prior to the transfer rather than the previous 14 days to name some amendments.[2]

Considering these circumstances, whilst it is possible for a new Government to overhaul this piece of legislation, it has been recently reviewed and left relatively unaltered. It would appear therefore, that although there clearly has been a desire to amend or repeal aspects of this legislation, it is unlikely for there to be any real or substantive changes to TUPE legislation in the UK. It would appear that the TUPE 2006 Regulations, as amended by the 2014 Regulations are to remain, at least in the foreseeable future.

---

1   Transfer of Undertakings, IDS, December 2015, Thomson Reuters (Professional) UK Limited, i – ii

2   *ibid*

Equality Rights/Discrimination

Employment law is a relatively new area of law, and discrimination law even more so. Prior to the Equality Act 2010 which unified and codified the legislation in this area, the date of each piece of legislation highlighted how new discrimination law was; Sex Discrimination Act 1976, Race Relations Act 1976, Disability Discrimination Act 1995, and Age discrimination was introduced in 2006 demonstrates how recent equality rights are in the UK.

It would be hugely surprising if any government now amended the discrimination legislation in any real or significant way. It is hard to imagine anything as blunt as a government repealing, for example, disability discrimination. Because much of the legislation and case law has been in place now for over a decade, it is hard to imagine any government changing the definition of disability, or creating uncertainty in this huge area of legislation. Even since 2010 there has been the introduction of further equality legislation and providing greater rights to employees, in a move both to provide greater flexibility to business and employees, but primarily to reduce the gender pay gap which exists within the UK.

Whilst there has been some scaremongering in regards to the fact that because there would not be any European Directives stopping the UK from repealing any legislation in regards to discrimination, there has been little discussion, desire or will to amend the Equality Act 2010 either within Parliament, the press or the public. In all likelihood, equality legislation is only likely to improve rather than regress over the remainder of the Parliament.

There is a strong push within Parliament to protect equality rights subsequent to Brexit. The Women and Equalities Select Committee published a report on ensuring strong equalities legislation after Brexit,[1] which was welcomed by the Equality and Diversity Forum, and a further push for the current equality legislation to remain once the UK has left the European Union.[2]

Agency Regulations

The Agency Workers Regulations 2010, which came into force on 1 October 2011, were introduced with a great amount of consternation at the time. The Temporary Agency Workers Directive from which the Agency Workers Regulations emerge, caused some upset across Europe, and not just the UK. Not all Directives receive such hostility and were only passed with amendments which are colloquially then named after the country who objected the loudest. Indeed, the so called 'Swedish derogation' was introduced in to the Directive due to the Swedish government's insistence in order to allow some inequality in pay between agency workers and employees, if nothing else.[3]

---

1   https://www.publications.parliament.uk/pa/cm201617/cmselect/cmwomeq/799/79902.htm
2   http://www.edf.org.uk/blog/wec-report-and-edf-response-ensuring-strong-equalities-legislation-after-brexit/
3   Agency Workers Regulations, Guidance, May 2011, Department for Business Innovation & Skills

The purpose of this Directive was to provide equality of treatment to individuals working for prolonged periods of time in the same location as employees, but who were not previously receiving the same remuneration, annual leave entitlement, pension contributions, breaks or benefits. In short, they were a response to companies having a core group of employees who simply directed long term agency workers in the role, but whom had very few rights, and suffered inequality of treatment to those who were employed by the company, but completed the same work as those employees but could be significantly worse off and could be dismissed on a whim.

Using the 'Swedish Derogation' was not seen as particularly enticing for agencies to use, as it would still require an agency to provide equality of treatment in virtually all matters except pay (such as rest breaks, holiday entitlement and pay, etc). However, although they would not have to pay the same wages as the employees who worked for the company the agency themselves would have to formally employ the individual, provide contractual rights on the location of work, hours of work, and minimum payments to be made to the employee in between assignments.

It therefore could become more expensive for an agency to formally employ the individual. It increased their liabilities as the agency worker (or now an employee) could gain employment rights to unfair dismissal and redundancy pay if they remained in employment with them for over two years. Also, because they would be formally placed on assignment, there was the risk of TUPE becoming an issue if the company chose to take the work 'in house' or moved to another agency worker provider. It could be argued that TUPE would not apply, but it could certainly increase uncertainty in this area of employment law.

Using agency workers allowed businesses to be flexible with its workforce, and to reduce or grow staffing numbers quickly, and have cheaper labour almost at their disposal. The Agency Workers Regulations 2010 removed this option if the worker was to remain on site for a period in excess of 12 week in the role.

Previously, companies were able to sidestep many employment rights and labilities that employees are able to gain and enjoy over time. If an agency worker displeased the company, the business simply informed the agency to send a replacement irrelevant of the length of time they may have been working there. On the proviso that it was not due to a certain set of circumstances, then it had low litigation risk in acting in this manner.

There is a strong argument in suggesting that the Agency Workers Regulations 2010 inadvertently created zero hours contracts, in which workers or employees have no contracted hours, but are employees of workers of the company rather than an agency and should receive parity of terms on a pro rata basis as other employees. Why go to an agency for potential employees, where they would gain equality over time in any event when you could simply employ individuals on a zero hours contract, and use them on an ad hoc whenever desired. For several years, zero hours contracts could have restrictive covenants to ban the individual working elsewhere. These contracts became more prevalent since

2011 onwards, to the extent where the S.153 Small Business, Enterprise and Employment Act 2015 was introduced to expressly prohibited zero hours contracts from having exclusivity covenants banning the worker or employee working for another company.

It would seem that companies have now moved away from the agency worker model to that of 'zero hours contracts' or to 'self-employed subcontractors' which have developed over recent years due to the growth in technology and to fill the void left by a reduction in agency workers. It is now often referred to as the 'gig economy'. Zero hours contracts can either provide 'worker' or 'employee' status. There is often no mutuality of obligation to provide or accept the work, but they received the benefits of being a worker or employee (otherwise the employer would fall foul of the Part-Time Worker Regulations[1]), but there was clear control over the individual in the workplace, and there was a clearer understanding of their status and employment relationship.

Where a problem has developed is the clear uncertainty over the status of these so called self-employed contractors, who have been working for companies such as Uber and Pimlico Plummers.[2] After several employment tribunal test cases, it would appear that the employment tribunals are believing that these people are not genuinely self-employed as alleged by these companies, but have 'worker' status, which entitles them to receive at least the National Minimum Wage, holiday pay, and other rights such as rest breaks as per the Working Time Regulations 1998. This has resulted in 'copycat litigation' being brought against similar organisations such as Hermes and Deliveroo.[3] Now that the gates have begun to open, it is likely to result in a flood of cases on the matter of employment status.

These cases are going to have not just a huge impact on the tax and financial liabilities of the businesses themselves, but to all similar, platform based 'on demand' technology companies. Although the litigation will takes years, along with the significant difficulties in calculating annual leave entitlement, and cross checking to see whether the individuals receives the National Minimum Wage during their period of work, the case law would all need to dramatically change in the higher courts in order for this practice to legitimately continue.

Employment Status

Due to the cases involved with employment status becoming more prominent in the press due to companies being judged to be labelling individuals incorrectly, it is likely that employment status will be given full consideration by the government. The Agency Workers Regulations appear to have resolved several inequality of treatment issues between employees and agency workers, but due

---

1   Part-Time Worker (Prevention of less favourable treatment) Regulations 2000 which is the UK implementation of Council Directive 98/23/EC
2   Aslam and others v Uber BV and others [2017] IRLR 4 ET and Pimlico Plumbers Ltd & Mullins v Smith [2017] EWCA Civ 51
3   https://www.theguardian.com/business/2017/jan/26/hermes-facing-legal-challenge-from-its-self-employed-workers and http://www.bbc.co.uk/news/uk-37905425

to the perhaps unintended consequence the individuals are now employees on zero hour contracts, or self-employed subcontractors working in the so called 'gig economy'. Not only has the expansion in the 'gig economy' dramatically increased over recent years by 70% in London alone since 2010, but arguably increased the precarity of work for individuals, and resulted in a significant sum in tax revenue not being collected by HMRC.[1]

The government has commissioned a report into employment status, which although completed in December 2015, was published only on 9 February 2017. It highlighted the current 'employment status' framework which is currently in place is long established, and developed over many decades. It highlights the danger that;

> 'Any attempt to change the framework substantially will be challenging, potentially resulting in a different set of issues being created'.[2]

In short, the proposals put forward are unclear, vague and have the potential to create more confusion than what is currently in place. One of the more radical proposals is to reverse the presumption on employment status so that they would automatically be entitled to 'employment status' unless another type of status could be proved. This is described as a 'game changer' by the report, but it still acknowledges that it would make many years to develop and implement. The other area for consideration was for reform in specific industry sectors or groups which could considered in more detail, but again, this would be over many years and unlikely to take place in the foreseeable future, even taking into consideration the recent high profile cases in employment status, and the fact that on each occasion they have so far found in favour of the individual rather than the organisation. What the spate of recent case on this area has demonstrated is that companies need to be absolutely sure that individuals are truly self-employed or else risk a host of holiday claims (albeit now capped at 2 years), National Minimum Wage claims, and perhaps most expensively, potential tax repercussions over many years.

Whilst there could be ideas of areas of discussion, such as removing 'worker' status from UK employment law, and merely having 'employees' or 'self-employed' individuals, this is not something that is likely to be seen in the foreseeable future.

There are other areas which could be vulnerable to repeal subsequent to Brexit, such as those regulations providing protection to fixed term or part time workers. The UK implemented the minimum requirements in order to comply with the Council Directives, but they do currently appeal to a more flexible workforce which could be in keeping with the 'gig economy'. There has also been little clamour for their removal and it is doubted whether any change would come soon after Brexit.

---

1   https://www.theguardian.com/money/2016/dec/09/londons-gig-economy-grown-more-than-70-since-2010-casual-workers
2   Employment Status Review, Department for Business innovation & Skills, December 2015, page 36

In summary, whilst European Directives have provided so much legislation and protection for workers within the UK, it is unlikely that these will all be repealed or amended once the UK leaves the European Union. In a post-Brexit world, the UK will not be bound to implement or retain European legislation. The UK Parliament and government will be responsible for legislation and protecting workers' rights or indeed choosing to amend or repeal legislation in order to provide business with greater flexibility and fewer risks. Legislation could therefore be more likely to fluctuate depending on the party in government at any one time, and it is possible that employment law will not have the stability that it has enjoyed due to being forced to remain in place due to European Directives, and perhaps become more of a politicalised area in years to come.

Peter Holmes is a non-practising barrister at Wirehouse Employer Services Limited. He has 10 years' experience in providing companies with practical advice on HR and employment law issues, and representing companies in employment tribunals throughout the UK and Northern Ireland.

For more information on Wirehouse Employer Services visit www.wirehouse-es. com

AMANDA FLINT, MERCER PLC

Brexit presents a variety of challenges for businesses in their capacity as employers. One of the major issues for employers is managing executives and employees through an extended period of uncertainty. This issue manifests itself in a number of different ways:

The trade agreement infrastructure will fall away when the UK leaves the European Union. There is extensive commentary on what that might mean for businesses but there is currently no clarity as to how a new infrastructure will be put in place. In particular, will this result in reduced output if markets start to shrink? If costs of sale increase or markets close up then it seems likely that the corresponding fall in profits will limit monies available for salary, benefits or other types of remuneration.

Currency fluctuations also distort business activities. If the depression in the value of the pound continues this is good news for exporters or companies with a significant overseas presence as the resulting foreign earnings will be more valuable for companies accounting in sterling. However, to the extent that raw materials are sourced outside the UK for sale locally, production costs will increase and profits will be eroded. As discussed in more detail below this has an impact for expatriate employees and when measuring performance targets for bonuses and long-term incentives.

One of the platforms for Brexit was the ability to control immigration into the UK. The freedom of movement within the EU was popularly perceived to result in an unwelcome volume of non-UK workers to the UK. However, it seems that if taking control of immigration reduces the number of workers coming into the country this could have a very negative effect on UK business:

Volume of workers – the UK has an aging population so if the supply of immigrants reduces there is a risk of a shortage of workers at all skill levels. This could also mean that by 2025 or even sooner, the ratio of active workers to retired workers will be insufficient to support the aging population which could have a significant social impact;

Skills shortage – even if the optimum level of the workforce is maintained, this may not avoid a skills shortage. Without freedom of movement in the EU, importing skills could become a much more costly and onerous burden on employers. For example, under the current rules, the employer typically has to demonstrate that non-EU immigrants are coming to the UK to undertake work where no suitable candidate can be found in the UK. This is not currently necessary for EU immigrants but if the same rules are applied to EU immigrants as those that apply to immigrants from all countries, the added bureaucracy will result in a greater burden for employers.

Flexibility – freedom of movement under EU rules provides UK employers with a labour pool from which they can access at will (subject to applicable UK employment laws) without any commitment, cost or formality. This allows UK employers to be nimble in staffing their business with the volume and appropriate level of people needed. Where freedom of movement is replaced by immigration requirements this will inevitably introduce cost, delay and process which is likely to result in UK companies being slow to react to changes affecting their businesses.

The impact of a weakened currency – if one of the outcomes of Brexit is that the value of Sterling remains at a low level for the medium term, this alone could affect the labour supply. One of the attractions of the UK for EU immigrants has been the opportunity to work and earn salaries in a strong currency. A weakened Sterling may mean that those EU immigrants are attracted to other EU countries and the numbers in the UK fall. Again, this reduction in the labour supply taken together with the other influences above could result in a shortage of labour for businesses.

Measuring performance in times of uncertainty can be difficult. Depending on the speed of change, performance measurement could be challenging even for annual bonuses measured over a one year period. It may also be particularly difficult to set performance targets for longer term incentive arrangements. For example, where a company has strategic objectives for expansion outside the UK, particularly in Europe, it may be difficult to predict at this stage how quickly and effectively this can be achieved. Profit or margin based performance targets may also need to be revised where the company relies on foreign imports for its production. Where a company has made awards with targets that have become unachievable post-Brexit, there is usually a mechanism within the plan rules to adjust that target. This is more than just a calculation adjustment. Shareholders, particularly institutional shareholders, are not enthusiastic about targets that are re-set if they appear to be easier to achieve than the existing performance targets. Such amendments need to be approached carefully in consultation with shareholders and other stakeholders to justify the change.

It will be interesting to see the effect of Brexit on the regulatory regime in the financial services industry. On the one hand, the UK is a world leading financial centre and as such leads the thinking on the regulation of pay in this sector. On the other hand, the EU takes a different approach to executive remuneration – the level of disclosure is generally lower than for UK listed companies and the degree of regulation is in some cases higher. There has been little enthusiasm for exceptions to be granted to the UK. For example, the Treasury attempted to challenge the bonus cap in the European Court but George Osborne confirmed in November 2014 that the case would be abandoned following an opinion from the European Court of Justice that the challenge should be rejected. Therefore, once exit from the EU takes effect there may in theory be an opportunity to scrap this rule. However, it is likely that this flexibility will be illusory. EU negotiators are likely to insist that the bonus cap continues to apply in London in return for allowing provisions that protect the City, such as access rights to the single market for financial services. In any event, the UK has embraced regulation for the financial services sector to help restore trust in its many financial institutions and in London as a financial centre. As a result, it is unlikely that the UK will start a process of deregulation. However it may have more flexibility to interpret those rules and post Exit to act more swiftly and appropriately where needed. To the extent that they do business within the EU, some financial services businesses may need or choose to continue to adhere to EU rules,

Government regulation of remuneration – one of the immediate political statements from Teresa May shortly after her appointment referred to curbs to executive pay. This was followed by a consultation paper that drew on shareholder engagement with executive pay, transparency on pay, the role of Remuneration Committees as well corporate governance in private companies. The consultation paper attracted comment from a wide variety of interest groups ranging from institutional investors to social enterprises.

Executive pay is a hot topic in the post referendum debate and there is an air of reproach – there is a view that the Brexit vote was a result of popular dissatisfaction with inequality – and the perceived high levels of executive pay bore a significant degree of responsibility for such dissatisfaction.

Managing through this period of uncertainty presents complex considerations and the reaction to these issues is set out in more detail below.

What was the initial reaction by employers to the referendum vote?

The Mercer 'Planning for Brexit: Talent Implications' report published in September 2016 shares the responses from senior Talent, HR and Reward specialists in 180 organisations.[1]

The initial findings showed a desire from the majority of employers to maintain freedom of movement within the EU. Short-term, employers were concerned

---

1   https://www.uk.mercer.com/our-thinking/brexit-hr-talent-implications.html

about resource levels to support additional activity as a result of the Brexit vote alongside maintenance of business as usual (e.g. developing new markets to compensate for a fall in profitability in relation to EU exports).

Unsurprisingly one of the main findings when considering the employee view was the high level of anxiety in the workplace as a result of the vote, with 72% of employers reporting concern being expressed by their employees. Dealing with the level of concern from employees on the outcomes of Brexit also gave rise to additional obligations on employers. 82% of survey respondents indicated that they felt responsible for communicating the implications of Brexit to employees. Communications from employers to date have focused on the robustness of the business and job security. However, it was interesting to see that many also highlighted opportunities to work abroad and international mobility as well as diversity as key issues. Employers seem to be at pains to stress that leaving the EU will not translate into a move away from a cosmopolitan, inclusive business culture

In anticipating the impact on executive pay, many employers responding to the survey were taking a cautious approach and looking for as much flexibility as possible to allow them to adapt to changing circumstances.

The short term reaction from employers in relation to executive pay, and indeed more broadly in terms of redesigning business plans, was to wait and see – only 11% were actively communicating openly due to the many uncertainties. Initial communications have focused on the economic outlook for organisations and job security.

Longer-term implications

Many of the participants envisaged a need to develop their existing workforce over the longer term so that they could be ready to fill talent pipelines as required. So, one of the unexpected by-products of Brexit is likely to be a greater concentration on development and training within the workforce. If this transpires, it will be an opportunity for employees to upskill and this is likely to be welcome in the context of the new world of work, where automation and digitalisation become increasingly prevalent meaning that employees will need to adapt.

Another obvious longer-term impact on workforce planning is the effect on companies' expatriate programmes. One third of the companies surveyed reported that UK located expatriates had already asked for additional pay to compensate for the weakening of Sterling. Few companies had changed their mobility programmes but acknowledged that salary and allowances would be adversely affected if the impact on Sterling continues long term. This would also increase costs for business – although it should be borne in mind that UK expatriates being paid in foreign currencies have benefited.

However, there was a great deal of concern expressed by EU nationals working in the UK, not only with regards to their residence status but also to the viability of their positions longer term. There was also an increase in employees eligible for permanent residence status making applications and asking employers for support in those applications.

Moreover, 58% of responding organisations anticipated a long term impact on their workforce planning; suggesting the natural tension between supply and demand will become even greater over the coming year.

Crucially for the UK, only a small minority of companies (around 10 percent) were considering moving some of their jobs from the UK to other locations at the time they were surveyed. It remains to be seen how companies will develop their location strategy outside the UK as greater clarity about the UK's Brexit strategy emerges.

The survey's core finding was that whilst employers have dealt with short term issues swiftly, they are poised to reshape their workforce strategy and corresponding programmes when the impact of leaving the EU is better understood.

The impact to employers of limiting immigration

The most significant concern is resourcing in an already stretched labour market. For many sectors the labour market is already under pressure. Organisations are increasingly concerned they will lose existing EU workers and not easily be able to hire new EU workers, in both critical skill areas and for lower level jobs where a high volume of workers is often needed.

Even before immigration restrictions are put in place, employers are very concerned that uncertainties caused by Brexit (both over the next few years and in the longer term) mean that net migration flows could reduce and may even reverse. After all, free movement is a two-way process. As and when economies recover in mainland EU and exert their own pressures on the labour markets, demand for immigrant workers in other EU countries may increase. If the weakness in sterling continues, the UK may become less attractive to migrant workers as their remittances of earnings back to their home country fall in value. Many European migrant workers have come to the UK attracted by the opportunity to earn more than in their home country and send earnings home. There is a danger that the economic, social and political fall-out of the referendum may reverse this trend even before any immigration restrictions are in place.

In addition, the UK already has a demographic time bomb to contend with. Since 1970 workforce growth has outpaced population growth. In the 15 years to 2015 the workforce and population growth has been 14% and 10% respectively. But whilst the population over the next 15 years to 2030 increases at a similar rate to the previous 15 years, there is a massive decline in workforce growth. Such reversals are rare in the UK's history.

Base case scenario

This scenario is based on the core migration scenario from Office of National Statistics'[1] population projections, including pre-Brexit migration assumptions. Our projections assume that net migration will fall progressively from current levels of 335,000 per year to 185,000 per year from 2020 onwards.

Great EU re-migration scenario

This scenario assumes that EU workers leave the country and net migration rapidly turns negative before 2020. Between 2017 and 2018 we assume net migration is zero and from thereon we assume it falls to 50,000:

UK-born net migration is kept constant at – 50,000 per year;

Non EU-born net migration falls to 50,000 from 2020 onwards; and

EU-born net migration falls to – 50,000 per year from 2020 onwards.

Under the Base Case Scenario population growth is at 8%, and the workforce grows at 5%. In contrast in the Great EU Re-Migration Scenario the population continues to grow by 3% but the workforce shrinks by 2%.

UK Population and Workforce Growth Projections (percentage change from 2015)

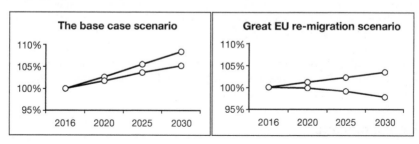

Top Line = Workforce, Bottom Line = Population

The differential is caused by the fact that the UK-born population in the UK is aging and increasingly leaving the workforce – and this is set to get worse. This is not a new phenomenon, the number of UK-born workers actually peaked in 2013 and has since been declining, but the impact of this has been masked by migration.

The effect of these changes affects the Aged Dependency Ratio – the number of people over age 65 compared to 1,000 of the population between 15 and 65. The resulting Age Dependency Ratios are expected to rise by 25% (from 277

---

1   Office for National Statistics

to 346) in the Base Case Scenario and by 34% (from 277 to 372) in the Great EU Re-Migration Scenario.

The concern is that in the absence of immigration from the EU the current level of employees in the workforce will be insufficient to support the aging population.

This issue should be factored into the considerations shaping immigration post-Brexit. The danger is that there is a political backlash stemming EU immigration. Substituting non-EU immigration such as Commonwealth immigration is one approach that has been mooted. However, this policy should be demand lead not politically driven. A highly motivated, well-educated workforce here on a temporary basis for a few years to grow personal wealth through valuable employment opportunities has contributed to the UK's growth. If this phenomenon is likely to be a good fit for the UK's requirements over the next 15 to 20 years then a new 'controlled' immigration policy should not block access to this flexible labour source.

The demographic issues are interesting to employers but outside of their control. So how businesses should be planning to address these potential issues?

At the extremes, businesses can either do nothing and address labour shortages as they arise or jump to solutions to fix future labour shortages. Both these extremes are probably ill-advised whilst the outcomes are so unclear. Solving labour shortage issues can be disruptive, resource intensive, require a cultural mind shift and potentially represent a high level of investment for the employer. However, whereas in the past many have had the luxury of hiring skilled workers as and when needed and at a reasonable price point, the workforce crisis outlined above could change all this dramatically.

A more measured approach would be for employers to use a manageable, four-step process – Define, Determine, Devise and Drive as set out in Mercer's Integrated People Planning™ process:

Define demand

What is the business strategy and what are the industry trends – there may be changes in consumer preferences, the regulatory climate and technology for example – how might this translate into workforce requirements in your business?

Identify the implications for the UK workforce:

- What UK jobs (and in what volume) are needed to fulfil current and future requirements?
- Prioritise the knowledge, skills and attributes that UK employees need to undertake these jobs?

Determine if there are any gaps in labour supply

Analyse the current position of the business' current UK workforce and the demographic and profile of these workers. If the current requirements remain unchanged, identify whether there is sufficient supply to satisfy business needs now and in the future.

Identify the potential impact of the age profile, staff attrition and net migration on the availability of workers on the ability to meet business need.

Consider which gaps can be easily closed by the external labour market within the UK, and which gaps represent a potential risk and require attention.

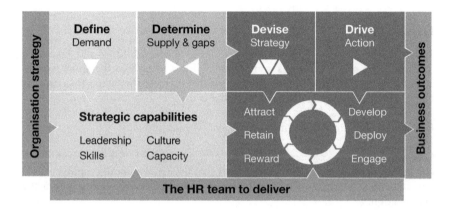

Devise strategy

Take a longer-term view on how to create the people the organisation needs – this is likely to be a longer term plan to take account of the fact that it can take years to develop a workforce with the right skills and capabilities.

Model and understand the options available for key roles that cannot be easily hired from the external labour market within the UK:

Location strategy: is it possible to move some elements of the business outside the UK? Identify the potential 'tipping point' which would indicate that this would be the correct strategy.

To what extent could automation be more cost effective than increasing labour costs/vacancies?

Can the business adapt to non-traditional talent? If the business is able to be flexible it may be able to attract a wider pool of candidates such as older workers, employees with a different technical qualification or retrain internal candidates.

To the extent that the business is likely to suffer skill shortages, it may want to invest in additional training to develop further skills. If this is viable, the business will need to consider what supplementary learning and development is needed to give employees the requisite qualifications and experiences.

To the extent that such a review as part of the exercise in Step 2 – Determine has identified potential gaps in its employee population either now or in the short to medium term, the business will need to prioritise its response. This will involve assessing the costs, resources and readiness of the organisation to meet the challenges identified and the impact of the changes.

Plan ahead for the people, processes and technology that HR will need to have to support the activities.

Drive action

Translate the strategy into actions, priorities, accountabilities and resources – identify the specific actions and responsibilities to take in the short term to ensure that longer-term goals are successfully met. At this stage it is case of being 'battle ready' rather than fighting the war.

Changing behavior and assumptions in assessing employees

One relatively low cost and potentially effective route is for organisations to challenge themselves on the assumptions that they make about employees and potential hires in relation to their abilities and aptitudes for roles within the organisation.

The first step is to understand fully the necessary and minimum requirements of the roles and to challenge assumptions. Often there is a tendency to rely heavily on past experiences – either personal or viewed in the environment that the managers or leaders have grown up in. Historical experience may not be the best gauge of the business needs. An analytical approach and breaking down the requirements of the various functions of current roles could deliver innovation around job design and flexibility. Breaking down assumptions and thinking differently is key.

A more flexible approach could result in organisations hiring non-traditional candidates – possible non-traditional categories include older workers, more women in managerial and technical roles, and people with disabilities, apprentices and graduates in roles previously filled by more experienced workers.

Hiring a wider spectrum of worker has a knock on effect on the value proposition made to the employee. What can be offered to them in terms of culture, working environment, teamwork and recognition other than pay? If the workforce encompasses a wider spectrum of worker, greater emphasis may be needed, for example on well-being including financial well-being as well as health. An unconventional work environment may bring additional stresses for employees and managing this dynamic productively will be key to success.

Reward structure will also need to be considered in more detail. For example how will pension provision be made for a wider spectrum workforce – will the defined contribution approach be of interest to a multi-demographic workforce or will a more innovative approach be needed to help employees at different stages of life save for retirement?

More and different types of training may be required for this multi-demographic. Employees from non-traditional backgrounds or for example older workers in a second career may not absorb traditional classroom style training. Different learning approaches to accommodate different learning styles may be necessary – for example more structured 'on the job training' with plenty of interaction may work better than passive training by video or lecture. A rethink of employee profile will therefore require a different approach and potentially additional investment in training. The talents and experience of the workforce may differ from the norm in the organisation but the benefits should be explored too. For example: more mature workers may be experienced in dispute resolution and collaborative working whilst newer entrants to the workplace can bring a fresh perspective and highly refined social networking media skills. If valued and nurtured, these skills can be very valuable.

A more flexible approach to the talent pool requires a certain degree of resilience from the organisation and the workers involved. If the business environment is not receptive to non-traditional talent those workers may leave the organisation and migrate to one where they will be valued. To be successful in this endeavour the organisation must ensure that its culture allows the non-conventional worker to thrive.

Lastly, to the extent that the organisation has an existing workforce that fulfils its business requirements, it is important that it retains those workers. Understanding what those existing workers value from their employment relationship and how the employment proposition can be improved is key to retention. Focus groups can be helpful to establish what employees' value and why they stay. Reward packages can be structured so as to be tailored to the individuals' requirements, for example, by an imaginative flexible benefits package or by a flexible approach to working hours or home working.

Dealing with currency fluctuations – executive pay

Currency fluctuations do not just affect expatriates, the UK business community tends to have an international outlook – either because it is operating in foreign markets and/or it is buying materials, goods, labour and services from those markets. Therefore from the perspective of Remuneration Committees, Brexit will have implications for executive pay including incentive target-setting.

Annual bonus pay-outs may be influenced by unhedged currency movements. Typically Sterling profits will be boosted for companies with significant overseas earnings. Conversely, companies that are primarily domestic may see their profits come under pressure as a result of rising import costs for goods or raw materials.

Currently, most UK listed companies operate long- term incentive plans that comprise awards of shares which are subject to performance targets before the shares are received. Performance targets typically involve a hybrid approach measuring profit growth and relative share price movements.

In the post-Brexit environment Remuneration Committees need to consider the performance targets applying to awards that have already been made but have not reached the end of their performance periods. And when making new awards, the Committee will need to consider whether a new approach to target-setting is necessary. The effects will vary by company and be based on factors such as the geographic spread of the company's revenues and costs, the company's reporting currency, the company's foreign exchange hedging policy and where shareholder return is measured in comparison to a group of other companies, whether those companies report in Sterling or in local currency.

Targets on existing awards:

The impact of unhedged currency movements on financial performance conditions such as earnings per share ('EPS') will be as described above for an annual bonus. Whether it is technically possible to adjust performance targets will depend on the Remuneration Policy set out in the company's Annual Report and Accounts (executive directors) and on the contractual terms contained in the plan Rules and set out in award letters. The implications are as follows.

Domestically-oriented businesses. In our experience, shareholders are wary of Remuneration Committees reducing targets in the mid-cycle of awards. Therefore, some UK-focused businesses (for example, those which rely on imported raw materials) may find that long-term incentive pay outs based on financial metrics will reduce, as generally no amendments to targets are likely. (The impact may affect multiple cycles of existing awards.)

Multinationals. Businesses with significant overseas earnings may see sterling profits boosted and therefore higher payments from long-term incentive based on financial metrics. Whilst some shareholders might like to see an adjustment to take this into account, Remuneration Committees tend to be reluctant to use their downward discretion to reduce windfall gains given how hard it is to exercise discretion in the other direction.

Some UK companies compare their total shareholder return ('TSR') performance with a group of international companies for the purposes of measuring performance for their long-term incentive awards. Only if TSR performance is greater than the average performance of the peer group will the long-term incentive award be paid out. The impact of currency movements depends on the situation, as follows:

In the case of multinationals, assuming TSR comparisons are made in common currency, the impact of Sterling depreciation might be broadly neutral. This is because any share price appreciation arising from increased Sterling earnings is to some degree cancelled out by the depreciation of Sterling when share price movements are compared in a common currency other than Sterling;

Domestically-oriented companies that make common currency TSR comparisons against international peers or Sterling comparisons against UK multinationals are likely to see reduced pay-outs;

Multinationals that make comparisons on a local currency basis are likely to see reduced pay outs.

In general, where currency movements are impacting business performance, Remuneration Committees may decide not to adjust targets for existing plan cycles except in the most extreme cases. However some companies are looking to adjust to make adjustments – see below.

Future targets:

The impact of Brexit should be considered as part of the wider review of financial targets required.

Most companies do not currently adjust for differences between actual and budgeted exchange rates when measuring financial performance for the purposes of their long-term incentive plan. If continued exchange rate instability is expected over the next few years, Remuneration Committees may wish to include discretion in the Policy to adjust vesting outcomes for exchange rates as appropriate. Remuneration policies for main market listed companies have to be put to shareholder vote every three years – this requirement was introduced relatively recently and many companies will be renewing their policies in 2017 so it will be interesting to see how many react to the exchange rate issue.

For relative TSR, we normally recommend that multinationals with international peers make comparisons on a common currency basis to ensure that currency movements are broadly neutral. The best approach for a UK-focused company will depend on the nature of its business and competitors.

Benchmarking

Where very senior or very specialist executives are being recruited from an international pool of talent, currency fluctuations can also affect benchmarks denominated in other currencies. This issue needs to be handled carefully as it can make UK executives look low paid in comparison to their peers internationally.[1]

There are a number of different ways of handling this issue – the first and most obvious approach is to consider seriously whether an international comparison is necessary or desirable. Where it is necessary – and in certain industries such as natural resources companies, executives are truly international – then an alternative approach may need to be taken. This might for example be addressed by using a constant/fixed/average currency rate or by reviewing the net-of-tax

---

1   http://content.mercer.com/Talent/Impact-of-Currency-Volatility-on-Compensation-Benchmarking.pdf

purchasing power in each relevant country to understand the full cost of living impact behind the headline figures.

Currency fluctuations are unpredictable so this issue does not warrant a rapid response – but if it seems that Sterling is likely to remain at a low level for the medium term an adjuster mechanism would be a sensible addition when looking at the currency impact on pay.

Executive pay

As mentioned at the beginning of this chapter one of the early reactions by the new Prime Minister to the Brexit vote was to characterise it as a protest against inequality and to attribute a degree of blame to perceived high levels of executive pay.

In response to this protest, in late November 2016 a green paper was issued by the Department for Business, Energy & Industrial Strategy. It noted that in 2013 reforms to the Companies Acts introduced a binding shareholder vote every three years on pay policy and an annual advisory vote on pay awards. In addition it also increased the reporting requirements for executive pay.

Although these reforms increased the transparency (and length) of Remuneration Committee reports in quoted company accounts, they did not remove the perception that executive pay has become increasingly disconnected both from the pay of ordinary workers and from the underlying performance of companies. The green paper probes the question as to whether further reforms are needed to demonstrate that companies are listening and acting on the views and concerns of shareholders – but also that they are taking account of wider stakeholders. Presumably this will include their employees and customers.

Whatever the view on Brexit, there is no doubt that executive pay has attracted a significant amount of press interest, most of it critical.

Interestingly however, institutional investors were not excessively active in the 2016 pay season. Remuneration Committee reports were approved by shareholders in 92% of companies so it seems that institutions were predominantly in agreement with pay awards – although there was an increase in the number of companies where the vote against was more than 20%. In the FTSE 350 only three companies had an advisory vote against their pay awards and only one had a majority vote against its remuneration policy. In fact, salary levels have not increased significantly over the last few years. Salary increases have been c. 2-3% per annum, broadly in line with those for the UK workforce as a whole. So, in 2016 there was no 'shareholder spring' and it seems that companies are largely adhering to institutional investor guidance and comment.

By the end of the 2016 a number of institutional investors had issued guidelines on their views on executive pay as well revised guidelines from the Investment Association (previously part of the Association of British Insurers).

On the whole, the 2013 reforms have had a positive impact: the existence of a binding policy has made it easier for Remuneration Committees to turn down requests for higher pay from executives and the 'single figure' disclosure of pay received has made it easier for investors to compare how pay has tracked performance over time and vote accordingly (see below).

One of the issues highlighted in the revised guidelines and by other commentators is the issue of quantum of executive pay. There are two aspects to these comments:

Pay ratio

We can be fairly certain the pay ratio disclosures will become a mandatory annual reporting requirement for UK PLCs within the next 12 months, with the intention of creating upwards pressure on workforce pay by revealing a measure of company's internal inequality.

However, the basic 'CEO pay ratio' proposal (ie the ratio of the Chief Executive Officer's pay to the median pay of an employee sample) is fraught with difficulty.

First, the ratio may be more a function of the type and demographics of a certain industry rather than a test of fairness. For example: a complex, international business which employs lots of part-time and temporary staff may have a very large ratio whilst a hedge fund would be likely to have a very high median pay level and so the ratio may be low. Whilst this draws attention to the fairness issue and calls for the duty of care to lower paid employees to be reinforced and widely communicated, it does not of itself suggest that pay is fairer in the latter organisation than in the former.

Another difficulty is the employee sample itself. If the employee sample is taken globally, companies with larger operations in developing regions are likely to have a larger ratio. Conversely if only UK employees are used to calculate the ratio, an inadvertent consequence might be that companies are incentivised to move higher paid jobs overseas.

A third question is what kind of CEO pay will be measured? If we use the single figure in any one year, long-term incentive payments and CEO changeovers will create huge volatility in the ratio and lend to misleading year on year comparisons.

Using mean employee pay would be better than using median pay. Using median figures would mean that the each company would have to rank the annualised pay of every employee. It would be easier to use mean pay figures as this requires knowing the full time equivalent headcount and total pay costs. This would have a lower administrative burden for the employer as existing reporting regulations and company processes tend to focus on mean averages rather than medians.

In addition, it would be instructive to require companies to disclose the proportion of their employees that are paid under the National Living Wage. The employee sample would need to be global and use a National Living Wage equivalent for each country so as not to encourage off-shoring of labour.

Both these factors could be measured against a selected peer group. An example of how the CEO pay ratio could be reported and also could reference the National Living Wage is set out below.

7.1 CEO Pay Ratio

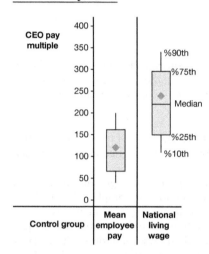

At Company A we are committed to balancing our collective desire for a fairer society with the commercial prerogative to attract, motivate and retain senior management of sufficient calibre.

Accordingly, we are happy to share our CEO's single figure (averaged over 3 years) as a multiple both of the average total remuneration received by our UK-based employees and of the National Living Wage.

Comparing our CEO pay ratio with our 19 industry peers, our CEO pay ratio versus mean employee pay is 9% greater than our peer group median. Similarly, our CEO pay ratio versus the National Living Wage is 10% greater than our peer group median.

Sector fees include:-

ABC Telecom, Lake Brothers, QWERTY Logistics, Sample Company, Allied Biscuit, Ankh-Sto PLC, Extensive Enterprise, Galaxy Corp, Globo-Chem Group, Mr. Sparkle, Globex Corporation, LexCorp, Luthor PLC, North Central Positronics, Omni Consumer Products, Praxis Group, Sombra Group, Sto Plains Holdings, Tessler-Ashpool

Potential CEO pays ratio disclosure

The link between employee pay and Chief Executive pay is not a logical cause and effect but can be viewed constructively if it is seen as a prompt to ensure that employees are well looked after.

Pay for performance

Arguably, the real issue is the actual and perceived link between pay and performance. Understandably, there are objections where executives who have not performed well receive high levels of pay. Some of this debate is around leavers – and the legal structure around executive pay should be effective enough to ensure that the Remuneration Committee has sufficient discretion in the Company's pay structures to ensure that poor performers who are leaving (or have left) the business do not receive excessive rewards.

This issue has been actively pursued by proxy agency Institutional Shareholder Services ('ISS') which in 2016 introduced pay for performance analysis for the largest 600 listed European companies and is currently doubling its coverage in the larger European countries including the UK. ISS looks at pay actually received by executives over 1, 3 and 5 year time periods versus the relevant company's TSR (which measures share price growth and dividends – the latter treated as reinvested in shares when the dividend is paid). ISS then undertakes 3 tests of whether pay is aligned to performance.

In its relative alignment test, it selects a comparator group for the relevant company and then ranks TSR and pay levels (averaged over 3 years). It identifies a zone of alignment between pay and performance: high pay and high performance is within the zone, but high pay and low performance is not. It also plots where the Chief Executive's pay falls within the group – see Figure 1 below.

Figure 1

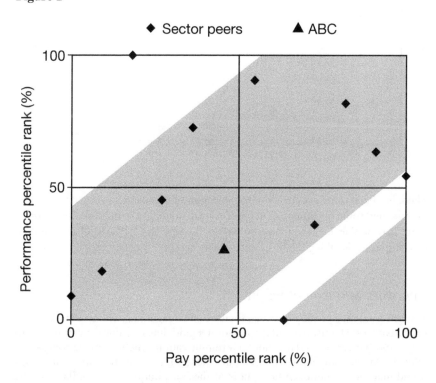

The assessment also looks at absolute alignment – how the Chief Executive's pay compares to the total shareholder return. In Figure 2 below pay exceeds performance in 2012 but is significantly lower for most of the other years. Performance has declined over time, but pay has declined more, so the company receives a positive score overall.

Figure 2

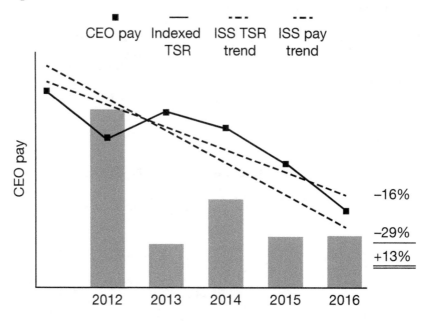

There has been some debate about the selection of comparable companies for this exercise and some fine tuning of the process will doubtless be helpful. But the main point here is that ISS (which represents approximately 21% of all institutional investor votes) is taking the link between pay and performance very seriously.

Investors and executive pay

The government's green paper also focuses on engagement with shareholders on executive pay. The Investment Association's guidelines encourage companies to engage with investors and to tailor their remuneration structures to the company's strategy. Many companies will welcome these suggestions but have sometimes found that their experience falls short of these aspirations – particularly in the case of companies outside the FTSE100. In some cases, institutional investors are not prepared to engage with companies on remuneration issues – or at least not in the time frame needed by the company. Another often voiced complaint is that the institutions themselves do not appear to have a 'joined up approach' between the buy-side and governance teams, with clients reporting that they hear different messages from each.

Pay levels disclosed in annual reports and accounts tend to fluctuate but this primarily is a function of performance and resulting fluctuations in the value of long-term incentive awards. Rewards under these plans can and should go up where performance is strong. This is why the ISS-style approach of comparing actual pay to performance is so valuable.

Fluctuating levels of executive pay

The green paper puts various questions around voting and sanctions to control pay policy but any share based incentive will give rise to fluctuations in the amounts received. The only way to control the amount that executives actually receive is to cap the value paid by an LTIP – rather than use the current approach which is to cap the number of shares. The problem with taking this approach is that it fails to align the executive appropriately with shareholders and to reward truly exceptional performance.

The danger with the approach in the green paper is that it could result in a system hidebound with complex regulation and restrictions which do not deliver a fair society in the UK and may ultimately reduce the competitiveness of UK-headquartered companies.

Of course simply lowering executive pay will not of itself benefit the lives of ordinary people and could have many adverse impacts – not least the decrease in income tax collected on LTIPs and other forms of remuneration. And in any event, the popular press are probably not the right arbiters of pay levels. We should also be mindful that in the post-Brexit environment, the UK needs to be nimble and competitive – this is not the time to weigh down organisations with additional bureaucracy. It should also be borne in mind that in the UK we have very high levels of disclosure and transparency on executive pay which exceed that of other European countries. Therefore, we approach this issue with 'clean hands'. That is not to say that the concerns are invalid – if the Brexit vote was a protest then it is important that it should be heard and that there should be an appropriate response.

In any case, regulation may not be the best approach. Practice can be very powerful – for example the Investment Association and ISS guidelines are not law but are almost universally adhered to by quoted companies. For example, as a result of investor pressure, many UK companies are starting to adopt a two year holding period requiring executives to continue to hold shares even after targets have been met. A longer term holding interest in the shares should add to the alignment with shareholders as executives, like shareholders, are affected in their pockets if the share price falls.

The other salient point in relation to executive pay is that the debate has focused almost exclusively on quoted companies – which adhere to high standards of corporate governance and are transparent about their pay. High pay is also present in other areas including large private companies, private equity funds, hedge funds, professional partnerships, entertainment and professional sport to give just a few examples.

If a vote for Brexit was a protest vote to highlight inequality – cutting executive pay is unlikely to improve the outlook for ordinary people. It would be more constructive for business to be encouraged to foster opportunity for all in the UK and to be held accountable for making a meaningful contribution – for example by offering apprenticeships or scholarships or making training available in the local community. Perhaps a measure of success in the post Brexit environment will be that our talented youngsters of the future aspire to be Chief Executives instead of dreaming of getting a break in professional football or becoming successful rock stars!

Conclusion

Employers have a wide spectrum of issues to consider in the post Brexit environment and we have seen that some of those issues require careful analysis and reassessment:

Sourcing high quality employees is always a challenge – if immigration slows significantly or if the supply of immigrants dries up because the UK ceases to be a conducive environment in which to live and work, then employers will need to start thinking about how they can attract and retain the people and/or re-shape their business (by for example automating where possible) to ensure that productivity is not impaired;

A softer currency may mean that managing these challenges is more complex and costly where the business has to pay more for foreign goods and services – but it may drive more UK businesses to expand internationally if there is pressure to generate foreign earnings;

Currency issues might affect measurement of executive pay and it will be important to ensure that such issues are dealt with effectively and with the minimum of fuss;

Executive pay has been the focus of much discontent – and therefore a measured reaction to the changes and a willingness to engage with a wider group of stakeholders will be increasingly important.

The post Brexit world may result in a paradigm shift for businesses. If this results in more flexible and agile businesses that can successfully change to adapt to circumstances, this could be a bed rock for future prosperity. A raft of new legislation to add to the burden on businesses in coping with Brexit will not be welcome, so government should be encouraged to make any changes through informal measures which may ultimately have more impact.

For more information on Mercer PLC visit www.uk.mercer.com/about-mercer/ lines-of-business/talent.html

SHALINI KHEMKA, E2EXCHANGE

E2E's mission is to be the main catalyst for entrepreneurial growth in UK and then internationally and its vision is to enable extraordinary entrepreneurship. It does so through very facilitating high quality connectivity between scale-up founders, super angel investors, high quality Non-Exec Directors and the UK's leading corporate organisations.

Under the E2E Group, E2E Invest, focuses on securing equity capital for scale-up businesses. E2E Exec, sources high calibre NED for scale-up companies and E2E Analytics uses the data on its 15,000+ scale-up community to intelligently connect its members.

One of the most contentious aspects of Brexit is what will happen to EU nationals already living in the UK. UK businesses need to recruit top talent to stay competitive and this can only be achieved if we remain open to EU workers and protect the rights of those already resident in the UK.

Yet the government has not been clear on whether it will do this. Earlier this week it was reported that the Prime Minister has drawn up plans to end freedom of movement rules as soon as Article 50 is triggered to prevent a sudden influx of EU nationals before Brexit actually happens. The government has also repeatedly resisted confirming that EU nationals already resident in the UK will be allowed to stay.

Thankfully, the House of Lords has now amended the draft Brexit bill to secure the rights of EU nationals already living in the UK. This is a major defeat for the government who wanted to keep their cards close to their chest, hoping to gain similar assurances from other EU countries about the rights of British citizens' resident abroad. Politically, this is also important for helping to warn off the threat of anti-immigrant UKIP and the right-wing of their own party.

The House of Lords amendment should be welcomed by British business and all those concerned about the future of the UK economy. Many UK businesses rely on EU workers to fill skill shortages and a recent survey by the Chartered Institute of Personnel and Development (CIPD) and the Adecco Group has found that sectors of the UK economy which are heavily dependent on EU labour are already starting to experience skills and labour shortages.

It is vitally important that we don't lose our best companies during Brexit and we have already seen warnings by the financial sector and others that they are considering migrating to the EU in the event of a 'hard' Brexit.

Ensuring that UK businesses maintain access to the single market will help, but keeping access to the EU talent pool is vital. However, that doesn't mean that we shouldn't also look at ways to upskill the British workforce. Having a larger choice of home grown and international talent can only benefit our businesses, and help keep them in the UK.

I work with numerous small and medium sized businesses (SMEs) on a day to day basis and despite the uncertainty and drop in the sterling against other currencies, SMEs remain resilient. A survey of 1,300 companies by Company Checking in November 2016 showed 50% expressing a view that Brexit had no effect on them so far, 30% said Brexit was a negative effect for their business and 15% said Brexit was positive. The rest didn't know. Indeed it is a waiting game, seeing how the economic and political uncertainty will pan out.

I help growth companies find investment and in this area, whilst there is worry, there is still plenty of lending and money going around. In particular, the Bank of England has announced approximately £500 million in funding to the Northern Powerhouse Fund and in times of uncertainty, SMEs in particular can create opportunities. Indeed, in the recession of 2008, during a financial crisis, some of the most successful companies were born and have adapted since to a changing world.

I believe the SMEs remain the engine room for the UK economy and cannot be ignored. In my organisation, I work collaboratively and introduce significant opportunities within our group.

Shalini founded E2Exchange (E2E) in 2011.

Shalini was an Investment Director at LDC, the private equity arm of Lloyds Banking Group and historically, she ran the Group's 'plain vanilla' International Trade Finance business. Prior to this, Shalini co-founded the world's first online 'bank to bank' trade finance company. She was a management accountant at Deutsche Bank and worked in various finance related roles for Bankers Trust, Natwest Bank and Coopers & Lybrand.

Shalini is a Member of the Mayor of London's Business Advisory Board. She is also a Director of the Centre for Entrepreneurs (CFE), a judge for the Great British Entrepreneurs Awards, a Champion for Tech London Advocate and an Ambassador for Recordsure. She was formerly on the Development Board of the Royal Philharmonic Orchestra and was a judge for IBM Smartcamp

For more information on E2Exhange visit www.e2exchange.com

ABHIJIT MUKHOPADHYAY, PRESIDENT (LEGAL) & GENERAL COUNSEL, HINDUJA GROUP

Introduction

At the Conservative Party conference held in October 2016, the British Prime Minister, Theresa May, announced that Article 50 would be triggered by the end of March 2017. This will begin formal negotiations with the European Union (EU) over Brexit, which must be completed within two years unless an extension is agreed by all 27 countries in the EU. Subsequently, the government introduced the Great Repeal Bill in the Queen's Speech this year (2017) enshrining all existing EU law into British law. The Bill would work by repealing the 1972 European Communities Act, which will take effect at the point of Brexit. Once Brexit has been completed the UK parliament will be able to keep, amend or cancel any EU legislation. The Bill would also end the jurisdiction of the European Court of Justice in the UK. Following the Supreme Court's decision on parliamentary voting based on the theory of Parliament's sovereignty, the House of Commons and the House of Lords have voted in favour of the Bill giving authority to the Prime Minister to trigger Article 50.

On 17 January 2017, Theresa May gave her anticipated 'Brexit' speech detailing the United Kingdom's exit strategy from the European Union. One of the more publicised statements made by the Prime Minister during her speech was the announcement that the United Kingdom 'could not possibly' be able to remain within the European single market following its exit from the European Union, suggesting that failing to do so would 'to all intents and purposes mean not leaving the EU at all'. The Prime Minister, however, made it clear that the fate of the EU citizens living in the UK would be put on hold pending negotiations with Brussels on the fate of British expats who are living in the EU. It is still unknown how the free movement of people will be dealt with on Britain's exit.

Single market

Mrs May's insinuation that remaining within the European single market would mean no major change following Brexit is reference to some of the proposed limitations that joining the single market has had on the United Kingdom, including the restrictions and 'disadvantages' that are placed on the United Kingdom as a member state which includes seemingly holding them back from being able to negotiate separately from the other member states when it comes to concluding international trade agreements with non-member states while continuing under the EU's common commercial policy; and the requirement of complying with the EU common customs tariffs leading to increases in the cost of goods from non-EU member states. It is still unknown how the movement of people and Britain's role with EU's customs tariff union would be dealt with. Industries have raised their apprehension against exiting from the customs tariff union.

The supposed bureaucracy of the EU, and the high economic costs that the United Kingdom is faced with in order to maintain their EU membership were other major discussion points throughout the referendum debate. However, arguably the most controversial and widely discussed topics within the referendum debates, and one of the key concerns for those in favour of leaving the EU, has been the topic of free movement of people, which has gone hand-in-hand with membership of the European single market.

During her speech, Theresa May insisted that she would push for the 'freest possible trade' that she could do with Europe, reiterating the fact that she did not wish to undermine the single market or the EU, but suggested against the EU 'punishing' the United Kingdom for their decision to leave implying that it would result in 'self-harm' for Europe. She even announced that Britain would not mind if negotiations fail because' no deal is better than a bad deal'.

Theresa May's 'Brexit speech' has introduced some clarity in the sense that it is now clear that there is a specific direction that the Prime Minister is hoping to see the United Kingdom heading towards seemingly 'hard' Brexit which will include a free-trade market outside of the EU's single market, and tighter controls over immigration as Article 50 is being triggered and the UK's withdrawal from the European Union begins. Be that as it may, these clarifications have hardly removed doubt that still persists and there are still underlying uncertainties that are likely plaguing many businesses and industries despite the Prime Minister and her government's attempts at giving the UK public some answers towards the next steps for the UK.

Impact on business

The impact of Brexit on businesses is quite uncertain. This is because neither the British government nor the EU have come out with their respective positions. Earlier Mrs. May had stated that 'Brexit means Brexit'. Business pundits were trying to decipher its meaning without success. If the United Kingdom no longer remains in the single market (which is a certainty now), what would be the country's position with regard to immigration? Both cannot go together as EU demands free movement of people if Britain wants to remain in the single market. There are demands from the Mayor of London and the Scottish First Minister to let them do business with the EU without any hindrance as is being done now. There are politicians in the government who hold diametrically opposite views. Be that as it may, the following could be the implications if 'Hard Brexit' is followed without any deal and at the time of writing this article, the government does not have a clue as to what would be the economic consequences or impact of no deal.

Sectoral implications

(a) Banking and Finance

There could be uncertainty for financial institutions. EU legislations give fundamental underpinning to capital markets, securitisation and banking lending. British financial institutions rely on fundamental legislation such as Markets in Financial Institutions Directives which give institutions the ability of availability of 'Passport' facility or conducting business throughout Europe without a license. It would be uncertain whether these financial institutions would be treated like their non-EU institutions or not. It could become more expensive and difficult for security issuers in the UK to offer securities around Europe. Institutions that conduct services such as deposit taking, lending and issuing may be affected. Along with this, London's premier status as the currency clearing market and euro clearing may be affected.

(b) Real Estate

Investors may defer major investment decisions until the details of Brexit are available. Some investors may implement pre-planned Brexit strategies they have put in place individually. Potential laws of free movement for workers could impact hotel and construction industries. However, uncertainty may create short-term opportunities as there may be a short-term boost for the property market in the UK. Depreciation in sterling could potentially increase demand for real estate especially from foreign investors.

(c) European Companies

The EU statute allows European public limited companies to be formed in any EU state which may be affected in the future.

354

(d)   Airlines

Airlines rely on EU derived traffic rights to fly freely to non-UK/EU destinations which may be affected. Virtually all protection regulations binding airline operations in the UK are based upon EU regulations which may be impacted. Safety and technical regulations for UK aerospace companies is predominantly within the remit of European Aviation Safety Agency. It is unclear whether this could be impacted or not.

(e)   Telecommunications

It is unclear what would be the policy agenda and its legislation with regard to mobile roaming rates and user's rates relating to electronic communication.

(f)   Oil and Gas

This industry is unlikely to be affected much since legislation covering oil and gas industry is unlikely to change. This is because most of the legislations are derived from international arrangements to which the UK is a party, such as the UN Convention on the Law of the Sea. Removal of EU competition laws may give UK some leeway to promulgate laws and regulations that give benefit to downstream industry. However, restrictions on the free movement of goods are likely to manifest themselves as tariffs and lack of freedom of movement of people may create a situation of skill shortage.

(g)   Construction

UK construction sector is heavily reliant on European workers and the tighter control on immigration is a concern. Impact of UK's formal exit from the EU and its current legislative framework would depend entirely on the agreement between EU countries and UK. If demand for labour outstrips supply, this will have implications on labour cost, which may impact the overall construction costs. Impact of the UK's formal exit from the EU and its current legislative framework will depend entirely on the terms which need to be agreed between the EU and the UK.

(h)   Immigration

This is a major area of concern for EU citizens in the UK. It is estimated that there are 3.5 million EU nationals who are presently working or residing in the UK. Will they be subject to any kind of visa control considering that immigration was a major issue at the Brexit referendum? Will there be some sort of visa regime for the movement of people from the EU to the UK and vice versa after Brexit? There is no clarity on this. This will have substantial impact on the businesses who may suddenly experience skill shortage.

(i)   Technology

Brexit will have an impact on UK law relating to technology to some extent. The wider effect of Brexit will be substantial on the UK technology sector because of substantial EU funding in this sector. Already concern has been expressed by the technology and research companies over their future funding.

(j) Financial Services

The UK legislative framework for the regulation of the financial services sector is currently derived from both domestic and EU level legislation. The EU-wide regulation of financial services consists of directives but requires UK member states to ratify them. It all depends on the negotiation as to how post-Brexit the financial services sector would be operating in the UK.

(k) Agricultural services

Presently the United Kingdom is under the 'Common Agricultural Policy' of the EU which may be affected unless the British government manages to clinch a good deal on it especially in the marine sector.

(l) Intellectual Property Rights

   i.   Presently, enforcement of intellectual property rights (IPRs) can be done on pan-EU basis. Once the UK leaves the EU, it may well be forced out of this unified system.

   ii.   UK designated European patents will continue to apply in the United Kingdom. However, on leaving the EU, the UK will no longer be able to participate in the new Unified Patent System. Assuming that Unitary Patent and the Unified Patent Court become active in 2017, UK businesses with these patents will still be able to use the Unified Patent Court for enforcement in other EU patent countries. This may of course undergo changes once the UK leaves the EU.

   iii.   Supplementary Protection Certificates are UK national rights granted by the IPO under Rules determined by EU regulation. The Great Repeal Bill, once enacted, will have the effect that all EU law applying to the UK at the day before Brexit will still apply as UK law going forward unless and until the position is changed by the Parliament.

   iv.   The Trade Secrets Directive adopted recently is due to be implemented into national law across EU member stated by 5 July 2018. Post Brexit one has to wait and see to understand its impact in the UK.

   v.   Whilst the UK system is similar in approach to the EU system, the EU regulations will cease to apply to the UK concerning plant breeders' rights post Brexit.

   vi.   EU trademarks will no longer cover the UK post Brexit since their effect is determined by the jurisdiction of the EU. To maintain the status quo, the government has to strike a deal whereby the future system will provide an equivalent right in the UK.

   vii.   Post Brexit, the EU Geographical Indications will no longer have effect in the UK. Similarly, Geographical Indications registered in the UK will not be eligible for making an application pan-EU.

    viii. Post Brexit provision will need to be made for the recognition of Community Registered Designs in a similar way to that for EU trademarks.

    ix. The General Data Protection Regulation will come into force on 25 May 2018. government's negotiations with the EU will determine the extent of its application in the UK.

    x. The EU Technology Transfer Block Exemption legislation has been used as a framework for providing licensing technology and other IPRs in the EU. To what extent the status quo will be maintained will depend upon the negation.

Government's Brexit White Paper

UK employers in general had been urged to look into the situations of EU-nationals that they employ following the Prime Minister's speech; now with the release of the government's awaited White Paper, and the confirmation that freedom of movement is to end, the ambiguity for its replacement is still in the air and it is still rather uncertain what this will mean for EU-nationals who have relied on freedom of movement to work within the UK, as well as the companies that have relied on them.

The 77-page 'Brexit White Paper', formally titled 'The United Kingdom's exit from and new partnership with the European Union' was published on 2 February 2017, with some of the major principles outlined within the document being:

- The UK taking control of their own statutes ending the jurisdiction of the Court of Justice of the European Union within the UK;
- Securing deals suitable for the entire UK including Scotland, Wales, Northern Ireland and the whole of England;
- Controlling the number of EU nationals coming to the UK;
- Trying to secure the status of EU nationals that are already living in the UK and UK nationals within other EU-member states;
- Ensuring they protect and enhance existing working rights;
- Ensuring a strategic partnership with the EU including a wide reaching and ambitious free trade agreement;
- And of course, a smooth exit from the EU.

London's position as Europe's best city for business

London has maintained a reputation globally as a key-figure for business in Europe, with most of Europe's largest companies having a presence there as well as many of Britain's own financial, investment, IT, and consultancy firms and service providers also being visible within the City. London's reputation as being one of the best cities for innovation and being an attractive city for business has been supported by the UK's place within the EU's single market which has also helped London gain the title of the 'gateway to Europe' which is likely the key factor for the banking sector's interest in London.

There are concerns that the UK's withdrawal of the European Trading Bloc will result in London losing the model that has helped them become the choice 'gateway to Europe' by financial service providers and businesses who may not see the City as viable anymore if the UK leaves the EU and it fails to secure a replacement to the current free-trade relationship that the UK has with the EU, allowing investors the opportunity to gain access to the rest of Europe's markets through London. The loss of London's reputation as 'the gateway to Europe' may also affect its reputation as the 'financial services capital' of Europe, at the moment it has been reported that almost 80% of foreign exchange transactions within the EU have been carried out in the UK with billions of pounds' worth of insurance services being traded daily.

A particular area of concern has been through the finance industry's response to the lack of clarification on the matter of 'passport rights'. The criticism has been directed at there being very little information provided to the finance industry on the proposed 'third country' status that is to be implemented as the UK exits the EU. As there is currently authorization developed and implemented through EU regulations that grant financial service providers and insurers the ability of providing their services across the other EU member states, the lack of clarity in relation to how these rights will be replaced is likely to be a cause for concern to UK firms, but also service providers across the other EU member states that have also been benefiting from these rights to provide their services to the UK.

The damaging effect that the uncertainty of Brexit has placed on London's position as the key-player in financial services in Europe has already began to show as major banks had confirmed their intentions to move thousands of jobs outside of London following Theresa May's 'Brexit speech'.

Likely impact on author's business group

The Hinduja Group is a well-diversified group operating in 10 business verticals, namely, automotive, foundries, lubricants, power and energy, banking and financial services, healthcare, business process outsourcing, explosives, real estate and media/entertainment. It employs more than 100,000 people in 50 countries around the world. It has been in existence for over 100 years and has been an international investor for many decades. The Group entered into Europe in the 1970s and has multi-billion dollar turnover from its businesses. It is also involved with charities in Asia, Europe and the USA. The Group has many manufacturing facilities in Asia, Europe and the USA. It is also a service provider in several Latin American countries as also in Canada. As one could see from the above, it is a largely diversified business Group. Its businesses and risks are equally spread. The Group exports its products mainly to Asian, African and Latin American countries as also to the United States. The Group does not export to Europe although it invests in Europe. The Group has investments in the UK in the field of automobile. It also runs business process outsourcing services in the UK. Since the automotive business in the UK largely sells its products in the UK and outside the EU, at the present moment, Brexit may not have a direct impact on the Group's business in the UK as well as in the EU. Be that as it may, the Group is investing in the construction and development of an iconic hotel in the city of London. The hotel is expected to become functional in a couple of years. By that time, hopefully, Brexit negotiations will be over and there will be clarity of its impact on the British economy. London is expected to continue as the global city and attract tourists from all over the world. It is also expected that the British government will ensure London's attractiveness as global financial sector to continue. It is also expected that the government will come out with ways and means to ensure that the tourist inflow to the city in particular, and to the UK in general, remain unchanged. As it is well known, tourism is a major contributor to the British economy. It is expected that post Brexit, the British government will try hard to strike trade deals with as many countries as possible including the Commonwealth countries. They are already in touch with the Indian government in this regard. The Group has major presence and investments in India and it hopes to play a major role in fostering business relationship between the two countries.

The Group owns the rights to a global brand in the lubricant sector and is a major producer of lubricants all over the world. It has production facility in a EU country which supplies to pan-European countries. There is a possibility that the brand will centralize its production in a EU country and market its products all over Europe.

In respect of the lubricant business, being a global brand, movement of people is essential. Therefore it has to be seen how the movement will be impacted post-Brexit. Since the business has customers in the UK, the likely impact of introduction of customers' tariffs on these products would be determined by the negotiations regarding the Customs Union. Likely future of the exchange rate between pounds sterling and euros also needs to be observed carefully.

It is yet to assess implications on its EU citizen employees who are working in the United Kingdom since their residential status is yet to be decided by the government which will become a part of negotiating deal.

However, the implications of Brexit on the Group's Intellectual Property Rights (IPRs) are yet to be seen. Presently the Group's many IPRs are registered in all the 28 EU countries under Community Registrations. IPRs of the lubricant brand of the Group are registered all over the world, including the EU. Likely impact of the IPRs post- Brexit has been dealt with in earlier paragraphs of this article. If the present regime of pan-EU registration and enforcement is maintained, the impact of IPRs post- Brexit will be minimal and if not, its impact will be substantial.

Conclusions

The Parliament has now voted in favour of giving Theresa May permission to trigger Article 50 and begin negotiations with the EU. The uncertainty as to what will be the implications when the UK leaves the EU still seems to be unclear. Although it may be years before EU concepts such as freedom of movement and the single market are completely abandoned within the UK, it is essential that the substitutes for these allow businesses and industries thriving within the UK at the present moment are developed in time which will give flexibility to the operating entities here to continue to conduct their operations globally including within Europe. This necessity will rely on the UK managing to obtain an impressive free trade deal that enables the UK to have flexible access to Europe. If an equivalence deal is actually accepted it could possibly give London the ability to maintain its 'gateway to Europe' status and also ensure that London remains a powerful city and favourable choice for global businesses. All of this is of course easier said than done as the UK may walk into any trade deal negotiations with Europe or the rest of the world with less to offer than before. It is now in the hands of the Prime Minister and the government to ensure that the UK remains open for business as usual. Britain is hoping to rely on her relationship with the Commonwealth countries to conclude favourable trade deals. However, trade deals with 60-odd countries will not be easy considering India has already asked for more visas for its businesses and students which the British government has not yet responded to. Negotiations with China (outside the Commonwealth) will also not be easy. Usually, it takes six to seven years to complete negotiations of a trade deal. India-EU negotiations are hanging in the balance for more than eight years without any substantive results. With a new President in the United States, it is not clear how the trade department there would favour an expedited trade deal with the United Kingdom considering former President Barack Obama's reluctance to allow the United Kingdom to jump the queue. It is also not clear what concessions the United Kingdom would offer in those trade deals especially in terms of free movement of people. In brief, watch and see is the only policy one could take till the negotiations are over in 2019. It is hoped that by that time Scotland will still remain a part of the United Kingdom and not continue to press for a vote for independence.

For more information on the Hinduja Group visit www.hindujagroup.com

DANA DENIS-SMITH, CEO, OBELISK LEGAL SUPPORT

And then, there were nearly none, to paraphrase Agatha Christie, one of Britain's most celebrated crime novelists. This 'disappearing act' might be just what will happen to the European-qualified lawyers that have practised in England and Wales in the last decade or so. If new immigration controls are brought in for EU nationals, those practitioners might no longer be able to continue to work in the UK once it exits the EU. Similarly, English qualified lawyers who operated on the continent might lose their right to practice there, even if they registered as European lawyers with the local bar associations. These 'talent' concerns are a new chapter for the English legal sector that has boomed in the last 25 years and has achieved an unrivalled global footprint. How can this be sustained if talent is a premium commodity in short supply in the face of technology advances and EU projects such as 'Find-a-Lawyer'.

'The EU is developing a powerful template for cross-border transactions across legal systems and languages, which is likely to become a world leader' said Jonathan Goldsmith.[1] 'English lawyers will continue to interact closely with European colleagues, and this will in due course extend to electronic

---

1   Jonathan Goldsmith, Law Society Gazette (13 February 2017).

transactions, even when we are outside the EU. The march of technology is such that what is possible now will soon become commonplace. Presumably in time we will regularly engage in cross-border electronic transactions outside the UK. Therefore, we should ensure that our systems are capable of making the eventual link-up.' We should ensure that our talent is capable of also linking in within that system and European qualified lawyers based in the UK could be just the link we need to ensure that the EU is not about to steal the UK's crown when it comes to ease of transacting internationally.

Ask anyone and they'd tell you – law is a people business and, like all service businesses, the quality of its talent is closely interlinked to the quality of service. A smaller pool of talent to choose from can have a huge impact on the legal sector – is it right that those of us who operate in the sector should be concerned? Will much of the transformation of the sector of the last years take a back step? How might a shrinking talent pool affect emerging innovative business models that deliver flexibility and affordability to cash-pressed clients and have challenged law firms to adapt or die?

Thus far, much of the debate and consultation around Brexit's implications on the legal sector have been framed around its effect on the size of the sector in the UK (will it shrink from its current £23 billion and will it result in job losses), the firms' global competitiveness and the sector's exportability (will English law stop being the contracting jurisdiction of choice?) and how will heavily EU regulated areas of law be affected (especially intellectual property, employment, human rights). Very little consideration has been given to the impact of the European legal talent that has helped the sector at various levels of seniority but particularly visible in the junior end, in paralegal work, as they sought to gain fuller access to the profession via the QLTT.

As the practice of law is still so centred on the people who deliver the services, a more important question emerges. Will Brexit lead to a flight of talent and how will firms prepare for any tightening of the labour market for such legal skills? This question strikes at the very heart of the business model operated by law firm partnerships – built around talent and their access to good quality lawyers. For a good while now, Europe has been feeding talent into these firms but this might all change if Britain decides to sacrifice freedom of movement post-Brexit, which is looking increasingly likely. The number of exempt European lawyers allowed to practice in England and Wales stands at 2,834, in addition to 640 registered European lawyers. These numbers are misleading, however, as many of the European qualified lawyers I have come across work as legal consultants to businesses where the jurisdiction of qualification is not as relevant and where it is not a requirements to register with the E&W regulator.

So what if European lawyers can no longer practice in the UK, some may say? There are plenty of local, talented English lawyers to step into their shoes. Currently the profession counts no less than 136,596 practising certificate holders according to February 2017 data from the SRA. Of those, just under 20% provide commercial and business legal services.

If not, they may argue, we will revert to the usual recruitment ground of Australia and New Zealand to fill the shoes of those forced or choosing to leave after Brexit. In February 2017 there were 2,234 registered foreign lawyers according to the SRA. In a profession that is all about people, as the legal industry is, planning strategically for talent is critical to business continuity. In the legal sector – just as we heard about the technology sector – a talent shortage as a result of Brexit will have a huge impact, on a sector that contributes a good £20 billion to the UK economy. At least in the short-to-medium term! Of course the market will adapt to these changes but a talent shock after Brexit should be ignored by law firms and general counsel at their peril.

Being laissez-faire about losing legal talent from the EU member states is a short-sighted view of how the reality of business tends to work. Running a business is all about people and changes in teams are disruptive and can have long-term effects. But when the service you deliver is centred on the capabilities of your people – losing talent can have a more devastating effect. What is the portrait of a European lawyer that we have seen coming through Obelisk Support? Educated and admitted to their local bar, they would have mainly worked in the in-house space in the UK after an initial stint in private practice in their own jurisdiction. Their skills – often dual-qualified, to include an English qualification and multilingual – are a good complement to the local talent in the UK. In a study conducted by Obelisk in 2013, we found that the most common language of English qualified lawyers working across the FTSE100 legal teams was French and multilingual ability was relatively poor across the board. But many other languages were absent and this can make supplying legal work internationally problematic not from the point of view of legal expertise alone, but also linguistically and culturally. International negotiations require not only an ability to draft and agree terms, but also to communicate with local business teams in an effective way.

Many businesses measure not just happiness at work, but also staff longevity and engagement. Should teams that have EU national lawyers be forced into being disrupted by their departure (it takes about six months to train someone into a job and probably near to 12 months to ensure they understand the business in which they are employed) will we end up with a war for talent, especially with the boom in corporate legal department jobs and international transactions, the increased global regulations around data protection and financial markets? The volume of legal work is increasing and yet the size of the English labour market is about to shrink. The mismatch will result in expensive resourcing for law firms and corporates alike.

In 1998, rule changes were brought in by the EU to make it easier to offer legal services between jurisdictions to support cross-border transactions (Directive 98/5/EC of the European Parliament and of the Council to facilitate practice of the profession of lawyer on a permanent basis in a Member State other than that in which the qualification was obtained, dated 16 February 1998).

Before this Directive, historically, each of the 28 member countries had a very 'national' legal system, with their own traditions, precedent rules and infrastructure. As the EU's single market expanded eastward and the body of EU generated legislation increased, this in turn required the legal talent to become more mobile and this is how the Solicitor's Regulatory Authority (SRA) introduced rules that allowed lawyers from other member states to start practising in the UK via either a QLTT transfer or, later, by registering on the register of European lawyers. A closer integration of legal systems across the EU member states made sense – especially as businesses sought new markets and English law was often used by counterparties. But in order to be globally competitive, law firms need not only closer integration of legal systems across the EU but EU talent was needed to give English law firms access to new markets to service. It was evident that panic has struck when a flurry of law firms started encouraging their lawyers to sign up to the Irish Bar immediately after the 23 June 2016 referendum. The Irish Bar was the closest link left between the EU legal system and that in England and Wales, not least because of the common origin of the two legal systems, originating in the Irish pre-independence years.

European lawyers have also been instrumental in the growth of the in-house profession where contract law is the main area of practice, which is found to be a transferrable skill irrespective of the jurisdiction of qualification. In the last decade, businesses have relied heavily on hiring legal consultants to be able to operate a more flexible staffing model at all levels. Many legal consultants are European lawyers, especially in large multinationals as those value the international experience and multilingual skills they bring. The flexibility of the contractor market has helped legal departments to manage larger volumes of legal work and control costs around the delivery of legal solutions to the business. Technology innovation in the legal sector has picked up in the last five years but the pace of adoption will have to change significantly to impact and transform the current working patterns both across law firms and in house team.

Britain has positioned its post-Brexit strategy as that of a global player – that might be so, and perhaps English law will remain a significant contracting tool for those transacting internationally beyond 2019. But if firms are to remain competitive on that global stage, they cannot be complacent about the nature of the talent they attract and need to continue to value diversity of backgrounds and skills. There is no doubt that a need by European lawyers to pass any immigration controls to join training programmes in the UK will impoverish the skills we have locally, in London and the UK. In the short term, law firms will no doubt recruit more people in their European offices to build up their teams and balance any fall out effects. Talent after Brexit is in danger of becoming more monolithic unless education establishments and law firms attach a strategic focus to recruiting candidates who are multilingual and are able to operate across international markets; their talent needs to be able to function across geographics, not just in their UK offices, and this should be a loud ask in any lobbying during the Brexit negotiations.

For more information on Obelisk Legal Support visit http://obelisksupport.com/

Appendix 1

PRIME MINISTER'S COMMONS STATEMENT ON TRIGGERING ARTICLE 50

29 March 2017

Theresa May gave a statement in Parliament on her letter notifying the European Council President of the UK's intention to leave the EU.

'Thank you Mr Speaker,

Today the government acts on the democratic will of the British people. And it acts, too, on the clear and convincing position of this House.

A few minutes ago in Brussels, the United Kingdom's Permanent Representative to the EU handed a letter to the President of the European Council on my behalf, confirming the government's decision to invoke Article 50 of the Treaty on European Union.

The Article 50 process is now underway. And in accordance with the wishes of the British people, the United Kingdom is leaving the European Union.

This is an historic moment from which there can be no turning back. Britain is leaving the European Union. We are going to make our own decisions and our own laws. We are going to take control of the things that matter most to us. And we are going to take this opportunity to build a stronger, fairer Britain – a country that our children and grandchildren are proud to call home. That is our ambition and our opportunity. That is what this government is determined to do.

Mr Speaker, at moments like these – great turning points in our national story – the choices we make define the character of our nation. We can choose to say the task ahead is too great. We can choose to turn our face to the past and believe it can't be done. Or we can look forward with optimism and hope – and to believe in the enduring power of the British spirit.

I choose to believe in Britain and that our best days lie ahead. And I do so because I am confident that we have the vision and the plan to use this moment to build a better Britain. For, leaving the European Union presents us with a unique opportunity. It is this generation's chance to shape a brighter future for our country. A chance to step back and ask ourselves what kind of country we want to be.

My answer is clear. I want the United Kingdom to emerge from this period of change stronger, fairer, more united and more outward-looking than ever before. I want us to be a secure, prosperous, tolerant country – a magnet for international talent and a home to the pioneers and innovators who will shape the world ahead.

I want us to be a truly Global Britain – the best friend and neighbour to our European partners, but a country that reaches beyond the borders of Europe too. A country that goes out into the world to build relationships with old friends and new allies alike.

And that is why I have set out a clear and ambitious plan for the negotiations ahead. It is a plan for a new deep and special partnership between Britain and the European Union. A partnership of values. A partnership of interests. A partnership based on cooperation in areas such as security and economic affairs. And a partnership that works in the best interests of the United Kingdom, the European Union and the wider world.

Because perhaps now more than ever, the world needs the liberal, democratic values of Europe – values that this United Kingdom shares. And that is why, while we are leaving the institutions of the European Union, we are not leaving Europe. We will remain a close friend and ally. We will be a committed partner. We will play our part to ensure that Europe is able to project its values and defend itself from security threats. And we will do all that we can to help the European Union prosper and succeed.

So Mr Speaker, in the letter that has been delivered to President Tusk today – copies of which I have placed in the library of the House – I have been clear that the deep and special partnership we seek is in the best interests of the United Kingdom and of the European Union too.

I have been clear that we will work constructively – in a spirit of sincere cooperation – to bring this partnership into being. And I have been clear that we should seek to agree the terms of this future partnership alongside those of our withdrawal, within the next 2 years.

I am ambitious for Britain. And the objectives I have set out for these negotiations remain. We will deliver certainty wherever possible so that business, the public sector and everybody else has as much clarity as we can provide as we move through the process. It is why, tomorrow, we will publish a White Paper confirming our plans to convert the 'acquis' into British law, so that everyone will know where they stand.

And it is why I have been clear that the government will put the final deal that is agreed between the UK and the EU to a vote in both Houses of Parliament before it comes into force. We will take control of our own laws and bring an end to the jurisdiction of the European Court of Justice in Britain. Leaving the European Union will mean that our laws will be made in Westminster, Edinburgh, Cardiff and Belfast. And those laws will be interpreted by judges not in Luxembourg, but in courts across this country.

We will strengthen the Union of the 4 nations that comprise our United Kingdom. We will negotiate as one United Kingdom, taking account of the specific interests of every nation and region of the UK and when it comes to the powers that we will take back from Europe, we will consult fully on which powers should reside in Westminster and which should be passed on to the devolved administrations.

But Mr Speaker, no decisions currently taken by the devolved administrations will be removed from them. And it is the expectation of the government that the devolved administrations in Scotland, Wales and Northern Ireland will see a significant increase in their decision-making power as a result of this process.

We want to maintain the common travel area with the Republic of Ireland. There should be no return to the borders of the past. We will control immigration so that we continue to attract the brightest and the best to work or study in Britain, but manage the process properly so that our immigration system serves the national interest.

We seek to guarantee the rights of EU citizens who are already living in Britain, and the rights of British nationals in other member states as early as we can. That is set out very clearly in the letter as an early priority for the talks ahead. We will ensure that workers' rights are fully protected and maintained. Indeed, under my leadership, not only will the government protect the rights of workers, we will build on them.

We will pursue a bold and ambitious free trade agreement with the European Union that allows for the freest possible trade in goods and services between Britain and the EU's member states; that gives British companies the maximum freedom to trade with and operate within European markets; and that lets European businesses do the same in Britain.

Because European leaders have said many times that we cannot 'cherry pick' and remain members of the single market without accepting the 4 freedoms that are indivisible. We respect that position. And as accepting those freedoms is incompatible with the democratically expressed will of the British people, we will no longer be members of the single market.

We are going to make sure that we can strike trade agreements with countries from outside the European Union too. Because important though our trade with the EU is and will remain, it is clear that the UK needs to increase significantly its trade with the fastest growing export markets in the world.

We hope to continue to collaborate with our European partners in the areas of science, education, research and technology, so that the UK is one of the best places for science and innovation. We seek continued cooperation with our European partners in important areas such as crime, terrorism and foreign affairs.

And it is our aim to deliver a smooth and orderly Brexit – reaching an agreement about our future partnership by the time the 2-year Article 50 process has concluded, then moving into a phased process of implementation in which Britain, the EU institutions and member states prepare for the new arrangements that will exist between us.

Mr Speaker, we understand that there will be consequences for the UK of leaving the EU. We know that we will lose influence over the rules that affect the European economy. We know that UK companies that trade with the EU will have to align with rules agreed by institutions of which we are no longer a part, just as we do in other overseas markets. We accept that.

However, we approach these talks constructively, respectfully, and in a spirit of sincere cooperation. For it is in the interests of both the United Kingdom and the European Union that we should use this process to deliver our objectives in a fair and orderly manner. It is in the interests of both the United Kingdom and the European Union that there should be as little disruption as possible. And it is in the interests of both the United Kingdom and the European Union that Europe should remain strong, prosperous and capable of projecting its values in the world.

At a time when the growth of global trade is slowing and there are signs that protectionist instincts are on the rise in many parts of the world, Europe has a responsibility to stand up for free trade in the interests of all our citizens.

With Europe's security more fragile today than at any time since the end of the Cold War, weakening our cooperation and failing to stand up for European values would be a costly mistake.

Our vote to leave the EU was no rejection of the values that we share as fellow Europeans. As a European country, we will continue to play our part in promoting and supporting those values – during the negotiations and once they are done.

We will continue to be reliable partners, willing allies and close friends. We want to continue to buy goods and services from the EU, and sell them ours. We want to trade with them as freely as possible, and work with one another to make sure we are all safer, more secure and more prosperous through continued friendship.

Indeed, in an increasingly unstable world, we must continue to forge the closest possible security co-operation to keep our people safe. We face the same global threats from terrorism and extremism. That message was only reinforced by the abhorrent attack on Westminster Bridge and this place last week.

So there should be no reason why we should not agree a new deep and special partnership between the UK and the EU that works for us all.

Mr Speaker, I know that this is a day of celebration for some and disappointment for others. The referendum last June was divisive at times. Not everyone shared the same point of view, or voted in the same way. The arguments on both side were passionate.

But, Mr Speaker, when I sit around the negotiating table in the months ahead, I will represent every person in the whole United Kingdom – young and old, rich and poor, city, town, country and all the villages and hamlets in between.

And yes, those EU nationals who have made this country their home and it is my fierce determination to get the right deal for every single person in this country. For, as we face the opportunities ahead of us on this momentous journey, our shared values, interests and ambitions can – and must – bring us together.

We all want to see a Britain that is stronger than it is today. We all want a country that is fairer so that everyone has the chance to succeed. We all want a nation that is safe and secure for our children and grandchildren. We all want to live in a truly Global Britain that gets out and builds relationships with old friends and new allies around the world.

These are the ambitions of this government's Plan for Britain. Ambitions that unite us, so that we are no longer defined by the vote we cast, but by our determination to make a success of the result.

We are one great union of people and nations with a proud history and a bright future. And now that the decision to leave has been made – and the process is underway – it is time to come together. For this great national moment needs a great national effort. An effort to shape a stronger future for Britain.

So let us do so together. Let us come together and work together. Let us together choose to believe in Britain with optimism and hope. For if we do, we can together make the most of the opportunities ahead. We can make a success of this moment. And we can together build a stronger, fairer, better Britain – a Britain our children and grandchildren are proud to call home.

I commend this statement to the House.'

Appendix 2

The full text of the Prime Minister's letter is set out below.

'On 23 June last year, the people of the United Kingdom voted to leave the European Union. As I have said before, that decision was no rejection of the values we share as fellow Europeans. Nor was it an attempt to do harm to the European Union or any of the remaining member states. On the contrary, the United Kingdom wants the European Union to succeed and prosper. Instead, the referendum was a vote to restore, as we see it, our national self-determination. We are leaving the European Union, but we are not leaving Europe – and we want to remain committed partners and allies to our friends across the continent.

Earlier this month, the United Kingdom Parliament confirmed the result of the referendum by voting with clear and convincing majorities in both of its Houses for the European Union (Notification of Withdrawal) Bill. The Bill was passed by Parliament on 13 March and it received Royal Assent from Her Majesty The Queen and became an Act of Parliament on 16 March.

Today, therefore, I am writing to give effect to the democratic decision of the people of the United Kingdom. I hereby notify the European Council in accordance with Article 50(2) of the Treaty on European Union of the United Kingdom's intention to withdraw from the European Union. In addition, in accordance with the same Article 50(2) as applied by Article 106a of the Treaty Establishing the European Atomic Energy Community, I hereby notify the European Council of the United Kingdom's intention to withdraw from the European Atomic Energy Community. References in this letter to the European Union should therefore be taken to include a reference to the European Atomic Energy Community.

This letter sets out the approach of Her Majesty's Government to the discussions we will have about the United Kingdom's departure from the European Union and about the deep and special partnership we hope to enjoy – as your closest friend and neighbour – with the European Union once we leave. We believe that these objectives are in the interests not only of the United Kingdom but of the European Union and the wider world too.

It is in the best interests of both the United Kingdom and the European Union that we should use the forthcoming process to deliver these objectives in a fair and orderly manner, and with as little disruption as possible on each side. We want to make sure that Europe remains strong and prosperous and is capable of projecting its values, leading in the world, and defending itself from security threats. We want the United Kingdom, through a new deep and special partnership with a strong European Union, to play its full part in achieving these goals. We therefore believe it is necessary to agree the terms of our future partnership alongside those of our withdrawal from the European Union.

The Government wants to approach our discussions with ambition, giving citizens and businesses in the United Kingdom and the European Union – and indeed from third countries around the world – as much certainty as possible, as early as possible. I would like to propose some principles that may help to shape our coming discussions, but before I do so, I should update you on the process we will be undertaking at home, in the United Kingdom.

The process in the United Kingdom

As I have announced already, the Government will bring forward legislation that will repeal the Act of Parliament – the European Communities Act 1972 – that gives effect to EU law in our country. This legislation will, wherever practical and appropriate, in effect convert the body of existing European Union law (the 'acquis') into UK law. This means there will be certainty for UK citizens and for anybody from the European Union who does business in the United Kingdom. The Government will consult on how we design and implement this legislation, and we will publish a White Paper tomorrow. We also intend to bring forward several other pieces of legislation that address specific issues relating to our departure from the European Union, also with a view to ensuring continuity and certainty, in particular for businesses. We will of course continue to fulfil our responsibilities as a member state while we remain a member of the European Union, and the legislation we propose will not come into effect until we leave.

From the start and throughout the discussions, we will negotiate as one United Kingdom, taking due account of the specific interests of every nation and region of the UK as we do so. When it comes to the return of powers back to the United Kingdom, we will consult fully on which powers should reside in Westminster and which should be devolved to Scotland, Wales and Northern Ireland. But it is the expectation of the Government that the outcome of this process will be a significant increase in the decision-making power of each devolved administration.

Negotiations between the United Kingdom and the European Union

The United Kingdom wants to agree with the European Union a deep and special partnership that takes in both economic and security cooperation. To achieve this, we believe it is necessary to agree the terms of our future partnership alongside those of our withdrawal from the EU.

If, however, we leave the European Union without an agreement the default position is that we would have to trade on World Trade Organisation terms. In security terms a failure to reach agreement would mean our cooperation in the fight against crime and terrorism would be weakened. In this kind of scenario, both the United Kingdom and the European Union would of course cope with the change, but it is not the outcome that either side should seek. We must therefore work hard to avoid that outcome.

It is for these reasons that we want to be able to agree a deep and special partnership, taking in both economic and security cooperation, but it is also because we want to play our part in making sure that Europe remains strong and prosperous and able to lead in the world, projecting its values and

372

defending itself from security threats. And we want the United Kingdom to play its full part in realising that vision for our continent.

Proposed principles for our discussions

Looking ahead to the discussions which we will soon begin, I would like to suggest some principles that we might agree to help make sure that the process is as smooth and successful as possible.

i. We should engage with one another constructively and respectfully, in a spirit of sincere cooperation

Since I became Prime Minister of the United Kingdom I have listened carefully to you, to my fellow EU Heads of Government and the Presidents of the European Commission and Parliament. That is why the United Kingdom does not seek membership of the single market: we understand and respect your position that the four freedoms of the single market are indivisible and there can be no 'cherry picking'. We also understand that there will be consequences for the UK of leaving the EU: we know that we will lose influence over the rules that affect the European economy. We also know that UK companies will, as they trade within the EU, have to align with rules agreed by institutions of which we are no longer a part – just as UK companies do in other overseas markets.

ii. We should always put our citizens first

There is obvious complexity in the discussions we are about to undertake, but we should remember that at the heart of our talks are the interests of all our citizens. There are, for example, many citizens of the remaining member states living in the United Kingdom, and UK citizens living elsewhere in the European Union, and we should aim to strike an early agreement about their rights.

iii. We should work towards securing a comprehensive agreement

We want to agree a deep and special partnership between the UK and the EU, taking in both economic and security cooperation. We will need to discuss how we determine a fair settlement of the UK's rights and obligations as a departing member state, in accordance with the law and in the spirit of the United Kingdom's continuing partnership with the EU. But we believe it is necessary to agree the terms of our future partnership alongside those of our withdrawal from the EU.

iv. We should work together to minimise disruption and give as much certainty as possible

Investors, businesses and citizens in both the UK and across the remaining 27 member states – and those from third countries around the world – want to be able to plan. In order to avoid any cliff-edge as we move from our current relationship to our future partnership, people and businesses in both the UK and the EU would benefit from implementation periods to adjust in a smooth and orderly way to new arrangements. It would help both sides to minimise unnecessary disruption if we agree this principle early in the process.

v. In particular, we must pay attention to the UK's unique relationship with the Republic of Ireland and the importance of the peace process in Northern Ireland

The Republic of Ireland is the only EU member state with a land border with the United Kingdom. We want to avoid a return to a hard border between our two countries, to be able to maintain the Common Travel Area between us, and to make sure that the UK's withdrawal from the EU does not harm the Republic of Ireland. We also have an important responsibility to make sure that nothing is done to jeopardise the peace process in Northern Ireland, and to continue to uphold the Belfast Agreement.

vi. We should begin technical talks on detailed policy areas as soon as possible, but we should prioritise the biggest challenges

Agreeing a high-level approach to the issues arising from our withdrawal will of course be an early priority. But we also propose a bold and ambitious Free Trade Agreement between the United Kingdom and the European Union. This should be of greater scope and ambition than any such agreement before it so that it covers sectors crucial to our linked economies such as financial services and network industries. This will require detailed technical talks, but as the UK is an existing EU member state, both sides have regulatory frameworks and standards that already match. We should therefore prioritise how we manage the evolution of our regulatory frameworks to maintain a fair and open trading environment, and how we resolve disputes. On the scope of the partnership between us – on both economic and security matters – my officials will put forward detailed proposals for deep, broad and dynamic cooperation.

vii. We should continue to work together to advance and protect our shared European values

Perhaps now more than ever, the world needs the liberal, democratic values of Europe. We want to play our part to ensure that Europe remains strong and prosperous and able to lead in the world, projecting its values and defending itself from security threats.

The task before us

As I have said, the Government of the United Kingdom wants to agree a deep and special partnership between the UK and the EU, taking in both economic and security cooperation. At a time when the growth of global trade is slowing and there are signs that protectionist instincts are on the rise in many parts of the world, Europe has a responsibility to stand up for free trade in the interest of all our citizens. Likewise, Europe's security is more fragile today than at any time since the end of the Cold War. Weakening our cooperation for the prosperity and protection of our citizens would be a costly mistake. The United Kingdom's objectives for our future partnership remain those set out in my Lancaster House speech of 17 January and the subsequent White Paper published on 2 February.

We recognise that it will be a challenge to reach such a comprehensive agreement within the two-year period set out for withdrawal discussions in the Treaty. But we believe it is necessary to agree the terms of our future partnership alongside those of our withdrawal from the EU. We start from a unique position in these discussions – close regulatory alignment, trust in one another's institutions, and a spirit of cooperation stretching back decades. It is for these reasons, and because the future partnership between the UK and the EU is of such importance to both sides, that I am sure it can be agreed in the time period set out by the Treaty.

The task before us is momentous but it should not be beyond us. After all, the institutions and the leaders of the European Union have succeeded in bringing together a continent blighted by war into a union of peaceful nations, and supported the transition of dictatorships to democracy. Together, I know we are capable of reaching an agreement about the UK's rights and obligations as a departing member state, while establishing a deep and special partnership that contributes towards the prosperity, security and global power of our continent.'

Appendix 3

EXTRACT FROM THE BREXIT PAPERS FROM THE BAR COUNCIL BREXIT WORKING GROUP

Paper 18 ('UK Tax')

(November 2016)[1]

1. Taxpayers, particular business taxpayers, need certainty as to the legal and fiscal position in order to make sensible commercial decisions as to investment, jobs, etc. Recent UK Governments have gone some way towards achieving this by outlining a 'Business Tax Road Map' which has sought to identify policy goals and broad routes to achieving such goals. That process is now under considerable pressure as a result of the vote to leave the EU, the current debate as to how and when to trigger Article 50 and the absence, as yet, of any published guidance as to how the Government sees the UK tax system developing in a post-Brexit world.

2. There is anecdotal evidence, at least, that some investment destined for the UK has been re-routed elsewhere or deferred and that plans are now well advanced to move businesses (and jobs) out of the UK if greater clarity is not achieved, particularly in the financial services sector. While tax is only one factor in such considerations it is an important one. What follows is an outline summary (no doubt incomplete) of the main issues that will need to be resolved over the next two years or so.

Customs duties

3. At present the UK is a part of the EU customs union which allows free of movement of goods between member states without any customs formalities or duties/tariffs. On leaving the EU the UK will need to decide if it is to remain inside the customs union and, assuming that it does not, the UK will need to introduce its own comprehensive customs code. This will require the UK to determine how it wishes to categorise goods, what goods will suffer what duties and how it is to operate customs formalities (clearance mechanisms, financial security for duties, registration requirements). As it is likely that duties/tariffs will be imposed on trade in goods between the UK and the remaining EU member states, the administrative costs of trading with the EU will increase.

4. Furthermore, the UK currently benefits from free trade agreements entered into by the EU with third countries which give access to preferential duty rates. Unless and until the UK has its own agreements

---

1   This paper originally appeared in the first edition of The Brexit Papers. It was authored by Jonathan Peacock QC and Hui Ling McCarthy of 11 New Square, and has been reproduced with kind permission of the Bar Council Brexit Working Group.

with such third countries, duty rates faced by UK exports are likely to increase.

Stamp duties

13. At present the UK is subject to the Capital Duties Directive which prevents, in some instances, EU member states charging indirect tax in respect of the raising of capital by companies (for example, by issuing shares or other securities). UK legislation currently imposes a 1.5% SDRT charge on issues of shares and securities to depositary receipt issuers and clearance services in certain circumstances. However, as a result of the Capital Duties Directive and decisions of the CJEU and the UK courts the UK no longer imposes this charge. Post-Brexit the UK would be free to impose this SDRT charge and also to impose a new capital duty.

Administration

14. At present the UK benefits from EU-wide administrative cooperation on exchanging information and tackling tax evasion, in particular in the form of the Mutual Assistance Directive which enables cross-EU border enforcement of tax debts. This will only be able to continue to the extent that the UK has or enters into bilateral agreements replicating this network.

Other issues

State aid

15. Assuming the UK is no longer part of the EU, the EEA and does not join EFTA, it will no longer be subject to EU law restrictions when seeking to grant state aid. The corollary of that, however, is that it will no longer have any recourse through the EU against member states introducing state aid that disadvantages UK businesses. The EU may well, however, in that situation seek to introduce some form of State aid or subsidy control in any trade agreement that is negotiated with the UK.

Grandfathering and transitional rules

17. Taxpayers, particularly businesses, will need to know well in advance of the post-Brexit new world becoming operational, when and in what circumstances there will be grandfathering and/or transitional rules.

Index